THE LION'S SHARE

THE
Lion's Share

The Story of an
Entertainment Empire

BY

BOSLEY CROWTHER

E. P. DUTTON & COMPANY, INC.

New York, 1957

TABLE OF CONTENTS

ACKNOWLEDGMENT

So MANY people have been helpful in providing information and material for this book that I must beg forgiveness for not mentioning every one of them. But a full list of those to whom I am grateful would be so ridiculously long that I fear it would irritate my publisher and provide you with no more entertaining reading than the telephone book.

However, I would be inexpressive if I did not record my particular thanks to Norma Shearer for priceless reminiscences and for making available letters and papers of Irving Thalberg that have shed light on his personality and career; to Irene Mayer Selznick for clear reflection on many affairs, for recondite information and some rare photographs; to Frances Marion, Victor Seastrom, Marshall Neilan, Carey Wilson, George Cukor, Anita Stewart, J. Robert Rubin, Al Lichtman, David O. Selznick, Douglas Shearer and—this is what I mean!

To Howard Dietz, Howard Strickling and their associates in the press departments of Loew's, Inc., and Metro-Goldwyn-Mayer, I am indebted for much assistance, and to countless company employes, from Nicholas Schenck and Dore Schary down the ladder, I am grateful for enlightening interviews.

As was inevitable in preparing a complicated book of this sort, much labor, skill and patience were required in researching vast accumulations of old newspapers, trade papers, magazines, court records, museum archives and photographic files. Most of this labor was done for me by my tenacious helper and friend, Harriet Davis Dryden. I cannot thank her enough.

And for photographs, I am indebted to the Film Library of the Museum of Modern Art in New York City, the Bettmann Archive, the Kelly-Springfield Tire Company and Metro-Goldwyn-Mayer.

LIST OF ILLUSTRATIONS

FOREWORD

IF EVER there was an occasion in the history of Hollywood that wrapped all the vainglory and the curious valor of that community into a ball, it was a gathering of studio employees that took place on a huge sound stage of the Metro-Goldwyn-Mayer establishment one day in February, 1949.

Dark clouds were conspicuously gathering over the famous California colony where for nearly forty years the making of motion pictures had wondrously grown. Attendance was off in the nation's theatres and the evidence was ever more plain that the new competitive medium of television was slicing permanently into the commerce of films.

Yet here, on the world's largest sound stage, beneath a cycloramic canopy of blue sky, was occurring a show that had the character of a parade of French nobility at Versailles. Close to 1,000 film salesmen and Hollywood newspapermen were ranked at long luncheon tables, partaking of a catered repast of stuffed squab, suitably garnished, and ice cream molded in the shape of the studio's trademark, the lion. And facing them, from two rows of tables and in front of a significantly higher tier of plump and well-dressed producers and executives of Metro-Goldwyn-Mayer, were fifty-eight stars and feature players (including one collie dog), who were all at the time under contract to this biggest studio in the world.

There were Clark Gable, Spencer Tracy, Greer Garson, Judy Garland, Deborah Kerr, Ava Gardner, Esther Williams, Katharine Hepburn, Gene Kelly and Jennifer Jones. There were also Wallace Beery, Walter Pidgeon, Fred Astaire, Frank Sinatra, Ethel and Lionel Barrymore, Ann Miller, Janet Leigh, Mario Lanza,

Jeanette MacDonald, Red Skelton and Lassie, the dog. And behind them, beaming proudly, was the fabulous Louis B. Mayer, boss of this glittering aggregation, flanked by his top associates.

The nominal reason for this regal and unblushingly boastful display of great and expensive talent was the celebration of the twenty-fifth anniversary of the formation of the studio. A quarter century earlier, shy some two months, the company had come into being with the merger of the old producing outfits of Metro, Goldwyn and Mayer. The union had been put forth as a measure for saving the first two companies, and its success was far from certain at the time it occurred. However, through skill, good fortune and great expansion in motion pictures and in the world, the company had come to a position of predominance in the realm of films.

But more than a silver anniversary was behind this extravagant display. It was also by way of being a defy of the prophets of woe. While clear-headed, realistic people were predicting that a fundamental change in the structure of the motion picture business was inevitable with the spread of video, the old and entrenched picture-makers were scornful of any such thought. There could be no deviation, they insisted, so long as the stars were theirs to shine.

The display of assembled magnificence was the response of the custodians of the Lion.

Already Mayer had told the salesmen that the inclination to cut the costs of producing films at a sacrifice in quality would be resisted by Metro-Goldwyn-Mayer. "Anybody can make pictures for less money," he said. This studio would continue to maintain quality and it would double its output in the next year. Bouquets were tossed, and Mayer paid tribute to Dore Schary, his new head of production, as "a tower of strength."

The whole show was in the grand tradition of Metro-Goldwyn-Mayer extravagance.

Less than three years later, Mayer had lost his job and the fine group of studio contract players was beginning to fade away. . . .

* * *

In retrospect, that famous luncheon can be seen as the climactic feast in the era of the star-studded glory of Metro-Goldwyn-Mayer. It was also an event that tagged the turning in a half-century tide in American films. It was a last fine display of studio solidarity on a scale that will probably never be seen again.

This book is offered as a story of the rise of the company that had the capacity and the audacity to put on such a display. As such, it is in essence a story of American films.

The history of motion pictures is so vast and industrially involved that one volume could not possibly contain all of it. Nor could it put flesh upon the bones of the many and complex operations that have characterized this great medium. For this history is more than a record of inventions and artistic growth, of social and commercial evolution—of Entertainment in its broadest sense. It is also a story of people, of remarkable personalities, of human aspiration, failing, generosity and greed. To understand the growth, the grandeur and the grotesqueries of American films, we must understand the people who made them and were carried along in their sweep.

In the hope of conveying this intelligence in sharp and dramatic terms, I have chosen to follow the development and the destinies of one film company. This is more than the company of Metro-Goldwyn-Mayer, as you will see. It is actually the company of Loew's, Inc., its parent and sponsor, which began with the modest aspirations of one man in the early days of the commerce of films.

I have chosen this company for three reasons. First, its history presents a clear and characteristic pattern of how the American film industry evolved. In the growth of the theatre empire of Loew's, Inc., and the producing facility of Metro-Goldwyn-Mayer is revealed, without too much corporate turmoil, the essential evolution of the whole.

Second, the distinctions of this company and the people who have worked in it add up to an overwhelming total of outstanding fascinations in American films.

Third, the sheer drama of the story of this particular company might almost have been concocted for presentation on the screen. The play and the sweep of forces and personalities, from the days of the penny arcades to the present, have been appropriately balanced and timed. Fate as well as contrivance has been responsible for the story of Loew's, Inc., and Metro-Goldwyn-Mayer.

And so, in the manner of the medium about which this book is concerned, let us quickly dissolve to our story. The lights fade and the drama begins.

CHAPTER I

THE MOVIES BEGIN

A FLUSH of nervous excitement tingled the full-house audience that sat in unexpected darkness in the New York vaudeville theatre of Koster & Bial on a balmy evening in April, 1896. The seventh turn on the variety program—the debonnaire Brothers Horn, assisted by Miss Charlotte Hallett—had just scampered off into the wings and all the lights in the big Herald Square show place had been significantly doused. Now had arrived the moment for the evening's grand surprise. What was billed as "Thomas A. Edison's Latest Marvel, the Vitascope" was about to be shown.

In the brief interval of total darkness, people giggled, whispered, squirmed. Nobody knew for certain just what was about to occur. Then, from the promenade gallery, where a curious contraption had been rigged—a contraption which the New York *Times* said resembled "the double turret of a big monitor"—there came "a loud buzzing and roaring," and a beam of light from it pierced the dark. The audience could not have been more startled if someone had hollered, "Fire!"

Astonished young ladies clutched their escorts; bug-eyed gentlemen stiffened in their chairs. Open-mouthed wonder seized the scattering of Broadway sports and theatrical swells. For the beam of light stabbing from the gallery was hitting a large gilt-framed screen set on the stage. And on that screen was appearing, for the first time in a New York theatre, a picture that *moved!*

There it was, just as real as a Rembrandt—a picture of two pretty girls, wearing *pink* and *blue* dresses and doing a dance with parasols! (The primitive film had been hand-tinted, which accounted for bits of color in the gowns.) The young ladies twirled and grimaced, as the theatre orchestra played. "The effect was the same," said the *Dramatic Mirror*, "as if the girls were on the stage."

The audience had barely absorbed the impact, when the magical scene as quickly changed. Now came a black-and-white picture of an angry ocean rolling upon a sandy shore. For this one, the orchestra segued into a mood piece suggesting the sea. As the surf tumbled forward in the picture, the patrons in the front rows squealed and

13

cringed, so captured were they with the illusion that what they were witnessing was real.

The image was sustained for several seconds. Then the scene again gave way to a swinging and slapping encounter between two low comedians. By now the audience was cheering—"vociferously," said the *Times*. . . . The brisk exhibition was concluded with a "skirt dance," performed by a tall blonde.

When the house lights came up, the blinking audience, incredulous and thrilled, broke into noisy applauding and shouting for Mr. Edison. The great man was in the audience but he prudently did not respond. He had good reason. His "latest marvel" had not been invented by him.

To be sure, Edison and his associates had perfected the first machine that showed moving pictures inside a cabinet and likewise the camera that photographed the spools of films. This amusing little peephole contraption had been put on commercial display in curio shops called "Edison parlors," along with Edison phonographs, two years before. But the Vitascope was an improvement upon the work of other inventors, working separately in those years. Edison had merely made an arrangement to acquire it and sponsor it with his name.

But this wasn't known that April evening. Indeed, it wasn't generally known for years, until the historian, Terry Ramsaye, revealed the record of inventive rivalries within the field. And even if the audience had known it, the effect would have surely been the same. All that mattered was that the patrons of the theatre had been treated to a new, sensational thrill.

There was something else they didn't know that evening—something salient in the forward march of man: they didn't know that this was the commencement of a new entertainment device that was eventually to dominate the area in which it was so modestly exposed. For that showing began the continuity of the exhibition of motion pictures in theatres which has persisted, with all its consequences, right up to this moment of time.

The Pursuit of Happiness

It may be hard for our present generations, accustomed and conditioned as we are to motion pictures as a highly developed means of broad communication in our lives, to calculate the amazement of first seeing pictures that moved or appreciate the wonder of their discovery in the entertainment world. To do so, it must be remembered that the human eye, in that day, was still unfamiliar with mechanical stimuli and that people themselves were but emerging into an age of marvels and thrills. The experience of getting entertainment from commercial pastimes was almost as new, for many millions, as was the impact of the electric light, the phonograph and the telephone.

Indeed, the facilities for mass diversion in this growing and prosperous land were just assuming large proportions as the nineteenth century drew to a close. The cities were filling with people who had money and time to spend on their own self-indulgence and amusement. And there were others eager to offer them interesting ways.

True, the theatre, the opera and concerts had served to divert the well-to-do in larger centers for many decades, and good stock companies and traveling troupes had peddled the favors of Thespis from the Eastern seaboard to the Pacific coast. Circuses, carnivals, camp meetings and lecturers with magic-lantern shows were also familiar attractions in smaller communities.

However, the entertainment moving rapidly to the fore as the favorite of the urban middle classes was that known as vaudeville. This form of theatrical diversion, which came to sudden bloom in the last two decades of the century, was also known as "family burlesque." It consisted of theatrical programs made up of assorted "acts"—comic and sentimental singers, dancers, jugglers, trained animals, acrobats, trick bicycle riders, magicians, contortionists, comedians—indeed, almost any sort of mummery calculated to intrigue the customers. Chains of vaudeville theatres and a system of rotating acts had been built up by shrewd commercial showmen, and ticket prices were kept within the range of what was charmingly mentioned as the "family pocketbook."

Naturally, the vaudeville managers—offshoots of P. T. Barnum, all— were constantly on the lookout for anything novel or odd. They dragged in all sorts of curiosities. One of their popular tours de force was a feature called "living pictures"—actors posing as famous paintings in large gilt frames. This quaint trick of tableaux making went over big with the crowds. Delight was provoked by the variety of the "pictures" and the dexterity with which they were changed. No wonder, then, that the development of mechanical pictures which actually *moved* caught the vaudeville managers' interest, as soon as they saw the things would work. To them, the new apparatus was plainly another "act." And no wonder that the patrons were naively overwhelmed.

As it happened, Albert Bial had been foresighted. He booked the Vitascope exclusively, to show as long as he chose to keep it at his theatre in New York, thus beginning the practice of "first run" that has prevailed in the commerce of films. But his rivals were enterprising, and they leaped for other machines that had been developed and pirated in the continuing inventors' war.

Less than three weeks after the inauguration of motion pictures at Koster & Bial's, Oscar Hammerstein booked a rival contraption (the Latham Eidoloscope) in his new variety theatre on Broadway. Then B. F. Keith, the vaudeville titan, installed the French Lumière machines in his Union Square Theatre in New York and got the Vitascope for his big houses in Boston and Philadelphia. By the end of that summer, there was scarcely a ranking vaudeville theatre in the United States that did not acquire some sort of variant of the "marvelous Vitascope."

And machines there were aplenty—all shapes and varieties of them. Inventors, mechanics and just plain tinkers rushed forward to meet the demand. What projectors weren't supplied by Edison and the Lumières were banged out by other enterprisers who were clever with calipers and tools. Edison soon had a formidable rival in American Biograph, and the market was also infested with Cinegraphs, Cinegraphoscopes, Kineopticons.

Nor was competition limited to the vaudeville theatres or to the leading manufacturers who made the films and projectors for them. As fast as apparatus was available—and that was very soon, in view of the ingenuity and acquisitiveness of humankind—traveling showmen, small-time lecturers and carnival entrepreneurs grabbed onto machines and spools of pictures and went forth to the country with them, carrying the new and thrilling marvel to towns and villages all over the land.

For such pioneering ventures, only modest investment was required. The current theatrical trade papers said so in eloquent come-on ads. "A complete outfit—Americanized Cinematograph—$50!" This typical offer appeared in the New York *Clipper*, an aptly named journal of the show world, in 1898. Films of brief duration such as *Circus Parade, Boxing Girls* or *Our Summer Boarder—Comic* could be bought outright for five dollars each. These represented the fashion and were "guaranteed not to peel." Characteristic was the promise made by a little Philadelphia optician, Sig Lubin, in offering projectors of his own devising: "You are bound to make a small fortune! Buy now and get in the push!"

Local opera houses, Pythian temples and even churches were adroitly used to display the transient attractions. Also black-topped tents—blackened to assure interior darkness—became the harbors of primitive picture shows. Many of the traveling exhibitors were previous "lecturers" with lantern slides. It was from such passing purveyors, who continued in business for years, that millions of pot-stove Americans first bought the magic of pictures that moved.

But for all the initial excitement and rush of activity—for all the vaudeville promotion and traffic of showmen on the road—the early venturings with moving pictures were blundering and confused. The formula for their employment was still completely obscure. After the first flush of newness, they rapidly lost novelty.

The reason is now quite obvious: more attention was being paid to the improvement of the machinery than to the improvement of the films. Most of the early pictures were made by the manufacturers of the machines, who functioned as film producers mainly to service the equipment they sold.

Outside of one positive inspiration to film a Passion Play on the part of Richard G. Hollaman, the proprietor of New York's Eden Musee—an inspiration which led, incidentally, to a number of Passion Play films that early cluttered the tent shows with Bible stories and forecast the later works of Cecil B. DeMille—there was no thought of using moving pictures to tell a dramatic tale. In fact, the Passion Play pictures were little more than series of scenes, usually accompanied by a "lecturer," who explained what was happening.

For the rest, the infant pictures consisted mostly of quaint and random views—*London Street Arabs Dancing and Singing, A Morning Dip in the Surf, The Geneva Exposition Cascade, Parade of the 96th French Infantry*—endless repetitions of mere movement, pictorial but devoid of surprise, as tedious to the accustomed observer as watching a balloon ascend for the fifteenth time.

And thus the motion pictures subsided from a thrilling novelty to an accepted piece of minor entertainment on conventional vaudeville bills. In fact, they became so monotonous in their routine weekly change that they were soon booked as supplemental items at the beginning or end of the bills. Eventually, they were known as "chasers"—the weakest "act" at the conclusion of the show to notify the customers that there wasn't any more.

How dismally anticlimactic was this sad state of affairs in the light of the enthusiasm that marked the beginning of films! "What is the future of the Kinetograph?" W.K.L. Dickson had rhetorically inquired in a pamphlet advertising the Edison camera in 1898. "Ask rather from what conceivable phase of the future it can be debarred. . . . It is the crown and flower of nineteenth century magic . . . the crystallization of eons of groping enchantments. . . . It is the earnest of the coming age."

Those were lofty words and prophetic, but it was still to be many years before the earnest of the coming age was realized and motion pictures came into their own. Then channels were opened into the future not so much by the pioneers of the machines or prosperous vaudeville showmen as by the swarm of little entrepreneurs of simple and cheap entertainment who moved in from the merchandising world. For it was ironically out of the garment business and down the grubby, crowded aisles of those newly popular emporiums of mechanical amusement, the penny arcades, that the oddly destined leaders of the American motion picture industry came.

Unpretentious among these opportunists was an amiable little man named Marcus Loew.

CHAPTER II

MARCUS LOEW IS WILLING

IT IS A significant feature of the American motion picture industry that it was grappled and guided into being by men from what we call the common herd—men from the moving masses of the people whose tastes they discovered and served. They were hobbled by no preconceptions of the canons of propriety and good form as then recognized and cherished in higher literary and theatrical realms. Their standards were picked up entirely from what they found the paying public would buy—and the public with which they had contact and to which they catered was the public with small change.

Among this incipient class of showmen there was not one to the manor born. Few of them had much education. Some couldn't even write or read. Immigrants and sons of immigrants in a fluid society which was peppered heavily with new Americans from whom Old World ties were quick to fall, these middlemen of amusement were prophetic of the culture-industry they came to run. They were the Carnegies of the movies.

Such was Marcus Loew.

Unlike a good many others of the early promoters of films, Loew did not have his birthplace in some middle-European or Russian town. Nobody pinned a steerage ticket to the lapel of his threadbare coat and sent him forth, with tears and kisses, to seek his fortune in the American promised land. He was born in a dark and dingy chamber of a slum on the lower East Side of New York, the son of a Jewish restaurant waiter and a widowed German girl. His father, Herman, had come from Austria only a few years before and had married the young Ida Sichel, who was already the mother of two small sons. They made their home in a tenement building at 173 Fourth Street, off Avenue B. It was there, on May 8, 1870, that Marcus arrived in the world.

In a burst of sentiment and poesy, one of Loew's panegyrists once wrote: "Over the modest crib of his baby years hung the star of destiny." If there was any such glittering adornment in the small and cluttered flat, it was not apparent or suspected. The Loew family— father, mother and three small boys, to which were later added a daughter, Fanny, and then Henry, another son—were pitifully poor people. And the state of their purse wasn't helped by the penchant of Herman for slipping small handouts to new Jewish immigrants in the tradition of the ghetto brotherhood. No wonder that, at the age of six, little Marcus—or Max, as he was known—was on the street selling newspapers, probably the *Irish World*. He and another youngster had their stand in front of Billy McGlory's old saloon at Hester Street near the Bowery, not far from Avenue B. It was there that the future movie magnate got his first bumps in business enterprise. The newsboys paid dearly for their position. Loew early learned the advantage of a good site.

The theatre, in this rococo era, was not exquisite on the lower East Side, but it flourished, and the newspaper merchants had a youthful taste for it. With a surplus of ten cents between them, they would buy one ticket to the second gallery of the old Bowery National Theatre —for *Butts the Boy Detective* or some such lurid favorite of the day. Then they would share the ticket between them, each boy seeing half of the show and exchanging information about it at the intermission and end.

During the three years he sold newspapers, young Marcus went by day to grammar school, hawked papers by night and, in the summer, worked for a pushcart peddler selling lemons to housewives and saloons. During that time, and for a few years after, he also received the conventional religious instruction given an orthodox Jewish boy. But, at nine, he put schooling behind him and got a job in a map-coloring plant pulling maps from under the big presses for thirty-five cents a day. A day was ten hours and the child laborer put in six days a week. Fortunately for him, his health and his future, that job didn't last very long. A strike for an increase in wages (which would have meant five cents a day more for the boy) was answered by the employer with a lockout. At ten, young Loew was unemployed.

At this point, a native ingenuity began to reveal itself. The youngster persuaded an older fellow who did odd jobs with a hand-printing press to take him in as an associate. The combination worked well and the lads dug up enough business to warrant purchase of a larger press. With this the oddly matched printers began publishing a neighborhood advertising throwaway sheet. It was grandly called the *East Side Advertiser*. Marcus, as the smaller of the two, scurried around soliciting advertisements and circulating the sheets while his partner did the heavy business of setting type and pumping the press. The division of labor was propitious. Marcus, well known in the neighborhood, had a gift for conning the ice-cream parlors, clothing shops and grocery stores into buying advertising. His partner had a talent for running the press. The publication had a circulation of 500 and the partners made a profit of close to twelve dollars a week.

Then fate entered in the form of a woman. The older partner took a wife who soon claimed her husband was doing more work and was entitled to more of the returns. The lad was no match for this termagant. The partnership was dissolved.

Next job for the undersized youngster was in an East Side gent's furnishing store, waiting on customers, running errands, sorting stock —working sometimes until midnight, six solid days of the week. His weekly wage was four dollars. Then the chance to earn a half-dollar more caused him to switch to a fur factory. It was a typical garment district sweat shop where the twelve-year-old boy was required to work for eleven and a half hours a day turning the crank on a heavy fur-cutting table because the place had no other form of power. Most of his slender earnings went into the family pocketbook. But this was a likely beginning in the garment industry, in a business which the shrewd, ambitious youngster figured worthwhile to learn.

Gambler in Furs

The garment industry, in that day—as at present—was attractive to those with a yen for speculation. Marcus was obviously one. Within six years of his entering employment in that Rivington Street fur firm, he had worked up through several levels, had learned a lot about furs and had saved enough money so that, at eighteen, he could start out on his own. With sixty-three hard-earned dollars—his first intoxicating capital—he became an independent broker, buying and selling pelts. At nineteen, he had failed. Something happened to the market and the neophyte was nipped.

This was nothing unusual in the fur business, where dealers were often ruined overnight by a sudden fluctuation in prices or an unpredictable change in styles. But Marcus Loew's attitude towards failure *was* unusual. After the routine bankruptcy, there was $1,800 still owed to his unhappy but unamazed creditors. Loew knocked them on their ears by telling them he intended to pay them anyhow. And he did. Going out as a salesman for another fur company, he earned $100 or more a week, out of which earnings he paid off his every debt in a few years.

Loew often said the assurance he gained from this odd experience was of priceless value to him in his later speculative career. His youthful discovery that failure, in itself, was no sin or shame and that tenacity could overcome it endowed him with a basic business poise. His characteristic of calculated daring stemmed from that failure in furs.

The immediate result, however, was an upsurge of confidence to ask a young lady's hand in marriage and start another fur business of his own. The young lady was Caroline Rosenheim, whose widowed mother had six daughters and a furniture store. Caroline and Marcus were married on March 4, 1894. That summer adversity again hit him. Loew went to the wall—only this time he squeaked through the wringer with seven dollars to spare. Then he went to work as a salesman for a furrier named Herman Baehr.

The association with Baehr was propitious. The older man was an expert with furs which he had learned as a boy in Germany. He knew how to buy them, to cut the goods, to manufacture garments. Loew knew how to sell. As a new team, they weathered the panic of 1895 and were thenceforth comparatively prosperous. Loew traveled, became familiar with merchants in cities through the East and Middle West. He was noted in the business as a salesman who could "push" a line of goods. Oftentimes orders he had sold would be returned to the busy loft factory of the firm in Union Square. Nothing daunted, Loew would go out and sell them over again.

Loew was apparently not content with the variable income the fur firm provided and the doubtful security it gave. He had felt the quick chill of failure and was regularly skating along the edge of a highly uncertain form of commerce. He knew the perversity of style. And though he had a taste for chance and venture—a penchant for audacity—there was a streak of caution in him that was matched in his partner, Baehr. As a dependable investment for his savings, Loew wanted something close to the ground, something that couldn't be lost in one bad season. Real estate was the best thing he could find.

Once he told a friend that the ambition, the sole ambition, of himself and his wife in those years was to have enough money to buy an interest in a good tenement or apartment house. Little could he have realized how spectacularly that self-preserving urge was to lead him to infinitely more fortune than he had spanned in his wildest dreams.

Fellow Well Met

For it was actually a modest investment, one of several that he and Baehr made, in a New York apartment building, on West 111th Street, that brought Loew into the orbit of the entertainment world. This is the way it happened: the fur salesman was standing one Sunday morning in front of his 111th Street building, looking it over with the appraising eye of an efficient landlord, when he noticed another gentleman looking at a building down the street. Instinctively, he approached his neighbor, began to converse with him and discovered that he, too, was an investor in the adjoining real estate.

The two compared notes. The stranger was frankly dissatisfied. He soon sensed, however, that he was talking to a man who knew whereof he spoke, so far as the business of managing real estate was concerned. It is also likely that Loew saw *he* was talking to a man who was pitifully inadequate in that ability but was doing all right otherwise. Indeed, it is safe to imagine that Loew clearly recognized his man and tactfully arranged the chance encounter, for Loew was an avid theatre fan and the stranger was an up-and-coming actor.

He was David Warfield, who had recently made a moderate hit as a shabby Jewish character in a revue called *The Merry Whirl.*

As a consequence of their sidewalk meeting and the acquaintanceship that developed between the two men, Loew was asked by Warfield if he would help with his real estate. Graciously, Loew accepted and the two soon became firm friends. Warfield often said later that he was struck by Loew's talent for finance and by his ability to make the property pay. Loew, in turn, was no doubt flattered to be the friend and adviser of a rising theatrical star. Warfield was yet to reach his zenith, but he was on the way.

The year of this fortunate encounter was 1899. For some time thereafter, Loew continued as a successful salesman of furs. But already another close friendship was drawing him toward his destiny.

On his selling trips West, the hustling Marcus had met Adolph Zukor and Morris Kohn, a pair of Chicago fur merchants anxious to move to New York. Loew helpfully gave them suggestions and found an apartment for the Zukor family when they moved. The amiable Loews and Zukors became block neighbors and intimate friends.

Now, Zukor and Kohn were also looking for something other than furs in which to make an investment. An opportunity came when a relative of Kohn invited them to put some money into a penny arcade. The principal promoter of this venture was a former Buffalo merchant, Mitchell Mark, who had attempted the new arcade business in Buffalo and in uptown New York City. Prospering in these locations, he wanted to try downtown New York and had his eye on a vacant dairy kitchen on Fourteenth Street, near thriving Union Square. But the holders of the property weren't eager to rent it to a hustler of arcades. They wanted a more reliable tenant. So Zukor and Kohn were invited to invest and sign the lease, which would be assurance, of a sort, that the rent would be paid.

The venture was readily attractive, for the novelty of penny arcades was rapidly gaining popularity under the label of "electric vaudeville." These bright little open-front "parlors," crowded with assorted machines that vended a variety of amusements and peephole motion pictures for a penny a vend, were especially appropriate and alluring to the curiosity-seeking sidewalk trade. Zukor and Kohn liked the prospect, so they joined with Mark and his group to form the Automatic Vaudeville Company, which opened its Fourteenth Street arcade in 1903.

Inevitably the venture intrigued Zukor's good friend, Marcus Loew. He closely watched the operation with a more than objective eye. He noted the easy luring of patrons and the clattering cascade of coins. Soon he took his resolution. When the company decided to expand and open other arcades in Philadelphia, Boston and Newark,

Loew asked to be let in. Zukor and Kohn, needing capital, readily agreed.

Since this was the entertainment business, Loew had talked it over with his friend, David Warfield, who was now starring grandly in David Belasco's *The Auctioneer*. Warfield was all for the venture and wanted to invest in it, too. Loew, parlaying his friendships, arranged it with Zukor and Kohn. Warfield got $15,000 worth of securities out of his safe deposit box and added that to Loew's lesser investment. They were in Automatic Vaudeville.

Through the winter and spring of 1904, Loew followed the fortunes of the arcades. Baehr, his conservative partner, was disapproving and aloof. Impressed by their parlors' prosperity, Loew thought of full-time occupation with them. But there wasn't room for him in the company. Besides, as he once explained, "Adolph didn't think I was worth $2,500 a year, and I had the same opinion of him."

About this time, Kohn concocted an ingenious device for performing the happy function of collecting the pennies from the machines. He rigged up a little electric railway with a train of open cars which ran around under the machines at regular intervals and caught the pennies as they were automatically dumped. The display became an added free attraction for the crowds. It was a literal and captivating spectacle of money rolling in.

Friends of Loew later insisted it was that ingenious electric train, groaning under carloads of pennies, that finally decided him. Any business that offered such immediate and obvious cash returns was irresistible to the fur merchant who had been battling with credits for years. He talked to Baehr and Warfield. Would they go along with him if he pulled his money out of the Zukor arcade and put it into one of his own? Baehr was not enthusiastic. He didn't want to lose his "outside" man, who he realized was largely responsible for the moderate prosperity of their firm. But Warfield again was agreeable. Loew looked around for a place. Soon he found one—a vacant store at 172 West Twenty-third Street, off the southeast corner of Seventh Avenue. He and Warfield removed their investments from Automatic Vaudeville. With a little more money raised from Loew's mother-in-law, from a merchant friend, Morris Drucker, and, indeed, with a small amount from Baehr, they dumped it together and started the People's Vaudeville Company on Nov. 14, 1904.

A lease was taken on the Twenty-third Street property, Loew fixed it up as an arcade, and it was opened for business in January, 1905. Loew was employed as general manager at $100 a week, plus profits, receivable in stock.

Thus the little furrier was started in the entertainment business—on his own.

CHAPTER III

FIRST LINKS IN A MIGHTY CHAIN

IN THE hands of a less ambitious salesman, that Twenty-third Street arcade might have been a sufficient establishment to satisfy his wants. But Loew was a lively operator and he saw some fast money in arcades. Within a few months he had opened two more in uptown New York. Now, with a "chain" of places, he disassociated himself from Baehr & Loew and moved the "offices" of the People's Vaudeville Company out of their Union Square fur loft to rooms above his penny establishment at 2172 Third Avenue. There, amid cluttered little Harlem shops and grocery stores, Loew's amusement business had its first formal home.

The simplicity of the setup did not discourage its occupants. Loew meant to run his organization as efficiently as if he were in furs. He had as lawyer, financial advisor and official secretary of the firm, Elek John Ludvigh, who was the Baehr & Loew attorney and also lawyer for Zukor's companies. It was Ludvigh, accustomed to the troubles of little firms in the garment industry, who guided Loew shrewdly and wisely in his financial and legal affairs for many years.

Loew also got a bookkeeper, David Bernstein, whom he hired away from a job as salesman for a carpet company at fourteen dollars a week. Bernstein, like Loew, was a poor boy who had never got beyond the eighth grade. He didn't know bookkeeping when Loew put him in the job. But he secretly hastened to study accounting from a correspondence school. Bernstein continued as a financial agent of Loew's companies for the next forty years.

The uptown neighborhood of Harlem was a prosperous middle-class residential area in those days. Loew had counted heavily on this when he spotted his arcades. He was always one for scouting any area into which he contemplated a move. In a few months, with a little more money and confidence, he opened a fourth arcade at 125th Street and Lenox Avenue.

During his travels as a fur salesman, Loew had made many firm friends, and it was probably from one of these—or perhaps from Warfield—that he heard of the next likely addition to his chain. It was a penny arcade in Cincinnati, on downtown Fountain Square—one of the several so-called Edisonias, operated by the penny-machine manufacturer, Herbert Mills. Loew went out to look at the Cincinnati arcade, figured he could make it go, rented it, hired a manager and reopened it as the Penny Hippodrome.

In later years, Loew often stated it was because of an experience at this arcade that he got into the business of showing motion pictures on screens. One Sunday afternoon, at the suggestion of his manager, he went across the river to Covington, Ky., to see a novel stunt being pulled by the owner of a local arcade. This fellow had rented an old projector and some films and was putting on shows in a room above his penny parlor. The admission was five cents a head.

The proprietor was the sole attendant. After selling tickets at the door, he would go inside, turn off the lights, start the projector and give a running explanation in a loud voice of what was happening on the screen, such as, "So-and-so is now going to be knocked down" or "This is where the burglar gets caught." The necessity for providing a narration betokened the patrons' naivete.

Loew was impressed with the performance and decided to try the same thing in his Cincinnati arcade. He and his manager put a projector and some folding chairs in an empty upstairs room. They got a Biograph comedy called *Hot Chestnuts* and a couple of other odds and ends that ran for no more than five minutes and opened for business on the next Sunday at the nickel scale.

The seating capacity of the "theatre" was a modest 110. On the opening day it attracted close to 5,000 customers! They lined up for hours to see the cheap show, which could have been seen on any vaudeville bill—but not for a nickel! That low price was what pulled the customers. The next week, the space was expanded. They put in 200 more chairs. The following Sunday they pushed more than 10,000 patrons through the room.

To Loew, this was absolutely magic. He didn't stop to explore the reasons for such a phenomenon. He hopped right back to New York and put a similar screen show in a vacant store adjacent to his Lenox Avenue arcade. The customers were "spilled" through an exit that gave into the arcade, so that they might relieve their pockets of any spare pennies in the familiar machines. The operation was immediately successful, so successful, indeed, that Loew shortly ordered the penny machines removed from his Twenty-third Street arcade and the place turned into a nickelodeon. His transition to theatre business was underway.

Loew's move was not original. For several years, there had been sporadic undertakings in different cities to run little picture shows, in connection with phonograph parlors or penny arcades, on a ten-cent or five-cent admission scale. And already the name Nickelodeon had been applied to one of these enterprises in a remodeled Pittsburgh store. The movement had become epidemic toward the end of 1905, and Loew was simply catching the infection when he converted his Twenty-third Street arcade.

For instance, his friend Adolph Zukor had withdrawn from Automatic Vaudeville and had opened his own nickelodeon, next door to the Fourteenth Street arcade. In Chicago, Aaron Jones, a Midwest showman whose career closely paralleled that of Loew, was converting his popular State Street arcade into a nickel theatre. In Kansas City, Louisville, San Francisco, other arcade owners were doing the same thing. And in Brooklyn, a former fur sponger, William Fox, was busily opening a chain of cheap "store shows."

The phenomenal popularity of these small places and their multiplication, beginning in 1905—there were 3,000 of them in the country by 1907, according to the *Motion Picture World*—was due to several factors, not least of which was the price. Another less fully realized factor was an extraordinary population change.

During the critical decade between 1900 and 1910, close to 9,000,000 immigrants crowded into the United States. The mark of 1,000,000 arrivals in one year was broken for the first time in 1905. This vast polyglot population, wide-eyed and with limited means, was particularly attracted to the little picture shows, which were cheap, sensational, and silent, presenting no language barriers.

Then, too, the character of the pictures had undergone an appropriate change from the crude photographs of mere movement that had become tiresome on vaudeville theatre bills. A measure of storytelling was now being got into the films. Little comic and melodramatic episodes were briefly but vigorously performed. *The Great Train Robbery*, produced by Edwin S. Porter for Edison in 1903, excited tremendous interest and started a rash of holdup films. Dozens of fly-by-night producers began crowding into the field which had been pretty well dominated by Edison, Biograph and Vitagraph, an early firm. Some of the newcomers prospered, such as Kalem, Selig and Essanay; others, working on shoestrings, rapidly fell by the way.

Also contributing to the eruption of the new motion picture "stores" was a semi-mechanical attraction known as the "scenic tour." This was a clattering contrivance that a couple of tinkers had fledged at Electric Park in Kansas City and "introduced" at the St. Louis Exposition in 1904. It consisted of a narrow room decorated to resemble the interior of a railway car, wherein motion pictures of scenic wonders were shown on a screen at the far end. When a "carload" of customers were seated, the lights were lowered, a whistle was blown, train noises were belched out of a phonograph and the seats were made to sway. Then, with the apparatus rocking and the customers rattling like seeds in a gourd, the screen was lighted with onrushing pictures of the scenic places of the world.

These "tours" were initially quite popular and hundreds of them were flung across the land, with showmen getting around the original patent by constructing variations of their own. Marcus Loew was briefly in the business of selling "scenic tours," in addition to operating a couple of his own. In fact, it was while he was promoting this apparatus that he came to know two men who were to be closely woven into the fabric of his life and companies. They were the Schenck brothers, Nicholas and Joe.

Pushers in Paradise

The brothers, who had come to this country from Russia in the 1880's as boys, were running an amusement park at the time Loew met them. It was a modest Elysium at the north end of Manhattan Island, known as Paradise Park. Its claim on that name was represented by the usual clutter of outdoor rides and a covered dancing pavilion where the proprietors got their profits from selling beer.

They had taken to this likely venture after trying many money-making schemes, including the ownership and operation of a drugstore on Third Avenue. But the entertainment business most intrigued them. They had been running their park for a couple of years when Loew met them and got a concession to set up a "scenic tour."

Much more important to him than any income got from that device was the opportunity this gave him to know and observe the Schencks. For he soon discovered in these brothers the sort of resourcefulness and energy that he knew were the rugged essentials in his own expanding entertainment realm.

Characteristic of the Schencks' aggressive natures was an experience Nick had about this time, an experience of such note in the family that it certainly did not escape the ears of Loew. He had undertaken as a side venture to put up a roller-coaster ride in the amusement-park area of Coney Island. The Red Devil was to be its name.

Although Nick had had no experience in erecting such a thing, he decided to save money on its construction by superintending it himself. A mechanic he employed had conned him into building it so it would operate from an electric third-rail, a form of roller-coaster propulsion that was cheaper but also quite new.

On the day Schenck was ready to test his layout, a man who had been silently watching him build came to him and said, "Take my advice, young fellow. Don't ride in that thing. You'll kill yourself."

Schenck understandably bridled. "Who are you?" he asked.

"My name is Thompson," said the stranger, "and I've built most of the scenic railways in the East. You've made a big mistake with this one. It should be operated with a chain."

The young promoter wilted. "You do not make me feel so good," he said. Now he perceived his folly in attempting the novel third-rail. Suddenly he saw his fine Red Devil turning into a literal ride of death and with it his large investment going down the drain.

At that point, young Nick did something he very seldom did—he went to a bar and swallowed three stiff slugs of liquor. Back he went to the Red Devil and shouted to the mechanic: "Start her up! I'll be damned if I'll listen to that fellow! I'll try it! Nobody else—just me!"

A car was brought into position. Schenck defiantly got in. The switch was thrown and the treacherous conveyance was started up the long grade. Just as it left the platform, a reckless workman jumped into the back seat, so Schenck had a loyal companion on his tentative life-or-death ride.

The perilous phase was that first pull up to the launching point. If the third-rail worked without slipping, the thing was presumably safe. Schenck held his breath and sweated as the car slowly moved up the grade. The last few feet were a nightmare. Then it was over the top and on its way. The agonized owner shouted. His companion hooted with joy as they raced around the inclines and came down toward the platform, safe and sound. Schenck, in his excitement, started to get up, when—bang!—his head struck a beam that someone had forgotten to saw off. His derby hat was crushed; his head remained.

The Red Devil at Coney Island became an extremely popular ride. . . .

After one summer of running the "scenic tour" at Paradise Park, Loew suggested that the Schenck brothers join him in People's Vaudeville. At first the boys were reluctant, but one of their several brothers, George, did take a job as manager of one of Loew's nickelodeons. Then, the following year, Nick accepted the proposition of Loew and went to work for him, on a tentative basis, at no fixed salary. Both brothers later succumbed when they entered a partnership with Loew in acquiring and operating the Lyric Theatre in Hoboken. The Schencks had the privilege of investing with Loew in his various deals. The arrangement added immeasurable manpower to his enlarging "family."

By this time, the busy little showman had swiftly progressed beyond the stage of mere nickelodeon operation or the peddling of "scenic tours." He had found a new entertainment formula in the combination of moving pictures and low-grade vaudeville.

His arriving at this was quick and clever. Early offered on the nickelodeon bills were interpolated presentations of illustrated songs. Ballad singers were put on between the pictures, accompanied by pianists and stereopticon slides. This expansion of cheap entertainment set a new "store show" style. The places that had such live performers were able to charge a dime.

Loew went along with this fashion, but he soon saw that the small size of the "stores" limited the attraction and the variety of such tabloid vaudeville. He sensed that he might get a jump on his competitors if he could do it on a somewhat larger scale.

The Royal Plunge

Sometime during the summer of 1907, he got wind that a real theatre could be had in the downtown section of Brooklyn for a modest cost. It was a place called Watson's Cozy Corner, at Pearl and Willoughby streets. It had been built by "Sliding Billy" Watson as a house for refined vaudeville, but it had degenerated swiftly into a mart of straight "beef-trust" burlesque.

Loew looked it over carefully. He wasn't a snap decision man. He talked to people in the neighborhood. Then he talked to his friends. He decided that, with some "fumigating," Watson's Cozy Corner could be made to serve the purpose of a ten-cent motion picture-vaudeville theatre that he had in mind.

But the house had a bad reputation which had to be overcome. Loew managed that by resorting to an imposed expediency. Before he had taken the theatre, it had been tentatively assigned for the following season to an Italian stock company. Loew decided to let the company continue as planned. In three months, it drenched the house with culture, and Loew was ready for the plunge.

He had changed the theatre's name to the Royal. Now he got together a bill of continuous vaudeville and pictures—small-time acts and sketchy little films. He did some local advertising and opened for business on a rainy January day.

The story of that opening was oft repeated by Loew—how one customer turned up in the theatre for the opening show, how Loew himself went to this customer and evasively tried to explain that this was a dress rehearsal, how the customer said he'd gladly pay ten cents to see a dress rehearsal and how the show thus had to go on. The first day's business was awful. They did much better the second day. Such a phenomenal jump in business foretold a ringing success, Loew wryly said.

He was right. With careful management and a fair selection of low-grade vaudeville—low in the sense that the performers were willing to work for small pay—the house turned in a profit of some $60,000 its first year. Loew attributed this to a policy of keeping his shows simple and clean. He frankly pitched his entertainment to the "family trade," on the theory that two or more members of a family made a better sales unit than one leering male. All through his life as a showman, Loew worked on this principle. He sought to provide amusement tuned to the tastes of "all."

The experience with the Royal was the clincher, so far as Loew was concerned. He saw the future for his sort of show business in larger theatres—theatres with enough seats to handle the necessary flow of trade, to warrant and pay for the presentation of more elaborate and thus more attractive bills. The grubby nickelodeons, with their small capacity and shabby atmosphere, might continue to draw a marginal business—and they did, for several more years. Loew himself kept a few going. But he saw the handwriting on their walls.

Indeed, they were marked for extinction by the axes of the pious as well as by the pressures of economics, which were more impressive to Loew. Scarcely had the rampant nickelodeons begun coming into vogue than the inevitable forces of righteousness began finding fault with them. Not only were the little show shops abused as firetraps and pestholes (which some were), but they were charged with completely upsetting the social balance and public morals.

As early as 1907, a local ordinance was obtained permitting the police of Chicago to close any nickelodeon in that city found showing "offensive" films. And in 1908—the same year in which Loew opened his Royal—Mayor George McClellan of New York started a war on the little "store shows." The attack was reactionary and relentless, and it might well have dealt a crippling blow to the early commerce of motion pictures if it had not been vigorously opposed by the defiant group of nickelodeon showmen, headed by William Fox and Marcus Loew. These little men formed clumsy forces and successfully defended their right to operate their places and show their pictures. The nickelodeons thus won a short reprieve.

But Loew, even though he joined the battle, had already gone beyond the limited idea of the "store shows." With his success at the Royal, he was looking around for other theatres in which he might put his "combination" bills. He soon came upon a couple that the Shubert Brothers held in New York. The Shuberts were smart operators who had assembled a formidable chain of legitimate theatres. A deal was made for Loew to operate the theatres, the Yorkville and the Lincoln Square, and he opened them, with bills featuring five acts of continuous vaudeville and assorted pictures, late in 1909. The price scale he now established was ten to twenty-five cents.

This tie-up of Loew with the Shuberts was a large step forward for him. It represented a liaison with the legitimate entertainment world.

And it also brought him into contact with sources of private finance that were now essential to the fulfillment of his ambition to get more theatres.

Capital Move

During the five years that he had been operating, Loew had gathered his working capital from friends and assorted associates, as his various enterprises took form. The idea was to keep his other ventures intact in case one didn't work. For instance, he had a scheme for rehearsing live actors and putting them behind motion picture screens to speak dialogue, thus achieving a sort of crude "talking pictures." It was called Humanova. It did not catch on.

But with his continuing prosperity and his ambitious plans, Loew found he needed a stronger corporate structure to support his bid for capital. He discussed it with his associates, Ludvigh and Zukor, who were connected with him in Humanova, in the Yorkville-Lincoln Square and other deals. The Schencks, who were now in business with him, were also in on the talks. They all agreed to pool their holdings and form a new company which would embrace the several companies that Loew and his various partners owned.

Thus in February, 1910, People's Vaudeville and the other companies were merged into Loew's Consolidated Enterprises. Stock in the new company was exchanged for that in the other holdings, and $200,000 worth of the new stock was sold to the Shuberts, who thus became important investors in the affairs of Loew.

Marcus, of course, was elected president of the new company. Zukor was elected treasurer, and Nicholas Schenck, secretary.

With this substantial financing, Loew was soon on the move, and in the next few years he greatly added to his theatrical chain. In October, 1910, he grandly opened his new National Theatre in the Bronx, which served as "flagship" of his growing circuit and a proving place for his "combination" bills. He also got the Harlem Casino and, in the following year, he made his biggest move of all. He boldly purchased the William Morris circuit of vaudeville theatres, which included the then very swanky American Music Hall on Forty-second Street in New York. By this surprising maneuver, which greatly startled the "big time" vaudeville world, the little man who was but six years out of the fur business became a figure in the field. He now moved his offices to the American Music Hall.

Within a month of this acquisition, he reorganized his company again further to extend his range for finance. Loew's Theatrical Enterprises was formed to take over Loew's Consolidated, with a capitalization of $5,000,000. Three shares of Loew's Theatrical

Loew's penny arcade at 2172 Third Avenue, New York City, above which were the first offices of his People's Vaudeville Company.

Loew's State Theater and office building at 1540 Broadway, the "lighthouse" and home of Loew's, Inc., following their opening in 1921.

Loew at 16, when he worked in a
fur-cutting factory on New York's
lower East Side.

Carrie and Marcus Loew at the entrance to their Long Island mansion,
shortly before his death.

Two ex-furriers, Adolph
Zukor and Marcus Loew,
top moguls in the new
movie industry, in Holly-
wood, 1923.

common stock, with a par value of $100, were given for one share of Loew's Consolidated. A further issue of $700,000 worth of common stock was then sold to private investors. The company was on high financial ground.

Although Loew at this time was becoming a rich and effective man in a surprisingly booming business, a contemporary observer of him said that he was "not exactly what is called a man of large vision.

"He did not look to the distant future for results, nor to far-away commercial fields. He was no railway king to figure on the growth of tributary cities and countrysides. But the things he was doing he knew through and through; he felt them stirring and living under his hands. He was quick to catch the meaning of every new thing that touched him, and he had the true gift of the creative mind, the gift of making small things grow. Also he had courage, a boundless courage which was born in him, which had not been beaten out of him by all his failures nor drowned out of him by the sudden flood of his success."

So wrote a journalist in the New York *Sun* in 1912.

This was a fair estimate of Marcus Loew in those years of theatrical growth. He had no intellectual pretensions, nor was he an egotistical man. A precipitate little figure with a large, bushy black mustache and big eyes which were usually beaming, he moved quickly and spoke in a voice that came surprisingly loud and deep from such a diminutive frame. When flamboyant writers and press agents began to dub him "the little Napoleon" of this or that—usually "the little Napoleon of small-time vaudeville"—he would cheerfully say: "Sure, I'm another Napoleon. I'm a little more than five feet tall and I don't weigh much."

It is remarkable, incidentally, how many "little Napoleons" there were in the group that pioneered the motion pictures. Zukor was such a small, slight man—a lean-faced and sharp-eyed little person who could almost slip through the slot of a coin machine. Unlike Loew, he was deliberate, mild-mannered, and spoke in a moderate voice. Joe Schenck used to call him "Creeping Jesus" because of the silence with which he got around.

Loew was a good-natured jokester. He disliked solemnity and often disconcerted the meetings of his directors by flipping matches when they were engaged in serious talk. He wouldn't sign a contract on Friday, wouldn't walk under a ladder and, in later years, he refused to undergo an operation because of some superstitious fear.

Although many of his associates were strong horse-players—notably the Schencks—Loew avoided that form of gambling. "I won't bet on anything that eats but can't talk," he often said. And he took umbrage when his name was mispronounced "Lowey." "You don't call a mule 'muley,'" he would say.

CHAPTER IV

THE PLOT THICKENS

KEEP in mind that Loew's staple was vaudeville entertainment in these years when he was engaged in putting together a powerful theatre chain. Even though motion pictures were increasingly popular between 1905 and 1912 and comprised the major portion of the programs in the nickelodeons, still they were minor items of entertainment merchandise, not yet fattened and dignified sufficiently to give them dominance on a real theatre bill.

This was due to two reasons. Prior to 1912, the impulse to make pictures longer than one or two reels was slight. The techniques of picture storytelling were still uninvitingly crude, and the average mind was not generally believed to be able to span more than a twenty-minute film. Shakespearean plays, operas and novels were compressed into florid pantomimes that ran no longer than such hack fabrications as A Dixie Mother, The Engineer's Sweetheart or Fighting Blood. When Vitagraph and George Kleine each came forward with incessant Biblical films that ran for more than two reels, they were obliged to release them serially, one reel at a time.

Their compulsion to do this betokened the second reason for the scanty size of films. That was the tough, restrictive influence of the so-called "Motion Picture Trust." The Trust—or the General Film Company as it was legally named—was a combination in which the earliest producers had joined to restrict to their own use the basic patents they variously held on cameras and thus squeeze out the new producers who had come in with the nickelodeons. These producing companies were Edison, Vitagraph, Biograph, Sig Lubin, George Kleine, Selig, Kalem, Essanay and Pathé and Melies of France. They issued their ultimatum against the encroachers in 1909.

One of their dictatorial rulings was that no picture more than one reel—later two reels—in length was to be released by its members. This was thought a good way to standardize the product and assure manufacture of a volume of films. The consumption of pictures by the nickelodeons, with their daily and semi-weekly changes of bills, was immense. And when the Trust found that its monopoly on the patents was not effective in stopping the production of bootleg films, it cracked down on the so-called "exchanges" which distributed the pictures to the exhibitors.

The exchanges were simply local dealers who bought the reels of pictures from the producers at a set price of ten cents a foot of film, regardless of how many prints of each subject they bought. The exchanges then rented the films to the exhibitors for as much as the traffic would bear. There were hundreds of exchanges through the country and their methods were whatever each chose. For instance, Marcus Loew had established his own People's Film Exchange to acquire pictures for his houses. He got his films that way for ten cents a foot. Then he sublet them to other small theatres and nickelodeons, however he could.

The Trust now took over from its members the selling of their films to the exchanges and stipulated that any exchange which handled bootleg films would not be permitted to acquire the indispensable product of the Trust. Indeed, it bought up many exchanges and operated them itself so as to tighten its hold on distribution. Furthermore, it dogmatically required from every house exhibiting its pictures a two dollar weekly license fee.

Although it was piously argued that these operations of the Trust were designed to "bring some order" into the haphazard commerce of films, it was obvious that they tended to create a monopoly for the group and for the exchanges they chose to sanction. This was all right by Marcus Loew. His People's Film Exchange was one of the soundest and was in good standing with the Trust. He stuck with its standardized pictures, which came cheap and were right for his combination bills. And he paid the license fees for his theatres. Loew was orderly.

But there were those who soon raised the devil against the rules and controls of the Trust. The potentials of this new and vital medium were not to be limited, they said. Within a year, a little fireball from Chicago, Carl Laemmle, was moving ahead in defying the lordly prohibitions against his making and distributing films. He got out his first Independent Motion Picture (Imp) production in 1909, and he put on a hot campaign to rally the small exchanges against the Trust. For several years, Laemmle's Imp company went at them hammer and tongs, making pictures and ridiculing "General Flimco." He was one of those who helped do it in.

Another resister on a different level was the strident and scrappy William Fox. He refused to allow his theatres to pay the demanded license fees. Pugnaciously, he started an anti-trust suit in 1910. After lengthy court hearings embracing several independent suits, the Trust was finally dissolved by the courts in 1915 as a violation of the Sherman Act.

However, its doom was sealed before that by the inexorable rise of rebels such as Imp and the persistence of the unrestrained film makers in turning out longer and comparatively better films. Adolph Zukor was in on this advancement. In 1912, he had resigned as treasurer of Loew's enterprises, sold the bulk of his stock holdings and devoted himself to the idea of getting into the production of multi-reel films.

Everybody's Doing It

With a little more confidence than cooperation, Zukor formed what he called the Famous Players Company for the purpose of making films of "famous plays with famous players." Then word came to him one day that the American rights to a four-reel French film, *Queen Elizabeth,* starring the divine Sarah Bernhardt, could be had. This was his opportunity! The world's most famous player, indeed, in a film that ran for four reels! Zukor grabbed the rights. Then he arranged with Daniel Frohman, a distinguished producer of plays, to go in with him in Famous Players and give *Queen Elizabeth* a big boost by opening for one performance at his legitimate Lyceum Theatre in New York. The première on July 12, 1912, was a historic "first." The elite of the theatre were there, and the prestige of motion pictures and the multi-reel film was vastly raised.

Developments hereafter were hectic. Already Laemmle's company, Imp, had merged with several other independents and formed the Universal Pictures Company, which made its first splash with *Traffic in Souls,* a six-reel exposé of white slavery. A group of Midwestern exchange men successfully launched the Mutual Company. And a fugitive from Biograph, Mack Sennett, began making a series of short farces for the independent Bison Company, called Keystone Comedies.

Then, in 1913, George Kleine, a member of the Trust, whose previous *Life of Moses* it had compelled to be released piece-reel, brought from Italy a film version of *Quo Vadis?* which was close to two hours long! The Trust declined to release it unless Kleine would let it out serially. He refused to do this and showed it to several exhibitors who were impressed—all save one, according to the historian, B.B. Hampton. That one was Marcus Loew. He walked out of the screening, says Hampton, agreeing with the gentlemen of the Trust that audiences would not hold interest in such a lengthy film. Kleine went ahead independently and rented the Astor Theatre in New York, where he opened *Quo Vadis?* on April 19, 1913, at a twenty-five to fifty cent scale to extraordinary popular acclaim—thus marking another milestone for films. Loew still felt the picture was too long.

It was not simply poor imagination that accounted for the reticence of Loew. It was mainly that he was doing nicely with short films and vaudeville. The little dramas featuring Mary Pickford, the girl with the golden curls; the tabloid westerns, the pie-throwing farces and the weekly serial films were fine for him. Longer pictures would disarrange his vaudeville programs and cost more money to book. Besides, he honestly figured that his audiences would not be interested.

Of course, his calculations were subject to subsequent change, as the march of events and competition were rapidly to compel. For the dynamic of the motion picture as a medium for lifting the human mind and emotions to flights of fancy and generating a great new culture of myth was just on the point of being discovered. The "movie age" was about to emerge.

Loew as a theatre man sensed it as a tide of mass interest setting in when he saw his competitors opening large theatres exclusively for films. Early in 1914, the Vitagraph Company acquired a legitimate theatre on Fourteenth Street and turned it into a showcase for its films, reopening it as the Vitagraph Theatre with a four-reel drama, *A Million Bid*. The scale of admission prices went from twenty cents to a dollar.

And then, in April, 1914, a major event occurred when Mitchell Mark, our old friend from Automatic Vaudeville and the Fourteenth Street penny arcade, opened his new Mark Strand Theatre on Broadway at Forty-seventh Street. This 3,300-seat show place—radically and startlingly designed by Thomas W. Lamb with a two-story rotunda and mezzanine promenade—"Continental in character," according to the press hurrahs—was the first theatre built from the ground up for the purpose of housing only films. It was launched with Selig's nine-reel version of *The Spoilers*, from a novel by Rex Beach.

That audience, that night was a gathering of social and theatrical swells the likes of which seldom turned out for the openings of the most distinguished plays. The occasion was, indeed, so dazzling that it moved Victor Watson to write in the New York *American* the next morning: "I must confess that when I saw the wonderful auditorium in all its costly togs, the one thought that came to my mind was that if anyone had told me two years ago that the time would come when the finest-looking people in town would be going to the biggest and newest theatre on Broadway *for the purpose of seeing motion pictures*, I would have sent them down to visit my friend, Dr. Menas Gregory, at Bellevue Hospital." Dr. Gregory was a psychiatrist.

The thought of 3,300 people packed into one theatre moved Marcus Loew even more strongly than the realization that they were there to see just films. He was in business, as he had said, "for the money there is in it," and he loved the sight of many customers.

It was probably the challenge of the Mark Strand which inspired him, in the summer of that year, to pull one of his gaudiest capers—the putting on of outdoor vaudeville-and-picture shows at Brooklyn's new ball park, Ebbets Field. On a split-profits arrangement with Charles Ebbet, the proud owner of the year-old park, Loew provided the entertainment which was played on a portable stage at midfield. On the opening night in June, some 21,000 customers jammed the place to see a Wild West show, the Dancing Kennedys, some tumblers and jugglers and Thomas Ince's spectacular six-reel drama, *The Wrath of the Gods*.

Loew was thrilled by the turnout and quickly tried the same in Boston at Braves Field. The novelty of shows in ball parks carried for a spell. (Outdoor picture shows in amusement parks were common—much like drive-in theatres today.) Then the fad faded and the ball-park shows were dropped. But Loew had the satisfaction of drawing "the largest crowd ever to see a vaudeville and moving picture show."

The Adolescent Stage

It was in the following year, 1915, that motion pictures may be said to have passed from a period of clumsy, sprawling childhood into a lusty, adolescent stage. For not only did the year witness much organization of producing groups, but it brought along the first almighty film that showed the raw power and narrative compass of the now unconfined medium. D. W. Griffith's *The Birth of a Nation*, directed and produced independently by him, was more of an experience for the millions who saw it than was their first bold glimpse of pictures that moved.

Tremendous was the impact of this saga of Reconstruction in the South. Though rampant in Southern sectionalism and Ku Klux Klan demagoguery, it was popular beyond all calculation. It played around the country—and around the world—time and again, first in two dollar two-a-day "road-showings" and then at prices right down the scale. It was seen by millions more people than had seen any one film before. It was hailed by scholars and intellectuals, as well as by the nickelodeon spawn. *The Birth of a Nation* established the picture drama as a considerable form of art. It put the multiple-reel attraction right up at the head of the class.

Now the gates were wide open and the field of picture making was clear. Scores of new producers and new producing combinations emerged, including two companies called Metro and Goldwyn, of which we will hear. The period between 1915 and 1919 was one in which there was violent tugging and tussling for advantage among the acting stars (who were obviously the chief attractions for the patrons), among the producing companies, among the distributors of the pictures and finally among the theatre men. The pressures of this evolution inevitably reached Marcus Loew.

The first pinch he felt from the lengthening and strengthening of films was a rise in the price he had to pay for them. Already the original scale of ten cents a foot for Trust products had been dropped, and fixed rental fees—so much per day or per week for a film—were in vogue. With the stars demanding larger salaries and the cost of making pictures going up, the rental fees demanded were also on the rise. Whereas in 1911, Loew was able to provide a theatre with an adequate bill of pictures for fifty dollars a week, his expense for this item was tripled and quadrupled in five years.

The rise in film rentals had a further and much more profound consequence in shaping the commerce of motion pictures and the destiny of Loew's company.

When Zukor's Famous Players and other producing outfits came to be, the standard way of distributing their pictures was through the existing exchanges or so-called "state right" men. The job of selling the pictures to the theatres was franchised to these men on a geographical basis, each one being granted exclusive right to handle a company's product in his area.

For example, the Schenck brothers and Dave Bernstein initially acquired the Southeastern state right to distribute the Famous Players pictures, beginning with *Queen Elizabeth*. They were doing all right on the quiet having dispatched a resourceful office boy named Eddie Mannix to move the prints of the Bernhardt picture around among the Southern theatres, when Marcus Loew heard of the side-line venture and compelled his enterprising employees to give it up. They sold their franchise for $2,500 to S. E. Lynch, who, in later years, by virtue of representing Zukor, became a multi-millionaire.

However, in 1916, Zukor's company—fortified by a merger with Jesse L. Lasky into the Famous Players-Lasky company—assumed direct control of the distribution of its pictures and thus achieved the first momentous integration of the production and distribution of films. Now it had full authority as to whom it would sell its pictures and for how much. This immediately made it the most formidable combination in the motion picture world. Its position was strengthened further by its galaxy of stars—such favorites as Pauline Frederick, Marie Doro and Marguerite Clark and the most popular of all, Mary Pickford, who made films for Zukor's distribution in her own independent company.

The Exhibitors Rise

With stars and bargaining position, Zukor was able—indeed, he *had*—to demand higher rentals for his pictures than had ever before been asked. This was a staggering development for the theatre men. So a group of important theatre owners throughout the country decided to try to protect themselves by joining together to finance the production of their own films. These were men who, like Loew, had assembled more or less strong theatre chains. They called their venture the First National Exhibitors Circuit. Independent producers were contracted to turn out films for it. Charlie Chaplin was signed to make a series of eight two-reel comedies for $125,000 each, and Mary Pickford was finally lured away from Zukor with a guarantee of $250,000 per film.

This move reversed the situation. Now the balance of bargaining power appeared to be tipping in the direction of the First National Exhibitors group. If the members of it could get along without the Famous Players-Lasky films, it was obvious that Zukor's outfit would have a hard time finding outlets for its films.

It was notable that Marcus Loew's theatres did not join the First National. Loew strung along with Zukor. He was not for getting himself involved. In the fall of 1918, for instance, he booked for his theatres the entire program of sixty feature films that Paramount was offering for the following year—what was then awesomely acknowledged as the biggest booking deal ever made. The know-it-alls nodded wisely. What, they asked, would one expect? Loew and Zukor still played cards together. Elek John Ludvigh was now with Zukor's firm as legal counsel but he still had a foot in Loew's camp. One of Ludvigh's bright lieutenants, Leopold Friedman, was a lawyer for Loew. The circumstantial evidence was convincing: Loew and Zukor had a deal!

However, the business of Loew's theatres was but a fraction of that required to keep Zukor's company in operation. He was forced to find a way to protect himself. One solution became apparent. It was to have his own theatres, to get control of sufficient first-class houses to assure adequate playing time for his films.

Progress from this point was precipitate. The World War had come to an end and theatre business was booming. Zukor went at his project with a will. Wherever a theatre was available, he leased it. When necessary, persuasion was applied. In the South, particularly, he conducted a vigorous theatre-getting campaign. S. A. Lynch was his boy in this area. He was the whipper-in. Not without reason were his agents referred to as the "dynamite squads."

This duel for power between Zukor and the First National Exhibitors group was leading to new consolidations that were disturbing to Marcus Loew. All through the years of evolution of motion pictures and the film industry, he had remained on the outside, so far as production and distributing were concerned. His People's Film Exchange had been abandoned in 1913, when he let it go to the dying Trust, thus ending his juvenile foray in the distribution of films. And his only ventures in the making of pictures had been investments in small affairs—in a little outfit of Roscoe ("Fatty") Arbuckle called Comique Films and a picture produced by Roland West called *Lost Souls.* Joe Schenck had left Loew's company in 1917 to become a producer on his own—making films for Lewis J. Selznick's company, with Schenck's new wife, Norma Talmadge, as star—and most of the Loew personnel had put in money. But Marcus was not intrigued.

His area of interest was theatres—building, buying, leasing, operating them. By 1919, he had assembled one of the nation's most estimable chains, with houses in Atlanta, Boston, Memphis, Baltimore, New Orleans, Birmingham, Montreal and Hamilton, Canada, plus several new ones around New York. All of them with a few exceptions, continued to operate successfully on his policy of small-time vaudeville and pictures at price scales now up to a fifty cent top.

Evolution at Work

So long as the business of motion pictures had remained generally categorized, with production, distribution and exhibition maintained in separate hands, Loew had been in a top position. His theatres gave him first-rate buying power. He was able to make deals for essential picture products more favorable than most of his competitors. Even the new consolidations of production and distribution that emerged, following the Famous Players-Paramount example, were not too menacing to the strong theatre man.

But now, as Loew saw evolution leading to such elaborate forms as bunches of theatres putting out tentacles to gather production facilities unto themselves and, more significantly, the strongest producer-distributor in motion pictures acquiring its own stout theatre arms, he sensed a development of total combines that could well leave him out in the cold. Even William Fox, whose chain of theatres had been expanded during these formative years, had gone into picture making as insurance of product for his theatres. Now Zukor's extension of the segments of his commercial control caused Loew to brood.

His first and instinctive inclination was to increase his theatre strength. Regardless of Zukor, this is what he would probably have done, anyhow. With characteristic candor, he went into partnership with Zukor, himself, in getting the Stillman Theatre in Cleveland. Next he made a deal to acquire the eighteen theatres of the Ackerman & Harris chain on the West Coast. But to do this he found it necessary to have further financing. This was in 1919—a significant year for Loew.

Now the matter of getting capital was different from what it had been when Loew last went after money, eight years previously. The bankers and brokerage houses were now quite happy to negotiate funds for the better producing companies and theatre properties.

Through two financial houses, Montgomery & Company and Van Emburgh & Atterbury, Loew arranged for a loan of $9,500,000. Loew's Theatrical Enterprises was absorbed into the new Loew's, Incorporated, which issued 700,000 shares of common stock at twenty-five dollars par value. Of these, 380,000 shares were transferred to the brokerage houses to secure the loan. The remaining 320,000 shares were used to redeem the common stock of Loew's Theatrical Enterprises at the rate of eight shares for one.

Loew's, Inc., was now Big Business. On its board of directors sat Charles E. Danforth of Van Emburgh & Atterbury, who had arranged the financial deal; Harvey Gibson, the eminent president of Liberty National Bank; W. C. Durant, the president of General Motors; Daniel Pomeroy, vice-president of Bankers Trust; James Perkins, another New York banker, and Lee Shubert, the theatrical man. Loew was not going to flip matches at meetings of this board.

With his financial house in order and his new theatre acquisitions made, Loew went to his board of directors in December, 1919, with a suggestion that he had been mulling for several months. It was that Loew's, Inc., acquire Metro, a modest producing company from which his chain of theatres occasionally picked up films. He offered two solid reasons for it: first, the industrial trend was obviously in the direction of integrated theatres and studios. If Loew's was to continue to have pictures to put on its vaudeville bills, it should definitely have its own certain and negotiable source of supply.

His second reason was a little more startling. There had recently occurred a change in the policy of selling the more important Famous Players-Lasky films. Now, instead of fixed rental prices for the use of these films, the distributor was going to charge a *percentage* of the first-run theatres' receipts. In other words, the rental would be in proportion to the amount the theatre took in. To Loew, this sounded murderous. He felt the time had come to make his own films.

CHAPTER V

LOEW BUYS A STUDIO

In Greek, the word "metro" means mother, or, more precisely, the womb. In Paris, it is the subway, a vital artery of urban life. Both of the meanings have been mentioned as inspiration for the name of the film company that Marcus Loew decided in 1919 that he should buy. But, alas, those conceits must be deflated. The name was lifted merely from a contraction of "metropolitan."

Metro was formed in 1915, in that lively transitional year when a number of new amalgamations of small producing companies were being made. It grew out of a previous combination that had been put together the year before by Al Lichtman, a clever young salesman who was to go far in the film industry.

Lichtman, then peddling films for Zukor, had the bright idea of getting a bunch of little exchanges around the country to put up money for the production of films. He saw that they were clamoring for pictures. By acting as a middleman, he would obtain backing from them for the small producers who would then sell their pictures exclusively through them.

The idea was commercially attractive. Some twenty-odd exchanges joined the scheme, and Lichtman lined up some likely products for his little Alco (Al Lichtman) Company. Among his initial offerings was a six-reel comedy, produced by Keystone and featuring three hopefuls, Marie Dressler, Mabel Normand and Charlie Chaplin. It was called *Tillie's Punctured Romance*.

But a not uncommon misfortune overtook the Alco Company. A light-fingered partner of Lichtman played a bit too freely with its funds. Within a few months of its formation, the company was broke and the venture, so sensibly started, was bound for bankruptcy court. Lichtman, strapped and discouraged, returned to the Zukor fold.

However, the Alco idea was not to be so supinely dropped. The exchange men who had given it faith and finance were anxious to see it carried on. A committee of swindled franchise holders was recruited to see what could be done. On this committee was a Boston exchange man by the name of L. B. Mayer.

Louis Burt Mayer, to adorn him with the full name he took for himself, was a minor figure in picture business when he entered the Alco group. His American Feature Film Company in Boston—which was just Mayer himself, at the time—played a decidedly second fiddle in the booming New England area. But the size of the swath he was then cutting was but a sliver of that he was to sweep as he moved in ever wider circles in the growing film industry.

Mayer, like the Schencks, was born in Russia and was brought by his parents, Jacob and Sara, to the Western world when he was but a child. The immigrant family settled in Saint John, New Brunswick; it was there that Louis grew up, in a friendly community that warmed to the poor Jewish family and to the doggedness that its oldest son showed.

Papa Mayer was in the scrap metal business, not too successfully, because the pickings were small in New Brunswick and he was not the go-getting sort. But Louis was. From his sturdy mother he got resourcefulness and pluck. He was out with a little wagon collecting scrap iron before he was eight years old. By the time he was thirteen or fourteen, he was running his father's junk yard and making deals which, because of his minority, the father had to approve. When a contract was made to raze an iron ship that lay sunk in the harbor of Saint John, Louis worked with the wreckers and divers engaged to cut it apart. The physique he developed as a youngster, handling scrap iron and wrecking ships, gave him the shape and the texture of a fireplug. He was short, thick and strong.

On business trips to Boston, young Mayer made assorted friends and got a taste for the city. In 1904, at the age of nineteen, he married Margaret Schenberg, a pleasant Boston girl, daughter of a synagogue cantor. He lived in Boston and, briefly, in Brooklyn with her, continuing in the scrap metal business and doing the best he could.

Whatever stray inclination it was that moved the impulsive young man to drop scrap metal and go into show business was probably much the same that moved Marcus Loew toward penny arcades and the Schenck brothers toward the cheap amusement parks. It was partly an urge to make money, partly a twist of temperament. Anyhow, the move came, three years later, when a Boston friend told Mayer of a "store show" that could be had in Haverhill, Mass., for little more than a song. Mayer went up and had a look at it. The place was called the Gem but, for fairly obvious reasons, it was known locally as the Germ. Mayer thought he could do something with it, put down a few hundred dollars to bind the deal, and went back to Boston resolved to become a theatre man.

The next few years were tough ones. Mayer moved his wife and two small daughters to Haverhill, cleaned up the ratty "store show" and renamed it the Orpheum. One of his first attractions in it was a hand-tinted Biblical film which his friends had warned him would be ruinous in the predominantly Roman Catholic factory town. But the picture did turn-away business, even though Mayer deliberately opened it during Lent.

The Orpheum fitfully prospered as a cheap vaudeville-picture place. Mayer himself sometimes went on as the singer, accompanying the familiar song slides. His wife often worked as the cashier and dutifully kept the books. In a little while, Mayer had accumulated enough money and experience to take over the better-class Colonial Theatre in Haverhill. Here he booked fancier attractions, such as the Boston Symphony. Later, he built his own theatres in nearby Lawrence and Lowell. Then, as a logical adjunct, he opened his own film exchange. He had been about a year in this side business when his chance came to join the Alco group.

Metro Is Born

It was on a cold night in January, 1915, that the franchise holders of stranded Alco met in the Hotel Claridge in New York to reorganize themselves. It didn't take much calculation to see that a new company could be formed for no more than it would cost to salvage Alco. So they voted to cut their losses and go ahead. It was agreed that working capital with which to finance films would be temporarily raised by having each member pay for his franchise, according to the estimated worth of the territory covered by his exchange. Stock was to be given the franchise holders in proportion to the amount of money they put in.

The Metro Pictures Corporation was chosen as the company's name and Richard Rowland, an exchange man from Pittsburgh, was elected president. Mayer was named secretary and Joe Engel, a New York franchise holder was treasurer. J. Robert Rubin was engaged as counsel for the newly started firm.

Rubin, a talented young lawyer from Syracuse, N.Y., had begun his career in the office of a conservative old New York legal firm and had angled toward public service. He had done an instructive hitch as an assistant district attorney in the aggressive reform administration of Mayor Charles S. Whitman, and later, had served as a Deputy Police Commissioner of New York City in charge of a reorganization of the detective bureau. One day, his good friend, Job Hedges, a Republican leader in New York, offered him the minor emolument of serving as counsel to the Alco receivership. Rubin casually took it and thus was fortuitously placed in contact with Mayer and Engel.

who got him as Metro's counselor and soon diverted his talents into a new and adventurous realm.

Most of the separate producers aligned with Alco went on with the new deal. There were Popular Plays and Players, which had Olga Petrova and Florence Reed as its top stars; B. A. Rolfe, who had Emily Stevens, Ethel Barrymore and William Faversham; Quality Pictures, with Francis X. Bushman, Marguerite Snow and, later, Beverly Bayne; and Dyreda Films, the producing company of J. Searle Dawley, who had been with Famous Players just two years previously.

The producing facilities of the various units were as numerous and scattered as were they themselves. Popular Plays and Players had its studio in New York, in a made-over church on Thirty-eighth Street. Dawley's Dyreda was located at Sixty-first Street and Broadway. It was this studio which shortly became the main Metro facility in the East. Quality Pictures, headed by Fred Balshofer, was located in Hollywood. Metro also had companies working in studios at Fort Lee, N. J.

The random state of its operations—and of film making, in general—was quaintly revealed by an advertisement that appeared in the *Motion Picture World* just two months after the company was formed:

> Responsible producers possessing or contemplating features of quality . . . desiring immediate marketing, wide distribution, through an organization composed of exchange men of acknowledged standing . . . submit their products to . . . 1465 Broadway.

The latter was the address of the home office, and it was here that Rowland dwelled, directing the business affairs of the company and presiding over the letting of contracts for films. The arrangement of compensations was that the home office received 10 per cent of the gross receipts that the exchanges got for the rental of the films. The remaining 90 per cent of each picture was to be divided equally between the exchanges and the producer after the exchanges had deducted whatever monies they had advanced.

By May, 1915, the company was announcing boastfully that it had got off to a fine start. *Satan Sanderson* was its first release in what it diligently strove to keep a schedule of one new film a week. The prospect of a steady flow of pictures was the commercial ideal.

Those first fine and often careless raptures of Metro, while not quite memorable, were typical of the fustian ferment and the dramatic tastes of the day. *The Heart of a Painted Woman, Shadows of a*

Great City, The Song of a Wage Slave, An Enemy to Society, Stork's Nest—these were some.

Ethel Barrymore was signed for eight pictures which she did in a couple of years. In one of these, she played a Russian princess; among the extras was a little Russian émigré, who also worked in New York as a tailor. As Leon Trotsky, he later achieved wider fame. Lionel Barrymore was also proudly listed as a Metro "star at large." He had just made a big hit in support of Pearl White in her classic serial, *The Exploits of Elaine*. Pert little Mary Miles Minter, whose alliterative name was contrived as a gesture of loyalty to Metro, did *Barbara Frietchie* with old Mrs. Thomas Whiffen of the stage. And Mr. and Mrs. Sidney Drew were lined up for a series of fifty-two one-reel husband-wife comedies, all to be made in one year!

The studio at Broadway and Sixty-first Street was a typical facility of the times. It was above a garage—a vast chamber, more than 200 feet long—with the shooting stage in the middle and offices around the sides. It was in this primitive atelier—a veritable crazy house of painted scenery, jumbled furniture, old-fashioned arc lights and hand cranked cameras—that the stars performed and the principal product of Metro came to elegant flower.

Thus the small company, torn from turbulence, tripped toward its destiny.

Mayer Cuts Loose

Through the first flowing years of Metro, Mayer dutifully served as a functioning distributor and officer, popping down regularly to New York from his headquarters in Boston to attend to company affairs. But the business of selling pictures was beginning to pall on him. His eager eyes were roving over the producing field. It was here, among the actors and creators, that he visioned excitement and wealth.

In late 1915, he assembled a syndicate which bought, for $25,000, the New England distribution rights to *The Birth of a Nation*. The picture was already showing in the area on a road-show basis, and Mayer was warned that it would be "played out." But he and his new exchange partner, Nathan Gordon, were convinced it would sell in regular theatres at popular prices to audiences that couldn't afford the road-show scales. They were right. They made a quarter million dollars by booking the picture for its "subsequent runs."

Now Mayer was ready to seek more fortune. The itch to produce was strong. It was just a matter of finding the right elements with which to begin. The essential for any average picture to be a success in those days was a star whose popularity was assured. The story and director were important. But the star drew the customers. Mayer knew this as well as anyone. His first aim was to catch a star.

Raiding for talent was common. Lewis Selznick had just despoiled Vitagraph of its beautiful and popular Clara Kimball Young and Joe Schenck was literally wooing Norma Talmadge away from Thomas Ince. Zukor was grabbing actors and actresses wherever he could. Mayer was not above indulging in this candidly cutthroat game.

He found his opportunity in the shape of another lovely star on the Vitagraph roster. She was Anita Stewart, the stunning actress who came to fame in *A Million Bid,* the picture with which Vitagraph had opened its New York theatre, three years before. Anita was brunette and slender, with an elegant, ladylike air. She was currently the rage in *The Goddess,* a serial with Earl Williams. And a goddess she was!

Mayer planned to snag Anita. Then, through a bizarre circumstance, he got a propitious introduction. There was a movie-mad dwarf in New York—a newspaper vender named Toby—who was one of Anita's wildest fans. He paid her the unrestrained attention of a mountebank to a Spanish queen. He fawned upon her, ran her errands and handed her photographs to the swells at the horse shows and the opera. Anita was flattered by him. Dwarfs were supposed to be lucky. She fancied him as her charm.

By coincidence, the little paper-peddler also became attached to Mayer. He would meet him on his trips down from Boston and often go to Grand Central Station to see him off. Mayer was pleased by this attention, and delighted when Toby would prate of the possibility of Mayer producing a picture starring the actress of his dreams.

It was this dwarf who took Mayer to Anita in 1917. The introduction led to dinners for Mayer at the Brooklyn home of the actress and her mother, where they talked about making films and Mayer drew dazzling word pictures of those he wanted to produce. His powers of persuasion were tremendous. Anita was doing well at Vitagraph. She was earning $1,000 a week, plus 10 per cent of the net profits of her pictures, which totaled close to $100,000 a year. Yet Mayer was able to persuade her that she should leave the established studio and make films with him.

His inducements were concrete and clever. In the first place, he agreed to form a company, Anita Stewart Productions, which would give her a distinction such as Mary Pickford had. He would pay her $2,000 a week, with the promise of better stories and directors. And, most important, he offered a fine advancement for Rudolph Cameron (Brennan), Anita's new leading man, to whom she was recently married and with whom she was madly in love. Rudy was to be made general manager and a director of the company and receive 12½ per cent of the profits. On those terms, Anita was sold.

J. Robert Rubin was now called on by Mayer to perform the legal rites. Rubin was counsel for Metro, and also served as lawyer for Mayer. The two had developed a friendship and mutual professional respect which were to last through many years and many crises in their constantly expanding affairs. Anita Stewart Productions was incorporated in September, 1917. Mayer and some Boston friends financed it, with Rubin in for a small share.

But with the announcement of the setup, a bit of hell broke loose. Vitagraph was boiling. It had a contract with Anita, it claimed, and that contract, by its calculation, still had a year to run. An injunction to restrain Anita from rendering service to the defendant was obtained. Then Vitagraph sued the alienator for $250,000 damages.

The threat to Mayer's prospects was awesome. He and Rubin maintained it was their understanding that Anita's contract was just about to expire.They expected to go right into picture making. Mayer had even given his star a sizable bonus when she signed her contract. Now, here they were in a snarl.

The court finally ruled in April that Anita should finish out her Vitagraph contract, which had until September to run. This meant she would have to make another couple of pictures, at the rate they made them then. But an automobile accident in the early summer banged up the actress a bit, and a deal was struck whereby she was released to Mayer two months ahead of time—provided he paid Vitagraph $70,000 for two unfinished Stewart films.

All things considered, Mayer's beginning as a producer was far from dull.

Once in the clear, he moved swiftly. Having put down a goodly sum for his star, he was ready to insure his gamble with a comparable parallel expense. He paid $15,000 for a magazine story by Owen Johnson called *Virtuous Wives*—"a truthful story of married life in New York society," the Mayer advertisements later said. He got the distinguished George Loane Tucker as director. Conway Tearle was engaged as leading man, and a supporting cast which included Mrs. DeWolf (Hedda) Hopper, Edwin Arden and William Boyd was hired. Space to produce the picture was rented, of all places, from Vitagraph.

Mayer couldn't come to terms with Rowland to have Metro distribute the film. So he pulled out of Metro and took his picture to the newly formed First National. A big ad campaign in the trade papers was put on to launch *Virtuous Wives* and it opened at the Strand Theatre in New York on December 29, 1918.

In reviewing this, the first of Mayer's productions, the New York *Times* observed:

> If it is a view of any kind of society, its only moral is that men and women may break as many middle-class commandments as they please without injury to their characters. Some of the people in the play are unforgivably stupid and others are as vain and vicious as good respectable folks can imagine, but everybody is miraculously reformed in the last reel and becomes virtuous and intelligent all because a little boy is nearly drowned.

Withal, the film was popular and reaped encouraging profits for all.

Mayer had Anita on a three-year contract, and both of them were leaning toward the West. It was out there in southern California that he thought he saw Fortune's beckoning hand. By this time, 1919, most of the top producers were located around Los Angeles, and Hollywood was becoming a glamorous and seductive name. Mayer moved out with Anita, her mother, Rudy Cameron and a small troupe and put together their next picture at a little rental studio.

After this, Mayer's mind was settled. He would stay in California and continue to produce. His family moved out from Boston, and he wound up his Eastern affairs. Although just another small producer, he was definitely on his way.

As for Toby, it is nice to be able to report that Mayer paid for his funeral when he died.

Rowland Rocks

The departure of Mayer from Metro was not a blow of disastrous consequence. But it is notable that about the time of his departure the company began to rock.

There had been a major change in its setup. Whereas, at the time it was formed, its franchise-holding distributors owned it and collectively determined its policies, this arrangement was slowly altered. As some of the individual exchanges failed, Metro itself absorbed them and operated them on its own. Eventually the parent company bought up all the franchises, in exchange for Metro stock, and thereafter did its own distributing and its own making of policy. Several of the original franchise holders, thus disassociated from control of this source of films, were in the combine that created the First National Exhibitors Circuit.

The superior position of the latter and of Zukor's company, which had theatres through which to release its pictures, was too much for Metro to buck. Rowland and his head of production, Maxwell

Karger, a bluff, bombastic man who had previously been a violinist with the Metropolitan Opera orchestra, tried to maintain themselves in business by producing cheap "program" films which cost no more than $15,000 or $20,000 each and "systematizing" production. This was a perilous policy, since such pictures could not get booking in the better theatres.

Later, they tried to match their rivals with a series of "special" films, elegantly called Screen Classics, for which they engaged such stars as Nazimova, Viola Dana, May Allison and Bert Lytell and upon which they spent more for production. Their quality was good, but the company lacked the theatre tie-ups to assure release for these top films. In the area of bruising competition, it was taking some damaging blows. Rowland and Rubin, his attorney, saw that the company would have to align itself with theatres to survive.

This was in the summer of 1919. On a fond hope, the two promoters went, hats in hand, to Adolph Zukor with a proposition that Metro be joined with his company. Zukor looked down his thin nose at them. "The only reason I'd have to take you in," he said, "would be to put you out of business." And he candidly indicated he didn't think it worth the cost. Thereupon Rowland and Rubin went to call on Marcus Loew.

Now, Loew, as we have already noted, was in a comparable spot as a theatre operator to that of Metro as a producing company. He needed a guaranteed supply of product to maintain his bargaining power, just as Metro needed theatres to give its pictures assured release. Loew pondered the proposition of Rowland and Rubin that he buy a half interest in their company.

Then he told them he wasn't interested in half of Metro but would like to buy the whole thing. Rowland and Rubin were interested. They got approval from their stockholders.

And that's how, in January, 1920, Loew bought a studio.

The terms of the deal were simple. Transfer was made for a flat sum of $3,100,000, payable with $1,500,000 of newly issued Loew's, Inc., stock which was passed along to the stockholders in Metro, and the remaining $1,600,000 was to be paid through the removal of 35 per cent of the profits realized from the sale of Metro pictures abroad.

This latter appeared an odd concession on Rowland's and Rubin's part. Metro's films were sold outright to independent exchanges in a few foreign countries. Gross receipts from all such distribution was seldom more than $50,000 a year. One man and a secretary in the Metro home office handled all foreign deals. But the full $1,600,000 was paid off to the Metro shareholders within four years. This was due to an immediate reorganization and build-up of foreign distribution under the direction of Marcus' son, Arthur Loew.

What Loew's, Inc., got for its money was Metro's new Hollywood studio—a tidy layout of white buildings with green shutters, clipped hedges and well-kept lawns at Cahuenga Boulevard and Romaine Street; its old New York studio, which had been closed since the winter of 1918 when wartime fuel shortages compelled the removal of all production to the West Coast; a formidable line-up of actors and directors, writers and cameramen; and a New York office which held together a network of Metro exchanges throughout the United States and Canada. In charge of the Hollywood studio was Joe Engel, one of the old Alco boys, with Bayard Veillier as his assistant. Max Karger remained as head of production and circulated between New York and the Coast.

LOEW STOCK OFFER

$21 per Share Partial Payment Plan
$20 per Share for Cash Outright

To My Friends and Patrons:

As you are probably aware, during the last few days there has been an unusual depression on the stock market.

This has produced an opportunity whereby I have been able to buy several thousand shares of Loew Stock at a lower price.

As long as the stock lasts it can be bought by you on the partial payment plan for $21.00 instead of $22.00 a share, and outright for cash at $20.00 a share.

Those who bought early in the week in this or any other New York Theatre will receive the same benefits and have the difference between what they paid refunded.

Yours very truly,

MARCUS LOEW.

Questions and Answers

Realizing that you will want to know more of the details before taking up this offer, certain important points are answered below.

Any further information can be obtained from our special representatives who will be at each of our Brooklyn and Bronx Theatres every afternoon and evening during Anniversary Week and until 11 P. M., November 22.

1. What is the Stock?

Ans.—The capital (and only) stock of Loew's, Inc., a company operating and controlling over one hundred Loew Theatres in the principal cities of U. S. and Canada. Loew's, Inc., also owns the Metro Pictures Corporation.

2. What does the Corporation Earn?

Ans.—Over $2,000,000 net earnings last year. Twenty-seven of our theatres are still under construction, for which capital has already been provided. As these get into operation, earnings next year are estimated at $4,000,-000, and the following year $6,000,000.

3. What Dividends does the Stock Pay?

Ans.—$2.00 per share per year. This is over 9% on your investment at the purchase price of $21.00 per share.

4. What are the terms of Stock Purchase?

Ans.—$21.00 per share, payable in installments covering six months if you desire. $4.00 per share now and $3.00 per share each month, commencing December 1.

5. What Interest on your Payments?

Ans.—Nine per cent (the dividend rate). This amounts to about 48 cents per share, which will be paid when you have completed your stock payments on May 1.

6. Why is Mr. Loew making this offer?

Ans.—He feels that Loew patrons appreciate the success of the Loew Theatres and may desire to become partners in the profits through stock ownership. This will also benefit the company because every patron who is a profit-sharing stockholder will be a Loew booster, even more than before.

Subscriptions Received at This Theatre
until 11 P. M., Monday Night, November 22.

This is one of the unique handbills which were circulated in Loew theatres in the fall of 1920 to advise patrons of the sale of Loew stock directly by representatives of the company in theatres. The stock-selling campaign, which would be *de trop* today, was also promoted by spielers who offered explanations of the satisfactions of being a Loew stockholder.

CHAPTER VI

THE MISERY OF METRO

Now THAT he owned a studio, Loew was full of confidence and hope. As he became more extended, he likewise became more verbose. Said he, after a visit to Hollywood in February to look over the company's acquisitions there:

"I have watched Metro closely since Richard Rowland announced his policy of 'fewer and better' pictures and started spending three months on a production instead of five weeks. The first Screen Classics impressed me with their beauty. Metro still retains its identity. Metro pictures will show in Loew houses. That is all the affiliation means to the public. But it means to me that, through my friend, Mr. Rowland, I will have a share in developing a powerful organization. I will leave the executive work to him. I plan for expansion of product. Metro will continue to make better pictures but it will make more of them."

Here Loew, exultantly predicting both quality and quantity in one breath, laid down the basic expectation of the theatre company from its studio. Pictures, pictures and still more pictures, that was the ceaseless demand of the theatre men upon their producing facility from the day Marcus Loew first visited the Coast.

Each of the films on Metro's schedule would cost at least $200,000, Loew said, and added that between fifty and seventy-five would be made during the coming year!

The schedule was ambitious. It included *The Heart of a Child,* starring the popular Nazimova; Bert Lytell in *Alias Jimmy Valentine; Old Lady 31,* from a play by Rachel Crothers; *Shore Acres,* with Alice Lake and Frank Brownlee; and *Polly With a Past,* as a vehicle for Ina Claire, Ralph Graves and Clifton Webb.

But in announcing the line-up of product, Loew barely mentioned what turned out to be the most valuable of all the projects. That was *The Four Horsemen of the Apocalypse.* This eventually potent picture, one of the historic silent films, came about under circumstances which smacked of Fortune smiling from above.

Conspicuous among the people who were important in Metro was a sturdy young lady named June Mathis, writer of scenarios. June was a child of the theatre, born of theatrical parents on the road and was herself a former actress in traveling stock companies and Broadway shows. As a consequence of some short-story writing and a friendship with Max Karger, she became a regular scenarist for Metro when the company was formed. Plump, not the least bit pretty, but dynamic and aggressive, she soon became the head of the scenario department at the old Sixty-first Street studio. June ground out scenarios by the bushel. Adaptations of plays and novels were her forte. She was one of the almost forgotten but influential productive people in silent films.

It was she who early insisted that Metro should make a picture from Blasco Ibanez' great popular novel of the First World War, *The Four Horsemen of the Apocalypse*. The novel had been read and considered by virtually every producer in the business, and the general opinion was that it could not be made into a successful film. They said the story was too elaborate, it would cost too much to do. And, besides, who wanted to see a picture about the grim and ugly business of war?

But June Mathis insisted. She kept at Karger; she beat on Rowland's door. A film version of *The Four Horsemen* was what she was determined to do. Finally, Rowland said he would buy it. In November, 1919, he made a deal with Ibanez' agent whereby he got the screen rights for $20,000, plus 10 per cent of the distributor's gross.

June was excited and went to work eagerly. On her own, she had spent one vacation discussing the possible film treatment with Ibanez. Now she had further notions. One was that the director should be a dark, handsome chap called Rex Ingram, who had made a couple of minor films.

This fellow, whose real name was Reginald Hitchcock, had studied sculpture at the Yale Fine Arts School and had done an assortment of odd jobs around Vitagraph's Brooklyn studio. From there he went to work for Carl Laemmle, and then went off to the World War. On his return, he got a job at Metro, where he directed some unimportant films. June Mathis saw and was attracted by the dark-eyed Irishman.

Again she prevailed upon Rowland and Karger to accept her choice. The virtually unknown director was assigned to *The Four Horsemen*. (It was just about now that the studio was taken over by Loew, and the possibility of having to abandon the picture was a brief, nerve-racking threat; that was completely dissipated after Loew's inspection visit to the Coast.) The next question now to be decided was who should play the leading role.

The certainty of who first suggested that the tempting part be played by a young actor of no distinction, Rudolph Valentino, is not clear. Ingram claimed he met the fellow when he was playing leads in second-rate Metro pictures and took a fancy to him.

June Mathis also claimed she had spotted the dark-skinned Italian with the cauliflower ear and immediately thought of him when *The Four Horsemen* came along. And Valentino himself occasionally mentioned that he immediately saw himself in the role and personally begged Max Karger for it when he learned that Metro was going to do the film.

In any case, it was definitely June Mathis who finally decided to put the swarthy Valentino in *The Four Horsemen,* for, in addition to writing the scenario, she was also in charge of production of the film. And it was she, along with Ingram, who suspected, as shooting progressed, that they had a hot thing in Valentino and so ordered that he be given more to do.

There was romance in the making of this picture at the old Metro Hollywood studio. Alice Terry, its leading lady, fell in love with Rex Ingram and married him, thus forming one of the famous husband-wife film-making teams. And June Mathis got a crush on Valentino, anticipating by a couple of years the devotion of at least half the females in this country, if not the world.

The Four Horsemen was several months before the camera. June Mathis and Ingram kept building it up, adding scenes, slipping in more material, enhancing the spectacle. Costs mounted. Max Karger and Joe Engel daily blew their tops. For his salient work in the picture, Valentino got $350 a week.

The film had its première at the Lyric Theatre in New York on March 6, 1921; it got a tremendous reception and became a sensational success, going ahead to earn several million dollars for Metro in the next few years. With it, Valentino was launched as a top-ranking star and Metro was briefly elevated as the "miracle studio."

There is a reliable recollection that when Marcus Loew first saw the film in a private showing, some time before its première, he was considerably doubtful and dismayed. He had the uncomfortable feeling it was too long and too involved.

The Penalty of Size

Poor Loew, he soon discovered that owning a studio and entering the realms of "big business" brought with them problems of which he had scarcely dreamed. One of the first came abruptly from a combine of theatre men who, while technically his competitors, he regarded as his friends.

The Motion Picture Theatre Owners of America, a new and expanding group of exhibitors who had no connection with the production or distribution of films, had already started hollering loudly about Zukor acquiring theatres and threatening to monopolize the business. Now, when Loew bought a studio and got for his chain of theatres first call on a substantial supply of films, they were bitter at him for making what they considered a similar combination in reverse.

The virulence of their resentment was vigorously manifested at the first annual convention of the outfit in the summer of 1920. Getting together in Cleveland, the exhibitors unrestrainedly charged that Zukor and Loew were evolving a "trust" as potentially strong as that which had briefly succeeded in controlling the industry ten years before.

Loew showed up at the meeting in his capacity as a theatre man and temporarily soothed his savage critics with amiable assurances that he had no dire intents. He was a good informal speaker and was personally liked by most theatre men. However, valid anxieties about the integration of producing companies and theatre chains continued among the exhibitors and were annually vocalized by them.

Then a clear case of power tactics being used to hurt an independent theatre man was exposed, and the adamant cynics felt their suspicions justified.

In Peekskill, N.Y., there was a theatre owned privately by Dave Bernstein and Nick Schenck, two of Loew's closest lieutenants. Although it was not a possession of Loew's, its films were booked by the regular booker for Loew's theatres and it was usually looked upon as an affiliate of Loew's.

During the summer of 1922, the owners of a newly opened rival theatre in Peekskill received a call from Bernstein. "You have made a big mistake," he said. "This town is not large enough for two theatres. I am going to give you a fight."

Thereupon he offered to sell them the theatre he and Schenck owned, and when they declined to buy it they discovered they could not get first-class films from the top distributors. A suit was brought by the new owners, and witnesses revealed that distributors would not service the new theatre because they feared displeasing the men of Loew's. The case was an open-and-shut instance of powerful position being used to hurt an independent exhibitor, the Appellate Division of the New York State Supreme Court found, and the court rebuked Bernstein in a stinging order that threatened resort to the criminal law.

Although Marcus Loew himself was innocent in the Peekskill affair, the action of his subordinates was seized upon by angry theatre men as a fair example of the sort of operation that could eventually ruin them. Shortly after this, the federal government chose to investigate the film industry, and a lengthy and complicated history of legal conflict with the government was begun.

Meanwhile, Loew was continuing with the expansion of his theatre chain and having his eyes uncomfortably opened to the difficulties of operating a studio. As he once told a group of exhibitors, "I will not stop expanding while I am alive." That drive to accumulate theatres was the encouraging impulse by which he and his nervous associates were sustained.

Shortly after the formation of Loew's, Inc., an extensive theatre-building program was launched in several Southern cities and four houses were acquired in the Bronx. Other emporiums were added over the next few years. But the one outstanding satisfaction in this continuing campaign was the opening of Loew's State Theatre at Broadway and Forty-fifth Street in New York. This major event in Loew's progress occurred on August 29, 1921, and fulfilled his dream of possessing a big vaudeville-picture palace in the nation's theatrical center, Times Square.

The theatre itself was an ornate 3,200-seat house in the nondescript style that was becoming oppressively characteristic of the architecture of the new temples of the movie age. Marble vestibules and stairways, a foyer fountain and French furniture manifested its elegance and pleased the heart of Loew. And the sixteen-story office building he had erected over it was as gratifying and meaningful as the new theatre. Herein was established the ultimate home of Loew's, Inc., anchoring the name in the area with a fine piece of real estate.

What an Exhibitor Doesn't Know

But the satisfactions that came with gathering theatres were clouded, in part, by the pains and headaches discovered in sponsoring the producing studio. Loew's was phenomenally fortunate in the profit and prestige that accrued to its newly acquired Metro company with *The Four Horsemen of the Apocalypse*. But that one film did not assure tranquillity nor a succession of other such miracles.

June Mathis and Ingram followed their initial triumph with a serious, heady film based upon Balzac's *Eugenie Grandet*. Valentino and Alice Terry were again the stars. Valentino also played opposite Nazimova in *Camille*. But that was the end of sweet concord. When assigned to his next film, the new idol asked a raise in salary from $350 to $450 a week. The studio heads finally settled for a raise of fifty dollars a week, which the star and his friend, June Mathis, considered an outright affront. Upon completion of the picture, Valentino and June Mathis pulled out and went over to Zukor's Famous Players where Valentino's first picture was *The Sheik.*

Ingram was nonchalant about it. He never had high regard for the acting talent of Valentino, attributing his appeal to the way he was photographed. He went right ahead and found another young actor in a modest little film called *The Rubaiyat of Omar Khayyám* and vowed to make him as much of a star by casting him to play Rupert of Hentzau in *The Prisoner of Zenda,* which was Ingram's next film. The actor's name was Ramon Samaniegas, but the studio feared it might be turned into something like Ham-n-eggs. So he was given Ramon Novarro as a new name.

Ingram was right; he was able to make the young man a new star, first in *The Prisoner of Zenda* and then in *Scaramouche.* But Novarro, for all his subsequent popularity, never had the magnetic quality possessed by Valentino, whom Metro lost over a matter of fifty dollars a week.

The departure of the lightly valued actor was less of an immediate loss than that of perky June Mathis, who was Metro's outstanding scenarist. She was not only the able adapter of Ingram's first spectacular films, but she also wrote many of the other better pictures turned out by the studio. Her contributions as a craftsman were missed tremendously.

At about this same time, Richard Rowland resigned as Metro's head, to move along to the First National. Shortly after, Max Karger died. Joe Engel was made head of production. The switch did not improve the output of the studio.

The dilemma was discouraging to Loew and his associates in New York. They made frequent excursions to the West Coast to try to figure what was wrong. The theatre men were discovering that there was more to running a studio than putting up a certain amount of money and commanding that great films be made. The dark rocks of temperament and dissension on which so many promising ventures had wrecked were looming in the pleasant buildings at Cahuenga Boulevard and Romaine.

"I've been surprised to learn how many things there are about this business that an exhibitor does not know," Loew said.

Loew personally made manful endeavors to keep the studio alive. He signed up the child star, Jackie Coogan, for 60 per cent of the profits of his films. He also made a deal with Buster Keaton, through Joe Schenck, the latter's brother-in-law, to have the dead-pan comedian provide Metro with a series of comedies. He even got around to making a contract with the independent producer, L. B. Mayer, to have him provide the company with four pictures a year.

But the ever increasing costs of production and a sag in business in 1923, following a national recession the previous year, made the future uncertain for Metro and other companies. Now the question that had been nagging the Loew people for the past couple of years, whether to hold onto the studio and endeavor to build up the quality of its films or abandon it as a poor risk, loomed for a showdown decision. The Metro product, as it stood, was not of sufficient distinction and money making virtues to warrant its adamant support. Indeed, it was with extreme reluctance that Nick Schenck agreed to play the Metro films in the best Loew theatres, of which he was now in charge.

And so the apparent advantage of owning a studio was assuming the proportions of a sad delusion for the efficiency-minded people of Loew's, when a new proposition was presented that had in it the elements of hope. It was, quite simply, that Loew's, Inc., take over the Goldwyn Company, one of the more important independent operations that spanned the field. The proposal was made to Marcus by Frank Joseph Godsol, president of Goldwyn, in Palm Beach in the winter of 1924. Immediately the prudent showman called Nick Schenck in New York. There were angles to this proposition that had to be carefully scanned. Not the least was the condition of the Goldwyn Company.

CHAPTER VII

THE OLD GOLDWYN COMPANY

ALTHOUGH the Goldwyn Pictures Corporation enjoyed a high repute for the quality of its productions and the eminence of its directors and stars, it was economically unstable and ridden by a weird executive group. Its network of thirty-one exchanges and a score of widely scattered theatres was extravagant and superfluous for the comparatively few films it released, and a battle for power among its officers had dealt it some damaging blows. Samuel Goldwyn, the company's fiery founder, had been shoved out two years previously, the fall-guy of pulverizing pressures which Joe Godsol had largely engineered. Under the latter's succeeding presidency, the air of disorder had not been cleared.

Ironically, the source of its product was a southern California studio which had been the scene of disaster for a prior conveyance of golden hopes. The big lot in Culver City, where the Goldwyn company's pictures were made, was originally the home of Triangle, the first ambitious attempt to consolidate the foremost picture makers in one reliable and efficient company. That arrangement had toppled in a short while, wrecked by strong wills and weak management. The Goldwyn company, successor to its domain, was afflicted with similar woes.

In many respects, this corporation mirrored the fitnesses and faults that showed up in organized movie making in the years after World War I. It was a typical sufferer from confusion in a tough transitional phase, wherein the single-minded men of the business were more and more pre-empting from the quixotic boys. Inevitably, its nature reflected the constant tensions that film commerce imposed and the powerful influence of the personalities of the people who ran the home offices and the studios.

To comprehend it fully, we must go back a few years to the entrance of Samuel Goldfish onto the rapidly changing motion picture scene.

This Goldfish—whose name became Goldwyn by a later transmutation, as we shall see—was an odd and invigorating impulse in the expansion of the film industry. As a youth, he had come from Poland (by way of Liverpool) and had apprenticed himself to a glove factory

61

in Gloversville, N.Y. By the time he was thirty, he had prospered to the point of owning a lucrative glove agency. It is said that he used to talk storekeepers into handling his line of goods, at small profit to themselves, just to have the prestige of selling his merchandise. But gloves were a mere warm-up for Goldfish. Show business captivated him from the moment he met, and married, Blanche Lasky, who had been a vaudeville performer with a brother-sister cornet team.

Blanche's brother, Jesse Lasky, was an amiable and wide-awake young man whose vision in the realms of entertainment extended beyond the mouth of his horn. He had managed several vaudeville ventures, when he and brother-in-law Sam got fascinated by the oncoming movies and decided in 1913 to give them a try. With a foot-loose young playwright-stage director named Cecil B. DeMille, they scratched together some $25,000, most of it put up by Sam, and hired a popular stage actor, Dustin Farnum, to make a movie of the play, *The Squaw Man*. They paid $10,000 for the film rights, a stupendous price in those days, then clattered off to Los Angeles, where they heard there were facilities for making pictures beyond the still possible obstruction of the Trust.

Goldfish was wryly philosophical. To Lasky, he said: "We've never produced a picture and this fellow DeMille has never directed one. We should be *great!*"

They weren't great, exactly, but they were fortunate. *The Squaw Man* came off successfully, returning to its fledgling producers twice as much money as they put in. Then Adolph Zukor got onto them and persuaded them to merge with his new Famous Players. Famous Players-Lasky was the result.

Now, for all Samuel Goldfish's ability—and let it be said, here and now, that his distinguished career of motion picture production under his later assumed Goldwyn name testifies not alone to his ability but to his magnificent and phenomenal staying powers—he was not, nor ever has been, a person who could long endure the disciplines of a team. His personality is studded with bristles. He must have been nurtured by a wolf. Indeed, he himself has claimed some kinship to that notoriously lone-prowling beast.

Zukor was president of the new company; Goldfish was chairman of the board. Each gentleman was of the opinion that he was the undisputed boss. While Goldfish was in California on a business trip the following year, Zukor told the board of directors that either Goldfish or he would have to go. When Goldfish returned, the directors invited him to resign. This he did—but he got $1,000,000 worth of stock of the company as his share. Of Zukor's maneuver, he said later: "I didn't think it was a very nice thing for him to do."

With wealth and a zeal for film making, Goldfish now turned his back on his brother-in-law, Lasky, and Zukor and started his own company. Towards the end of 1916, he joined with Edgar and Archibald Selwyn to form the Goldwyn Pictures Corporation, which took its euphonious name from the first syllable of the Goldfish and the last syllable of the Selwyn names. Goldfish put up his million dollars; the Selwyns, well-known on Broadway as successful stage producers, put up mainly the motion picture rights to an impressive and valuable portfolio of their successful plays.

The partners in the new Goldwyn company were high in their enthusiasm for films. They were determined to lift from Famous Players-Lasky its own original policy of distinguished players in quality plays. They combed the theatre for talent and recruited a roster of stars which included Jane Cowl, Maxine Elliott, Madge Kennedy, Mary Garden, Mae Marsh and—as a concession to the masses—Mabel Normand, the Keystone comedy queen. As directors, they got such current journeymen as John S. Robertson, Charles Thomas Horan and Edwin L. Hollywood, and they assembled a scenario department that gleamed with popular writers of the day. It was headed by Margaret Mayo, Edgar Selwyn's wife, herself the author of several hit plays, and it included Irvin S. Cobb, Edward Childs Carpenter, Edith Ellis, Arthur Train and Roi Cooper Megrue. Goldfish had absorbed from the glove business a wholesome respect for good material in his merchandise.

A glass-domed studio was leased at Fort Lee, N.J., across the Hudson River from New York, and Arthur Hopkins, who was later to become one of Broadway's most respected play producers, was put in charge. The first film turned out by the company was an adaptation of Miss Mayo's romantic play, *Polly of the Circus*, with Mae Marsh and Vernon Steele as its stars. It was released in September, 1917. Immediately thereafter came such sentiment-loaded items as *Baby Mine* with Madge Kennedy, *The Fighting Odds* with Maxine Elliott, *The Spreading Dawn* with Jane Cowl and, at the year's end, there was dished up a super-production of Anatole France's *Thais*. The handsome opera singer, Mary Garden, was cast as the Athenian courtesan.

To promote his new company, Goldfish did a striking and audacious thing. He ran a series of full-page advertisements in the *Saturday Evening Post*. National advertising of motion pictures was just beginning to be explored, and the use of the magazine medium was a considerable intimation of class. The tone of the ads conveyed this. Emphasis was on beauty and *brains*. "Pictures Built Upon the Strong Foundation of Intelligence and Refinement," they proclaimed.

The pitch was conspicuously directed to a higher level of public discrimination and taste.

Notable in the Goldwyn advertisements was the trade-mark—a recumbent lion, stretched out in lordly profile and framed in a flowing loop of film. Across the film was a motto in Latin, "*Ars Gratia Artis*"—intended to say: "Art Is Beholden to the Artists." This struck a decidedly new note in the ballyhooing of films.

Leo Is Whelped

The birth of the lion as a trade-mark cannot be noted historically without a postscript on the accouchement, for the beast was to grow and range, and the doctor by whom it was delivered was to have a lot to do with its later care.

When the Goldwyn company was started, the job of preparing its ads was placed with a New York agency, wherein was employed a bright young man fresh out of Columbia University, Howard Dietz. Dietz got his job by winning a contest in ad-writing for Fatima cigarettes. His ad showed two dudes at a party. One said: "Isn't this a boring affair?" The other replied: "Do you think so? Then have a Fatima." Very chic!

Obviously, any ad-writer with such a fine sense of style and elegance was qualified to conceive a trade-mark for the proud new picture company. Dietz was given the assignment. He pondered it carefully. Animals were popular as emblems for the product of various studios. Pathé had a rooster. Selig's Bison company had a buffalo. Metro used a parrot that tossed the letters of the Metro name into the air. (The possible innuendo of the parrot was apparently a matter of slight concern.) Dietz, disdainful of the trivial, bethought himself of the lion, king of the beasts and, incidentally, the mascot of Columbia University. Here was his inspiration. To give the trade-mark some tone, he dreamed up the Latin motto and tossed it in with the lion. Morris Rosenbaum, a commercial artist, drew the finished designs, which the Goldwyn company accepted. And that's how Leo was born. Neither it nor Dietz cut a figure of any notable importance for several years.

The early films of the Goldwyn company met with encouraging success—so much so that new talent was recruited and the company expanded normally. Geraldine Farrar, the beautiful opera singer, whom Goldfish had previously signed to play for the Lasky company in *Carmen* and other films, was wooed into his new outfit. Her first whirl was in *The Turn of the Wheel*. Later she was teamed with Lou Tellegen, a handsome hero, in a number of florid films. The masculine wheel horse of the company was the rugged, good-natured Tom

Louis B. Mayer, the Haverhill (Mass.) theater owner, and his wife in their first car, a model-T Ford, circa 1910.

The new producer of Anita Stewart pictures, Mayer, brings a location company back to Los Angeles from the Northwest (1920). L. to r.: Miss Stewart, Mrs. Mayer, Rudolph Cameron, Mrs. Stewart, Mayer's secretary and himself (in glasses and straw hat).

The extraordinary and influential June Mathis and her beloved Rudolph Valentino during the filming of Metro's "The Four Horsemen of the Apocalypse" (1920).

Rex Ingram, in dress indicative of his eccentricity, directs an outdoor scene for "The Four Horsemen of the Apocalypse."

Moore, brother of actors Matt and Owen. Tom was shuttled briskly among the elegant Goldwyn actresses. He never made much money, but he had a lot of fun. An odd cuss from Oklahoma by the name of Will Rogers was introduced in *Laughing Bill Hyde*. He did moderately well in a series of Goldwyn comedies. And Tallulah Bankhead, the pretty daughter of a Congressman from Alabama, was plucked from a magazine beauty contest and starred in *Thirty A Week*.

Two developments in 1918 were of historic account. One was that Samuel Goldfish decided to change his name. Intrigued with the sleek neologism which he and the Selwyns contrived as the appellation of their outfit, he petitioned the courts to let him take it as his own. Since the name was copyrighted, it was necessary to get the company's consent. Goldfish, as president, consented. Permission was granted by the courts. The change was a tacit indication of Goldfish's taking on of class, which was somewhat inhibited and embarrassed by the piscatorial tag. As Judge Learned Hand later put it, with reference to this change—and with a courteous nod toward the producer—"A self-made man may prefer a self-made name."

The other development in 1918 was that the Goldwyn company leased the Culver City studio of Triangle, which had been lying idle for almost a year, and began to transfer its Eastern production to that West Coast facility. The place had a colorful background which is interesting to this report because it is part of the complicated lineage of a mighty film company.

The Culver City Lot

Back in the days when movie makers were drifting gypsylike to the West Coast and the Los Angelinos were discovering that theirs was more than just a drowsy market town, a citizen named Harry Culver had conceived the extravagant idea of promoting a real estate development by offering to give away land to anybody who would use the acreage to build a movie studio. In the middle of a vast, flat, sun-baked area lying midway between Los Angeles and seaside Venice, he erected a seven-story hotel, from the top of which he urged his prospects to scan the virtually desolate countryside, which he bravely named Culver City. Harry Culver had vanity and hopes.

Lured by his generosity and the sweep of the Culver City range, several skipjack producers of one-reel westerns moved out and staked claims. Then Thomas Ince, who had his pioneer Inceville studio out where Sunset Boulevard now reaches the sea, took advantage of Culver's reckless offer and snagged a sixteen-acre parcel of land out along dusty Washington Boulevard, which was then little more than a country road running through the fields. The year was 1915. Ince was a top director at that time, famed for his William S. Hart westerns and such early features as *The Alien* and *The Wrath of the Gods*. On the land acquired from Culver, he constructed a "modern" studio— five glass-enclosed stages for "indoor" filming, with collateral offices, workshops and dressing rooms.

By the time this spectacular plant was ready, Ince and his company had become one of the equilateral elements in Triangle, the daring combine which Harry Aitken formed with D. W. Griffith and Mack Sennett as the two other geometric sides. This eminent company was established on the theory that the best directors in the country would be joined with the best available acting talent to assure a flow of the best possible films. The purpose was that Triangle should be the Tiffany of the movie industry. It was a hopeful and reasonable project. The Culver City studio of Ince became its home.

The hapless career of Triangle—its rocketing rise and fall—is one of the glaring examples of reckless management in the early days of films. Leading stage actors were imported: De Wolf Hopper, Sir Herbert Beerbohm Tree, Billie Burke, Julia Dean, Raymond Hitchcock, Willie Collier, Joe Weber and Lew Fields. They were paid extraordinary salaries for the comparatively little work they did and they were put in such inappropriate items as film versions of *Don Quixote* and *Macbeth*. It soon became painfully evident that mere theatrical prestige and conventional stage material were not necessarily sure-fire on the screen.

Furthermore, Zukor and others began raiding the Triangle fold, which included the idolized "Bill" Hart, young Douglas Fairbanks, the Talmadge sisters, Bessie Barriscale, Olive Thomas, Charles Ray, and Lillian and Dorothy Gish. And the dispositions of the partners did not make for studio harmony. Griffith pulled out in 1916. Ince later went, with several stars. Sennett was left with a large debt. The management was changed, and the Culver City studio was abandoned. After a few years, Triangle expired. It is ironic that all this should have happened on the lot where Metro-Goldwyn-Mayer now is.

The layout in Culver City on the day the Goldwyn company moved in was puny in comparison with the vast plant that spreads out from there today, blanketing many additional acres with great sound stages, laboratories and standing sets. But it was, for the times and the necessities, a large and imposing studio. A high white wall and a three-story office building, fronted by a white colonnade, faced on Washington Boulevard. Behind them were six glassed-in stages of the sort that were used in those days to get natural light on indoor shooting, and a clutter of other buildings and sets. The new tenants soon had the place humming. Appropriately, the first Goldwyn film completed there was a comedy starring Tom Moore. Eight months later, Goldwyn bought the property outright, moved all production from the East coast and gave up his Fort Lee studio.

It is hard to pinpoint precisely when the troubles of the Goldwyn company began, but its operations were erratic from 1919 on. In that year, Goldwyn formed a new unit—Eminent Authors it was called—which reflected his pronounced regard for writers. "The story is the important part of this business," he said. Among the eminent authors who worked for him were Rex Beach, Rupert Hughes, Mary Roberts Rinehart, Gouverneur Morris, Gertrude Atherton and Octavus Roy Cohen. There was always a suspicion that their scenarios were a bit too eminent for the average public taste.

In any event, the usual problem of all expanding picture-making firms, that of commanding sufficient capital to finance a steady inventory of films, began to bedevil the Goldwyn company after World War I. Costs were rising and the competition of First National and Famous Players-Lasky was strong. The artful Goldwyn had already done some fishing in the abundant Wall Street pool, from which other picture promoters were pulling sizable funds. Now he was lured into an alliance which spelled eventual misery and doom.

Fabulous Joe Godsol

When Lee and J. J. Shubert and a third theatrical producer, A. H. (Al) Woods, came to him with a fine-feathered gentleman who was reputed to have untold wealth and a genius for raising more of it, Goldwyn eagerly clasped them to his breast and put them on his board of directors, confident of the capital they would fetch. Little did he reckon the fateful consequences of this move. For the gentleman, Frank Joseph Godsol, a relative by marriage of Woods, was about as helpful to Goldwyn as a rattlesnake might have been.

It would not be accurate to term him a man of mystery, since his devious commercial depredations had been widely publicized over a period of years. Only a short while before he infiltrated into the Goldwyn company, he had been the center of a scandal concerning a wartime purchasing commission from France, and during the consequent wrangling over that issue he had languished for several weeks in a Washington jail. Even at the time he joined Goldwyn, he was under a military indictment in France.

Dark-haired, handsome, athletic, a bon vivant and sport, Godsol had moved in the liveliest circles in Europe's leading capitals and resorts. Although born in Cleveland, Ohio, he had transferred abroad as a young man and had made a career of high-class swindling in several appropriate fields. One of his earlier difficulties came from promoting imitation pearls, which he and his hoodwinking henchmen neglected to mention were artificial. The Paris Commercial Tribunal hauled him up for this in 1905. "The most colossal fake in the history of jewelry" is what it was termed in the trade.

There is no need to recollect in detail the episodes of Godsol's wartime career, which led to his being arrested on charges of embezzlement by the government of France. His own comment to the court (which freed him) sums him up.

"I am no angel; I seek no halos," he explained.

This was the gentleman who moved in on Goldwyn's company.

Ironically, the capital which Godsol was expected to bring in did not materialize according to schedule, even though he had been made a vice-president of the company and a member of the executive committee. So Goldwyn had to go fishing again. This time he cast his line in a potent preserve of private riches—that of the du Pont family of Delaware. By a vigorous exercise of his salesman's talents—and by agreeing to use the du Pont raw film—he got two of the manifold cousins, Henry F. and Eugene E. du Pont, to put up some $3,000,000 to carry the company along. The two du Ponts and a retinue of affiliated bankers, including E. V. R. Thayer, president of Chase National in New York, who came in with them, were added to the Goldwyn board.

This instituted a period of fantastic confusion and strain. The bickerings of that bizarre board of directors were unbelievable. Goldwyn was mercilessly harried, and, being a volatile sort, he did not react with behavior that was helpful to compromise. One time, a director interrupted, just as he was about to propose a plan, and told him that he (the director) was against it, no matter *what* it was. "I had to stop making pictures and spend all my time explaining things," Goldwyn complained. His most severe critic was Godsol. He was a very tough man.

And, as though the executive alignment was not sufficiently fraught, it became even more so with the acquisition by the company of a half interest in the big new Capitol Theatre in New York. This was accomplished in May, 1920. It was in line with the company's desire to establish some theatre affiliations and was considered quite a coup. It was that, especially for the gentlemen who owned the Capitol.

This elaborate 4,500-seat theatre had been built the year before by a syndicate assembled by Messmore Kendall. It was on a plot of land at Broadway and Fiftieth Street, bought from the Wendel estate for $1,000,000. The theatre itself cost $900,000 to build, bringing the entire cost to $1,900,000. There were the usual predictions that the new picture palace would fail, that it was "too far uptown," but it did well from the night of its gala opening on November 8, 1919.

Under the circumstances, the Goldwyn people felt they had an excellent deal when they were able to buy a half-interest in the theatre—for $1,900,000, which reimbursed the syndicate for the total cost. However, a part of it was paid in stock of the Goldwyn company. So Kendall and other members of the syndicate which included T. Coleman du Pont, another member of the Delaware family, were also placed on the Goldwyn company board.

Within a few months, a crisis of major proportions occurred. A cyclical decline in the movie business caused distress to the company. The du Ponts, concerned for their investment, urged that it be reorganized. Goldwyn resisted the suggestion and, in thorough exasperation, resigned. Kendall tried to effect a reorganization, with Coleman du Pont as the new president. But this didn't work, and Goldwyn, somewhat cooled off, was persuaded to return. Eighteen months passed. Another depression in the movie industry brought more woe. Whereupon Goldwyn, under further harassment from Godsol, now strong with the du Ponts, finally uttered his immortal declaration, "You may include me out!" and departed for good. This ultimate leave-taking happened in March, 1922. One month later, the elegant Godsol was elected president. Goldwyn, though thoroughly routed, still held onto a small block of stock.

The departure of Goldwyn from the company to which he had given his name—or, at least, the nicer half of it—precipitated another nasty quarrel. Going on to independent film making, he was enjoined by the Goldwyn company from putting his name on any pictures he made in his new circumstance. He vigorously challenged the injunction. Eventually, it was agreed, after a considerable amount of legal battling, that he might use the name if he made it perfectly clear in every commercial usage that he, Samuel Goldwyn, was "not now connected with Goldwyn Pictures." This explicit explanation had to be made with the words "Not Now" in letters exactly as large as those of the Goldwyn name. Such an obvious juxtaposition of "Samuel Goldwyn" and "Not Now" went hard with the man who had formed the company and had made its name his own.

Godsol's Grief

It must be said for Godsol that, once he got control of the guillotined Goldwyn company, he made vigorous and valiant moves to improve its financial condition and boost its productive potency. He was not a creative film man; he frankly admitted that. His singular talent was for business, and he tried to put it to use.

Perceiving that an economic weakness was the small output of the studio in relation to the number of exchanges and the distribution machinery the company maintained, Godsol worked to build up production. He went after William Randolph Hearst, the powerful publisher, who owned Cosmopolitan Pictures, in which Marion Davies was the favored star, and got the contract to distribute the product of Hearst's studio. Cosmopolitan, which made its pictures in New York City, had released through Paramount. Godsol also arranged to distribute Distinctive's pictures and those of some minor producers.

Further, he got June Mathis to come to the Culver City plant in charge of the scenario department. She had continued to spark successful films at Famous Players-Lasky after leaving the Metro lot. June moved in with her usual determination, and put some ambitious projects into the works. One of these was a motion picture version of the great popular novel and stage spectacle, *Ben Hur*, which was destined to be historic. Of that we will hear more anon.

The odds defeated Godsol. The increasing cost of making films, which brought on the general industry crisis in the black fall of 1923; the expense of its distributing operations; and the large debt burden the company bore as a consequence of its earlier expansions were too much to overcome. The period of executive chaos and studio extravagance had taken its toll.

An attempt to sell the company to First National was made in 1922; it fell through when the latter decided to build and operate its own studio. A financial reorganization in the spring of 1923 was again a stopgap maneuver; the company's stock, which sold at a high of 22 in June, was down to 8¼ by the end of the year. Godsol endeavored to excuse it by saying that he was "building up the Goldwyn company's business and not the stock market." But his dodge didn't fool anyone.

Ordered to take a rest in Florida in January, 1924, Godsol encountered Lee Shubert, who had put some money into the Goldwyn company when he went in. Shubert was also a heavy investor and a member of the board of directors of Loew's. It was Shubert who helpfully suggested that Godsol have a talk with Marcus Loew, also wintering in Palm Beach. Shubert was well aware of the Loew company's indecision as to whether to build up its production facilities or sell out. Godsol recognized the implications and immediately called upon Loew.

CHAPTER VIII

THE MAYER GROUP

Now, the chance to acquire the Goldwyn company offered these attractive aspects to the people of Loew's: First, the production facilities of the big Culver City studio, with its line-up of stars and directors, were auspicious for the contemplated move toward more and classier pictures that Loew and his associates had in mind.

Further, there was the prospect of acquiring with the Goldwyn company the scattering of affiliated theatres that it had picked up in a period of five years. These included the handsome Miller and California in Los Angeles, the Ascher circuit in and around Chicago and, most particularly, the potent Capitol in New York. Marcus Loew looked upon this house with a peculiarly covetous eye.

But there were two big things to be considered in putting together a deal to acquire the Goldwyn company. One was the matter of cost. Loew's was a frugal organization. Its success was due, in part, to a genius for picking up potentially valuable properties at bargain prices and making them pay. Nick Schenck was expert at this business, and the job of negotiating for the Goldwyn company fell largely to him. Loew was now suffering a heart ailment and was not up to the kind of bargaining he so enjoyed.

The second and more important consideration was that of discovering a man who could head the big producing operation that would be the consequence of the deal. Schenck had already made a thorough check on the management of Metro and had found that Joe Engel, then head of the studio, was not adequate to the job. Studio management, Schenck figured, required a man with a creative bent, but, above all, it sternly demanded competence in handling people and a hard-headedness in business affairs.

Schenck discussed the problem with Robert Rubin, who had come over to Loew's as one of its legal counsel when Metro was acquired. They agreed that the studio head of the Goldwyn company was also weak. Abe Lehr, while a kindly, courteous person, was considered a poor executive. If a deal was made to get the Goldwyn company, a new man to run the studio would have to be found.

Rubin had a suggestion. As legal counsel for Loew's, he was dutifully mindful of its welfare. But he was also mindful of the welfare of another of his clients, his old friend, Louis B. Mayer, with whom he had continued as counselor and financial partner ever since Mayer had gone into producing on his own. When the deal for the Goldwyn Company began to take promising form, Rubin telephoned Mayer in California and urged him to make a quick trip to New York. He figured there might be something doing in the way of a double-barreled deal—a merger of Metro and Goldwyn under the management of Mayer.

This was a calculation that made good sense on several counts, not least of which was the nature and qualifications of Mayer himself. This tough and resourceful go-getter had been doing remarkably well in the five years that he had been making pictures, following his move to the West Coast. The films he produced with Anita Stewart, his first and most fortunate star, had brought him profits and assurance. The affable Miss Stewart soon learned that working for Mayer was quite different from working at leisurely Vitagraph. He kept her in constant operation. The idea was to get pictures made, regardless of the nerves and the temperaments of the stars and directors who did the work.

In the three years that she had a contract with Mayer, Miss Stewart made fifteen films. They were hard years for her. She didn't like her stories. Mayer and Rudolph Cameron, her husband, quarreled. At the end of the period of her contract, tired and discouraged, she retired. Later, she made some films for Hearst's Cosmopolitan company, but her career never again reached the height it attained when she worked with Mayer.

Marshall Neilan, who directed Miss Stewart in several films for Mayer, was often annoyed at the way the producer would show up on the sets, demanding to know whether they were following schedule, what they were doing and why. Being himself a volatile person, Neilan would irritably protest that Mayer was interfering with production, that he was causing costly delays. But the slight expense probably profited the producer. He was learning how movies were made.

Flush with the early success of the Stewart pictures, Mayer established his own Louis B. Mayer Production Company, which aptly had its first residence in what was known as the Selig Zoo, a Hollywood studio-menagerie generally rented for animal films. Here he made many soulful pictures, such as *The Song of Life, The Child Thou Gavest Me, One Clear Call*—solemn and sentimental "dramas," characteristic of that era of the silent screen.

The mawkishness of these pictures reflected the emotional nature of Mayer. He was immensely sentimental. Tears sprang quickly to his eyes and he developed a disposition toward broad theatrical gestures and displays. More than once, in heated encounters with directors and stars at the Selig Zoo, he would be overcome with emotion and go off into fainting spells. In such crises, his loyal secretary, Florence Browning, would casually dash cold water into his face, and he would come to, muttering "Where am I?" after sufficient pause for alarm.

The ambiguities of Mayer's nature were memorably revealed in the handling of one of the first films he made with Mildred Harris Chaplin, whom he signed in 1919 to star under an arrangement similar to that he had with Anita Stewart. The picture was *Polly of the Storm Country*, a touching tale of strife between poor "squatters" and rich landowners, in which the pretty heroine—a "squatter," of course—brought understanding to the feudists and snagged herself a landowner mate because of her exalting recollection of her dead grandmother's faith in love as a remedy for all woes.

At the time Mayer signed Mildred Harris Chaplin, she was eighteen years old and estranged from her husband, Charlie Chaplin, from whom she was later divorced. This circumstance caused bitter feelings over her use of the Chaplin name. The popular comedian suspected, with ample reason, that she and Mayer were trading on his fame. A suggestion for exploiting *Polly of the Storm Country*, published in the *Motion Picture World*, gave support to this notion. It said:

"Mildred Harris Chaplin is still new enough as a star to be exploited as the famous comedian's wife. She will attract more attention that way than by referring to her ability."

The matter came to a crisis in a characteristic episode. One pleasant evening, Mayer and a party of guests, which included the visiting Robert Rubin, arrived to have dinner in the dining room of the old Alexandria Hotel in Hollywood. Chaplin happened to be there. Some unpleasant remarks were passed between the resentful comedian and the producer. Chaplin invited Mayer to remove his glasses. Mayer did so with one hand. With the other, he clipped Chaplin on the jaw. Rubin, a mild-mannered gentleman, witnessed this chivalrous display. He thereafter resisted all suggestions of his partner that he move his office to the West Coast.

Mayer's ability to assemble talent was manifested in these years by the people he brought to his own new studio at 3200 Mission Road. Directors Fred Niblo, Reginald Barker, Hobart Henley and John Stahl were enlisted to make pictures for him. He inveigled such beautiful ladies as Renee Adoree, Kathleen MacDonald and Barbara LaMarr. Frances Marion, Bess Meredyth and Kathleen Norris were among the writers he engaged. But by far the most fortunate association that he made was with the boyish Irving Thalberg, whom he got to come to work for him.

Today the name of Thalberg is sacred in Hollywood. There is scarcely a person in the community who does not hallow the reputation of the man, even those who never knew him when he was living or arrived long after he was gone. So rapid was the quick absorption of this bright youth into the medium, and so commanding and constructive was his impact upon the business of manufacturing films, that his career represents the grand fulfillment of professional Hollywood's sublime ideal. Everyone in the place knows of him, and most of them think of him as a sort of god.

A person unfamiliar with the circumstances and the climate in which movies are made might find it hard to comprehend this reverence for a producer long since dead. It might seem foolish and phony, or, at the best, naive, in a community as materialistic and ego-ridden as Hollywood is. That may be. There is no way of telling how much the lasting cult of Thalberg is a compound of genuine admiration for what he was and what he did, or a wistful, almost pitiful, manifestation of the community's hunger for comforting symbols of its own worth.

Thalberg is dead now. He has been dead a long time. And legends gain luster through the years. Most that went into the making of his legend will be told here, for you to judge. . . .

Wonder Boy

The young man who joined Mayer, however, in February, 1923, was but an eager and elementary promise of the figure he was to become. He was still shy his twenty-fourth birthday when he joined the organization of Mayer. One thing that always gave him stature in Hollywood eyes was his phenomenally youthful start.

What made the successful film producer back in that wonderful span of years when American motion pictures were rising to triumphant forms? What physical or chemical factors went into the shaping of the mind that had the tuning to catch the wave lengths of mass interest and popular taste? What traits of personality endowed one with the power to encourage the best from creative people in the complex job of planning and putting together worthwhile films? These are difficult questions. Millions of dollars were thrown away trying to find ready-made answers crystallized and consummated in little men. But if Irving Thalberg could be taken as a prime example of the optimum result, then a middle-class, middle-income background was the first desirable factor to demand.

Thalberg was born in Brooklyn, N.Y., on May 30, 1899, and was raised in the average modest comfort of a Flatbush-section home. His father, William, was a moderately successful lace importer, with an office in New York, and his mother, Henrietta, was a housewife with lots of energy and a stubborn resolve.

Indeed, it was to his mother that Irving Thalberg probably owed not only the fact that he was in movies but that he ever amounted to anything at all. For a siege of rheumatic fever that took him in his seventeenth year, on top of a discouraging series of boyhood illnesses, put him to bed for six months, just a few aggravating months before he was due to graduate with possible honors from Brooklyn Boys High. During this time, a less Spartan mother might have cribbed and coddled her darling boy to the point of spoiling him completely for any further aggressiveness in this world.

Not so Henrietta Thalberg. She would remind Irving every day, as soon as his illness had passed its climax, that he wasn't getting anywhere lying in bed, and that she certainly did not intend to be the mother of a useless invalid. She would fetch him books from the library, get his teachers to give him homework to do and even come around occasionally to hear his lessons. The method worked. The boy, who had already been prodded through the lower grades of school, saw that objection was useless and made himself get well.

Naturally, it had been expected that he would go to college, perhaps to study law. Henrietta fondly visioned a solid respectable profession for him. But his heart had been strained by the rheumatic fever—a strain that Thalberg lived with all his life—and further formal education was feared too hard for him to take. So he started his career by doing light occasional work in the small department store of his maternal grandfather, H. Heymann, while studying typing and shorthand at night. Later he studied Spanish at a Brooklyn commercial school. Then he got a job as secretary with a New York importing firm. Within a year, he earned a promotion to assistant manager of a department, but that soon palled. Commerce did not appeal to him. With the arrival of summer, he threw up the job and went to his grandmother's vacation cottage at Edgemere, L.I., to relax and muse.

By chance, a summer neighbor was Carl Laemmle, pint-size head of Universal and a power in the motion picture world. The opportunity was one that Henrietta, with her eye for opportunities, could not miss. She soon dropped a hint to Mrs. Laemmle that maybe her husband might give Irving a job. Laemmle came through with an offer. Irving said thanks, he would see. A few weeks later, he went into the Universal office in New York and was given a minor secretarial job.

What followed sounds so fabulous and foolish that it has to be prefaced with the note that Carl Laemmle was a man of infinite whimsies and charmingly quixotic moves. He was, indeed, an original of the legendary madcap movie industry tycoon. For less than two years, young Thalberg worked as a secretary in the old Universal offices at 1600 Broadway in New York, serving first under D. B. Lederman, assistant to Laemmle, and then under Laemmle himself. The lad was diligent and thoughtful. He would leave notes to Laemmle about the company's films, offering comments and suggestions. The boss was impressed with him.

Then one day Irving called home excitedly. Laemmle was departing that night for a visit to the West Coast and wanted to take his young secretary with him to get some work done on the train. Could Henrietta bring his bag to the station? She could—and she did! Indeed, they had all been waiting for just such a break for the boy. Irving, boiling with excitement, kissed his mother and father goodby at the train, and off he went to Hollywood. It must be remembered that, in 1919, when Thalberg first arrived in Hollywood, the innovation of feature-length pictures had come only some five years before. Picture making was still in an expanding and experimental stage. Nobody knew too much about it. Everybody had a lot to learn.

Universal, at that time, was existing in a particularly chaotic state, due to the casualness of Laemmle and his inability (or his unwillingness) to establish a firm command. The operation of the studio, in the San Fernando Valley north of Hollywood, was amazingly loose and haphazard. Isidore Bernstein, the supposed general manager, often had to share authority with people sent out from New York. Laemmle, himself a frequent visitor, attempted to run the place when he was there. Directors and assorted supervisors did pretty much as they pleased.

Thus it complicated matters further when, a few months after Laemmle and his young secretary arrived, the boss decided to go to Europe and left Thalberg in his stead at the studio. The situation was ticklish, since Laemmle characteristically failed to designate whether Bernstein or the ex-secretary was in charge. This uncertainty demanded of Thalberg, boyish and inexperienced as he was, a summoning of smartness and gumption that makes one wonder at the resources in his slight frame. But he was the son of Henrietta, and this necessity to assert himself or fail was the challenge that brought out his mettle and set the pattern for his career.

His and the studio's major problem was the *enfant terrible* of the time, the fabulous Erich von Stroheim, screen writer, director and actor. Von Stroheim had made himself solid with Laemmle the year before by writing, directing and starring in *Blind Husbands,* a sleek, seductive film that proved both novel and sensational when it opened in New York. In July 1920, he began shooting his now legendary *Foolish Wives* and at this point his path and that of Thalberg first came to a violent cross.

The reports of the making of this picture (the money spent, the time consumed, the battles that raged when von Stroheim demanded the most precise and costly details) contributed much to the early impressions of recklessness and extravagance in Hollywood. The picture was before the cameras for almost a year and cost over $1,000,000, which was incredible then. The Universal people were frantic. Von Stroheim was uncontrollable. Right in the middle was Thalberg, then just twenty-one.

Letters which the frail, harassed young man wrote to Laemmle, who was then abroad, picture his dogged efforts to curb von Stroheim and establish his own control as head of the studio. Slowly, stubbornly and shrewdly, he made his authority supreme first by his tireless persistence and then by his knowledge of films. In a surprisingly short time, Thalberg was running the Universal studio, getting out a good program of pictures and earning Hollywood fame as a "wonder boy."

Even so, the young man grew impatient with his Universal job. There were causes of irritation. Laemmle's appreciation of him was apparently not too high. He paid Thalberg, as studio manager, only $450 a week, considering this ample remuneration for a man who had started as a secretary at thirty dollars a week only five years before. Further, a romance between Thalberg and Rosabelle Laemmle, the dark, attractive daughter of Carl, was not panning out as Papa expected and his paternal attitude was cool. Thalberg began looking quietly for another job. His eye fell on Mayer. In this producer, he saw a promising man.

Meetings between Mayer and Thalberg happened to occur frequently in the home of E. B. Loeb, the lawyer for Universal and also the West Coast lawyer for Mayer. The two talked pictures intently. Mayer was greatly impressed. Pretty soon he was contemplating taking Thalberg into a producing partnership, giving him his own unit in the Mayer company and 20 per cent of the profits of the films he made. However, Mayer's eastern counselor, Robert Rubin advised that he not move so fast. "Wait awhile," he suggested. "Try him on straight salary for six months." The suggestion was taken. Mayer offered Thalberg $600 a week to come in with him as an associate. Thalberg happily agreed. For a third again as much as he had been earning, Thalberg joined Mayer in February, 1923.

The smooth and successful cooperation between Mayer and Thalberg in the one year that they were working together as an independent outfit at Mayer's Mission Road studio is attested by the several respectable and financially successful films they produced and the happy recollections of some of the people who were with them at the time. One of these was a clever young actress who was hired to play minor roles, with little more thought for her prospects than that she might turn out some day to be a star on the strength of a pretty face, a modest talent and a refined and gentle charm. No one at that particular juncture suspected the more important role that Norma Shearer was to play in the destinies of Irving Thalberg and Mayer—no one, with the possible exception of Norma Shearer, that is.

Working Girl

Hers had been pretty much the routine of the hard-working, conscientious girl, determined to make a living and be somebody in the entertainment world. An early ambition to be a pianist, pursued with diligence during her teens in Montreal, where she was born, was cut short when her well-to-do father failed in business and she had to get out on her own.

With money from the sale of her piano, she and her sister, Athole, went to New York, chaperoned by their mother, and sought employment as extras in films. Their first jobs were in a shoestring series of two-reel comedies set in a girls' boarding school. They were made in a studio in Mount Vernon, N.Y., and later on location in Raleigh, N.C. While there, the producer went broke, and Norma, her sister and the rest of the "school girls" day-coached back to New York.

For the next several years, the patient Norma had her ups and downs, modeling for photographers between film jobs and trying to work up courage to go to Hollywood. One of her modeling triumphs was as the anonymous Miss Lotta Miles, the pretty girl whose smiling face on billboards was wreathed artistically in a Kelly-Springfield automobile tire.

Good luck finally tapped her. Within a few days, in 1923, she was offered Hollywood jobs by two producers, and her agent, Edward Small, told her he thought he might get her a chance with L. B. Mayer. She waited in painful anxiety. Then the offer came. It was for a six-months term, with options, at $150 a week. Norma had no hesitation. She and her mother were off to the Coast.

On arrival, they registered grandly at the famous old Hollywood Hotel, and then took themselves serenely to the Mayer studio on Mission Road. They waited while the telephone girl announced them.

A few minutes later, a nice young chap whom Norma took to be an office boy came out and invited them to follow him. He showed them down a short passage, into a small office and held chairs for them. Then, when they were seated, he went around and sat down himself behind the desk. Only then did it dawn upon Norma that this polite and pleasant young man was not an office boy. It was Irving Thalberg, the associate of Mayer.

Amused at her obvious confusion, Thalberg told the young actress that he had been her watchful admirer for some time. This was very flattering, and Norma was soon at her ease. In a few minutes, Mayer came into the office and the Shearers were formally introduced. When they left the office later, Mrs. Shearer whispered into Norma's ear, "Wouldn't it be wonderful if you married that nice young man!"

However, her first assignments did not lend much hope to that design. A test for the lead in a John Stahl picture fizzled when Norma overdressed in a beaded gown. Stahl took one startled look at her and dumped her in a minor role. And her next job came near disaster when the director, Reginald Barker, harried her for being uncertain and nervous, which only made her more so. Providentially, it was discovered, after a week of shooting, that the camera work was bad and that the whole thing would have to be done over. Thalberg took Norma aside and politely but firmly told her that she would have to do much better or her contract would be dropped. This sent her back for the fresh start with a grim determination to make good. She did, and her option was picked up.

A succession of loan-outs followed. In the course of her first exciting year as a contract player with Mayer's company, Norma appeared in eight films. And all through that year she was working with a concentrated effort to improve, to distinguish herself as an actress. She was fired with a passion to succeed. In a little Chevrolet roadster she bought when her contract was renewed, she would drive along the Hollywood boulevards, look at the new movie mansions and dream of the day when she would have one. Her castle-building was as candid and unrestrained as a child's. . . .

Such were the destined people in the organization of Louis B. Mayer when he was looked upon as a likely candidate for the job of running a big studio for Loew's.

The Merger Is Arranged

The three-way negotiations among Godsol, Nick Schenck and Mayer continued from January until April. In March, the rumors began to spread. They ranged from hints that Loew's would distribute the Goldwyn company's pictures to accurate, though incomplete, predictions that the Metro and Goldwyn studios would be joined. But no one, outside the participants (and a few silent advisers, such as Joe Schenck), foresaw the magnitude of the merger that was publicly announced on April 17, 1924.

The major step in the transaction was the absorption of the Goldwyn Pictures Corporation by Loew's, Inc., with the Goldwyn company being purchased through a straight exchange of stock. A new producing company, the Metro-Goldwyn Pictures Corporation, was formed. The common stock of this corporation was given to Loew's, Inc., in exchange for the Metro company. The preferred stock was given to the Goldwyn shareholders in exchange for their shares, one for one. The value of the latter shares was figured at $5,000,000. It was thus, without the passing of any actual monies, that the Goldwyn company was acquired.

By this transaction, Loew's, Inc., obtained, through possession of the voting stock, control of the Metro-Goldwyn Corporation, which was to be a merger of the two studios in the big Culver City plant that was owned by the Goldwyn company. It also obtained the theatres and exchanges of the latter company. In the light of subsequent developments, it was a bargain beyond compare.

At the same time, the Goldwyn stockholders were handsomely recompensed. The preferred stock of the new corporation was to pay a 7 per cent cumulative dividend.

Only one major Goldwyn stockholder refused to accept the exchange. That one was Samuel Goldwyn. He did not approve the deal, and arrangements had to be made by the Goldwyn company trustees to buy in his shares for cash. Thus, through one of those perversities that the unpredictable Goldwyn often displayed, he was not even a stockholder in the new company that continued his patented name.

The second big step in the transaction was the arrangement that was made with Mayer and his associates, Thalberg and Robert Rubin, to direct the production operations of the Metro-Goldwyn company. These three men, constituting the so-called "Mayer group," were put under a personal-service contract for three years, with options. It called for Mayer to serve as vice-president and general manager of the new producing company at a salary of $1,500 a week. Thalberg to act as second vice-president and "supervisor of production" at $650 a week, and Rubin to serve as secretary (with his office in New York) at $600 a week. The physical properties and some of the personnel contracts of the Mayer company were purchased outright by Metro-Goldwyn for $75,000. This employment of Mayer and his associates was the big surprise in the deal.

In order to maintain Mayer s identity, it was agreed that he might choose whether to inscribe the pictures of the studio with the credit line, "Produced by Louis B. Mayer for the Metro-Goldwyn Corporaation" or "Produced by Metro-Goldwyn-Mayer." He eventually chose the latter, and thus the familiar name came into common usage and later was adopted as the official name of the studio.

But the significant and what proved in time to be the critical corollary in this contract was a private understanding that the "Mayer group" would receive, in addition to salaries, a further compensation of 20 per cent of the profits of all the pictures turned out by the studio. (A picture's profits were to be calculated after the payment of all production and distribution costs and the withholding of sufficient monies to pay an annual dividend of at least two dollars a share on the common stock.)

Such a formidable inducement to the heads of the studio seemed a sensible one to Loew and Schenck. The company would survive only on profitable pictures, and if this managerial group could provide it with such pictures, the bonus would be amply justified.

Not mentioned in the contract, because it was a private partnership arrangement among Mayer, Thalberg and Rubin themselves, was the division they would make of the profits within their group. They agreed that Mayer was to receive a little better than half, or 53 per cent. Rubin would receive 27 per cent and Thalberg would receive 20 per cent. It soon became evident that this was an underestimation of Thalberg's worth, and it wasn't long before he was saying so to his partners, in no uncertain terms. Indeed, the whole "Mayer group" arrangement was a cause of periodic private strife. By it, as was later discovered, "the seeds of friction" were sown.

But no one had any thoughts of friction when the deal was all arranged and Marcus Loew got the approval of his board of directors and proudly announced it to the press. A glowing future was envisioned for Metro-Goldwyn and its parent, Loew's, Inc.

How important was to be that future to the development of the American film industry was a matter that even the most sanguine prophet could not at that time foresee.

CHAPTER IX

THE LAUNCHING OF METRO-GOLDWYN

MAYER was eager and impatient to get the new company on the road. Even though the terms of the merger specified that he and his group would not take over operation of the Culver City studio until May 17, 1924, he moved most of his own studio equipment to the big Goldwyn plant within a week. And on April 26, which was a Saturday, he bade a formal dedication of the place to the future greatness and glory of Metro-Goldwyn—and Mayer.

Forecasting a flair for ceremonials which he was to develop and delight in through the years, he ordered a studio turnout and a becomingly boastful display. A platform draped with bunting was set up on the studio lawn, and stars and distinguished guests were piled upon it in a glittering and grandiose array. John Gilbert, Mae Murray, Lon Chaney, Ramon Novarro, Antonio Moreno and Lillian Gish (who happened to be there as a visitor) were ranked with the Mayor of Culver City and the Admiral of the Pacific Fleet. A Navy band boomed appropriate music. Telegrams of congratulations were received from President Coolidge and Secretary of Commerce Herbert Hoover. A shower of roses from the Governor of California was dropped from a circling plane.

The moment of exaltation came when Abraham Lehr, vice-president of the Goldwyn company and head of the studio, presented Mayer with a large key, symbolic of handing over the property. Mayer, somewhat choked with emotion, accepted it solemnly.

"I hope," he said, "that it is given me to live up to this great trust. It has been my argument and practice that each picture should teach a lesson, should have a reason for existence. With seventeen of the greatest directors in the industry calling this great institution their home, I feel that this aim will be carried out. . . . This is a great moment for me. I accept this solemn trust and pledge the best that I have to give."

The mood of solemnity was lightened when Will Rogers arrived on horseback and apologized for being tardy. He explained that he had left home without his chewing gum and had to get it. The amiable Will, who had risen to stardom in Goldwyn pictures, then proceeded to present smaller keys to Mayer's waiting lieutenants, Irving Thalberg and a new man, Harry Rapf. Neither man dared attempt to top Mayer's eloquence.

Noting a wretched crayon portrait of Marcus Loew, which some studio artist had hastily done and hung at the front of the platform, Will observed laconically, "If the new boss could see *that,* he would probably call the whole thing off!"

This crack was a pointed reminder of the actual proprietors of the studio. Neither Loew nor Nick Schenck was present. Both were in New York. But Joe Schenck, Nick's watchful brother, now producing at United Artists, was on hand.

In the midst of the hopeful ceremonies, one pregnant and embarrassing incident occurred. Marshall Neilan, a top Goldwyn company director, who was then at the point of wrapping up the final shooting on his adaptation of Thomas Hardy's *Tess of the D'Urbervilles,* grew bored and impatient with the speechmaking. Pacing up and down outside the crowd, he sent an assistant among the spectators to summon the members of his troupe. Then, when his people were assembled, he ordered them into waiting automobiles and, with no endeavor to conceal, deliberately drove off to the set.

The departure created a brief disturbance. There was some snickering at the obvious slight to Mayer, who was not oblivious of it. Neilan had disregarded Mayer ever since he had directed the new producer's first Anita Stewart films. In common with most of the top directors, he frankly scorned what they called the "money men." So his act of leaving the ceremonies was defiant of the new management.

It was, indeed, in the nature of the opening shot in a latent war between the producers and the bolder directors that was to rumble in the studio for years. For despite Mayer's lofty boasting of "the seventeen greatest directors" in his talk, he had some distinct misgivings about the status and authority of those gentlemen. These were to be manifested rather sharply as time went on.

High hopes flowed in the opening speeches, but there was much anxiety among the 600 Goldwyn company employees who thronged the studio lawn that April afternoon. The prospects of who would continue in the merged outfit were far from clear, as, indeed, were the long-range prospects of the new producing company.

Joe Engel, who had been head man at Metro, had already got the sack. Abe Lehr, an amiable gentleman, was kept on briefly at Culver

City in a nominal role. Then, with a small financial settlement, he was politely let go. Both men, casualties of the progress of industrialization in the making of films, slowly faded into the background of a quickly forgetful Hollywood.

Mayer was tough and unrelenting. He had been hired to operate the studio on an efficient and profitable basis, and that he intended to do. He himself had been accustomed to producing some eight or ten pictures a year. Now, with Thalberg and Rapf as his associates, he was to be called on to turn out one a week!

In that day, the word "producer" was applied particularly to the head of the studio—to the man in charge of a producing company, such as a Lasky, a Goldwyn or a Mayer. The man who was immediate overseer and coordinator of production on a film was known as a "supervisor." His was largely a managerial job, though he had much to do with selecting stories, picking casts and approving what was done.

However, in most situations, the major creative job was in the hands of the director. He was the person who conceived the overall character of the picture and instructed the writers, the designers, the cameraman, the actors and finally the cutters in bringing it to his desire. He guided the performance of the whole thing and was responsible for its eventual quality. Especially was this true of the top directors. They were the undisputed masters of their films. Such men as Rex Ingram, Marshall Neilan, Reginald Barker, Hobart Henley, Fred Niblo and, of course, the great Erich von Stroheim took little supervision from anyone.

In the light of the demanding complications of producing a picture today, it seems incredible that Mayer could have thought of making fifty films a year with only two working supervisors, Thalberg and Rapf. Yet that was his confident intention. And the remarkable thing is he pulled it off—at least, in the first year of his tenure, which was the toughest year of all.

His treasure, as it turned out, was Thalberg. It was this slender, boyish-looking chap with the dark hair, the pale complexion, the squared-off shoulders and the pipestem legs who came to provide the imagination and the creative impulse for the "Mayer group." At the start, he superintended the production of *every* picture turned out by the studio. Rapf supervised the lesser items, under Thalberg's watchful eye.

This Rapf was a curious colleague. Brought up in the world of vaudeville, where he worked as a booker and agent, he got into movie making through the door of the old Lewis Selznick Select company and then became head of production at the small Warner studio.

Mayer hired him away from the latter just before the merger occurred. Rapf was a man of meagre schooling and frankly inelegant tastes.

Yet, somehow, this boorish fellow did possess the instinctive drives and the capacities for hard work and detailed labor that made him valuable as a foreman in producing films. He had an odd sense of the mass audience, a slave driver's callous faculties, and he himself was a tireless worker. Thalberg was Mayer's productive right hand; Rapf was his left.

First Film

The first film begun in Culver City under the new management was a remarkably faithful adaptation of Leonid Andreyev's play, *He Who Gets Slapped*. This stark and ironic drama about a sensitive, oppressed scientist who abandoned his career to become a clown in the circus and died in defending the honor of a circus girl had been produced on Broadway by the Theatre Guild in 1922. As a play, it was moderately popular, but was more of a *succes d'estime*. That such a drama should have been chosen for the first film produced by Metro-Goldwyn was coincidence.

Even before announcement of the merger, Mayer and Thalberg were laying out lines for possible productions on which they might proceed. One of the actors they had placed under contract and for whom they would need a vehicle was Lon Chaney, the popular performer of weird and grotesque characters who was on the wave of his recent success for Universal in *The Hunchback of Notre Dame*. Chaney's horrifying performance of the piteous and deformed bell ringer in the Paris cathedral was one of the most memorable of that era. Another role of a grotesque sort was wanted for him.

One day, Mayer and Thalberg were in the office of Abe Lehr when Victor Seastrom, a Swedish director under contract to the Goldwyn company, was brought in to meet them and to be told of the impending merger. He frankly told Thalberg he was not pleased with the picture he was about to shoot, and Thalberg, who was exceedingly friendly, promised to find something better for him to do. A few days later, he sent Seastrom a copy of *He Who Gets Slapped*. The director was enthusiastic. Here was the sort of thing that matched precisely his penchant for poetic imagery and subtle moods. He went to work at once on a scenario, which he wrote in Swedish. When it was done, it was translated into English and then was given a final polishing by Carey Wilson, one of the writers on the Goldwyn company list.

Thalberg was pleased. He immediately cast Chaney in the role of the scientist-turned-clown, and Norma Shearer, brought over with the Mayer contract players, was cast to play the circus girl. John Gilbert, the handsome young actor who had come along in Fox and Goldwyn films, was given the role of a circus performer who truly loved the girl.

Thus *He Who Gets Slapped* was ready to go before the camera as the first film under the new setup of the merged companies. Thalberg was supervisor, but he did not interfere. Seastrom barely saw him during the shooting of the film. It was finished within a few months and was presented at the Capitol Theatre in New York in November, with a big stage show in celebration of the fifth anniversary of the theatre.

The serene and propitious experience which was had with *He Who Gets Slapped* was anything but typical of the first few months of studio activities. Confusion and conflict were common. The organization of schedules and the handling of equipment were slow. Directors would hijack cameras and lights from the sets of other directors, who would hijack them back again. It took some months for the shakedown and smoothing out of operations to occur.

Most difficult were some problems inherited from the Goldwyn company. Marshall Neilan was a brilliant director, and his *Tess of the D'Urbervilles* was one of the boasted projects to which Metro-Goldwyn fell heir. This film from the Thomas Hardy novel had the talented Blanche Sweet as its star, and was intended to be a quality production. A camera crew had been sent to England to get authentic exterior long shots of Stonehenge and the Hardy country to give it genuine atmosphere. With Neilan as the director, a film of great prestige was presumed.

When Mayer saw the finished film, however, he was far from satisfied with the literal and tragic ending wherein poor Tess was hanged. He felt sure the American public would not accept this inevitable irony. He insisted that Neilan prepare a "happy ending," which Neilan reluctantly did. He shot one scene. In it Tess' husband— a role which Conrad Nagel played—awaited the report of her execution. Suddenly a messenger arrived with the news (conveyed in a subtitle) that she had been reprieved. There was a bit of rejoicing on the part of the husband and that was the end of the film.

At a preview in San Francisco, which Neilan demanded, both endings were shown and the audience was asked for its opinion. It preferred the tragic one. So the film was released with that conclusion. However, Mayer stuck to his belief and arranged that exhibitors be given the choice of which ending they would show. Neilan was incensed at this perversion. He went abroad in the summer of 1924 to shoot another film for the company—*The Sporting Venus*, a Scottish romance with a new actor, Ronald Colman, and Miss Sweet. While in England, he took occasion to give Thomas Hardy a showing of *Tess*. Hardy was reported pleased with it, with the original ending, of course. But when he heard of the erroneous ending, the author complained bitterly. He said it had been agreed when he sold the screen rights that not a word or situation would be changed. "But what could I do," he said, sadly, expressing the futility that many authors were to feel when confronted with Hollywood mutations of their works. "I am an old man and have no defense against this sort of thing."

The clash was the first of several that Neilan had with the "money men." When his contract expired, he went to First National, where he continued as a figure until the end of silent films.

Another of the top directors who could not abide the change was Rex Ingram. He had been a lord at Metro ever since his sensational triumph with *The Four Horsemen of the Apocalypse*, which he had followed with *The Prisoner of Zenda*, *Scaramouche* and several other films of slightly lesser profit but no less pre-eminence and renown. Ingram was a king among the silent film directors, in a class with Griffith and DeMille.

Even before the merger, he was getting impatient with Hollywood. Far places and strange voices called him. He had a passionate urge to roam. Marcus Loew had conceded him permission to produce *The Arab* in North Africa, and Ingram, on completing this picture, returned home in March, 1924.

Back just in time to witness the merger, Ingram let it be known that he was no longer interested in making pictures in Hollywood. He didn't like Mayer or Thalberg. He resented the organization they compelled. He gloomily intoned the prediction that Griffith was said to have made to him: "Rex, you and I are building on sand." Already he saw that the freedom of the director to do as he pleased was being cramped by the authority of the "front office," which was closing in with the establishment of Mayer.

With financial backing provided independently by Marcus Loew and Nick Schenck, Ingram returned to Europe and set up shop in the south of France. Here he made in succession his distinguished *Mare Nostrum*, *The Magician* and *The Garden of Allah*, in all of which his wife, Alice Terry, starred. Metro-Goldwyn distributed them.

The arrival of sound finished Ingram. His passion for pictorial form, so eloquent in the silent movies, appeared old-fashioned in early talking films. He stayed on the French Riviera, but he occasionally went back to Hollywood, and it was there that he died of a stroke on July 22, 1950, at the age of fifty-eight.

Directorial Didos

Another significant departure from the directorial ranks within the first year after the merger was that of Erich von Stroheim, the man with whom Thalberg had such trouble at Universal. Von Stroheim had gone directly from there to the Goldwyn company to do a film of Frank Norris' brutal and realistic novel, *McTeague*, and was present at Culver City when Thalberg moved over with Mayer.

Von Stroheim was a raw and ruthless realist so far as his taste in dramatic subjects was concerned. He believed in making pictures of the literal and sordid aspects of life, not of romantic illusions, which were largely the silent movies' stock in trade. *McTeague* was a harsh, relentless story of a man's gross lust for gold. It ended with his brutal extinction in Death Valley, whither he had been pursued for murdering his equally greedy wife.

For the sake of authenticity, von Stroheim insisted on shooting the film in San Francisco and Death Valley, where the story occurred. Even though the picture was silent, he made the actors speak dialogue with as much precision and expression as if they were acting in a play. He took his people to Death Valley to shoot the final, torturing scenes in the hottest part of the summer of 1923. He wanted the suffering to be apparent. And for that he felt it had to be real.

It was—and so was the suffering of the Goldwyn company when the picture was finally completed in December, 1923. Not only did the filming take nine months and cost close to $500,000, but in von Stroheim's first edit of it, it ran to the unconscionable length of forty-two reels! Von Stroheim was told to cut it to a length that would be reasonable. He cut it to twenty-four reels. This, he said, was the absolute minimum in which justice to the story could be done. Twenty-four reels would have taken something in the neighborhood of four hours to show. When the studio insisted, the director snorted and walked away. June Mathis, the story editor at the Goldwyn company, trimmed it to ten reels and gave it the name *Greed*. It was this chopped-down version that was inherited by Metro-Goldwyn for release.

Von Stroheim and his ardent admirers tended in later years to blame Mayer and Thalberg for the callous "mutilation" of his mammoth masterpiece. The charge was not wholly legitimate. It is true that Mayer and Thalberg refused, during months of arguing and wrangling, to permit any of the eliminated footage to be restored, and they held up release of the picture until December, 1924. But the cuts had been made before they got it. And their consideration was mainly one of passing along a picture in a length they thought commercially practical.

However, their troubles with von Stroheim were not at an end with *Greed*. His contract was taken over, along with those of the other directors of the Goldwyn company, and something had to be found for him to do. Eventually, he was assigned to make a picture based on the operetta, *The Merry Widow*, of Franz Lehár, for which he himself was allowed to write the scenario.

This frivolous bit of Viennese make-believe about the wealthy young widow who was in love with the handsome Ruritanian guardsman was an odd thing for the director of *Greed*. But von Stroheim was not one to let his imagination be clobbered with whipped cream. He spiced the innocent fable with many flashes of sly, suggestive wit and worked in some naughty business for the lecherous husband of the heroine before he died. Mae Murray, a Goldwyn company siren, and John Gilbert were assigned the leading roles. The picture went before the cameras late in 1924.

Right away trouble began happening. Early along in the affair, von Stroheim conceived a cold aversion to his blonde and seductive star. They wrangled and fought through the schedule. When they came to film the famous *Merry Widow* waltz, von Stroheim snorted contemptuously, muttered something unpleasant and walked away. The next day he and the actress were on the carpet before Thalberg and Mayer. Miss Murray bitterly complained that the director often turned his back when she was playing a scene and said, "Tell me when the damn thing is done!"

But the big blowup came when Miss Murray insisted that a special entrance be filmed to introduce the waltz sequence. Von Stroheim refused to "make a path to the star"—that is, to open an aisle among the other dancers so she could be fully seen. She called him "a dirty Hun." With that he marched out of the studio and refused to continue with Miss Murray in the film.

This was to Mayer's satisfaction. Von Stroheim's contract, like those of other Goldwyn company directors, said that he would receive a percentage of the profits of his pictures but would forfeit his percentage if he resigned. Mayer hastily put Monta Bell, one of the lesser directors, on the film.

The next day, there was an open rebellion by the stagehands and extras on the set. They were on the side of von Stroheim and refused to work with Bell. Mayer was hurriedly summoned. When he appeared to take command, the rebels, supported by other studio workers, jeered and threatened him. Whereupon Eddie Mannix, a former bouncer at the Schenck brothers' Palisades Park who had just been sent out to the studio to serve as an aide to Mayer, clipped the nearest insurgent on the jaw. The exercise sobered the gathering and cooler heads prevailed. Miss Murray was persuaded to apologize to von Stroheim and they finished the film.

However, the rupture was final. Von Stroheim had previously tangled with Mayer when the director expressed the bland opinion that practically all women are whores. Mayer, who gallantly considered himself the champion of the female sex, vaulted his desk and smote the blasphemer. He, too, regarded von Stroheim as a "dirty Hun."

Inevitably, *The Merry Widow* ran to excessive length in its first cut. Thalberg was vastly irritated at the interminableness and impurity of some of the episodes. One scene which had the heroine's lecherous husband (Edward Connelly) drooling over a rack of slippers collected from compliant women, particularly annoyed Thalberg.

"What's all this stuff?" he asked von Stroheim.

"He has a fetish for feet," the director said.

"And you have a fetish for footage!" snapped Thalberg.

The two could not agree. Von Stroheim wanted the film released substantially as he had shot it. Thalberg insisted that it be cut, especially in some of the more suggestive and unwholesome passages. Whereupon von Stroheim agreed to waive his right to edit the picture if he be relieved of his contract. He was. And with that he took his departure from Metro-Goldwyn and Mayer.

As for Miss Murray, her ability to get along with her directors did not improve in her following picture. That was an item called *The Masked Bride*, which Joseph von Sternberg, a young man of considerable promise, had been assigned to direct. He had shot about half the picture when Miss Murray complained to Harry Rapf, who was supervising this one, that von Sternberg was trying to show her how to dance. Rapf called the director on the carpet and bluntly ordered him to let the actress dance as she chose. He also said, rather forcefully, that he wasn't pleased with some of the inventive things von Sternberg was doing with the film. Whereupon the indignant director shook the dust of the lot off his feet. He went right away to Famous Players and later to Germany, where he "discovered" Marlene Dietrich, made *The Blue Angel* and became a rage.

Miss Murray made one more film, *Valencia*, at the Metro-Goldwyn Studio. Then she, too, took her departure. The temperamental types were being flushed.

CHAPTER X

THE SAGA OF *BEN HUR*

OF ALL the challenging problems that the Goldwyn company brought, by far the most mammoth and momentous was that of the production of *Ben Hur*. This vast and ambitious project, which was already being filmed in Italy, had been started by Godsol at the time he was making a valiant try to save the Goldwyn company. It was a heroic gamble. No production of comparable dimensions had ever been launched. No one had dared start a picture as costly as would plainly be *Ben Hur*.

The history of this production is a saga of motion picture enterprise that stands as a consequential chapter in the overall history of American films. *Ben Hur* marked a notable milestone in the advancement of Hollywood. And in the heat of its achievement and presentation was hammered out a telling triumph for Metro-Goldwyn-Mayer.

Ever since storytelling in movies had been discovered and rendered practical, makers and promoters of pictures had been casting covetous eyes upon General Lew Wallace's famed novel, *Ben Hur—A Tale of the Christ*. This bulging fable of the early Christian era was first published in 1880 and had sold several million copies throughout the world. It was one of the all-time "best sellers," the *Gone With the Wind* of its day.

The story was made for dramatics. A young and wealthy Jew, Ben Hur, who lived with his widowed mother and sister in Jerusalem, was accused by his Roman friend, Messala, of trying to assassinate the new Roman governor. His property was confiscated, his mother and sister were cast in jail, and he himself was condemned as a slave to the Roman galley ships for the rest of his life. In the course of a naval battle with pirates, however, he managed to escape and save the Roman admiral, Arrius, who thereupon adopted him as his son.

Returning to the East a few years later, Ben Hur discovered true love in the person of Esther, the daughter of an old and faithful family friend. Through this friend he was able to recover his fortune and challenge Messala, his cruel nemesis, in a great chariot race for the championship of the East in the coliseum at Antioch. In a thundering, exciting contest, Ben Hur upset Messala's chariot and won. He was then the most famous and wealthy of Roman subjects in that part of the world.

But grief for his lost mother and sister plagued him, and with Esther he tirelessly sought to find them, meanwhile occupying himself secretly in raising a Galilean army to place the man Jesus on a temporal Jewish throne. Then Esther found his mother and sister for him. They were horribly diseased with leprosy. When Jesus cured them by a miracle, Ben Hur abandoned his mission and became a Christian.

The theatrical rights to the story were obtained from General Wallace in 1899 by the powerful producing firm of Klaw & Erlanger, which staged the dramatization sumptuously with numerous scenes, great mobs of extras, singing choruses and a chariot race with real horses on a treadmill in the center of the stage. The play ran for years on Broadway and was toured widely with road companies all over the world. This was the strong theatrical property that the movie makers were eager to obtain.

One of the novel features of the theatrical contract was that Klaw & Erlanger were bound to produce the play *somewhere* every season or otherwise forfeit the dramatic rights. This was a minor stipulation when the play was having great success and road companies were playing it all over. But, as the years went by and the popularity of the play began to wane, it became more and more of a gamble to send out a company every year. However, the prospect of sharing in the sale of screen rights, which assumed greater proportions as films increased in size, emboldened the producers to continue to mount shows, even when they sometimes lost money. This is the reason *Ben Hur* was played year after year by some company long after it was rendered obsolete by increasingly spectacular films.

The pay-off was worth it, however. In 1919, the eagerness of Douglas Fairbanks to obtain the screen rights caused General Wallace's son, the executor of his estate, to realize that the time had come to sell. After some legal wrangling with Erlanger, Wallace indicated he would part with his entire rights to the novel for $400,000. More interest began to show. There was talk of Adolph Zukor buying the rights for a film to be made by Max Reinhardt, the great German stage director. D. W. Griffith was said to be interested. Whereupon, Erlanger quietly moved to obtain the screen rights for his own disposal. All he needed was the money to swing the deal.

He obtained it in a most surprising quarter. Vincent Astor and Robert Walton Goelet, two of New York's most eminent citizens and wealthy owners of real estate, were interested in a gamble on the prospect. They agreed sub rosa to put up $600,000—$200,000 from Astor and $400,000 from Goelet. Whereupon Erlanger, in association with Charles Dillingham and Florenz Ziegfeld, formed the Classical

Cinematograph Corporation, in which Erlanger, Dillingham, Ziegfeld and Astor each owned a one-sixth share and Goelet owned one-third. With the $600,000 from the two "angels," the corporation purchased the rights to *Ben Hur* from the estate of General Wallace and from the publishers, Harper & Brothers. Now the object was to get someone to make it into a film.

The same came along the next year, 1922. It was Godsol, who was eager for a story to capture great attention and prestige. Erlanger and his partners wanted at least $1,000,000 for a flat sale of screen rights to *Ben Hur*. The price was out of the question, so far as the Goldwyn company was concerned—or anyone else, for that matter. Fairbanks and Zukor had said "no." So Godsol's only chance of obtaining the screen rights was to make a novel deal, which would be in the nature of an extraordinary gamble. This he decided to do.

He agreed to finance a production of *Ben Hur* as a film, the same to "be of a caliber equal to *The Birth of a Nation* or *Orphans of the Storm* or *Way Down East*," all famous Griffith films—and to share the gross receipts of said production equally with the Classical Cinematograph Corporation. In other words, for the use of the story and title, Godsol agreed to pay *one-half* of all the money earned by the picture. It was, beyond any question, the most fantastic story deal ever made. No wonder Marcus Loew stated flatly, a few years later, to an audience at the Harvard Business School, "It is a contract I do not want to claim credit for."

Since it was in the original contract with General Wallace that the stage production was not to show the figure of Christ nor re-enact the Crucifixion, Erlanger insisted that these terms be included in the picture deal. He also reserved for himself full approval of the director, cast, scenario and finished film.

In the course of negotiations, June Mathis, who was head of the scenario department of the Goldwyn company, got friendly with old Abe Erlanger and soon convinced him that she alone was the only screen writer who had the feeling and talent to translate the greatness and grandeur of his pet *Ben Hur*. Erlanger stipulated to Godsol that the ubiquitous Miss Mathis should be in charge of the writing and production of the picture. Godsol willingly agreed.

The assignment inspired Miss Mathis with an enthusiasm beyond any she had known. She was determined that *Ben Hur* should be the greatest and most magnificent motion picture ever made. Nothing would do, she insisted, but that it be produced in Italy, the only place where the spirit and atmosphere of the Roman Empire could be obtained. J.J. Cohn of the studio cost department was sent abroad to reconnoiter the field. He returned with a negative opinion of the practicality of shooting in Rome. However, Miss Mathis was insistent, and she transmitted her enthusiasm to the company heads. "Major" Edward Bowes, vice-president of the Goldwyn company, to whom Cohn reported, was serene.

"We can do it in Rome for $600,000," the always expansive "Major" said.

"How?" inquired Cohn, a stubborn realist.

"That's the director's worry," Bowes replied.

The gentleman upon whom this "worry" quite unexpectedly fell was the handsome and dignified Charles Brabin, one of whose claims to renown was the fact that he was the husband of Theda Bara, the first and perhaps the most famous of all the sultry vampires of the screen.

Brabin and Bowes left for Rome in the fall of 1923. On the ship going over they became chummy and had some stimulating talks about what they wanted to do. Brabin munificently suggested that a reproduction of Jerusalem's Joppa Gate should be built three times as high as the original, so that the mob of people surrounding the far-off figure of Christ in the scene of his march on the road to Calvary would be dwarfed by this symbol of Rome. Bowes thought the idea terrific. This they would have to do. However, he firmly reminded Brabin that the budget for the picture was $750,000—no more! The director was apprehensive. And he had no scenario, as yet. Miss Mathis had given him nothing but an outline. He began to smell trouble ahead.

The company was finally assembled in Italy early in 1924. June Mathis went over in February. George Walsh, a veteran outdoor star (and brother of Raoul Walsh), whom she had selected to play the key role of Ben Hur, followed in a few days. Francis X. Bushman, who would play the anti-Semite, Messala; May McAvoy, who would be Esther; Carmel Myers, enrolled as the pagan vampire and mistress of Messala who tried to lure Ben Hur—all arrived in the next few weeks, along with technicians and cameramen. Mussolini, in the first flush of his triumphs, gave orders that every assistance be extended to the company.

While waiting for the sets and studio to be ready, Brabin went to Egypt to shoot some desert scenes. And, as spring came, he took his company down the coast to the village of Anzio, the village which years later was to be the locale of one of the bloodiest beachhead struggles of World War II. Here he hoped to shoot the scenes of the battle of the Roman and pirate galleys offshore. Then it was discovered that no barges or anything that might be used to resemble galleys were available.

Just at this time, the merger of the companies occurred, and the completion of the production of *Ben Hur* became the responsibility of Metro-Goldwyn—and Mayer.

Actually, Mayer and Thalberg were dubious of the enterprise from the start, considering it to be another of the grandiose and inefficient vagaries of Godsol's extravagant company. Thalberg said he could not see why the film should have been made in Italy. He said that he could do it better in Culver City and at considerably less expense. However, the New York executives were disposed to continue the production abroad. Marcus Loew seemed to feel the foreign venture was a challenge to his new company's prestige. There was also the little matter of the agreements with Abe Erlanger.

Even so, it was obvious that some changes in personnel would have to be made. No "rushes" of what had been shot had come back from Italy, and no one knew what was going on. Thalberg, sensing the stalemate, had secretly assigned the writer, Bess Meredyth, to prepare a new scenario as soon as the merger was certain and had gone into huddles with Mayer about a new director and star.

Then, in June, under a veil of some mystery, a small group left Hollywood for New York. It included Fred Niblo, the director who had made pictures for Mayer on Mission Road; Ramon Novarro, the popular Metro actor; Bess Meredyth, Carey Wilson and Mayer. Wilson, another writer, had been assigned by Thalberg at the last minute to assist with the scenario. It was sensed that something important in the matter of *Ben Hur* was afoot.

In New York, the fact was admitted that they were going to Italy "to look over the situation." Marcus Loew, in his now sententious vein, gave out information that Brabin was "ill" and that possibly Niblo would be selected to "take over this stupendous production." The Hollywood group, minus Mayer, was joined by Mr. and Mrs. Loew, Mr. and Mrs. J. Robert Rubin and Joe Dannenberg, a favorite pinochle playing friend of Loew, when it sailed for Europe aboard the *Leviathan*. That the die had been cast was fairly clear when Mayer was heard to shout to Niblo, as the ship pulled away from the pier: "And be sure to get plenty of camels in it! Lots of camels!" That was the clue.

When the party arrived, Loew and Rubin broke the news to the nervous company. Niblo was to replace Brabin as director (Brabin had already been sent home), and Ramon Novarro was to replace George Walsh in the title role.

As for Miss Mathis, she was given a graceful opportunity to withdraw. Loew was still deeply grateful to her for *The Four Horsemen of the Apocalypse*. She cried a bit but took it bravely, considering all that she had done to instigate interest and excitement for a bang-up production of *Ben Hur*. She stayed on in Rome until August to be near one of the handsome cameramen, Silvanio Balboni, with whom she was having a romance and to whom she was later wed.

We cannot take leave of June Mathis without a brief and wistful word on the finis of this extraordinary woman whose activities were fatefully interwoven with the developing fortunes of Loew's. On her return to Hollywood in August, she made arrangements to write two new films for Rudolph Valentino, but she soon quarreled with the new Mrs. Valentino, Natacha Rambova, and the deal was off. Miss Mathis then went to First National.

Three years later, she and her grandmother were attending a performance of a play in New York, when June slumped over with a cry, "I am dying, I am dying!" and expired from a heart attack.

Little known is the fact that Valentino, who had died just ten months before, had been buried in a crypt in the Hollywood Cemetery which June Mathis provided for him. When she died, her body, sent from New York, was placed next to his. Thus she and her beloved Rudy finally lay side by side in death. . . .

When In Rome

During the hot weeks of July and early August, production was at a standstill in Rome. Niblo was taking over, and Miss Meredyth and Wilson were finishing their scenario. Loew, after a week of observation, had decided to let the company remain in Italy. The decision was one with which Rubin of the "Mayer group" did not concur.

On his return to New York in August, Loew predicted that *Ben Hur* would be the greatest picture ever. Asked when it would be completed, he said: "They tell me in January." Then he added wryly, "But they didn't say what year."

Mayer went to Italy in September to give the whole project a look. With his wife, his two daughters and the family physician, he arrived just in time to see the filming of the big sea battle sequence, which still remained to be done.

For the shooting of this important action, the entire production unit had been moved from Anzio to Livorno, where better facilities and more extras were to be had. Extras were used by the hundreds as galley slaves and soldiers in the battle scenes.

On the day of the big enactment, which Niblo had determined to shoot several thousand yards offshore, it was arranged that one of the fourteen galleys was to appear to take fire and burn, while the people aboard it, under direction, were to dive spectacularly into the sea.

The Goldwyn Company is launched in 1916. Samuel Goldfish (later Goldwyn) surrounded by his "staff." From l. to r.: Edith Ellis, Roi Cooper Megrue, Crosby Gaige, Ralph Ince, Goldwyn, Edgar Selwyn, Arthur Hopkins, Robert W. Chambers, Irvin S. Cobb and Margaret Mayo.

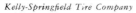

Miss Lotta Miles of 1918: Norma Shearer, when she was alternating between photographer's model and small roles in movies.

A beaming Irving Thalberg, flanked by his parents, and Norma Shearer with her mother, at their wedding on September 29, 1927.

This spindling young man on a California beach in 1922 is Irving G. Thalberg, director-general of Universal Studio.

When the fires were lit in oil drums, however, the oar holes created an unexpected draft and the flames were sucked lengthwise through the galley. In a flash, the craft was truly ablaze, and the terrified extras, without waiting for instructions, tumbled pell-mell into the sea. There were several minutes of genuine frenzy as rescue launches rushed in to save the floundering men.

Here was a bad situation. Suppose some of the men were lost. In Italy, it went hard with an employer if a workman was killed on the job. And even though all the extras signed for the sea scenes had sworn they could swim, it was obvious during the melee that some of them, greedy for the bonus pay, had lied.

When the frightened and exhausted people had finally been got back to shore, changed out of their dripping costumes and sent off to their homes, three sets of unclaimed clothing were found remaining in the extras' dressing room. It plainly appeared that three Italians had, indeed, been drowned.

The unit manager took desperate measures. Without saying anything to the police, he secretly rowed the telltale bundles out to sea that night and sank them in a weighted bag. Two days later, the missing extras, still in the costumes of Roman soldiers, showed up and demanded their clothes. They had been picked up by a fishing vessel and landed down the coast. The unit manager happily reimbursed them for the mysterious loss of their things.

Mayer was provoked by the evident wastage. When he returned to Rome, he looked at the "rushes" of the footage that Niblo had shot and stated bluntly that he was displeased. Niblo hit the ceiling and said he would resign. Mayer came back at him hotly: "You haven't resigned; you've been removed!" The rift was patched up, however, and Mayer and his family took off for a European tour.

All the difficulties were not the fault of the Americans. The tense political atmosphere in Italy accounted for much dissension among the Italians. One day, violent rioting broke out between the pro-Fascist and anti-Fascist workmen, when the latter, who were in the majority, tried to force a half holiday in honor of the Socialist deputy, Matteotti, who had been slain by Mussolini's thugs. Several times, the Fascist foreman at Livorno darkly threatened to have Niblo killed for not giving sole preference to Fascist members. There were frequent acts of obstruction and sabotage.

Finally in January 1925, the company was ordered home. All along, Thalberg had been against the Italian adventure. "I could make the whole thing right here for $800,000," he said. A couple of million dollars had been blown in Italy. To cut these unprecedented expenses and confess to a fiasco took decisive nerve. But Mayer and Thalberg were realistic. Marcus Loew now agreed.

Actually, the fourteen months of fiddling in Rome and Italy was not a total waste. In the final assembly of *Ben Hur*, there turned up considerable footage that had been shot abroad. All the scenes of and in the galleys, including the big battle at sea, were those that were shot off Livorno at such tremendous cost. The Joppa Gate sequences, jammed with extras and bulging with spectacle, were made in Rome, as were many other pieces. The only things wasted were money, energy—and time.

And a good bit more of them still had to be put out when the company returned to Hollywood. Immediately Thalberg decided there was no use returning to Rome to shoot the chariot race, as they had expected to do. A bigger and better Antioch Coliseum could be built in Culver City, he said, and he forthwith gave instructions that one should be raised. On a big open lot off Venice Boulevard, at La Cienega, the structure was built at a further cost of $300,000. It was, when completed, the biggest movie set erected up to that time.

While it was building, the company completed the rest of the tie-in stuff—the prefatory story of Mary and Joseph, the raising of the Galilean legions, and such. Thalberg excited some amazement when he selected Betty Bronson to play the role of the Virgin Mary. Miss Bronson's chief distinctions up to then were her cute performances in *Peter Pan* and *A Kiss For Cinderella*. She was later praised for the "soulfulness" of her interpretation of the Mother of Christ.

Incidentally, the Biblical inserts were filmed in the crude Technicolor of the day. These color sequences drew high approval when the picture was released.

The Chariot Race

When the coliseum was finished, the big day for the chariot race was set, and, after weeks of detailed preparations, all thoughts and energies were now devoted to this conclusive event. Some 3,000 extras were recruited to fill the mammoth set. The going pay for these extras was $3.50 a day, plus lunch.

To play the Roman horse guard that paraded before the chariot race, a crack cavalry troop was borrowed from the Praesidio in Monterey. The soldiers, mounted on beautiful matched bays, wore shining Roman costumes. Stunt men were got to ride in the twelve chariots, each drawn by four powerful horses, that were to race around the coliseum track.

Forty-two cameras were located in various strategic spots all over the huge set. These were more cameras than they owned in Culver City—more than had ever been used on one job. When they got all the cameramen together, many on loan from other studios, it looked like a full convention of the American Society of Cinematographers.

When the big day came—it was a Saturday—the extras crowded the old Venice Short Line trolley cars, flocking to Culver City to take part in the big event. Virtually every director and star in Hollywood knocked off that day and went out to watch. There was a festival air about the happening. It was a historic occurrence in the community. The entire motion picture colony had a vital interest in the achievement of this film, not to mention a burning curiosity about this mammoth episode.

Zero hour for starting the shooting was 11 A.M. At 10:30, Thalberg looked at the 3,000 extras banked in the seats of the coliseum and said there were not enough. Studio runners went scurrying madly through the onlookers gaping outside the lot and pulled in another 300.

To be filmed on this day of shooting was the panoramic spectacle of the actual race, the massiveness of the crowded coliseum and the colorful aspects of the Roman holiday. The dramatic close-ups of Ramon Novarro and Francis X. Bushman driving their chariots, which would be cut into the race sequence afterwards, were shot separately from the race itself, of course. To assure that the cowboy stunt men who drove the chariots would make it a real show, a bonus of $150 was offered to the one who came in first.

With everything set, Director Niblo, stationed on a high tower from which he could command the whole business, gave the signal for the race to begin. Buglers blew their summons. Huge tapestries were flung back and out dashed the twelve lumbering chariots. They lined up for the start and were off. As they thundered around the coliseum, dust flew, the crowds roared and the cameras whirred. The excitement was surely as high as it had ever been at a race in Roman days.

Then a phenomenon happened. As the heavy chariots were swinging into a turn, the wheel on one driven by Mickey Millerick, a famous stunt cowboy, worked loose and the vehicle began to careen. On a wild swerve, it banged into another. The two rolled over in a heap, and, as the spectators gasped in sudden horror, two more chariots and teams crashed into the wreck. Four chariots, sixteen horses and four drivers ended up in a spectacular shambles. And not a man nor an animal was hurt!

It was a flash of fortuitous action that no one would have dared try to stage as it occurred—not with the Society for the Prevention of

Cruelty to Animals watching the whole thing rigidly. Yet it was a feature that added incalculably to the realism of the spectacle. The cameramen were checked to make sure they had got it. Fortunately, they had. . . .

The rest of the saga of *Ben Hur* is a recount of triumphs and rewards. The vast amount of footage, taken over a period of some eighteen months, was edited into twelve reels. It was provided with a special musical score, written by David Mendoza and William Axt, to be played by the pit orchestra. An elaborate advance publicity campaign on the lines of *The Birth of a Nation* ballyhoo was given it, and its grand première was held at the George M. Cohan Theatre in New York City on the evening of December 30, 1925.

The reception was thunderously approving. A glittering audience of theatrical and society nobs actually burst into shouting and applauding during the chariot race. The film was shown on a two-a-day basis, with two intermissions during its two-hour-and-eight-minute running time—the first intermission after the sequence of the sea battle and the second after the chariot race. *Ben Hur* stayed for a year on Broadway, while it was being road-shown (two-a-day) in other cities. It did not go into general release until the fall of 1927.

Among the perennially popular legends of the motion picture industry have been those concerning the cost and the earnings of *Ben Hur*. The general impression has been that it "cleaned up" for Metro-Goldwyn-Mayer. Actually, the total negative cost of the picture—not including the royalties paid to the Classical Cinematograph Company—was just short of $4,000,000.

On the other hand, the gross earnings (including those from an unsuccessful reissue, released in 1931, with dubbed sound) were $9,386,000. With 35 per cent subtracted from that figure to cover distribution costs, the total net earnings came to approximately $6,100,000. Since this was divided equally with the Classical Cinematograph Company, the ultimate money return to Metro-Goldwyn was almost $1,000,000 less than the negative costs.

However, the total venture was far from unprofitable to the studio and to Loew's. The vast commercial prestige redounding to the company through having this picture was a tremendous, incalculable boon.

But, of course, in the final reckonings, the individuals who really profited from *Ben Hur* were the fortunate gentlemen of the Classical Cinematograph Company, who shared among themselves more than $3,000,000 in royalties—the Messrs. Erlanger, Ziegfeld and Dillingham and especially the "silent" and generally unsuspected partners, Vincent Astor and Robert Walton Goelet.

CHAPTER XI

EARLY STARS IN THE CONSTELLATION OF LEO

BY THE time *Ben Hur* reached the screen, the raising of Metro-Goldwyn-Mayer into the ranks of the top producing companies had been remarkably engineered. The accomplishment of this elevation was due to a number of things—to good fortune, to the acumen of Thalberg and to the managerial competence of Mayer. The foresight and wisdom of these landreeves in gathering talent and putting it to work were the secrets of their advancement, if such can be considered recondite. Evidence of their smartness was most apparent in the galaxy of stars that they early began to assemble and use intelligently.

Although the era of the great star ascendance at Metro-Goldwyn-Mayer was to come in the 1930's, the firmament was notably bright and was constantly being further brightened in the five-year period between the studio merger and the coming of sound. One of the most important and now most sadly forgotten of those stars was the great Lon Chaney, whom even the cinema esthetes now tend to dismiss as a sort of freak.

The neglect is unjust and unperceptive, for the actor was, in his time, an artist of real imagination and extraordinary histrionic skill. He was a full-fledged phenomenon in a period when the movies were truly finding wings.

Chaney, a strange, ambiguous fellow, started his movie career in 1913 and learned his business in more than a hundred assorted films. His forte was unusual make-up and the creation of grotesque characters, such as the fake cripple, Frog, in George Loane Tucker's historic, *The Miracle Man;* the blind sailor, Pew, in *Treasure Island* and Fagin in Jackie Coogan's *Oliver Twist.* He had a fine sense of timing, and his skill at pantomime emerged from the fact that both his parents were deaf-mutes, with whom he was able to communicate only by mimicry and signs. For all his competence, however, Chaney was no better than a feature player when, in 1923, through one of the last acts of Irving Thalberg at Universal, he was cast to play the role of the mad and misshapen bell ringer in *The Hunchback of Notre Dame.*

With his performance in this great shocker, which took the public by storm, Chaney commanded wide attention and the distinction of starring roles. Thalberg got him to sign a one-year contract with the new Metro-Goldwyn company, where, as we have seen, his first role was in the unusual *He Who Gets Slapped.* His next film was *The Monster,* in which he played a mad scientist. Thalberg was obviously probing to place his unique skill.

It was at this point that a director, Tod Browning, whom Thalberg had known at Universal, came to him with a story, *The Unholy Three,* which he begged that he be permitted to direct, with Chaney starred. *The Unholy Three* was a weird tale of criminals in a circus—a ventriloquist, a strong man and a dwarf—so bizarre and freakishly diabolic that most of the people to whom Browning had tried to sell it thought it hopelessly absurd. But Thalberg was captivated by it. He sensed a perfect Chaney vehicle. He took a gamble, bought the story and hired Browning to direct.

The consequences were momentous. In the first place, *The Unholy Three* came forth a smashing picture, full of surprising and electrifying twists. Chaney was brilliantly malevolent as the clever ventriloquist-crook who committed his crimes disguised as a nice old lady, with the dwarf disguised as a baby in his arms. *The Unholy Three* grossed over $2,000,000 and was hailed as one of the best films of 1925.

But of further advantage to the studio, Thalberg discovered with it a striking harmony between Browning's imagination and Chaney's versatility. After a return to Universal to do *The Phantom of the Opera,* Chaney had a happy collaboration with Browning and an uninterrupted succession of films for Metro-Goldwyn-Mayer.

It was from this association that Chaney particularly advanced his reputation as "the man of a thousand faces" and his penchant for oddity. In *The Blackbird* he was a crippled clergyman who lapsed into a Cockney thief; in *The Road to Mandalay* he was a felon with a sickeningly glaring dead eye; in *The Unknown* he feigned an armless knife-thrower; in *London After Midnight* he played the dual roles of a Scotland Yard detective and a human vampire of exceptionally horrible mien. To make his eyes pop as the latter, he rigged up a punishing device that stretched fine wires across his eyelids. He would go to any extreme to look grotesque.

Yet Chaney himself was an amazingly gentle and self-effacing man, devoted to his profession as very few actors ever are. He stubbornly shunned the Hollywood limelight and would not let himself be publicized as anything but the make-believe character he was playing at the time. He wore caps in the style of circus performers and made his friends among the studio stage crews. One day someone saw him risking his life on the roof of a building, trying to put some baby birds back in a nest.

It was strongly revealing of his nature that his favorite role, and one of his best, was that of a tough Marine sergeant with a heart of gold in *Tell It To the Marines*. This film, which had Chaney gruffly nurturing a young recruit, played by William Haines, was directed by George Hill, who was given the assignment by Thalberg to allow for a change of pace.

Chaney, one of the greats of the Nineteen Twenties—and certainly one of the blessings of Metro-Goldwyn-Mayer—barely outlived silent pictures. Like Charlie Chaplin, he resisted the change to sound. He wished to be sure of the new medium, and sure of himself, before he moved. "Just as I am the man of a thousand faces, I want to be the man of a thousand voices," he said.

In 1930, he and Thalberg agreed that he should make his debut in talking pictures in a remake of *The Unholy Three*. Again, in the role of the ventriloquist, he was able to project the voices of the dummy, the old lady, the baby and a parrot, in addition to his own. The film was a success, despite the worries and misgivings of the star.

But that was the last film made by Chaney. Even then he was mortally ill, ironically of throat cancer. His last day on the set, he suggested they get a photograph of the company. It was made, with the stage crew happily rubbing elbows with the star. Then Chaney shook hands with everybody and departed, never to return. He died on August 26, 1930, at the age of forty-four. At the hour of his funeral, a Marine guard lowered the American flag at the studio and a bugler sounded taps, in remembrance of his beloved performance in *Tell It To the Marines*. At the services, they played "mood music" identified with his favorite films. . . .

Jack-Be-Nimble

Perhaps even more important to the public and to the studio as a star was John Gilbert, whom Thalberg helped immensely to gain greatness and glory in *The Big Parade*.

Gilbert was made for the movies and the movies were made for him—at least, as they were in that era when they and he were fairly young. He was a born barnstormer who first saw the light of day in a cheap rooming house in Logan, Utah, where his mother,, a minor actress, stopped off to have her unwanted baby before catching up with her touring show. At fourteen, the boy was an orphan, roaming the country alone. At sixteen, he was a two-dollar-a-day "bit" player at the old Tom Ince studio.

It was later, while acting at Triangle, that he got a yen to write and direct and landed a job as an assistant to the distinguished director, Maurice Tourneur. From that job, he sold himself adroitly to a New York millionaire, Jules Brulatour, to make pictures starring the latter's friend, Hope Hampton, an ex-sales girl. The only trouble with this arrangement was that he had to move to New York, which was highly inconvenient and disturbing because he was in love with the beautiful actress, Leatrice Joy. Finally, with characteristic rashness, he chucked his $500-a-week job and hurried back to Hollywood to marry the waiting Miss Joy.

The couple eloped to Tia Juana and were spliced by a Mexican judge. There was one little hitch, however. Gilbert had a former wife, from whom he wasn't fully divorced. When he and his bride returned to Hollywood and took up residence in a Laurel Canyon home, the gossips began to cackle and eyebrows were raised by the press. About this time, Rudolph Valentino was almost jailed for marrying Natacha Rambova in Mexico before being unhitched from a former wife, so Gilbert and Miss Joy quickly parted. A year later, they were married legally.

Meanwhile, the rambunctious Gilbert was resuming his acting career at the Fox studio in such swashy pictures as *The Count of Monte Cristo, Cameo Kirby* and *The Brute Man.* He then joined the Goldwyn company in 1923, and it was there that Thalberg found him and resolved to develop him as a star. From *He Who Gets Slapped,* Thalberg put him in *His Hour* with Aileen Pringle; *The Snob* with Norma Shearer; *The Wife of the Centaur,* with Eleanor Boardman, and *The Merry Widow,* all within a year. It was while he was finishing the latter that Thalberg selected him to play in *The Big Parade.*

This film, which now is remembered as one of the classics of the silent screen, originated in the mind of King Vidor, a young director from the Goldwyn company. One day, in a conversation with Thalberg, Vidor said he would like to make a film about war—not the usual heroic type of war film but a realistic account of the experiences of one man. Thalberg liked the idea. He may have judiciously recalled the amazing success of Rex Ingram's *The Four Horsemen of the Apocalypse.*

The studio owned *Plumes,* a war story by Laurence Stallings, who was hired to do a scenario with Vidor and another writer, Harry Behn. What they came up with bore little or no resemblance to *Plumes.* It was scheduled to be made on a low budget (about $200,000) and was titled *The Big Parade.*

The picture had been shooting for two weeks when the realization emerged that something uncommon was cooking. Quietly the word

began to spread that Vidor had a winner and Gilbert started telling
friends, "This one is going to play the Egyptian!" that being the name
of a big theatre in Los Angeles.

A rough cut of the film was shown to Thalberg and members of
his family in Coronado one week end. He was down there for a rest
and a local theatre was borrowed for the showing; that's how im-
promptu it was. Thalberg was overwhelmed by it. On Monday morning he got together with Mayer and insisted that more money be
budgeted to make it a really big film. Mayer got the money for him
and the whole latter half of the film, with its famous scenes of the
battle of the Argonne Forest, was greatly augmented by Vidor and
his crew.

When the picture was completed and the Loew's sale force saw
what it had, the original plan to sell it as a straight "Jack Gilbert
special" was hastily revised. A big promotion campaign was started
and the picture was given its première in simultaneous showings at
the Capitol and Astor Theatres in New York on November 19, 1925.
It stayed for ninety-six weeks at the Astor, which was a record for
longevity (until it was broken a quarter century later by a British
film, *The Red Shoes,* which ran for more than two years in one theatre
in New York). It earned millions of dollars, great prestige and made a
top star of John Gilbert. Thalberg's hunch to build it up paid off.

Among other of the studio's busy male stars—Ramon Novarro,
Conrad Nagel, William Haines—there was also the popular Buster
Keaton, one of the great comics of the silent screen. Keaton's former
contract with Metro was extended to the new company and brought
him within the orbit of the Culver City plant.

The comedian's individual unit occupied a bungalow just outside
the east gate (on the site where the Irving Thalberg Memorial Building now stands), and this was the mecca for all the funsters and genial
cutups within studio range. They called it Keaton's Kennel, and here
the comedian was top dog, with a whole swarm of practical jokers
and "gag men" to help him dream up sight-gags for his films. Keaton
would summon his butler, Willie, by solemnly striking a mammoth
Chinese gong. The hotfoot and sneezing powder were regularly employed. Yet, out of this contiguous madhouse there came to Metro-
Goldwyn-Mayer those memorable Keaton comedies, *The Navigator,*
Battling Butler and *Go West.* It is another of the ironies of movies
that Keaton's slapstick did not survive sound.

The Lovely Ladies

Rivaling the male stars for pre-eminence at the burgeoning studio
were the lovely and luscious ladies whom Mayer and Thalberg main-

tained on the rolls—Mae Murray, Norma Shearer, Eleanor Board-man, Aileen Pringle, Renee Adoree, Mae Busch, Kathleen Key, Hedda Hopper, Carmel Myers, Claire Windsor and such as those. Mayer's notions on the feminine factor in pictures were beautifully and char-acteristically put in answering an interviewer in this period as to his feelings about sex in films.

"Of course we shall have sex," he answered. "As long as we have men and women in the world, we'll have sex. And I approve of it. We'll have sex in motion pictures, and I want it there." (This personal endorsement of the primal impulse was not a surprise to Hollywood.)

"But," Mayer carefully added, "it will be normal, real beautiful sex—the sex that is common to the people in the audience, to me and to you. A man and a woman are in love with one another. That's sex, and it's beautiful."

The pious distinction was sufficient to permit ample range for the studio's stars.

Somewhat above and apart from the latter, but definitely a figure in the group, was Marion Davies, whose status in the studio was very special and classified. She was the star of Cosmopolitan Pictures, one of the many cultural indulgences of William Randolph Hearst, which had formerly released through the Goldwyn company and was con-tinued as a contractual adjunct of Metro-Goldwyn-Mayer.

Miss Davies was a pleasing combination of fragile beauty and gamin qualities whose acting talents had been best demonstrated in the costumed cutups of *When Knighthood Was in Flower*. Her transfer to Culver City from her previous area of operations in New York was an event in Hollywood society comparable to the arrival of a royal household and its queen.

A fourteen-room bungalow was built for her near the front of the studio lot, and there, in this elaborate pavilion, she and Hearst held frequent court. Virtually everyone of distinction who visited Holly-wood was invited there to lunch and to see Miss Davies or some of the other stars at work. Mayer was usually present and took great delight in these affairs.

Unfortunately, the films of Miss Davies were not among the more impressive or profitable releases of the studio. They included such frothy items as *Zander the Great, Lights of Old Broadway, Beverly of Graustark* and *The Red Mill*. This caused some considerable grumbling among certain elements of the company's personnel.

Finally, at a company sales convention in Los Angeles in 1927, the displeasure was brought to the floor when Mayer made so bold as to ask the salesmen if any of them had questions they would like to put to him.

"Why do we handle Miss Davies' pictures?" one intrepid salesman bluntly asked.

The question startled the gathering, and for a moment Mayer did not reply. He obviously had not expected to be so candidly taxed. But he bravely rose to the occasion. First he mentioned the modest success of one of Miss Davies' pictures. Then he reminded his audience that the actress was the close, dear friend of Mr. Hearst, the powerful publisher whose friendship and newspapers were of help to the studio.

"Furthermore," Mayer continued, "I would like to remind you gentlemen that Mr. Hearst is the son of that great patriot, former United States Senator from California, the late George Hearst." And with that he launched into an eloquent account of how George Hearst had left Missouri as a young man, made the perilous overland journey to California, opened great mining territory and contributed vastly to the building of the American West.

"This," said Mayer, "is the point I wish to impress upon you gentlemen here today. We live in a land of opportunity. God bless America!"

Tears sprang to his eyes and his voice quavered, as he addressed himself directly to the salesman, "Does that answer your question?"

"It does," said the poor guy and sat down.

Exactly one year after the merger, Nicholas Schenck proudly announced that the great Lillian Gish had been added to the roster of Metro-Goldwyn stars. She was put under contract to make six pictures for $800,000. This was a coup which attested to the rise in the studio's prestige, for Miss Gish had a place in the world of movies comparable to that in the theatre of a Sarah Bernhardt or an Eleanora Duse.

She was the winsome actress who had first come to eminence in *The Birth of a Nation* and had continued as Griffith's luminous star in *Way Down East, Orphans of the Storm* and *Broken Blossoms.* More recently, she had been in *The White Sister* and *Romola,* two exceedingly dignified films that were produced in Italy by an unfortunate gentleman, Charles Duell. Miss Gish's association with him had been erratic and highly publicized.

Naturally, a vehicle befitting her distinction had to be found for her debut as an adornment of Metro-Goldwyn-Mayer. Thalberg suggested a film version of Puccini's opera, *La Boheme,* with John Gilbert to play Rudolphe and King Vidor to direct. They had just completed *The Big Parade.*

The preparation and the shooting of *La Boheme* was an experience on the lot. Miss Gish had been schooled by Griffith to have integrity in details and moods. She insisted upon careful rehearsals—on bare stages, or even outdoors. She was a tremendous stickler for lighting, and was slavishly obedient to her own special cameraman.

Her interesting eccentricities were accepted as artistry. But on one point Miss Gish's creative impulse carried a little too far. She suggested that at no time in the picture should Mimi and Rudolphe kiss; the contact would shatter the illusion and expectation of the audience she said. Vidor went along with it, while Gilbert, utterly confused (but impressed with his new rank as an artist), restrained himself out of deference to his great colleague.

However, when a rough cut of the picture was shown to Thalberg and Mayer, the latter demanded loudly to know where the love scenes were. Vidor explained Miss Gish's theory. Mayer was utterly appalled. Didn't they realize the public expected Gilbert to make emphatic love! The requisition was heeded, and several scenes were ordered reshot so that Gilbert could give to Rudolphe the proper ardor and physical approach.

La Boheme was hailed on all sides as an achievement of the highest order in the art of the screen. One week after it was completed, Miss Gish started to play Hester Prynne in a film of Nathaniel Hawthorne's *The Scarlet Letter*, much to the anxiety of Mayer. He feared that churchmen and the public would not tolerate this tale of an adulteress. Miss Gish reassured him by getting approval from several church organizations, which said they would depend upon her taste.

The Scarlet Letter was also lauded as a fine film, one of the best of 1926, but Miss Gish followed with two less noble items, *Annie Laurie* and *The Enemy*. Her last picture for the studio was an extraordinary effort called *The Wind*, a strange, depressing drama of life on a windswept farm. It was done under the direction of Victor Seastrom, who had directed *The Scarlet Letter*, too, and was largely a film of pure motion. It was mainly artistry.

The salesmen were baffled by it, and while they were pondering how to sell it, sound came in. The studio finally dubbed sound effects on it, and also a happy end. But long before they finally released it, Miss Gish departed the studio. With one picture still owed, her contract was canceled by mutual consent. That was the only experience of the great Miss Gish at Metro-Goldwyn-Mayer, but she contributed her share to its prestige in those critical years.

CHAPTER XII

ENTER GRETA GARBO

THE departure of Lillian Gish from the studio, trailing her aura of artistry, did not leave a void as perceptible as it might have a short while previously. For even while she was in Culver City—indeed, shortly after she arrived—there came on the lot a young actress who soon was plucking the laurels from her brow. Although Miss Gish breathed the essence of purity and this new girl was an essential femme fatale, there was a comparable uncommonness about them. Greta Garbo was the newcomer.

Since the movies are a medium of illusion, the personality of the performer has always been a tremendous and often dominating factor in accomplishing their effects. The thing which the actor or actress represents to the audience and the degree to which he or she represents it actually accounts for much of a picture's consequence. These qualities of the performer, these personality elements which emanate, are sometimes difficult to fathom, to anticipate or analyze. But they go to make up the sum and substance of the dramatic vibrance of a film.

The intangible thing which Greta Garbo brought to the motion picture screen has been delved into and dissected with desperate diligence over the passing years. It has been seen as a physical, a social, a philosophical, a mystical quality, as a matter of beauty, of custom, of abstract morality, of genes. But whatever it was, it is certain that it was not categorically foreseen when the actress was brought to this country from Sweden in 1925. The circumstances which conspired to land her in Culver City were due quite as much to chance and good fortune as to clear and marvelous vision. The good fortune was largely Metro-Goldwyn-Mayer's.

There have been many stories, many legends, of how Greta Garbo came to be enrolled to make movies in Hollywood. And these stories have had a lot to do with the accumulation of the sense of fatalism that has been a strong part of her personality.

There certainly was no great mystery about the lady when she was first brought to Hollywood. She was a simple, shy European actress with ambition and promise but no conspicuous talent or chic. And the oft-told story that Mayer signed her simply to get Mauritz Stiller, her Swedish director, is wrong. Mayer spotted her as a girl with promise the first time he saw her on the screen.

Greta Garbo was the daughter of poor parents by the name of Gustafson, and went to work at fourteen soaping faces in a Stockholm barber shop. It was the sort of job that put her in the way of being close to men, and she probably got some basic notions of them even at that early age. Later she worked as a sales girl in a Stockholm department store, appeared in a couple of advertising movies and then enrolled at the Royal Dramatic School. Here she was "discovered" by Stiller, who was second to Victor Seastrom as the foremost director in Swedish films.

Stiller, a large, expansive person, engaged the untried student in 1923 to play the second female lead in *The Story of Gosta Berling,* an adaptation of a novel by Selma Lagerloff, which he had inherited when Seastrom left Sweden to work for the Goldwyn company in Hollywood. Greta, who was given the name of Garbo by Stiller as a more exciting tag than Gustafson, had the role of a lovely, honorable woman who finally saved a dissolute minister from absolute ruin. The minister was played by Lars Hanson (who later played a similar role in *The Scarlet Letter* to Lillian Gish's Hester Prynne), and one of the girls who helped this minister to go to the devil was played by Greta's close friend Mona Martensen. *The Story of Gosta Berling* came off successfully; Stiller was vastly pleased with it and considerably enhanced thereby.

In the early 1920's, the hub of European film culture was Berlin, and thither went Stiller with his picture—and with Greta—when it was ready for release. In Berlin, the eighteen-year-old actress was hired (with Stiller's consent) to play in another picture under the direction of G. W. Pabst. It was a stark and cynical drama of Vienna after World War I. They called it *Joyless Street.* In it the youthful Greta had the role of a prostitute. (This film was later shown in this country, under the title of *Street of Sorrow* as a sort of "educational" sex show. M. Sayle Taylor, who was later the Voice of Experience on the radio, was a "lecturer" with it in the Midwest.)

As a consequence of this association, the youthful Greta was early imbued with the European sense of serious endeavor and mature artistry in films. She was in contact with the top film people of Sweden and Germany through her close companionship with Stiller, which was absorbing and absolute. Neither had any particular interest in far-away Hollywood. . . .

While on his trip to Europe late in 1924 to look over the production of *Ben Hur* and make his first continental "tour," Louis Mayer had his eye out for talent. The Europeans, still recovering from World War I, were making many interesting pictures and were developing their own group of stars. On his way through Paris, Mayer had instructed the company's representative there, Alf Aaronson, to send some likely pictures and suggested names of talent to consider while he was in Rome. Aaronson sent, among other things, a couple of Stiller films—one a lovely picture about Lapland in which reindeer largely prevailed.

Mayer sent word to Aaronson that he admired the picture but would like to see what Stiller could do with people. So later, when Mayer was in Berlin, Aaronson arranged for Stiller to call upon him and show him *The Story of Gosta Berling.*

It makes a provocative image, the giant Stiller and the short, stocky, Mayer sitting down in a projection room in Berlin for one of the more momentous screenings in the history of films. Stiller could not speak English, and an interpreter was there. Mayer was not too hopeful about the subject. It was a little too heavy for his taste. However, he admired the direction and was mildly interested when Mona Martensen appeared. Then Greta Garbo came into the picture. Mayer sat up and looked.

"Who is she?" he asked.

Stiller roared, "Watch the picture!" "Watch the direction!" He thought Mayer was only struck by the actress' beauty and had designs on her. Mayer assured him that he was interested in the ensemble. When the showing was ended, a meeting was arranged.

Mayer met the couple for Sunday dinner in the spacious dining room of the Adlon Hotel in Berlin. Stiller forehandedly arranged that Greta should sit opposite Mayer, who arrived after the two were seated. His first impression of the actual girl was not good. Her arms were fat and he caught a glimpse of thick ankles. But her face was alive and wonderful.

"Tell her," he said to Stiller, "that in America our men don't like fat women." Stiller passed the information to Greta. She accepted it thoughtfully.

At that table, in the Adlon Hotel in Berlin, Mayer arranged the deal for Stiller to come to Culver City and bring Greta Garbo with him.

Thus the legend that the youthful actress was hired at Stiller's insistence is wrong. Mayer was never so intent upon directors that he couldn't spot a potential star.

Six months passed before Stiller and Greta arrived in the United States. When they did, they were not greeted with any special excitement or huzzahs. Greta struck those who saw her as a rather prosaic girl. Her hair was stringy, her face was solemn and her apparel was anything but chic. The fellows in the New York publicity office figured that Mayer had hired a dog. The word that she was on contract for $400 a week occasioned some dismal head-shaking. They saw her headed the other way at the end of a year.

There is no evidence or recollection of exactly what Thalberg thought when he got his first look at Greta, but Mayer was agreeably surprised when she arrived in Hollywood and he discovered that she had reduced. Now she was trim and angular. She had heeded his advice.

Greta's first picture assignment was in a story of Blasco Ibanez, *The Torrent,* in which Ricardo Cortez was placed to play opposite her. It told of a Spanish peasant girl who became a great opera star and the exquisite toast of all Europe, yet loved only one man—the son of her family's landlord—and he was stubbornly forbidden to marry her. Stiller was not chosen to direct it. The assignment fell to Monta Bell. It was a routine tear-jerker for those days. But Greta came off very well. When it opened at the Capitol Theatre in New York on February 21, 1926, the picture was mildly regarded but Greta received some flattering reviews.

Meanwhile, however, the actress had been having her trials in Hollywood. First, she was bewildered and unhappy at not having Stiller to direct her first film. He, a proud and somewhat arrogant European, was inclined to be supercilious toward the methods and product of Hollywood. Furthermore, Pete Smith, head of studio publicity, made the mistake at the start of trying to publicize Greta in the conventional baby-star way. He got her into a turtle-neck sweater and running pants (which showed her knobby knees) and took her over to the athletic field of the University of Southern California to pose for fan magazine pictures with the husky brutes of the track team. This was extremely confusing and embarrassing to the foreign girl. Also, despite her scant English, Smith let her be interviewed. The sessions with reporters were agonizing, and the consequent stories humiliated her. In a short time, she was tearfully beseeching that she not be interviewed. Smith had to give in to her wishes. She soon had a reputation of being top-lofty toward the press.

The next assignment for Greta found her in another Ibanez yarn, this one called *The Temptress* with Antonio Moreno as her leading man. This time Stiller was put on to direct her, but filming had not proceeded a week before it was concluded by Mayer and Thalberg that he simply would not do. He spent too much time on details of Greta's role, and he was obviously out to make something arty in the allusive European style. This was futile, because the story was just another potboiler about the ruin of a Latin lover by a femme fatale. The studio heads were suddenly suspicious that they had another von Stroheim on their hands. After a painful session with Thalberg, Stiller was removed. Fred Niblo, fresh from *Ben Hur,* was put on to finish the film. The public swarmed to see it when it opened late in 1926, and the magnetism that Greta had developed was tangibly and gratifyingly revealed.

Before *The Temptress* was on the screens, however, the most convulsive event in the career of Greta Garbo had happened. She had met Jack Gilbert and begun a mad romance with him.

The circumstances were prophetic. For her third American film, Greta was assigned to an adaptation of Hermann Sudermann's novel, *The Undying Past.* It was a routine story of a young German matron's fateful seduction by a handsome, light-hearted blade. They retitled it *Flesh and the Devil* and Clarence Brown was assigned to direct. More important, the high-riding Gilbert was picked to be Greta's new leading man. Mayer and Thalberg were ready to shoot the works this time.

But by now the actress had become conscious of her importance to the studio, and she was still strongly under the sway of the side-tracked Stiller, who insisted that she was being "ruined" in cheap love-story films. So she put up some brief resistance when *Flesh and the Devil* was picked for her, and she stubbornly stayed away from the studio while preparations were being made to shoot the film.

"Who the hell is this dame?" Gilbert grumbled, as days went by and Greta did not appear. Brown, who knew Jack from the Tourneur days—he had introduced him to Leatrice Joy, indeed—patiently soothed the outraged actor. Finally, Greta showed up for work one day. Brown tactfully suggested to Gilbert that he might step over to her dressing room to be introduced.

"To hell with her," snorted Gilbert. "Let her come meet me!"

So Brown brought the diffident Swedish actress over to meet the great star of *The Big Parade.*

The Grand Passion

Their first scene together that day was in the German railway station. Then they did the memorable scene in the outdoor arbor, after the destined lovers had met at the ball. Here the director had them do a bit of flirtatious business with a cigarette. Suddenly, as Brown put it, "the buttons began to pop." Gilbert, the gay caballero, was entranced with the laconic Swede. He developed a tempestuous passion for her. And she was intrigued by him.

Of course she was. The gay and smiling Gilbert was now at the

peak of his powers, full of the fire of a stallion and the ingenuousness
of a child. He was romance in all its masculine magic, the paragon
of dash and grace—reckless, naive and boastful. That Gilbert was
quite a lad!

He was extremely considerate and helpful to Greta during the
shooting of the film, acceding to shots that favored her and giving
valuable advice. The love scenes, which were sensational when the
film was released, were played with genuine ardor. Brown often felt
a little in the way.

The romance of Gilbert and Garbo was so luridly publicized that
it was difficult for anybody to get a clear picture of it. Perhaps the
two participants found it a bit difficult themselves. This was the sort
of glamorous legend on which the illusions of the movies were built.
It was impossible to tell where make-believe left off and red-hot
reality began.

A sceptic might well have imagined that the rumors of the romance
were contrived to attract interest to the couple's first film together.
Certainly the nature of *Flesh and the Devil* was such that suspicions
were justified. It was pure dime-store boudoir fiction in the tradition
of Elinor Glyn. Yet it made a spectacular killing and established
Gilbert and Garbo as the screen's most popular love team.

In the course of her rapid absorption into the culture of Hollywood, Greta acquired an acute sophistication so far as payment for
her services was concerned. Her original contract with the studio
called for a salary of $400 a week for a year (one year, by custom in
the business, being forty weeks). Her contract carried an option for
renewal at $600 a week for the second year and $750 a week for the
third.

While working in *Flesh and the Devil,* which was a little more
than a year after her arrival in this country and while she was in the
$600 a week bracket of her contract, Greta issued her first demand
for a revision of its terms. She thought it would be only proper for
the studio to raise her salary to $5,000 a week! This was a shattering
suggestion. When *Flesh and the Devil* was done, Greta refused to
move on to another picture called *Women Love Diamonds.* She
walked out of the studio and stayed away for seven months. Stiller,
who by now had moved over to Famous Players-Lasky, happily
encouraged her.

During this period of holdout, Greta was persuaded by Gilbert to
get a business manager, Harry Edington. He went into negotiations
with Mayer, whose inclination was to force the Swedish actress to
be reasonable—or else. However, there was a little matter which
previously had been overlooked. When Greta had signed her original

contract, she was not of legal age, and there was the question of whether the studio could hold her to the deal, if she chose to leave. Rather than risk that possibility, Mayer finally agreed to tear up her previous contract and signed her to a new one at $5,000 a week. It was not a regrettable decision as circumstances later proved. Immediately Greta was rushed into a new film with Gilbert, *Love.*

This was a popularized version of *Anna Karenina,* the Tolstoi novel, prepared by Frances Marion and directed by Edmund Goulding. The title clearly expressed the matter anticipated by the public in the film. By now, the Gilbert-Garbo romance was not only the talk of Hollywood but the subject of spicy news items and gossip retailed in the press. One story even had it that Gilbert, crazy with love and jealousy, had climbed one night to the balcony of the hotel where Greta lived in Santa Monica and had taken a shot at Stiller, whom he was supposed to have caught with her.

The public effect of such a story was much more favorable to the commerce of the couple's films than might have been that of the true story of what actually transpired.

It seems that Gilbert and Greta were in one of those phases when they were on the verge of marrying, but the lady would not summon her resolve, and Jack was exceedingly touchy. One night they were talking things out during a dinner at Jack's new home. He was getting along all right. Jack had a wonderful way of looking at Greta when she was sitting with him in a room and sighing, "Gee-bo you are *so* beautiful!"—to which she would reply ecstatically, "Dear Ya-quee!"

While they were talking this evening, the butler came in to announce that Stiller was outside, calling for Miss Garbo. The director had previously arranged to pick her up to go to a concert or some such function, as Gilbert understood. However, when Greta started to go out, Jack ran downstairs after her, beseeching her to abandon the engagement. And as she got into Stiller's car, he impetuously tried to restrain her. Stiller gave him a little push. Gilbert fell back, amazed and angry. Then Stiller and Greta drove away.

"He tried to shove me down the canyon!" Gilbert howled into the night, then went inside to console himself with brandy and brood upon the torments of a man in love. Some hours later, he got the brilliant idea of calling on Greta at her Santa Monica hotel. The clerk of the Miramar would not admit him, for several reasons which were perfectly clear, so Gilbert went outside the building and tried to climb to the actress' suite. He later claimed that he did reach her balcony and was about to enter the lady's bower when Stiller, raging, rushed forth and tried to push him over the balustrade. But what actually happened was that Gilbert did try to climb the building, fell when he had got up a bit and wounded himself inconsequentially. Angry and bleeding, he went calling upon friends, routing them out and maundering about Stiller's imagined assault. That is how the most pathetic story of Jack's futile courtship spread.

There was also the story of how the couple started to elope. This was in 1927, and there was a nation-wide titter over it. They got into an auto and headed for Mexico, which had been the scene of the previous Gilbert hijink with his now divorced wife, Leatrice Joy. But along the way, Greta lost interest and requested her ardent swain to permit her to visit a ladies restroom. There she gave him the slip and took a train back to Hollywood, thus leaving the world-famous screen lover in an angry and baffled state. It was after this dismal fiasco that the ardor of the romance cooled.

But not before Gilbert and Greta had been established in the public mind as lovers as eminent and mighty as Heloise and Abélard. Their amour was literally the ideal of lovelorn females all over the world, wherever the right to dream of luxury and self-indulgence was a privilege of the general populace. "Garbo-Gilberting" was minted by Walter Winchell, the popular gossipeer, as a common expression for being in love, and it was given wide circulation in the fan magazines. It was significant that the pictures Greta played in with Gilbert were among her most popular of all.

After *Love,* Greta gained a concession from the studio. It was that she might appear in a film under the direction of Victor Seastrom and with her old friend, Lars Hanson, as her leading man. This was a semi-biography of Sara Bernhardt. *The Divine Woman* was its name, and it was adapted from a play called *Starlight.* The prospect was promising, but the picture that finally came forth was a weak and inadequate pastiche.

A mood of despair and fatalism was settling upon Greta now. Stiller's final, defeating disappointment came when he was not allowed to direct her in *The Divine Woman,* and he returned to Sweden, an ill and lonely man. Shortly before he left, he wrote an article for *Variety* in which he painfully said, "I have not yet reached a position in American film affairs that will permit me to boast." And then he pitifully added, "Had I remained in Europe, I think I would have continued to make pictures that the public looked upon as representative of life."

With Stiller gone and her romance with Gilbert faded, Greta was very much alone. She saw few people and accepted what Mayer and Thalberg gave her to do. Her next was *The Mysterious Lady,* a thoroughly undistinguished thing, and then she appeared again with Gilbert in *A Woman of Affairs.* This was taken from *The Green Hat* of Michael Arlen, and once more Greta was in the way of playing a fallen woman. She went at it stoically, which was very much evident in her acting of the later commercially successful film.

She was finishing another, *Wild Orchids,* when word came on November 8, 1928, that Stiller had died in Stockholm. Greta was doing a scene with Nils Asther when the message arrived. She went off by herself for several minutes, then returned and finished the scene. One month later, with that picture completed, she departed Hollywood for New York, where she kept herself rigidly secluded. Then she took a ship for home. She had been in America less than four years, in which brief time she had become a world-famous and wealthy movie actress. Now that flamboyant phase of her life was done.

CHAPTER XIII

THE EMERGENCE OF THALBERG

BY THE setup of the studio, Mayer was the overall boss, with Thalberg his nominal assistant in charge of the actual production of films. It was a delicate division of authority, but it worked out harmoniously because each man respected the competence of the other in his acknowledged sphere. Mayer handled the large administrative problems and maintained the difficult relations with the home office in New York. Thalberg devoted himself entirely to the creative functions of the studio. The arrangement was ideally productive in those beginning and growing years.

No one perceived this more quickly and clearly than did Thalberg and Mayer. As soon as the studio's output evidenced strength and popularity, they began agitating for more compensation for what they did. The allocation by the home office of $500,000 for expansion of the studio's facilities in the summer of 1925 was the cue for their first maneuvers to get their positions improved.

Even though the "Mayer group" contract had a year and a half to go, they got Loew's, Inc., to modify it so that their compensations were upped. The salary of Mayer was raised from $1,500 to $2,500 a week, Thalberg's from $650 to $2,000 and Rubin's from $600 to $1,000, and it was specifically guaranteed that the group's compensation from their percentage of the profits of the pictures would not fall below $500,000 a year. This was on the positive understanding that the studio would produce no less than forty-four pictures a year.

Schenck, who arranged the modification, tried first to get the group to accept a deal for drawing against their anticipated profits, but the gentlemen were too smart for that. So Schenck "studied the situation quite a bit," as he put it, and came to the conclusion that "there was no risk for us to satisfy them."

"My concern was that they should be happy and deliver results," he said. "If you keep them satisfied in that line of business (it is all creative work), you will get results."

Schenck was right. The compensation from the percentage of profits never fell below the guarantee.

However, dissatisfaction continued. Again, in the fall of 1926, Mayer told Schenck that they would lose Thalberg unless some better arrangement for compensation was made. So this time Thalberg's salary was jumped to $4,000 a week and it was guaranteed that his personal compensation from salary and percentages would not fall below $400,000 annually. Within less than three years, the young producer (he was then twenty-seven) had obtained a rather impressive acknowledgment of his value to Metro-Goldwyn-Mayer.

At the same time, Mayer and Rubin saw to it that they were rewarded, too. It was their stubborn contention that the compensation of the "Mayer group" was unfairly reduced by the large amount deducted from the company's income for the cost of distributing the films. They also felt that they should receive some of the benefit of the money earned by the company's films in Loew theatres. So it was arranged that the computation of their percentage should henceforth be made on the basis of the combined profits of Loew's, Inc., and Metro-Goldwyn-Mayer.

With these arrangements, which were extended to run to 1932, the dissatisfactions of Thalberg were pacified, for the nonce. In a letter to Schenck he said amicably that he was "perfectly happy and content," and would be "for the remainder of the period of the present agreement" and that he could now feel that his future was "assured."

Thalberg was a hard worker, but he knew how to look out for himself.

In the supervision of production, he was assisted as time went on by an augmenting group of young associates who became deeply attached and devoted to him. In addition to Harry Rapf and Hunt Stromberg, another supervisor who was hired by Mayer in 1925, he had a special corps of lieutenants who worked directly in production with him. These included, at the outset, Bernard Hyman, Albert Lewin and Paul Bern—a triumvirate of able and loyal companions with intelligence and taste.

Hyman, a native of West Virginia, had put in a little time at Yale and had worked as a film salesman and story reader at Universal, where he and Thalberg first met. Their personal friendship continued when Thalberg went over to Mayer. With the merger, Thalberg got Hyman to Culver City to work with him. There was little about the former reader to suggest the Hollywood "type." He was modest, reserved, soft-spoken, good-natured and essentially shy. These were qualities Thalberg respected, and Hyman fitted comfortably into his pattern of studio command.

Lewin, too, was unusual. He had attended New York University with the twin sons of Marcus Loew, and had taught English for a spell at Wisconsin before switching his interests to Hollywood. There he had worked as a reader at the Goldwyn company and then become a scenarist at Metro. He had written the scenario for *Bread,* from a novel by Charles Norris, and it was before the camera under the direction of Victor Schertzinger, when the merger occurred. Thalberg liked the scenario. However, he challenged one point. Lewin defended it strongly. Thalberg admired his spunk. Several months later, after Lewin had tried to work independently with the deposed Joe Engel and failed, he was called by Thalberg to Culver City. * Thalberg respected him for having a mind of his own.

The third member of the Thalberg circle was the urbane and elegant Paul Bern, a clever and fascinating worldling in a community where urbanity was rare. Bern had come to this country from Germany as a boy and had started as a film cutter for the Goldwyn company in New York. Later, he was a cutter, editor and scenarist at the studio in Hollywood, but left when June Mathis became story editor.

In the course of his getting about the community, Thalberg met the little man. Bern was small, dark, delicate and neat in appearance. Bern contributed a sophistication—a savoir-faire—in which Thalberg himself was shy. He was witty and self-possessed, a man of wide and exotic interests. Thalberg drew a lot from him.

Their companionship extended into the realm of social life, in which Thalberg participated gaily in his Hollywood bachelor years. He made his home with his family—his dynamic mother, Henrietta; his gentle father, his sister, Sylvia, who became a writer, and a clutch of transient relatives. The family had moved to Hollywood when it was evident that Irving was there to stay, and had occupied a succession of rented houses. Henrietta was not sufficiently impressed with the real estate to buy.

Man About Town

Among Thalberg's other male companions were the gay and exciting Hawks brothers, Howard and Kenneth, both of whom were rising young directors and conspicuous men about town. King Vidor, John Gilbert and Jack Conway, a director, also made company with the group in their card playing, party going and night-owling—what there was of it—in those days. Henrietta was darkly suspicious. She sometimes spoke of Irving's friends as "bums" and semi-seriously predicted that they would lead her adored son to ruin!

Of that there was not much danger. Thalberg, by nature and by concern for his curiously frail constitution, which was a hang-over from the illness of his youth, did not go for dissipation. He enjoyed parties, and fun, was an avid and inveterate card player, at which he gambled for rather heavy stakes; but he seldom drank, except at studio Christmas parties, and didn't even smoke. He was the sort who carried his own exhilaration, when he was in the mood to be gay. His most serious form of dissipation was driving fast in automobiles.

This vice, which was curiously chronic among many of the famous folk of Hollywood (Greta Garbo was tagged twice for speeding before she had been in the community a year), was one which Thalberg, for a long time, had to indulge vicariously. It took him a while to master the operation of an automobile. And, even when he did, he preferred to have someone drive for him.

Shortly after the merger, he took a liking to the studio shoeshine boy—a beaming Negro known familiarly as Kid Slickem—and soon got him as servant and chauffeur. Slickem was a natural-born performer, as well as an obliging servitor. He made himself a studied adornment of Thalberg's big white Marmon touring car. "I'se like a fly setting on a milk bottle, when I'se driving that car," he would say. Thalberg was amused and boastful of the oddity of his footman-chauffeur.

During his early attachment to Carl Laemmle, Thalberg started going with Carl's daughter, Rosabelle. And it wasn't long before the gossips were buzzing that Rosabelle and Irving were a romantic thing. They were—and so they continued, off and on, for several years. Two or three times in the course of the courtship it was understood that they were engaged. This was not to Henrietta's liking. She would scoff, in the family circle, at "that Rosabelle!"

"Why should my boy Irving marry *her?*" she would say.

But, then, Henrietta was that way about most of Irving's girls. When he began going around with Constance Talmadge, she was blisteringly critical of her. Connie was breezy and vivacious. She loved parties, as Irving did. She had been married and divorced and was a leader of the gay set in the movie colony. Irving was fascinated by her. She was complementary in his life to Paul Bern. The romance with Connie was probably the closest Thalberg came to being a blade. He went around with other screen actresses—Bessie Love was notable for awhile—but his friends pretty generally acknowledged that he had none of the proclivities of a rake.

Thalberg's interest in Norma Shearer was professional, and nothing more, for a year or so after the merger.

Norma had done very nicely—though not spectacularly—in a succession of the less conspicuous but not unprofitable films of the studio. After *He Who Gets Slapped*, she appeared with Gilbert and Conrad Nagel in *The Snob*, and then in a string of silent dramas such as *Lady of the Night, Tower of Lies, His Secretary, The Devil's Circus* and

The Waning Sex. She was not on a level of stardom with Mae Murray, Marion Davies or Lillian Gish, but she had definitely reached the eminence of a star of the second magnitude, on a level with Eleanor Boardman, Claire Windsor, Pauline Starke—or a new girl they called Joan Crawford, who was taken on in 1925. Her admiration for Thalberg was extended from afar.

That first Christmas Eve at Culver City, she had been working late on the back lot and was weary, depressed and lonesome when she finally returned to her dressing room. The studio party was over and most everyone had gone home. Norma was fit to loathe Christmas. Then her telephone rang. It was Thalberg.

"I hear you had to work late," he said, "so I just called to wish you a Merry Christmas!"

Norma floated home that night on a cloud.

She was naturally an object of admiration of a great many suitors in Hollywood. Harry D'Arrast, who directed for Charlie Chaplin, was one of her persistent beaus. So was her leading man, Lew Cody. She was rumored engaged many times. She did not sit at home and mope for Thalberg. Norma got around.

One day, Thalberg's secretary called her.

"Mr. Thalberg would like to know if you would care to go to the opening of *The Gold Rush* with him?"

"Tell Mr. Thalberg I'd be delighted," Norma replied. When she hung up, she smiled at herself in the mirror. "I'm going to get him!" she said.

Thalberg called for her that evening in a brand-new limousine. Slickem was happily driving, and Thalberg looked proud and boyish in the back seat of the elegant car. After the première of the Chaplin picture, they went dancing at the Cocoanut Grove. It was a happy and jolly evening. Norma played her hand well. Thereafter, she went with him for dinners and parties at his home. She was sweet and attentive to Henrietta, who soon grew to like the pretty star.

However, the romance with Connie Talmadge flared a few times more, and Henrietta counseled Norma to take a more aggressive line. But Norma smiled benignly. "I am Irving's spare tire," she would say.

Then, of course, it happened. One night at the Cocoanut Grove, while they were dancing, Irving casually said to Norma, "Don't you think it's about time we got married?" She played along with the attitude. "If you are proposing," she parried, "you're not using the right dialogue." He assured her he meant it. The engagement was announced at a dinner party at Mayer's home. And on September 29, 1927, Norma Shearer and Irving Thalberg were wed.

Norma, realizing the attachment of Irving to his family, agreed that they would all live together, so they found and rented a new home prior to the wedding. It was the old house of actress Pauline Frederick—a modest and not too pretty villa on Sunset Boulevard. The wedding was held in the garden. Mayer was Thalberg's best man. His groomsmen included King Vidor, Norma's brother Douglas (who gave the bride away) and Jack Conway. Norma had as her bridesmaids Mayer's young daughters, Edith and Irene; her sister, Athole, who later married Howard Hawks; Irving's sister, Sylvia, and Marion Davies.

The wedding turned out to be a little more elaborate than at first intended. As such things do, it grew—especially when Miss Davies and Louella Parsons enthusiastically moved in. Among other things, Miss Davies ordered a dazzling diamond bracelet from a fashionable jeweler in New York. It arrived by special messenger just as the ceremony was about to begin. Marion gayly ripped off the wrappings and clamped the magnificent jewelry on an amazed and somewhat nonplussed Norma's wrist.

That night, when Norma was preparing to retire at the Del Monte, California, hotel, where she and Irving were honeymooning, she found she couldn't get the bracelet off her wrist. The catch was stuck. She and Irving pulled and tussled with it to no avail. She had to wear the bracelet to bed. The next morning, they found a jeweler who freed her from the Hearst-Davies gift.

The new home and family arrangements worked out very well. Henrietta took over the house and the planning of the meals. Norma was free to go to the studio, without a domestic care. The only slight inconvenience was that the bedrooms of Irving and Norma (in Hollywood, husbands and wives invariably have separate bedrooms) were at opposite ends of the house, with the rest of the family scattered in bedrooms in between. It required some considerable traveling to effect a connubial rendezvous.

CHAPTER XIV

EAST IS EAST—THE BUSINESS END

THE COMMERCE of motion pictures in the mid-1920's had reached a point where a producing company's prosperity was determined by something more than its ability to turn out good pictures. Success had come to depend upon a closely integrated organization of all facilities to assure the efficient flow of pictures out of the studio and through the theatres.

Marcus Loew put it in a nutshell. "A star picture of the first grade costs anywhere from $150,000 to $300,000," he said, which was a general indication of the total investment in a feature film. "When such sums are tied up, it is essential to control proper channels of distribution so that the money can be turned over."

Here was the basic anxiety. So many films were being made in the already overgrown and continually expanding industry—some 750 were turned out in 1923—that a producer who hadn't firm arrangements for the exhibition of his films couldn't even be sure of getting them placed on the market, let alone recovering his investment or a reasonable profit from them. The mediocrity of the average picture made it necessary to have assured "channels" for selling it, if the investment was to be secured. The premise was that if the film was shown in enough theatres, it would earn enough to pay off, at least.

By far, the most powerful and effective organization in the business of "channeling" films was now Adolph Zukor's Famous Players-Lasky Company which, through Paramount, its distributing arm, and its increasingly large chain of theatres, was not only making a generally better grade of films but was giving them wide distribution. Zukor, who owned or controlled some 200 well-placed theatres, commanded the top position in the United States and was, in large measure, able to dictate commercial terms.

The most conspicuous and momentous trade practice that his sales forces introduced was that known as "block booking." This compelled that a theatre, in order to get any of the Famous Players pictures, had to book whole blocks of that studio's output for the year, the sizes and contents of the blocks determined by the distributor. Thus was playing time—or, at least, a rental assured for weak films as well as strong. This practice had become conventional with the large producer-distributors by 1924.

At the urgent behest of theatre owners, the Federal Trade Commission had begun in 1923 an exhaustive investigation of Famous Players-Lasky and its subsidiaries. In the course of these slow investigations, it was often and forcibly charged that the companies of Loew and Zukor were in a secret conspiracy to exchange preferential bookings of the pictures of their two companies among their theatres. That is to say, the pictures of Famous Players-Lasky were arbitrarily given prior release to the theatres of Loew in those areas where Loew houses did not overlap with the theatres of Zukor. Likewise, Zukor's theatres were said to have first call on the best films of Metro-Goldwyn-Mayer.

Conspiracy may have been a harsh word to apply to the sort of business done by the two old penny-arcade partners. They used harsh words in those days, especially when the existence of one's theatres and livelihood was at stake. But there was no doubt that Loew and Zukor were selling each other films with close and preferential bookings. This was reasonable, from their point of view. Their companies had top pictures and many of the best theatres. What they did of this sort was shrewd business on the part of both companies.

Following the studio merger, Loew continued to build new theatres around the country and acquire control or booking arrangements with other ones. His chain had an even 100 houses in 1924. By 1927, he had run it to 144.

New theatres in New York City, Brooklyn and the New York metropolitan area strengthened Loew's hand in meeting the competition of his most formidable and increasing rival in the exhibition field, the similar combination movie-vaudeville houses of the B. F. Keith-Albee chain. Keith-Albee had been late in coming to the combination idea. They had held out for straight vaudeville programs in all their theatres until 1923. But the advantage Loew's had was too apparent, and old man Albee finally put in films. The rivalry of the two chains for pictures and for vaudeville acts continued hot for several years.

Loew added theatres in many other key cities in the mid-1920's. Six houses were acquired in Cleveland, three in New Orleans, three in Baltimore, three in Pittsburgh, two in Toronto and single theatres in Syracuse, Buffalo, New Haven, New London, Chicago, Kalamazoo, Akron, Flint, Saginaw, Evansville (Ind.) and London, Ontario. The race for accumulating power continued unaffected by any thought of an end to the era of boom.

In 1925, Adolph Zukor made a major maneuver in the motion picture world. Faced with the frightening prospect of a government monopoly suit, he shrewdly separated the theatres of the Famous Players-Lasky company and merged them with the 500 houses independently

owned or controlled by the great Chicago theatre chain of Balaban
& Katz. The consequent theatre operating company, known as the
Paramount-Publix chain, was owned largely by Famous Players-
Lasky, which held and acquired two-thirds of its stock. But it was
nominally a separate company.

This maneuver was followed with the announcemnt that Paramount-Publix intended to build a handsome new theatre and office
building in the heart of Times Square in New York, which indicated
that Paramount-Publix was aiming to challenge Loew's theatre
standing in the area. Already Zukor owned three houses on Broadway—the Rivoli, the Rialto and the Criterion. Loew's people viewed
the move with some concern, fearing that Paramount-Publix might
mean to move into the rich neighborhood and surburban area of
New York.

To add a touch of irony, the new Paramount building was to go
on the site of the old Putnam Building, in which Loew had maintained headquarters for many years. Threatened friction was avoided,
however, when Loew made a tacit agreement with Zukor and Katz
that any future building they might do in the New York suburban
area would be owned jointly by Paramount-Publix and Loew's.

Loew, ever cautious and conservative, regarded Zukor's ambitious
moves with anxiety and misgiving. He would stand at the window
of his office across the way and gaze down into the hole they were
excavating for the new Paramount building and theatre, shake his
head sadly and mutter, "Adolph is digging his grave." How close and
ironic was his prediction remained to be seen.

Soon after the Paramount Building was completed, an incident
occurred which provided a bright illumination of the capriciousness
of the industry. To celebrate the eighth anniversary of the Capitol
Theatre, a four-million-candlepower searchlight was rigged as a
magic lantern on its roof and made to throw a huge sign proclaim-
ing "GO TO THE CAPITOL" on the sides of buildings along Broadway. Inevitably, the new Paramount skyscraper presented a most
tempting "screen," and somehow the gleaming "billboard" seemed
to linger most frequently there.

At once, there was an open squabble as to whether this rampant
impudence of throwing an advertisement for one theatre upon the
property of a competitor was against the law. For several nights it
continued, while the argument raged by day. Then the Capitol
abandoned its frank skylarking, with a sly acknowledgment that it
was "a little gay."

But the irony was that the searchlight magic lantern was being
hawked by a little outfit, of which Harry E. Aitken, the former

president of the once dominant Triangle producing company, was the head. It was Zukor's "raids" on the stars and directors of Triangle that had a lot to do with that company's collapse. How appropriate it was that Aitken's searchlight should briefly cause the mighty Zukor some slight dismay!

New Groupings

The Paramount-Publix merger was the peak of a new wave of aggressive groupings of companies within the film industry. In that same year, the Vitagraph Company, which had previously attempted to survive by forming a consolidation with Selig, Lubin and Essanay, sold out to Warner Brothers.

The next year, the Producers Distributing Company of Cecil B. DeMille and W. W. Hodkinson, both ex-victims of Zukor's voracity, joined up to supply motion pictures to the Keith-Albee and the Orpheum chains of vaudeville theatres, thus beginning the association out of which the Radio-Keith-Orpheum combine came. On the same day, the Stanley Company greatly enlarged its independent theatre chain by taking in the Fabian theatres of New Jersey, the big Mark Strand in New York and the Rowland and Clark houses around Pittsburgh. One year later, Stanley was to join with the West Coast Theatre Company, a California chain, to take control of First National, thus completing another typical absorption of producing facilities by a theatre group.

Inexorably, the motion picture industry was shaping itself into the forms of pyramidal combinations that commercial experience proved the most efficient and effective devices for the grappling of control. Manifold elaborations were envisioned and discussed. The field was again fair for the promoters and the architects of schemes. At one stage, it was even rumored that a giant amalgamation was to be made by First National, Famous Players-Lasky, United Artists and Metro-Goldwyn-Mayer! While such a thing was fantastic and preposterous— a super-colossal movie trust—it was seriously reported as a possibility. That was the current state of mind.

Already Loew's was embarked on a program of expansion abroad which was to lead in future years to great enrichment and international prestige. The program was inaugurated in 1920, when Arthur Loew, one of the twin sons of Marcus, took over the then one-man job of directing the foreign distribution of the Metro company's films.

At first, the handling of these pictures in Great Britain, France, Sweden, Denmark, Germany and Spain was franchised to local distributors, just as the functions of distribution were originally farmed to state-rights agents in the United States, with the films sold outright to the franchise holders in each country. But this system was soon changed to one of allowing a percentage of the rentals to be taken by the distributor.

Great Britain, for instance, which was the most productive market for American films, was franchised to Sir William Jury, a colorful Cockney character, who made a fine thing of his privilege during the seven years it was held by him. Sir William was by bent a pigeon fancier and had little perspicacity or taste for the qualities of motion pictures. Example: he stubbornly refused to release *The Four Horsemen of the Apocalypse* in Great Britain until Loew had thoroughly proved it would be popular with the British people by independently renting a theatre in London and showing it there. Sir William had a curious notion that it would offend the British sense of morality.

Shortly after this experience, Marcus Loew was in Europe to look at *Ben Hur*. He stopped off in London on his way home and bought the old Tivoli Theatre there. This was the first important theatre acquired by Loew abroad. Three years later, in 1927, the franchise to Sir William was withdrawn—he was paid $620,000 for what was then his one-half interest—and the Loew company henceforth did its own distributing. At that time, the gross revenues of the company from the British market were about $900,000 a year.

It was three years before this that the company's first full-scale operation in a foreign country had been inaugurated. This was in France, where it took over the Gaumont circuit of exchanges and theatres and ran them for a few years. No money was paid to Gaumont for them. The Culver Export Company, which was the wholly owned subsidiary of Loew's, Inc., set up for handling its foreign business, simply guaranteed an annual profit to Gaumont, based on a percentage of the gross business done. Schenck and others in New York were apprehensive about the arrangement and sent a couple of lawyers to France to try to talk the veteran Leon Gaumont out of the deal he had made with Arthur Loew. But the old Frenchman stubbornly stuck to it. The arrangement looked good to him. And, indeed, it turned out to be quite happy and profitable for Loew's. However, the company later sold its contract with Gaumont when sound motion pictures came in and France threatened to place restrictions on the import of American films.

With the foreign market booming in the 1920's, Arthur Loew went on to place company exchanges in South Africa and Australia, challenging established film agencies there. He also made a brief and unsuccessful stab at running a group of theatres in Brazil. Although Marcus Loew had once mentioned that the company did not aim to

Harry Rapf, Louis B. Mayer and Irving Thalberg with the prophetic "key" presented to Mayer at the dedication of the Metro-Goldwyn-Mayer studio on April 26, 1924.

Lon Chaney (in clown costume), Norma Shearer, Director Victor Seastrom and John Gilbert outside a glass-enclosed stage during the filming of "He Who Gets Slapped," first production launched under the new regime. Behind Chaney is George Davis, a famous European clown who helped coach him for his role.

The Culver City lot in 1918, about the time it was taken over from Triangle by the Goldwyn company. This view is looking east along wide-open Washington and Culver Boulevards.

The same lot as it is today, looking west. At lower left is the Irving G. Thalberg Memorial Building, which houses studio executives, producers and writers and is known facetiously as "the Iron Lung."

be "competitive" in the foreign field, the already established distributing agencies in the various countries soon discovered that it definitely was. Particularly, in South Africa it was evident that Loew's had moved in to stay when it built Loew's Metro, its first theatre constructed from the ground up in a foreign country, in Johannesburg.

Thus were the foundations laid for the later great international trade of Loew's.

Carried on the Wind

It is easy to see now that the character of mass entertainment was on a wave of vast and incalculable alteration during these turgid years. But then the men closest to it were slow to recognize change. The miracle of radio telephony that was sprung after World War I evolved during the middle 1920's into the great popular medium of broadcast radio, and the big black horns, squawking music and news announcements, became the focuses of excited attention and interest in American homes. Theatre men let the new mechanism creep up on them without showing undue alarm.

The behavior of Loew's was indicative. In 1923, when the radio field was still wide open and broadcasting was truly spontaneous and unrehearsed, Loew's bought a small independent station in Brooklyn, with the call letters WHN, for the purpose of using it merely to advertise the local Loew theatre programs. The tiny studio was moved bag and baggage to the Loew's State Building in New York, and the vaudeville acts that were booked for the Loew circuit were its principal talent pool. The performers were not paid for their radio services; this was regarded as mere publicity. The opportunity to air themselves on the new gadget was considered more than adequate recompense.

Then, while the company was pondering whether to pick up stations in other cities where it operated theatres and extend the pattern of the functioning of WHN, the smart promoters of network combinations, backed by big money interests, moved in and organized the broadcasting business on a large industrial-advertising scale. With the formation of the National Broadcasting Company in 1926, and the subsequent assembly of nationwide stations into the Columbia and Mutual chains, the chief purveyance of radio entertainment was settled in other hands and the chance of theatre men to get control of this increasingly competitive medium was gone. Even so, the Loew people were still thinking about the assembly of a radio chain when sound motion pictures came surging upwards in 1927 and chased the thought of it out of their heads. A mildly profitable reminder of the chance that got away has been the company's continued possession over the years of its one radio station, now WMGM.

But the prospect of momentous changes did not penetrate Loew's in the years when radio was wobbling through its bawling infancy. Vaudeville and silent motion pictures seemed so firmly and fittingly fixed as the ideal in popular entertainment that their sovereignty could not be disturbed. And no company was more successful with the "combination" program than was Loew's. As the *Motion Picture World* richly put it, the success of the company was due to the efficiency and regularity of its operations, "like the maneuvers of a crack army division."

Said the paper:

> The supply of movies is assured and standardized. The vaude-
> ville acts are routed uniformly, the strength of each is known and
> the proper balance of a bill is fixed. The public knows what it
> will get for its money, week after week. Thus the Loew line is
> held.

The grenadiers of Napoleon seemed no more invincible.

The summer of 1927, that golden summer, turned out to be the simultaneous zenith of vaudeville, silent films and Marcus Loew. In twenty-three years, the former furrier and ambitious real estate man, had risen to fame and fortune with these two popular entertainment forms. Now, as momentous circumstances gathered to change the shape of things, they stood at the peak of their possession of a realm and an era that were soon to go.

Strangely enough, the gravest problem that the motion picture businessmen perceived in the midst of this autumnal summer was one that really did not reach them—then. That was a federal court order which ominously decreed that the prevalent practice of "block booking" was in restraint of trade. This was the final distillation of the Federal Trade Commission's inquiries into the operation of Paramount and others that had extended over a period of five years. In a suit brought by the Trade Commission, the court ordered the distributors to cease the practice of wholesale merchandising by which they assured the unloading of their stocks of films.

Actually, the order was resisted and evaded at first, until, as a consequence of further legal action, the distributors were released from the order by the courts in 1932. But at the time it seemed to the big distributors to be a disastrous blow. They saw the very keystones of the arches of their hegemony being removed.

In what was ironically fated to be the last public statement of Marcus Loew, he stubbornly challenged the wisdom and the practicality of this decree. From his home in Glen Cove, Long Island, on

July 11, the day of the decree, he passed the word that "any other way than block booking" would be prohibitive.

"An executive"—he had grown quite fond of that word—"wouldn't even buy one picture at a time," he said. "Such a practice would be analogous to limiting a jewelry salesman to selling one article of jewelry to a store on one trip to a city . . . or a plum salesman to selling one plum at a time."

For all the conspicuous development of the individuality of films, Marcus Loew, the respected showman, still thought of them as bulk merchandise, like manufactured jewelry, or plums. He had not come to sense the real distinction of the creations that his company made and sold. Nor was he unique in his obtuseness to the variations in the values of separate films. His was the usual way of thinking by the "businessmen" in the industry. *Product* was what they were selling, not individual gems. They thought of entertainment in terms of the assembly line. Indeed, Loew assured the reporter who called him about the court decree that the only producer who did not sell by block booking was the "small" producer of single films. "And he," Loew said, with shattering candor, "is gradually being weeded out."

Such was the final public comment of the cheerful little showman who had come up from the slums of New York's East Side, up from the penny arcades, the nickelodeons and the small-time vaudeville houses to be the boss of a powerful theatre chain and then the king of a motion picture empire that was being extended around the world. For Marcus Loew's days were now numbered. In 1923, he had suffered a heart attack which had caused him to transfer some of his command. Nicholas Schenck, Dave Bernstein, Robert Rubin and other lieutenants assumed his chores.

"How do you manage to carry on your innumerable enterprises and keep alive?" an interviewer asked him the following year.

"I make somebody else do it. Let the other fellow go crazy," he blithely said.

In his earlier years, Loew had played tennis—not well but vigorously. He and his circle of cronies used to have violent round-robin "tournaments" on Sunday afternoons. The categories of trophies were always ordered so that everybody got a prize. That was characteristic of his good-humored joshing of his friends. Now, on his doctor's orders, he switched from tennis to golf.

"I want to live and enjoy my business, not let it kill me," he explained. "Every day, from four-thirty on, it's the golf links for me!"

However, on a trip to the West Coast in the fall of 1926, Loew contracted pneumonia, which hit him very hard. He was several weeks convalescing. That winter, as usual, he and his wife spent at the Alba in Palm Beach. There, on March 4, they celebrated their thirty-third wedding anniversary with a small group of old friends from New York. The ladies got orchids as favors, the men got fountain-pen sets. It was a cheerful, neighborly gathering, reminiscent of some of the happy parties at the Loews' former West End Avenue home.

The Last of the 'Little Napoleon'

As spring came on, they returned to Pembroke, the mansion and estate at Glen Cove that Loew had bought right after the merger of Metro-Goldwyn-Mayer. The house was a formidable red-stone palace containing some thirty-five rooms and commanding an expanse of forty-six acres on a point jutting into Long Island Sound. It was originally the property of one J. J. Delameter, a fabulous financial adventurer. Loew bought it from the latter's daughter for $500,000. Within its elaborate surroundings of greenhouses, formal gardens and small golf course, the genial little landlord tried uncertainly to act the big tycoon. An elegant and haughty English butler practically ruled the menage. He baffled and awed his employer and extracted fabulous tips from the guests, many of whom were less affluent old neighbors from earlier days in New York.

A guest who had spent a week end there a year or so after Loew had bought the place was returning to New York on Monday morning with his host aboard the latter's yacht—a sixty-foot cruiser, the *Caroline*, named for Mrs. Loew. As the boat pulled out from the landing and headed down Long Island Sound, the guest, looking back at Pembroke, remarked what a handsome place it was.

"Yes," Loew acknowledged. He paused, then murmured, "But Caroline isn't there."

The guest was naturally puzzled. They had just had breakfast with Mrs. Loew. What did her husband mean by that remark?

"Oh, she lives there, all right," Loew answered. "But she never really moved out here with me. That's just her face and her body. Her heart still lives in New York."

Such was the vast, impressive dwelling to which the one-time insignificant theatre man, "the little Napoleon of the small-time," returned from Palm Beach that last bright spring.

In August of the succeeding summer, Nicholas Schenck was married for the second time. He took as his bride Pansy Wilcox, a West Virginian, whom Schenck had met the year before at the marriage of her sister, a pretty show girl, to Edgar Selwyn—his second wife. Schenck and his bride were quietly married at Palisades, New Jersey, close by the amusement park which he and his brother, Joe, still owned independently. Then they had taken a house at Saratoga while the racing season was on. Schenck was—and is—a passionate horse-player, usually for heavy stakes.

A few weeks after their arrival, Loew went up to visit them, with a nurse in close attendance, for his health was now very poor. He had been there only a few days when his strength began to fail and it was decided that he should be moved back to Glen Cove as gently as possible. His yacht was called from New York to pick him up at Albany, and on the Saturday and Sunday before Labor Day he was brought home leisurely aboard it.

The *Caroline* was met at the Pembroke landing by Loew's physician, Dr. Bell, who, as soon as the patient was debarked from it, dispatched it across Long Island Sound to Westport, Connecticut, to pick up the eminent heart specialist, Dr. George Baehr. Dr. Baehr was the son of Loew's old partner in the fur firm of Baehr & Loew.

The physicians stayed close to the bedroom of the very sick man that night. Shortly after six on Labor Day morning, while the rest of the household slept, the nurse noticed a slight uneasiness of the patient, then a fluttering of his pulse. She hastily summoned the doctors. Loew was dead when they reached the room. So, at the age of fifty-seven, he came to a peaceful end in an elegant mansion on Long Island, far from the tenement in which he was born.

The funeral, three days later, was an event of impressive magnitude. Loew was actually the first of the big movie magnates to go. Nicholas Schenck took personal charge of the funeral and saw that the proper respects were paid. The services were held in the main reception hall of Pembroke, beginning at 11 A.M. Virtually everyone of power or importance in the motion picture and theatrical worlds was there. More than 2,500 persons attempted to attend. The gates to the estate had to be locked shut after the capacity of mourners had crowded in.

It was said that a quarter million dollars worth of flowers was delivered to the home. One huge floral design, sent by the managers of Loew theatres across the country, was in the form of a proscenium arch, with the simple words, THE LAST CURTAIN, inscribed across it in flowers. As the funeral party was leaving the mansion, Loew's very close and loyal actor friend, David Warfield, was seized with a fit of weeping. Possibly he recalled that long ago Sunday morning when they met in front of an apartment house in New York. He became so severely affected that Adolph Zukor and Robert Rubin had to help him to a car. Onlookers were thoroughly shaken. Sentiments were strong and unconcealed.

All the Loew theatres in the nation remained closed that day until after the funeral. Those that had orchestras or pipe organs opened their programs with the playing of *Lead Kindly Light*. The family said that had been Loew's favorite hymn ever since he first heard it at the funeral of President McKinley, back in the days when he was peddling furs. Other competing theatres around the country suspended their programs at the funeral hour.

At 2 P.M. just as the burial service was ending in Maimonedes Cemetery in Cypress Hills, N.T. Granlund broadcast a memorial tribute over Loew's radio station, WHN. "To know Marcus Loew was to love him," N.T.G. solemnly said. "He was a man without an enemy."

"He would have been successful in a legitimate business," Will Rogers wrote.

"He was burned out with worrying for his stockholders," the trade paper *Variety* touchingly claimed.

This was poetic license. In the fiscal year before Loew died, his company showed a net income of more than $6,000,000, which was nothing to cause him great concern. Loew stock remained firm on the market when the exchange opened the day after his death.

It was later found that Loew's will had been drawn in 1912. Because of his lasting superstitions, he had not changed it since that time. "In the event that the net value of my estate exceeds $200,000 . . ." the will began. A conservative estimate put it at $30,000,000. It was left to his family and friends.

Two weeks after Loew's death, the directors of Loew's, Inc., named Nicholas Schenck president. Dave Bernstein continued as treasurer. Loew's "boys" were set to carry on.

CHAPTER XV

THE CRASH OF SOUND

It was an odd and fateful coincidence that the death of Marcus Loew and the succession of Nicholas Schenck to the presidency of Loew's, Inc., came precisely when they did. For, in every respect, the film industry, which Loew had helped to build, had come to the end of an era. He died just as it was about to close.

Already the ever-loudening thunder and lightning of movies with sound had unsuspectedly signaled the onset of the technical storm that was to rock the entire picture business and vastly change the characteristics of films. The silent movies and their kind of illusion were soon to go by the board in a rush of electrification that would further mechanize and alter the entire entertainment world. Vaudeville as Marcus Loew had known it and used it to build an empire was doomed; the mechanism of the talking motion picture was to complete the eclipse of the old commercial stage. How immense were to be the alterations in the techniques of making films and in the mass communication of culture was beyond the power of anyone to see.

Simultaneously, another illusion, that of endless prosperity in an America that had boomed through the 1920's was about to be blown to smithereens. The stock market "crash" and the Great Depression, which were to desolate a nation grown obese on rash industrial expansion, greedy speculation and needled beer, were making up for their entrance when Marcus Loew finished his turn. Film companies that had overextended in the years of prosperity were to collapse under financial strains that were to torture the transforming industry, and men who had spiraled to high positions were to be plunged into personal ruin.

That Loew died on the eve of these great changes was a strange—perhaps merciful—irony. The responsibility of facing the hard dilemmas and the big decisions was passed to Nicholas Schenck.

The first of these, as indicated, was the mechanical onrush of sound, which—like so many new departures—caused confusion and resentment when it came. Indeed, it was stubbornly resisted by most of the experts in the industry, including the experienced policy makers of Loew's and Metro-Goldwyn-Mayer. And the eventual compulsion and achievement of an audible and vocal screen were brought about less by the industry desiring it than by factors that forced its hand.

Much that has been written in recollection of the conversion of the screen to sound has given the sketchy impression that this occurrence was brought about on an inspiration of the Warner Brothers, who achieved it single-handedly with the presentation of *The Jazz Singer* in Vitaphone. The notion conveyed by such abridging is that *The Jazz Singer* was a miracle that touched the screen one fateful evening in 1927 and an immediate transformation then occurred.

This is an unfortunate impression—particularly in these days when the screen is undergoing an evolution comparable to the prolonged change to sound. For the factors that brought the transformation were actually extensive and involved, beyond the manipulation of any individual will. They included the forward push of science in the new electronic age that was as inexorable and compelling as it was in the period of invention when movies were born. They also included the factor of competition within the industry, which was simply a matter of one showman trying to find a livelier freak than the last. And, finally, they included the factor of audience psychology, which again was prepared by parallel forces for the acceptance of something new. That sound and voice became accretions of pictures that simply moved was an eventuality as inevitable as the development of language by Man.

For years—ever since the invention of the motion picture, indeed— the scientists had been attempting to equip the image with sound. Thomas Edison had tried it. So had Leon Gaumont in France. Even little Carl Laemmle had come up with a German combination of phonograph and motion picture called a Synchroscope. But for various mechanical reasons—the most persistent of which was the fact that they lacked effective amplifying equipment—none had proved practical.

Then, in the middle 1920's, the diligent engineers of the Western Electric Company, which was the developing and manufacturing arm of the great American Telephone and Telegraph Company—or the Bell System, as it was known—had advanced their prolonged researches in the electrical transmission of sound to the point where they were confidently able to propose to the manufacturers of movies that they could now make the screen audible. The key to their offered mechanism was a miracle device called the audion, which had been invented by Dr. Lee de Forest in 1906. This device had initially provided the Bell System with a relay amplifier that allowed a revolutionary extension and speed-up of its long-distance telephone lines.

Later, perfected by de Forest and other engineers as the vacuum tube, it became the crucial apparatus that made possible the radio telephone.

In the line of industrial research, the Western Electric engineers then sought to discover other uses to which their amplifiers might be put. They perfected the public address system, which was dramatically proved when it was used to amplify the speech of President Harding at his inauguration in 1921. They developed electrical phonograph recording. Then they got around to perfecting a system for equipping the motion picture with sound.

This system was based upon a technique of recording the sound on discs, much like phonograph records, which were played in synchronization with the film, the sound being projected from amplified horns behind the screen. The device was first offered to the film industry in 1924, the memorable year in which the merger of Metro, Goldwyn and Mayer occurred.

Even though this Western Electric system had been promisingly demonstrated in a short film, experimentally made by the company to show its own activities, and even though broadcast radio was rapidly reaching into the nation's homes, the major motion picture companies rejected it, one by one. In later years, it was easy to ridicule the men of the motion picture business who took such a negative attitude. But their reluctance was not as pig-headed or illogical as has been implied by those critics whose hindsight is more lucid than their memories of the way things were.

In the first place, a state of equilibrium had been reached in the film industry by the middle 1920's; production was largely controlled by companies that owned big theatre circuits. If they encouraged the promotion of sound, (according to their calculations) it would not only be expensive in the exploratory stage but, if the experiments proved propitious, it would cost them tremendous sums to re-equip their studios and their theatres to handle films with sound. This would place in jeopardy their large stocks of silent films. As shrewd businessmen, they saw no reason to take this seemingly foolish risk.

And who could be sure that the public would really want sound in films, even if it was developed to a mechanically perfect state? In all the previous attempts and enterprises to make the screen audible—including the dimly remembered Humanova "talking pictures" promoted by Adolph Zukor and Marcus Loew, away back in the days of the nickelodeons—the devices had not caught on. It was too much for the hard-headed magnates to imagine they should do so now.

Furthermore, there is this to be remembered: the uncertain prospect of an audible screen did not envision the "talking photoplay" as it later came to be. The art of the silent motion picture, based firmly upon graphic pantomime, had become so established and familiar that it was extremely difficult to conceive how a fluent method—let alone an artistic improvement—could be achieved by having the actors speak words. The extent of the advantages first envisioned by those who were trying to sell sound was that it would be used to provide "theme music" and realistic sound effects on feature-length films.

Finally, there was a natural instinct on the part of theatre men to be suspicious of anything as radical and mechanically complex as sound. Already Lee de Forest, who had experimented with sound films on his own, apart from the laboratory research of Western Electric, had hit the market with a highly touted system wherein the sound was recorded directly on the edge of the film. He played it in several theatres and auditoriums in 1924. But his talking films had what the critics termed a distracting "hollow, hornlike quality." They helped to discourage the industry people. If de Forest couldn't make sound work, who could?

Then, briefly marked at the moment and almost forgotten today, was an embarrassing mishap that Metro-Goldwyn-Mayer had with an experiment in synchronized sound. In 1925, Douglas Shearer, the brother of Norma Shearer, went to Hollywood to pay a visit to his mother and sisters. Shearer, a young engineer, had been eagerly following developments in radio telephony and amplified sound. Out of a fertile imagination, he conceived a wild idea for a combined "scientific" experiment and publicity venture which he persuaded the studio people to try.

The idea was to combine the mechanism of the marvelous new broadcast radio with a silent motion picture to achieve the effect of a "talking" film. The studio had a new picture, *Slave of Fashion*, in which Norma and Lew Cody were the stars. Shearer got Pete Smith, the studio press agent, to have a special trailer prepared for it. This trailer had the stars doing a little act and exchanging conversation. It was arranged that it should be shown in several theatres in the Los Angeles area at exactly the same time on a certain evening. Simultaneous with the showings, the two stars would speak the dialogue of the trailer into a microphone at radio station KFI, and this dialogue, broadcast by radio, would be picked up by sets in the theatres and transmitted to the audiences through amplified horns behind the screens.

The novelty of the thing was intriguing, and it attracted a lot of newspaper attention in advance. But the execution was deadly. Success depended upon a complicated arrangement for matching the radio broadcast with the trailer showings by means of synchronized watches and metronomes in the radio studio and the theatre projection booths. Inevitably, there were miscalculations and some weird effects occurred, such as the voice of Norma being heard speaking while the lips of Cody were seen to move. Naturally, audiences found it a little ludicrous.

Even so, Shearer was excited by the possibilities he foresaw for sound, and he tried to persuade Mayer to employ him for further experiments. But Mayer was understandably distrustful. He saw no practical future in this sort of folderol. So Shearer, rebuffed but hopeful, got a job with Warner Brothers as a property man, determined to stay in Hollywood until something good turned up.

Such was the state of indifference of the major companies in 1925.

Breaking the Barrier

But the scientists were persistent, and finally, in June of that year, they got a response from Warner Brothers, one of the lesser producing outfits, then playing a lone and far from winning hand. Led by Sam and Harry Warner (and with money raised by Walter J. Rich), the studio agreed to join with Western Electric and its newly formed research unit, Bell Laboratories, Inc., to promote the Western Electric sound system, which they labeled Vitaphone. Together they set up the Vitaphone Corporation to perfect and market it.

All through the fall and winter of 1925-26, the engineers and picture makers from the Warner West Coast studio worked at the project in Brooklyn and at the Manhattan Opera House in New York. Reports of their slow and fitful progress circulated idly in the trade. There was no elaborate expectation that they would come up with anything great. The people at Loew's were happily busy counting their phenomenal returns from such popular silent dramas as *The Merry Widow, The Big Parade* and *Ben Hur.* They sensed no cause to be interested in what the little Warners did.

Then, on the muggy, showery evening of August 5, 1926, there occurred at the Warner Theatre in New York the event that was to inaugurate great change. That was the first public showing of the outcome of the experiments with Vitaphone.

The program on which the picture makers and the engineers had labored for so long—and for which the opening night audience paid ten dollars a head to behold—was introduced with a short film presenting Will H. Hays, the eminent president of the Motion Picture Producers and Distributors of America. Mr. Hays expressed interest and gratification in the new device that was to be seen. The audience showed audible amazement at the clear reproduction of his voice.

This was followed by a series of screen performances by such distinguished operatic and concert stars as Anna Case, Giovanni Martinelli, Mischa Elman and Efrem Zimbalist. These performers were used because Western Electric was tied in with the Victor Recording Company, to whom they were under contract as recording artists, and their talents were believed the tops in sounds. To each successive performer the audience responded with explosive applause. However, the sensation on the program was a new John Barrymore film, *Don Juan,* which was equipped with a carefully recorded Vitaphone synchronized musical score.

The house was packed with celebrities that evening, including most of the leading men of the industry. Marcus Loew wasn't able to make it, but Nicholas Schenck was there. He joined in the loud and general chorus of unstinted praise for Vitaphone. "It is very marvelous and has great possibilities," he told an interviewer at the close. Speculation was immediate and eager as to what its future—if any—would be.

Film Daily expressed the current thinking:

> It seems beyond human conception that the smallest theatre in the smallest hamlet of this country can exhibit *Don Juan* with an orchestral accompaniment of 107 men of the New York Philharmonic Orchestra. This is what the Vitaphone has done. Metropolitan Opera stars . . . spreading their artistry to the far-flung corners of the world for untold millions to hear and enjoy—the Vitaphone has done this, too. Can there be any doubt that a momentous event has come to pass in the industry?

The anticipation was prophetic, but realization was to take much toil—and time.

In the first flush of their single New York triumph, the Warners leaped to the idea of setting up a national chain of special theatres for the exclusive showing of their Vitaphone films. A monopoly of the new entertainment was their evident aim. But Western Electric, which owned the basic patents and was to manufacture the equipment, had other ideas. As the mere promoter of the apparatus, it wished to make its use universal.

The industry was in no hurry, however. The enthusiasm of that opening night was not to be forthwith translated into revolutionary change.

In October, the Warners presented a second series of Vitaphone shorts, along with a second feature picture, *The Better 'Ole,* equipped with a synchronized musical score. The audience response was even better than it had been for the first program. This was obviously due to the more plebeian and popular nature of the shorts. Instead of operatic artists, the performers on this second bill were such familiar entertainers as Elsie Janis, Willie and Eugene Howard, Georgie Jessel and Al Jolson doing such stuff as they regularly did in vaudeville. The heaviest thing on the program was Reinald Werrenrath singing *The Long, Long Trail*.

This was coming closer to discovering the popular potentialities of sound. But still there was no contemplation of the use of dramatic dialogue. The nearest to it was the proposal that "spoken subtitles" might be put into the otherwise vocally silent synchronized films. The Warners now swung to the policy that all exhibitors "of standing" who chose to install Vitaphone equipment in their theatres would be welcome to rent films. A dozen theatres around the country were equipped by the end of 1926. None were Loew's.

However, there was now one other film man besides Sam and Harry Warner who believed there was a bright and commercially profitable future, if not an undeniable destiny, for sound. He was William Fox, the restless rover who had pioneered in nickelodeons at the same time as Marcus Loew and was now the absolute sovereign of Fox Films and Fox Theatres. Fox was relentlessly embarking on a campaign to accumulate more power, and he believed that a way to do it was to get ahead of the competition with sound.

Just two weeks before the first public demonstration of Vitaphone—at about the time the aged Thomas Edison was telling reporters there was no future for motion pictures that made a noise—Fox formed a company for the purpose of promoting a sound system developed by Theodore Case. This system, like that of de Forest, worked on the principle of the sound being recorded directly on the film. The sound waves, picked up by a microphone, were transferred into electrical vibrations which, in turn, were changed into light variations that were "photographed" on the edge of the film. When the film was projected, the process was reversed and the recreated sound waves were transmitted to the audience from amplified speakers behind the screen. The Fox-Case system was given an intriguing name: Movietone.

The one weakness of this system was its amplifying unit, so Fox-Case was compelled to make a deal with Western Electric to obtain its superior amplifiers. Thus Western Electric became master of the key equipment used in both Vitaphone and Movietone. This gave a strategic advantage to the electrical company.

The critical importance of its position and the scope of its intentions were clear when, in January, 1927, Western Electric withdrew from the Vitaphone Corporation and formed its own subsidiary company, Electrical Research Products, Inc.—thereafter known as ERPI.

Its aim was the manufacture, rental and sale of equipment for the recording and projecting of sound. Thenceforth, the Vitaphone Corporation was simply the Warners' facility for producing films.

The Patents War Is On

With this development, it was evident that control of the machinery of sound would be as much of a consideration as its practicality. Already Westinghouse and General Electric were coming forward with sound systems of their own, as were several other promoters. The major companies, outside of Warners and Fox, were in a spot where they had to decide which—if any—of the rival systems they would adopt. Prudently, the five top companies, led by Paramount and Metro-Goldwyn-Mayer, and including Universal, First National and Producers Distributing, agreed to stick together and make no final or conclusive move until they had examined and settled upon one system to be used by all.

Their policy of watchful waiting plus some cautious experimenting on the part of Paramount, continued as Fox came forward with its first Movietone films in newsreel form, and the Warners, impatient and anxious, turned out more Vitaphone shorts, plus one other feature picture, *When a Man Loves*, with a synchronized score.

Then, in the spring and summer of 1927, there came a drop of truly alarming proportions in public attendance at films. For no then apparent reason, patronage fell away off and the concern of industry leaders was with matters more pressing than sound. The standard economy measure of salary cuts was ordered in the studios. Personnel troubles developed, and, for the first time, Hollywood had a major labor crisis on its hands.

On top of all this, the court decision abolishing block-booking was handed down and a Federal Trade Conference on industry practices was ominously ordered to be held in New York. In the face of such accumulated troubles, the industry leaders virtually thanked their lucky stars that, at least, they hadn't got themselves committed to the expense and uncertainty of sound.

Of course, it is always hard to fathom the tides of public taste. Fluctuations in movie attendance have invariably baffled theatre men. But it is safe to surmise, from this distance and from the evidence of later events, that the 1927 plunge in business was due in some measure to ennui and impatience with silent films.

The illusions of soundless movies had prevailed as entertainment and as art so long as the public was unaccustomed to being stimulated by mechanical music and voice. But as soon as the public's ears were opened by the device of the radio, as they were, during the mid-1920's, to an extent that was profound, and people's minds were stimulated to create images to match what they heard, a vague sense of the lack of aural content in motion pictures began to be felt. A subtle psychological rejection of the incongruity of the silent screen occurred.

This feeling of insufficiency undoubtedly contributed much to the public's deviation from movie going in that critical year. This is actually what theatre men were blaming when they cried out, as they did, with characteristic resentment, against "the menace of radio." But the matter was too abstract and devious for their understanding then. Circumstances beyond their calculation had to bring them around to a discovery of the necessity and the commercial salvation that lay in sound.

Then, on the ordinary evening of October 5, there occurred the event that has been universally reckoned the big turning point for sound. It was the première of *The Jazz Singer* at the Warner Theatre in New York—a film made mighty by the mere fact that in it Al Jolson spoke a few lines and sang two songs.

The drama itself was mediocre. It had to do with a Jewish rabbi's son who defied his orthodox father's wishes that he become a cantor in the synagogue. Instead, he became a night-club singer. In the end, however, he fulfilled his parent's dying prayer by singing the traditional lament, the *Kol Nidre*, at his funeral.

The whole thing was thoroughly sentimental and Jolson, who played the role of the "jazz singer," gave it all the gusto of his minstrel-man style and his unctuous voice. The initial line of dialogue did not come until the picture was well along. Then Jolson, made up in blackface, said, "You ain't heard nothin' yet, folks!" (he was supposedly addressing a night-club audience), and began bellowing *Mammy*, a maudlin song.

The people in the theatre were transported. For the first time, the poignant sentiments of a character in a movie were audibly conveyed. The voice wrought the simple magic of making emotion eloquent and real. It added another dimension to the image of the person on the screen. When Jolson finally sang the *Kol Nidre*, tears flowed copiously. When it was done, they found the actor in the audience and made him go up and take bows.

For all the enthusiasm at the *Jazz Singer* première, there was no particular excitement in trade circles the following day. Industry men were much more worked up about the pending conference on trade practices. (At that conference, which followed in a few days, there was not a single resolution mentioning sound.) The general feeling was that *The Jazz Singer* was just another good synchronized film. The emphasis on economy was still strong in the industry. The cost of equipping a theatre to project Vitaphone and Movietone, both now manufactured by ERPI, ran from $8,000 to $15,000. This was an expense that could be risked by only the more successful theatres, of which there were very few. By the end of 1927, three months after *The Jazz Singer* was first shown, there were no more than 157 houses throughout the country "wired for sound."

However, events that winter hastened the inevitable change. The most compelling was the success of *The Jazz Singer* everywhere it was shown with sound. It played for as long as eight weeks in some cities where three to four weeks was an excellent run, and it did as well—or better—on repeat engagements as it did the first time round. The Warners were finally collecting the winnings from their gamble on Vitaphone. Theatre owners, overwhelmed by the public's interest, began clamoring to get their houses "wired."

Simultaneously, it became apparent that General Electric and Westinghouse, now combined with the Radio Corporation of America, were set to push their sound system, Photophone. They acquired a substantial interest in the film distributing firm of F.B.O. Inexorably the policy makers of major companies were forced to move.

On May 15, 1928, Paramount, United Artists and Metro-Goldwyn-Mayer signed with ERPI to install its equipment in their studios at a cost to the latter company of $100,000 a year. They agreed the system used would be Movietone. Nicholas Schenck announced shortly thereafter that 15 to 20 per cent of the pictures to be made that year at Culver City would be in sound; also that $3,000,000 would be spent immediately to wire the Loew theatres.

Thus the major forces of the motion picture industry crossed the Rubicon of sound.

CHAPTER XVI

THE LION'S FIRST ROARS

As soon as the businessmen made their decision, the great problem of harnessing and adapting sound to the medium of motion pictures fell to the people at the studio, to the writers, directors, technicians, the actors and producers who made the films.

In June, 1927, Irving Thalberg had said, "The talking motion picture has its place, as has color photography, but I do not believe [it] will ever replace the silent drama any more than I believe colored photography will replace entirely the present black-and-white." Now it was up to Thalberg, as much as anyone, to find out if it would.

Already Paramount, which had tested the General Electric system with its *Wings,* had a good sound department started. Mayer and Thalberg, falling in, assigned Douglas Shearer, who had been brought back to the studio in the camera department, to go East to the Bell Laboratories and acquire all the knowledge he could about sound. He was to have the job of top technician. Eddie Mannix was named to take charge of a new sound department in Culver City, and "Major" Edward Bowes was to run a studio for the making of Metro-Movietone shorts in New York.

Taking their cue from the initial experiences of Warner and Fox, Thalberg and Mayer decided that the studio's first venture with sound would be by way of equipping one of their finished silent films with a synchronized score. For the purpose, they picked a good one—*White Shadows in the South Seas.*

Even at the time of its selection for what came to be a distinguished role in the history of the company, this film had already been the center of a tempest that is worth remembering. When Thalberg scheduled the picture for production in 1927, he made the particular specification that it should be filmed in the South Seas. A method of pictorial storytelling against authentic backgrounds was being pursued by him, and he chose as particularly suitable for such treatment the then best-selling tales of the South Pacific, written by Frederick William O'Brien.

Emerging at the time as a director was Robert Flaherty, whose *Nanook of the North* and *Moana* had excitingly revealed a new and sensitive artist at capturing the poetry of primitive peoples on film.

Thalberg got interested in him and signed him to direct *White Shadows in the South Seas,* with the promise that he would be allowed to shoot the whole thing in Tahiti, where the beautiful *Moana* was made.

But a stubborn mistrust on the part of Mayer towards directors with suspected temperaments—and Flaherty was already known to be one who took plenty of time—caused him to insist that another director be sent along as "studio representative" and "associate" to Flaherty. The man who got this assignment was W. S. (Woody) Van Dyke, a spirited young fellow whose previous work for the studio had been mainly directing low-budget westerns, starring the cowboy actor, Tim McCoy.

No sooner had the company reached Tahiti than trouble began. Flaherty was disgusted at the requirement that he use the Hollywood actor, Monte Blue, and the Mexican actress, Raquel Torres, to play the leading Polynesian roles. He was further vexed at the romantic and synthetic scenario. His hope was to gather his story as he went along—which, of course, was out of the question to the practical-minded men at the studio.

After a few weeks of aggravated shooting, Flaherty threw in the sponge, was released from his contract by cable and indignantly returned home. Van Dyke, a notorious "one-take shooter," was left to finish the film. Thanks to cameraman Clyde De Vinna, he got some scenic stuff of the South Seas, but the weak story and atrocious acting drained the picture of "poetry."

Thus did the great Robert Flaherty, later hailed as the dean of documentary films, have his one classic experience with Metro-Goldwyn-Mayer. And thus did "Woody" Van Dyke acquire for himself a new prestige.

No sound recording equipment had yet been installed at the studio. So they sent a print of *White Shadows* East with Shearer to the Victor Recording Company at Camden, New Jersey, and it was there that the first musical score for a Metro-Goldwyn-Mayer film was prepared. For this first job, the synchronized score was put on discs, in the method of Vitaphone. Some sound effects of breaking surf, shouts and wailing—and one word of dialogue, "hello"—were also dubbed. This first of the company's sound pictures was presented at the Astor Theatre in New York on July 31, 1928. It was crude, but it drew the customers.

It also had another distinction. It was the first film introduced by the roaring Metro-Goldwyn-Mayer lion.

While in the East, Shearer recruited a crew of some twenty technicians and engineers which he took back to the studio as the nucleus of a sound department. Everything was now technological. The monster of sound was fearsome. No move was made without "technical advice." Professor Verne Knudson, an expert on acoustics at the University of California in Los Angeles, was engaged to design new sound stages. He advised construction of huge brick-and-concrete barns, set on twenty-foot-deep concrete pilings to guard against "vibration." Forts could not have been built more firmly. Later it was found that thoroughly sound-proof buildings could be had by simply enclosing rock-wool insulation between two shells of light materials. But those first two sound stages, constructed in the summer of 1928, were put up like storage warehouses, which is what they are actually used for today. They stand on the lot as silent monuments to the terror and confusion of the taking-on of sound.

Even before the completion of its sound stages, Metro-Goldwyn-Mayer proceeded with its program of sound pictures by arranging with Paramount to use the recording facilities already installed at that studio. It was there that the dialogue sequences for the company's first "talking picture" were prepared. The picture was the already completed silent rendering of the old favorite, *Alias Jimmy Valentine*, in which the leading male roles were taken by William Haines and Lionel Barrymore.

Haines was one of the most active and popular of the young stars of Metro-Goldwyn-Mayer. He had started with the old Goldwyn company and had plugged his way through countless comedies and assorted silent dramas to a point of great favor with the fans. But he was so overwhelmed with anxiety as he stood up to a microphone for the first time that he almost collapsed when some joker, in the dead-silent studio, sneezed. Barrymore, who was a veteran stage actor and had already appeared in the Warners' part-dialogue film, *The Lion and the Mouse*, helped to steady the nerves of the star. It took them several days to complete the synchronized dialogue that was dubbed onto the last two reels of the film.

The ordeal was piteous and prophetic, for Haines, who was the studio's first top star to do lines in the new sound pictures, was one of the first of many to go because he was completely unable to make the fans like his strangely high-pitched voice. Without knowing it, he was embarking on his way out with *Alias Jimmy Valentine*. On the other hand, Barrymore, his supporter, who had been a middling screen actor up to this time, went on to become a famous and beloved talking-picture star at Metro-Goldwyn-Mayer.

This matter of the quality of their voices suddenly became the grave concern not only of the actors but of the heads of the studios as well. They were eager to reassure the public of the vocal magnificence of their stars. Thalberg hastened to get out a short film, which was presented with *Alias Jimmy Valentine* at the Astor Theatre in New York in November, 1928, in which top stars such as Norma Shearer, John Gilbert and Joan Crawford were permitted to make their vocal bows. The problem of voice was to be a challenge—and an enigma—for the next few years.

First Call for Musicians

More pressing at the moment, however, were the problems of simply licking the mechanics of sound, setting up facilities for its production and learning what to do with it. Obviously, a need for music—lots of music—was initially imposed, and it soon became clear that special composers and arrangers would be required. The crude jobs of putting together music for the first synchronized films of the studio were done by orchestrators picked up in Los Angeles. But Shearer soon found that the complexities of matching music to scenes, of cutting sound tracks to fit the cutting of the pictures, called for a new kind of musical specialist.

He explained this to Thalberg and Mannix. Thalberg could not understand why music could not be recorded to play as a mere accompaniment, as it did with silent films. It took a good deal of persuasion and demonstration to bring him around to the realization that a music department would have to be set up at the studio. When he got it, he called in Martin Broones, a young composer of musical shows, to head up a new department and then sent a call to New York for the top arrangers and the whole music library of the Capitol Theatre to be hurried out to the Coast. In October, the Robbins Music Company was purchased outright in order to obtain its catalogue of songs. The task of turning out music became as pressing as turning out scripts.

Here was another great problem. What sort of dramatic material—and what sort of preparation of it—would be most suitable for sound? The writers and directors soon discovered that action, which was the heart of silent films, had to be virtually abandoned to make way for dialogue. This was a form of expression that the old scenarists found hard to understand.

As Chapin Hall said in an article published in the New York *Times* on July 8, 1928,

> A new type of story will have to be devised—something that will bridge the gap between action and talk. Present sound films are interesting as novelties, but as pictures they are flops. The abrupt changes of tempo when the words stop and the action resumes is a terrific strain on the credulity of the customers.

The rigidness of the scenes with dialogue was forced, to a large extent, by the bulk and the immobility of the early sound equipment. The cameras were set inside "greenhouses"—big glass-enclosed, sound-proof booths, designed to muffle the whir of the cameras so it would not be picked up by the microphones. The camera operators almost suffocated when they wedged into these coops to shoot a scene. The things were so heavy and cumbersome that they could not be moved during a shot. Each "take" had to be made from a fixed position, with the camera held steadily on the scene.

Likewise, the microphones were so crude, in comparison with what they later came to be, that the actors had to stand close beside them and not move too much one way or the other when they talked. The trick was to hide the microphones at predetermined spots on the set where the director wished the actors to speak their lines. The consequence was that the actors were always immobile when they spoke.

Some slight relief from this rigidity was afforded with the invention of the "boom"—a long, movable pole from the end of which a microphone was suspended directly above the actor's head. (Naturally, the "boom" and the microphone were kept just out of the camera's range.) By virtue of it, the actors could move around more freely, as the microphone was made to follow them.

Credit for conceiving this apparatus has been given generally to Lionel Barrymore, who—doubling, as he did, as a director—is supposed to have called for a fishing pole and suspended a microphone from it while directing an early sound short. But the man who actually had the brilliant idea was Eddie Mannix. He went on a set one day where a team of string instrumentalists, the Hollywood Trio, was trying to do a number for a short with the microphone hanging above them from a crude sort of movable gauntry frame. The thing was exceedingly clumsy, and the carpenters who had built it simply couldn't make it work. Mannix watched for a few minutes, then suggested that they try rigging up an apparatus on the order of an old-fashioned well sweep on which to swing the microphone. The carpenters hastily followed his suggestion, using a long timber, weighted with a sandbag on one end. It filled the bill very nicely. That was the birth of the "boom."

Through those fearful months of exploration, during the summer and fall of 1928, Thalberg had some misgivings, but he maintained an enthusiastic front and constantly pepped up his associates who inclined to frustration and despair.

"Keep this in mind," he would tell them. "We know as much about sound as anybody does."

That wasn't too much encouragement, but it stated the case accurately.

The obvious convenience of music as a means of conveying sound led to the selection of stories in which songs could be used dramatically. The Warners had run to night-club stories. Thalberg was one of the first to sense the possibilities of a musical-comedy film.

The studio was still in the phase of putting synchronized scores and dialogue on its already finished silent pictures such as *Our Dancing Daughters, The Bellamy Trial, While the City Sleeps, The Wind, Lady of Chance* and *The Bridge of San Luis Rey,* when work was started on what turned out to be its first all-talking film and the first of a long line of musicals, which became a specialty of Metro-Goldwyn-Mayer.

Eddie Goulding, a versatile director, had sold Thalberg a story about a vaudeville sister-team, somewhat like the famed Duncan Sisters. It was a conventional sentimental tale of the heartbreaks and successes of show people, but Thalberg liked it and ordered it made. Then sound came and he decided it would be done as the studio's first all-talking film. Lawrence Weingarten, who had just wed Thalberg's sister, Sylvia, was assigned to supervise. They were ready to go when Thalberg decided it should have some special musical numbers as well. This presented a question of who would write the songs.

A popular and resourceful title-writer at the studio was Ralph Spence. He suggested the assignment be given to two friends of his who were then putting on tabloid stage shows at a palaestra called the Orange Grove Theatre in Los Angeles. Thalberg called in the two fellows and assigned them to write some songs. He was so casual about it that he didn't even catch their names. He referred to them as "the real estate man and the piano player." They were Nacio Herb Brown and Arthur Freed.

The first song they did was a little number they called *Broadway Melody.* Then they did one for a chorus dance routine. This was called *The Wedding of the Painted Doll.* A third was a romantic ditty, *You Were Meant For Me.*

Before they were turned in to Thalberg, he had been approached by one of the mob of Tin Pan Alley tunesmiths who flocked to Hollywood with the coming of sound. This fellow—a sturdy little hustler by the name of Billy Rose—wanted to sell a batch of his songs for the picture. Thalberg agreed to listen to them, and Rose turned up with an orchestra to play his repertoire. This made quite a difference. Thalberg was almost convinced.

However, he told Brown and Freed that he would give them an equal chance to prove their songs. So they arranged to play them on a radio broadcast from the Los Angeles station, KFI. Thalberg, Norma Shearer and Weingarten went to the studio to hear the numbers done. Brown played the piano, Freed sang the words. Even so, Thalberg decided that theirs were the songs he would use. Thus what came to be a memorable musical score was first presented to the public as an audition on the radio.

Norman Houston and James Gleason wrote the dialogue for the picture. Harry Beaumont directed it, and its stars were Bessie Love, Anita Page and Charles King. It took all of thirty days to shoot it, and its total cost was $350,000, including the use of color for the big chorus production number to *The Wedding of the Painted Doll.*

The decision to use color on that number was a bold one for Thalberg to make, but he topped it when he later ordered the completed sequence to be reshot. He had been in New York when they first filmed it and looked at the footage on his return. He thought it smacked too much of a stage number that had been photographed literally from one spot. He was right. The task of shooting from the "greenhouse" had inhibited the camera work. Thalberg got a dance director to lay out new routines that would be interesting when viewed from different angles. "Now do it over again," he said.

The effort was eminently worth it. The number was vastly improved by the essentially cinematic treatment. Thalberg's instincts were sound.

The aim was to call the picture *Whoopee*, but Florenz Ziegfeld got ahead of them by putting that tag on the musical show he presented that winter on Broadway. So they settled for calling it by the title of its song, *The Broadway Melody.* It was given its première at Grauman's Chinese Theatre in Los Angeles on February 1, 1929, to become the first definite musical picture out of any studio. It was followed in April by Universal's *Showboat*, and in May by Paramount's *The Cocoanuts* and R.K.O.'s *Rio Rita*, all done from stage musicals. An original, *The Broadway Melody*, came first.

The Mother of Invention

They made a discovery while redoing the *Painted Dolls* number that was to be of invaluable convenience and economy in the future making of musical films. When Thalberg ordered the original footage tossed into the ash can, it occurred to Douglas Shearer that it would be a shame and a waste to abandon the musical recording that had been made along with it. Not only was it a good recording, but it would cost a lot of money to call back a full orchestra to play the music while they were shooting the scene again.

Shearer told Thalberg he had an idea: why not shoot the scene to an amplified play-back of the recording and then match the footage and the recording in the cutting-room? Thalberg was persuaded they could do it, and the experiment was successfully tried. Thus the technique of "pre-scoring" was devised on the first musical film. Later, they discovered it was practical even to record vocal numbers in advance and then have the performer synchronize his (or her) lip movements to the play-back while the scene was being photographed.

An amusing reverse of this procedure, which occurred about the same time, resulted in a later famous song being saved for posterity. Woody Van Dyke was back in the South Seas shooting another Polynesian romance—this one called *The Pagan*. Ramon Novarro and Renee Adoree were its stars. It was being shot "silent" but dialogue was to be dubbed later in the studio. In keeping with the new convention, Novarro had to do a song, so they got Brown and Freed to write a number and sent the lyrics out for the star to "mouth" in the close-up scenes.

All went well, but when the picture was completed and the company had returned, the word began to spread that the song was no good and they should have a better one. (Jealousy and sabotage among song writers had been extended to Hollywood.) But then they realized they couldn't change it, because new lyrics would not synchronize with the already photographed movement of Novarro's lips in the close-up shots. So that's how *The Pagan Love Song* was saved from being tossed in the can.

Simultaneous with the preparation of *The Broadway Melody*, Thalberg and his people were making ready their first "all-talking" dramatic film. It was to be *The Trial of Mary Dugan*, which had been a recently popular courtroom play on Broadway, and Thalberg had the confidence and valor to cast his wife, Norma Shearer, in the leading role. Naturally, a play that had been proved before audiences was regarded as safe—or as safe as could be expected—for an initial try with dialogue.

Even so, Thalberg was ultra-cautious in making preparations for it. He was reluctant, at first, to let Norma do it, because of the type of the character. It was that of a show girl on trial for murder—a rather brassy, unseemly role. She persuaded him to let her try it by demonstrating that she could do a few scenes after practicing them with Bayard Veillier, the original playwright, who was brought out to direct.

However, that wasn't enough for Thalberg. He assembled a hand-picked cast which included Lewis Stone, H. B. Warner and Raymond Hackett, all veterans of the stage, and he had them rehearse the play for two weeks on an improvised courtroom set. Then he had them act it before a studio audience. He said, "They'll be the jury; I'll be the judge." The performance went off nicely. Thalberg said, "Go ahead, do the film."

Actually, the picture was not too different from a straight photograph of the staged play. It was "not blessed with any great abundance of imagination from the cinematic viewpoint," as one reviewer said. However, it was judged "highly effective" when it was released in March, 1929, and Norma was found to "reveal herself quite able to meet the requirements of that tempermental device, the microphone."

CHAPTER XVII

A FOX TRIES TO SWALLOW THE LION

IN THE midst of the industry's confusion in the late fall of 1928, while the studios and theatres were struggling with the problems of switching to sound, weird and perplexing rumors began to circulate that something important was cooking between Loew's, Inc., and William Fox. These were disquieting rumors, because by now it was evident that Fox was boldly and candidly maneuvering to get control of the whole industry, and the one company that seemed most dependable as a barrier against him was Loew's. That a deal might be making up between them was a grave and disturbing thought.

Fox, a notoriously savage lone wolf since the days when he ripped into the Trust and went on to become a big producer and owner of theatres, had greatly expanded his holdings since 1924 and had worked himself into a strong position by his initial promotion of Movietone. Starting his campaign by acquiring a heavy interest in a Chicago theatre chain, he made his intentions apparent in 1925 by buying an influential holding in the West Coast Theatres, Inc.

This strong group of independent houses owned a key franchise in the First National, and Fox's sudden wedging into it caused the other franchise holders justifiable alarm. Through a firm of New York bankers, they formed a corporation, Wesco, to buy up the remaining holdings in West Coast Theatres and five small chains, primarily for the purpose of overwhelming Fox. But two years later, when it appeared that First National was going to pieces in the slump preceding sound, the bankers got nervous and unloaded to the very fellow they were out to foil. Thus Fox picked up all the Wesco theatres and a key franchise in First National.

Meanwhile, the crafty operator had taken the precaution to set himself up so that his huge personal holdings were divided between his new Fox Theatres Corporation and his original Fox Films. By this forehand maneuver, he protected his studio from loss in case his theatre pyramid should tumble. And he precluded (he thought) the possible charge of "trust." His shrewd legal counsel, Saul Rogers, had a long memory.

This was just the beginning. In March 1927, Fox made a sensational splatter by buying the new Roxy Theatre in New York, two weeks after this spectacular show place had had its elaborate opening. He used the 6,000-seat theatre—"the Cathedral of Motion Pictures," it was tagged—as the bejeweled and impressive showcase for oncoming Movietone. A year later, he moved into New England by getting the twenty houses of the Poli chain.

Then, in good time, lawyer Rogers and another henchman, A. C. Blumenthal, began putting together a circuit of some 130 theatres in and around New York, which was known as Fox Metropolitan Theatres when it was launched in January 1929.

It was during the assembly of this circuit that the rumors of a deal with Loew's began to spread.

At once, the suspected parties came out with unqualified denials. "Were it not for the fact that such reports are apt to do harm," said Nicholas Schenck, "this newest rumor would be the most ridiculously amusing gossip that I have heard in years." And Fox parried questions succinctly. "I have no interest in acquiring the (Loew's) chain," he said.

However, industry people put little faith in denials, and speculation was rampant as to what might be in the air. It was even suggested as likely that there would be a giant merger of Loew's and Fox, in which Joe Schenck's United Artists and mighty Paramount would have to join to survive.

"But then anything is possible these days," quipped *Variety*. "It's merging time!"

That was the frightening realization. A few months previously, the Radio Corporation of America had firmed-up its place in the field of films by organizing Radio-Keith-Orpheum, through a merger of the producing company, FBO, and the Keith-Albee-Orpheum circuit of theatres. Warner Brothers was expanding mightily by acquiring the powerful group of Stanley Theatres in a move to consolidate its gains with sound. The dread was that everybody might soon be caught in this race for power. Rumors were that both R.K.O. and Warners were anxious to consolidate with Loew's.

Thus, there was acute anticipation when the portentous word went out on an ordinarily idle Sunday morning, March 3, 1929, that William Fox would have an important announcement to make at four o'clock that afternoon. Reporters flocked to his sumptuous offices above the Roxy Theatre at the appointed hour. Fox entered precisely at the moment an antique clock in the room struck four. He was flanked on one side by Winfield Sheehan, his resourceful right-hand man, and on the other by Nicholas Schenck and Dave Bernstein, the wizard treasurer of Loew's, Inc.

With an air of elaborate formality, Fox first introduced himself and the three gentlemen with him (who were known to everybody in the room). Next he gave the impatient reporters a brief resume of his career, which was not untinged with a suggestion of the genius of William Fox. Then he came to his announcement. It was, bluntly, that he had got control of Loew's Inc., by acquiring "a substantial block" of its common stock.

Despite all the rumors that went before it, the announcement exploded like a bomb. Not a reporter in the room was expecting such an incredible piece of news. That Loew's Inc., a top major company, should fall under the control of Fox was almost as hard to imagine as that the United States should fall into the hands of Mexico. Here was a healthy organization whose income had been soaring every year since it accomplished the highly successful merger of Metro-Goldwyn-Mayer. Its annual report, issued in September, had shown a profit of over $8,500,000 for the preceding fiscal year. How did this lionlike corporation become a prey for the wily Fox—and why?

Schenck was bland and noncommittal, other than to confirm the accuracy of Fox's statement, plus the further assurance that Loew's, Inc., would continue in operation as an "independent entity." (The next day, he explained that the erstwhile rivals would thenceforth "make their plans with full knowledge of each others commitments," thus coordinating their affairs.) However, a second statement, issued that day by Arthur Loew, gave an initial inkling of what had actually occurred.

Loew said that he, his brother David, their mother and their father's estate had pooled all their common stock holdings in the company, amounting to some 230,000 shares, and had sold them to Fox for a consideration that was then unspecified.

This seemed a candid explanation—until it was realized that there were more than 1,300,000 outstanding common shares and that a block of 230,000 would scarcely constitute control. It looked as though Fox was bluffing—unless he had got a lot of shares from somewhere else.

It took a few days for the reporters to collect enough details to assure them that Fox wasn't bluffing and that the sell-out wasn't entirely by the Loews. And, as the full story fell together, it caused amazement, indignation and wrath.

Briefly, this is what happened (though some of the facts reported here did not become general knowledge for months—or even years):

Back in October, Fox's henchman, Blumenthal, had a sudden hunch that he might be able to arrange it so that his boss could grab a controlling block of Loew's shares. (Blumenthal, though a semi-midget, was never at a loss for big ideas.) He talked it over with his employer, to whom the chance of getting the Loew's theatres was as tempting as the chance of getting Metro-Goldwyn-Mayer. Fox gave Blumenthal the green light to see what he could do, with the understanding that he would have to move in secret and pay above the market price for the shares.

Blumenthal, keen at such maneuvering, went to Nicholas Schenck and said that he was able to make an attractive offer for a big block of Loew's stock. At first, Schenck was cool and suspicious. After all, how did he know whether this was a serious proposition or merely an attempt by Fox to spy? He tested the offer by suggesting that $125 a share was the price that would have to be paid for such a delivery. The stock was then selling on the market at around sixty-three.

Fox balked at the high figure. Schenck wouldn't budge. The conversations were continued. Many times, Schenck attempted to call them off. Finally, Fox agreed to pay him $125 a share for a block of 400,000. He knew that R.K.O. and Warners were also eager to get control of Loew's.

Now Schenck was faced with the problem of collecting the 400,000 shares. He had already put the proposition squarely to Arthur Loew. Loew had decided with his mother and brother that they would relinquish their shares to Schenck at $102.50, which was some forty dollars above the market price. The family felt this would give them a handsome profit and they could then diversify their funds, rather than keep them concentrated in the uncertain film industry. The difference between what they got and the price that Fox would pay would constitute a bonus to Schenck for arranging the deal.

Next, he and Bernstein, whom he brought in as his associate in the enterprise, bent to the task of gathering the remaining 170,000 shares. Neither of them was a big stockholder, despite the positions they held. Between them, they got together some 45,000 shares. So, with secrecy and caution, they judiciously approached other selected stockholders and invited them in on the juicy deal.

David Warfield, the old friend of the founder and now a director of the company, was attracted by the proposition. He put in some 38,000 shares. The Shuberts, who had been Loew stockholders since 1910, put in 17,000 more. All the Loew, Schenck and Bernstein relatives who held shares (and they were legion!) were cut in. They were paid up to $105 a share for their holdings. The balance went to Schenck and Bernstein.

The secrecy of the operation was, indeed, so successful that Robert Rubin, one of the company's legal counsel and Eastern representative of the "Mayer group," did not know what was happening.

Schenck studiously put him off, when he asked about the rumors. He was as surprised as anyone at the ultimate news.

As soon as Schenck had the stock assembled, the exchange of it was arranged. Arthur Loew was then in London to attend the grand opening of the company's new Empire Theatre. The night before the big occasion, he got a message from Schenck to come right home. He boarded the *Berengaria* the next morning, leaving his London people mystified.

The exchange took place in a banking office in New York on February 28. It was a strictly private transaction; no brokers' fees, no ticker flash. Schenck and Arthur Loew delivered the stock certificates, Fox delivered the cash. That is to say, he delivered $15,000,000 which he had borrowed from the American Telephone and Telegraph Company's ERPI as a token of their faith in pending negotiations to get sound film patents from him. The remaining money was being assembled from various investment houses and banks and from the sale of new shares in Fox Theatres Corporation, to which the Loew shares were carefully consigned. Until this money was delivered, the Loew shares were held by the bank. That day the Loew's stock closed on the market at eighty-four.

Thus the transaction was completed and made ready for announcement on March 3.

The industry's amazement was as nothing to the fury of Mayer and Thalberg, who, like Rubin, had got no indication of what was pending from Schenck or from the Loews. Mayer was en route to Washington for the inauguration of President Hoover on March 4, when the word reached him in New Orleans. He telephoned Schenck in New York. What did this mean, he demanded—selling the company to Fox? And why weren't he and his partners notified of the deal?

Later that week, Mayer and Thalberg descended on New York, Mayer coming up from Washington and Thalberg rushing in from the Coast. Their anger was deep and dangerous. They boldly and bluntly charged Schenck with selling the company down the river and claimed their contracts were thereby null and void.

There was a point to their anger. They held, not unreasonably, that much of the company's prosperity in the past four years had been due to the general quality of the pictures turned out by the studio. For this, of course, they took credit. That Schenck should then realize upon the increased value of the company by engineering the sale of control to Fox, for no other evident purpose than to make a profit for himself and his friends, seemed to them a piece of

personal opportunism that woefully betrayed the "Mayer group."
By this maneuver, Schenck opened an ugly and unforgettable wound.

That matter of Schenck's and Bernstein's profit was particularly
galling when it was realized that they had picked up for themselves
in "bonuses" some $9,000,000 or more. Ruefully, it was remembered
that Schenck had solemnly proclaimed, at the time he took over the
presidency of the company, less than two years before: "There shall
be no personal aggrandizement. The organization rises above any
one individual."

Even though Mayer and Thalberg hollered, there was nothing
they could do. The fact that Fox had become a big stockholder did
not affect the corporate structure of Loew's, Inc. Their contract was
still in operation, and had three years to run. What might be done
about it later would probably depend upon Fox. For the time being,
he assured them he had no intention of attempting to disturb the
conspicuously successful operation of the studio. Indeed, he hoped
to maintain it as the facility for producing "class" films. His own
studio would be devoted to making "cheaper" films, he said.

Whatever private arrangements, if any, were made by Schenck to
pacify the irate producers have never been fully revealed. Mayer and
Rubin have insisted that they did not take a cent of the sizable share
of the "bonus" that Schenck and Bernstein later offered to pass along
to them. Mayer and others have stated that Thalberg did accept
$250,000 as a token of gratitude. It is fair to believe that he did so,
for, shortly after, he returned to the studio in a relaxed state of mind
and with assurance to the anxious personnel that "the integrity of
the Metro-Goldwyn-Mayer organization will be preserved." But
to close friends, he muttered grimly, "If Winnie Sheehan walks into
my office, I walk out!"

Meanwhile, Mayer remained impassive to the studied endeavors
of Fox to make a respectful friend of him, and he candidly reminded
his "new boss" (as Sheehan jauntily put it) that the acquisition of the
Loew's shares might get him into trouble with the Justice Department of the United States.

"They're very particular about companies getting too damn big,"
he said.

Fox dismissed the warning. "We've already got their okay," he
replied. "And, besides, my friend Greenfield in Philadelphia has the
President in his back pocket."

Albert M. Greenfield, the chairman of the Bankers Security Corporation, was a close friend of Fox, and had put up $10,000,000 to
go toward the purchase of the Loew shares.

"I don't know anybody who has the President of the United States in his back pocket," Mayer snapped. Fox was touching upon a subject that was especially close to him.

For two or three years, Mayer had been playing a private but ardent hand in Republican politics in California. Through Ida Koverman, a lady of rare political talent and influence, he had met Herbert Hoover shortly after the 1924 Presidential campaign, and, in his vigorous fashion, had made the gentleman a close personal friend. Indeed, he had introduced him to William Randolph Hearst and had been influential in urging Hearst's support of Hoover as the Republican Presidential candidate in 1928. Mayer himself was a delegate from California to the Republican National convention that year and had helped to nominate Hoover. He had connections, too.

In fact, his acceptability was conspicuously indicated within a few days when he, his wife and their two daughters went to Washington to spend the night as the guests of the Hoovers in the White House. They were the first overnight guests to be entertained unofficially by the Hoovers in their new domicile. At that particular juncture, this was a definite coup for Mayer. He said he had been offered the ambassadorship to Turkey by the President. That was, perhaps, an overstatement of a suggestion made in jest. What was more important, he had been able to let a word drop here and there of his distinct disapproval and suspicions of the legality of the Fox deal.

There were no further surprises or even rumblings during the next few months. Fox gave no indication that he meant to consolidate his gain. For all that was evident to outsiders, he was just another stockholder in Loew's. What he might do in the future was anybody's guess.

Actually, he had his own worries. He was privately told by Harry Stuart of Halsey, Stuart & Company, investment bankers, who had also loaned him money for the Loew's buy, that he still didn't have enough shares to assure himself of unchallenged control. So he secretly went into the open market and began buying up additional shares until he had 260,000 more tucked away. These were bought in small lots on huge margins and were registered in various names to disguise their actual possessor. Fox used all his available cash for these purchases.

And still he was tirelessly predacious. In May, 1929, he arranged with Isador Ostrer to buy control of the Gaumont chain of 300 theatres in Great Britain for $20,000,000. Again he had to borrow for this venture. But money was easy to get in those last days of extravagant boom and inflation. Fox was way over his head.

Off to Rome for the filming of "Ben Hur." Marcus Loew (rear row, in cap) departs aboard the *Leviathan*. In this party of voyagers and well-wishers are, front row l. to r., "Major" Bowes, Ramon Novarro, Louis B. Mayer, Nicholas Schenck and J. Robert Rubin; rear row, l. to r., Mrs. Rubin, Joe Dannenberg, Mrs. David Loew, Mrs. Marcus Loew, David Loew, Alice Terry, David Warfield, Enid Bennett, Loew, J. E. D. Meador and Fred Niblo.

Museum of Modern Art Film Library

The chariot race in "Ben Hur" as it was finally filmed in the huge set constructed in Los Angeles to represent the Circus at Antioch.

Museum of Modern Art Film Library

John Gilbert and Lillian Gish in "La Boheme" (1925).

Mae Murray on an outing in 1924.

Greta Garbo and Gilbert in "Flesh and the Devil" (1926), when their w o r l d - f a m o u s infatuation began.

Then fate, which all so often has played a remarkable hand in the fortunes of Loew's, Inc., pulled a lever, and the downfall of Fox began.

Hue and Cry

On July 17, he was driving to play golf on Long Island when his car was in a serious collision. The chauffeur was killed and Fox was badly hurt. He was laid up for weeks, during which time the consolidation of Loew's and Fox was delayed and a plan for the permanent financing of all his short-term commitments was put off. His affairs were in hopeless confusion when, on October 24—Black Thursday in American financial history—the stock market crash began.

Fox tottered back to his office to face a barrage of calls from brokers who were screaming for him to cover the margins on his stock. The Loew shares were tumbling in value, and the bankers who were holding most of those he had bought in the big Loew-Schenck bundle were dogging him about their loans. He soon sold his First National franchise to Warner Brothers in a desperate reach for cash to cover his margins. But he stubbornly clung to his Loew's shares as the anchor of his hopes.

Then, on November 27, the unkindest cut of all came. The Justice Department instituted a dual suit against Fox and Warners for operating as trusts—Fox because of the Loew holdings and Warner Brothers because of its acquisition of First National. Fox was particularly baffled, because he thought, as he had previously told Mayer, that his ownership of shares would be permitted. He later claimed that a change of personnel in the Justice Department between administrations had caused reversal of the ruling given him. He also blamed Mayer for talking against him on that trip to Washington. Mayer frankly acknowledged that he had done so. Fox was not one of his friends.

Anyhow, the immense accumulation of troubles and woes for Fox was more than he could shoulder. In December, he was compelled to relinquish control of both his companies, Fox Theatres Corporation and Fox Films, to a board of trustees, which was headed by Harry Stuart, and John Otterson, the president of ERPI, whose organizations were large Fox creditors. The lawyers for the trustees were the firm of the recent Secretary of State, Charles Evans Hughes.

It would be pointless now to struggle through the long and involved account of Fox's legal and financial writhings and twistings to avoid his ultimate doom. (He came to the end of his dark passage in 1942 when he went to the penitentiary for attempting to bribe a federal judge.) So complex and factious is the story—so laced with

Fox's own outraged complaints that he was the helpless victim of "big business" buccaneers—that it would take a book to tell it. Indeed, it is told in a book, written by Upton Sinclair, which is strongly sympathetic to Fox.

For the purposes of this present story, there are only three things to record as considerable consequences of the strange William Fox episode.

The first is merely in the nature of an instructive irony. It is that Fox got indigestion when he tried to eat the lion. The major mistake in his maneuvering was that he extended himself to capture Loew's and then greedily attempted to hold on to it when the peril of his position was plain. Had he abandoned his ambition and dumped his Loew stock in the 1929 crash, he might have saved himself from downfall. But he wasn't that kind of man.

The second is that the block of 660,900 Loew shares that Fox was forced to put in the hands of trustees was still a controlling interest in Loew's, Inc. And its thus being in the hands of bankers during the subsequent depression years, as it was via various legal routings, had considerable influence upon the caution and circumspection with which Nicholas Schenck and the board of directors administered the company. Later, when this block was finally split up among the banks and other Fox creditors who slowly drained it off into the market during 1934, the consequence was that it dribbled into thousands of investors' hands and Loew's common became, in the 1930's, the most widely held motion picture stock.

The third and perhaps the most unfortunate result of the Fox affair was the hurt that it caused in the relations of the company's top personnel. Mayer, Thalberg and Rubin were inevitably made to feel that an internecine rivalry existed between them and the Schenck cabal in New York. The wound of this candid revelation was eventually to be closed, by the application of one salve or another, and the company was to flourish through the years. But the scar of that wound remained sensitive. It was never to be entirely healed. And it was frequently reopened and expanded. It was finally ruptured beyond repair.

CHAPTER XVIII

PUTTING THINGS ON A SOUND BASIS

IT WAS a cool and determined Irving Thalberg who went back to Culver City in March, 1929, following his lacerating run-in with Schenck over the Fox deal in New York. That cold-blooded pecuniary experience was behind them, so far as he was concerned, and now he was ready to bend his efforts to the one job of turning out films.

Sound still remained a hovering challenge to the creative people in the studio, and there continued to be serious questions as to whether it would become a universal or even a lasting thing. "My personal opinion is that the silent film will never be eliminated," said Nicholas Schenck in a by-line piece published in *Film Daily* as late as May 20, 1929. And he cited the continuing success of the silent versions of such pictures as *Our Dancing Daughters* and *The Duke Steps Out,* as evidence that the public was still paying to see silent films.

The reason for that was simple. Not more than one-fourth of the country's theatres (estimated on the basis of seating capacity) were wired for sound at the time. The rest were waiting for equipment or their owners were vacillating as to whether to risk the cost. There were those who followed Schenck in his opinion that the medium would continue half silent, half sound.

It was to reassure the unwired theatres (and also to protect itself) that Metro-Goldwyn-Mayer announced in April that the fifty "dialogue pictures" it intended to produce that year would also be released in silent versions, except where the nature of the film demanded sound. It announced, too, that foreign-language versions of a few would be made at the same time, pointing with pride to the number of its star performers who could speak foreign tongues. (Actually, the studio did make several complete Spanish and German versions of its films, usually with different casts, over the next few years, but the practice was abandoned when the dubbing of foreign voices was found more practical.)

For all the anxiety of others, Thalberg confidently proclaimed that the season of 1929-30 would be "the greatest" in the history of the studio. He had assured himself by this time that he and his people could do good things with sound. The fact that his prophecy was actually borne out was due to something more than luck. Under the driving direction and inspiration of this intense man who was yet a few months shy of thirty, the whole assemblage of a mighty studio did accomplish the job of delivering a surpassing schedule of sound films that first year.

Already *The Broadway Melody* and *The Trial of Mary Dugan* were out as pilots for other film producers, as well as for Metro-Goldwyn-Mayer. *Madame X* followed shortly. It was a rendering of a mawkish French play about a wayward wife and mother, in which Ruth Chatterton was starred. Lionel Barrymore directed it with forgivable staginess. (Barrymore then had ambitions to be a director in the new medium.) *Madame X* was an unrestrained tear-jerker, to the deep satisfaction of Mayer. But it also pleased the public and was voted one of the best films of the year.

So was *The Last of Mrs. Cheney*, which came along in July—the second of Norma Shearer's "talkies," likewise based on a popular play. In making it, Thalberg ordered they do exactly as they did in making *The Trial of Mary Dugan*—that is, rehearse it as they would a play and present it before a studio audience before shooting a foot of it.

Sidney Franklin was the director, and he and his writer, Claudine West, departed considerably from the stage play of Frederick Lonsdale in preparing it for the screen. Furthermore, they all took rehearsals lightly, including Norma, so that when Thalberg came down to see them run through their performance, they gave an abominable show. Thalberg watched in stony silence. At the conclusion, he said, "Now *that's* done, you'll do *The Last of Mrs. Cheney*. But, before you do, I want to see each one of you separately in my office!" So up they all trooped, including Norma, and were politely made certain that the head of production had no patience for such nonsense. They went to work, then, and made a film.

Also, another outstanding Metro-Goldwyn-Mayer picture of that year was King Vidor's *Hallelujah*, which was extraordinary and memorable because it departed entirely from the conventions of that or any other studio. It told a story of cotton-picking Negroes in the south—a poignant tale of humble, impoverished people, rendered more touching by some beautiful singing of Negro spirituals.

Vidor had been a studio favorite since *The Big Parade*. He had just turned in the last great silent picture of Metro-Goldwyn-Mayer—*The Crowd*. But the thing that recommended *Hallelujah* to Thalberg above all else—even above an offer made by Vidor to Nicholas Schenck to gamble his own salary in the production—was the fact that it was a story told with music. The dramatic potential of song was still the one proven insurance that all the studios were depending upon.

A good proportion of the pictures laid down by Metro-Goldwyn-Mayer that year had somebody singing in them. They were either straight musical shows or music was used as communication to do the service of words. Lawrence Tibbett, the Metropolitan Opera baritone, was hustled out to Culver City to do *The Rogue Song* of Franz Lehár. Three-quarters of it was music, and audiences were quite amused when Tibbett, stripped to the waist and being horse-whipped, poured out his agony in song. This sort of operatic behavior was something that movie audiences had to become accustomed to. Tibbett was next teamed with Grace Moore, another Metropolitan Opera recruit, in a remarkably gaudy version of the stage musical, *New Moon*.

Marion Davies, whose first talking picture was the uncertain *Marianne*, was swept into the musical spiral in *The Florodora Girl*. Ramon Novarro, still the most romantic male star of Metro-Goldwyn-Mayer, did *Call of the Flesh*. In this elaborate heartbreak story he played a Spanish opera singer whose big success was with the farewell aria of *Pagliacci*, which Mayer persisted in referring to as *Laugh, Clown, Laugh*. And Joan Crawford, who was now the studio's answer to Paramount's Clara Bow, was starred in a rapid succession of films about jazz-mad girls.

Meanwhile, the hearty reception of *The Broadway Melody* had inspired the throwing together of another fast musical which they called *The Hollywood Revue*.

The job of assemblying this potpourri of songs and vaudeville turns fell to that ex-vaudevillian and work horse of the studio, Harry Rapf. He got his old pal, Gus Edwards, to write the music and play a role in it. Practically every star in the studio (except Garbo) did a turn, from Buster Keaton playing a sozzled submariner to Norma Shearer and John Gilbert doing the balcony scene from *Romeo and Juliet*. William Haines, Joan Crawford, Marion Davies, Bessie Love and Charles King did songs and skits. Conrad Nagel and Jack Benny were masters of ceremonies. There was an Albertina Rasch ballet and a lot of trick camera effects. The most memorable of its song numbers was one that Nacio Herb Brown and Arthur Freed dashed off to fill a spot after the rest of the picture was finished. It was called *Singing in the Rain*.

So loaded with gusto was it that Brooks Atkinson, the drama critic of the New York *Times*, departed from his usual watch over the legitimate theatre to see it and observe, "If the sound film can approximate the theatre in so many respects, you begin to foresee the

ease with which they will dominate the routine entertainment of the
country . . . and the influence they may have when they develop an
artistic form."

Those sweet words were more reflective than the film makers
themselves were inclined to be. Their endeavors to score in the new
sound medium caused them to splurge without artistic heed. The
very thing that helped make their pictures novel was doomed to
make them dull. Within a year, they had flooded the screen with so
much music that the public grew surfeited and bored. Then that
first great tide of musical pictures was quickly permitted to ebb. Soon
it was considered thoroughly dangerous to make a picture with songs.

Trader Horn

Fortunately, Thalberg and his associates had followed other lines
in exploring the possibilities of dialogue and sound. One of these
was, appropriately, in the direction of travel and exploration in a
foreign land. It was to make a sound-picture based on the popular
autobiography of an African peddler, *Trader Horn*.

Thalberg and Mayer agreed that this one should be filmed in
Africa, where they could get shots of genuine wild animals and make
recordings of genuine animal sounds. It was to be done primarily
for the novelty and excitement of the locale. Woody Van Dyke, who
had made his reputation with *White Shadows in the South Seas*, was
assigned to direct.

A scenario was quickly slapped together—a transparent and flexible
adventure tale of a search by Trader Horn and a young hunter for a
fabled "white goddess" in the African wilds. It gave suspicious indica-
tions of having been inspired by the early *Tarzan* films. Its one virtue,
in the eyes of Mayer and Thalberg, was that its cast was small. Only
three actors would be taken on the trip to Africa. Harry Carey, a
veteran hand at Westerns, was signed to play Trader Horn and
Duncan Renaldo, a minor romantic actor, was recruited to play his
companion. Who was to be the White Goddess? This was maintained
a mystery.

Obviously Mayer and Thalberg were unwilling to assign one of
their valuable females for such a precarious jaunt. The dangers and
discomforts of traveling in Africa were no joke. And, of course, the
studio couldn't afford to side-track one of its popular feminine stars
for several months. Then Howard Strickling, the new head of
publicity, came up with a brilliant idea. Why not a "White Goddess
Contest" to pick the actress from a panel of vying blondes?

The idea was supported, the contest was advertised and, on the
appointed day, the blondes assembled at the Culver City studio.

There were hundreds of them, all shapes and sizes—some of them not so blonde. Individual screen tests were out of the question, so a phony mass screen test was arranged. Van Dyke ordered a camera mounted on a truck and told the girls to line up. He was going to ride down the row of hopefuls and pretend to photograph them.

All went well until one blonde spitfire suspected that the whole thing was a fake, stepped out of line when the camera reached her and gave Van Dyke a piece of her mind. He was impressed with her spirit. This was White Goddess character.

"Have that girl come to my office!" he bawled. She did—and she was signed for the role.

The young lady's name was Constance Woodruff, but she called herself Edwina Booth. She was no relation of the famous Shakesperian actor, though she liked to claim she was. Her only experience in films had been as an extra. She was put under contract at $100 a week.

The company of thirty people, including sound technicians and crew, departed Culver City in March, 1929. They sailed from New York a few days later aboard the *Ile de France*. Several tons of sound recording apparatus, including a nine-ton generator and a couple of trucks, were in the mass of paraphernalia that was shipped to Africa. Everything from rifles to flyswatters, from iceless refrigerators to portable radio sets, was sent on that roving expedition. Van Dyke took a quarter million feet of unexposed film. For his own private entertainment, he also took a couple of trunks of bathtub gin.

From France, the company went on to East Africa and entered the big-game country through Nairobi, where a well-known white hunter, Major W. V. D. Dickinson, was engaged to lead the way. A doctor whose qualifications were later challenged was also signed on for the tour.

The story of that expedition, which was the first big journey into Africa made by a Hollywood company, is a record of mad happenings. One might get the impression from it that Van Dyke, who had been a gold miner, lumberjack, engine-oiler and soldier of fortune, was on a pleasure trip all his own.

In the course of rounding up footage of wild animals in their habitat, native tribes in ceremonial regalia and the members of the cast clomping about in the bush, he enjoyed himself immensely, indulging in such coy practical jokes as dragging ropes over the beds of sleeping persons to imitate snakes and feeding a baboon gin.

The discomforts endured by the company were more distressing than Van Dyke's pranks. Virtually every one came down with fever of some sort at some time. Among the mishaps and misfortunes later complained of by Edwina Booth, who was one of three women in the outfit—the other two were Mrs. Carey and a script girl—were a case of sunstroke, a brain concussion got from a fall out of a tree, recurring bouts of dysentery and a touch of malaria. The doctor treated everything with whiskey. Van Dyke treated his own ailments with gin. The company was in Africa for seven months. It brought back 200,000 feet of exposed film.

Even so, it was realized by Van Dyke before he returned that he was probably in the soup. He knew he had plenty of footage, but did he have a film? Naturally, he saw no "rushes" (developed footage) of what he had shot, since they had no laboratory facilities for developing the film in the wilds. He also knew that his primitive sound equipment was frequently at fault. So he shot as much as he could get that was remotely interesting and hoped they could make something of it at the studio.

His anxieties were justified. When Mayer and Thalberg got a look at the developed film, Thalberg shook his head gravely, Mayer hooted in disgust.

"What are we going to do with *this*?" he hollered. "Cut it into travelogues?"

Thalberg pondered the problem. "We'll just have to fix it," he said. And he ordered Van Dyke and his company to keep on working on the thing.

There were two faults with the footage. One was that the animal scenes, while authentic, were lacking the sort of movement and drama that audiences assumed. The other was that the human adventure story was spotty and unresolved. It would require some further development and pulling together with connecting scenes.

The first fault was corrected in a way that was as old and familiar as the device by which the pioneer film maker, Colonel Selig, got even with Theodore Roosevelt. Roosevelt refused to take Selig as a cameraman on one of his African big-game hunting trips, so Selig got ahead of the old Rough Rider by shooting a fake "African" film in the Chicago zoo.

Van Dyke did something of the same sort. With the help of the experienced studio staff, he collected a batch of animals on the back lot and tried to make them perform. When that didn't prove satisfactory, he sent a unit off to Mexico, beyond the watch of the Society for the Prevention of Cruelty to Animals, to get some exciting scenes.

That proved satisfactory.

A cage of lions was turned loose in a well-disguised outdoor pen. The animals were starved for a few days and then thrown a couple of chunks of dead meat. When they didn't fight over it with sufficient ferocity, they were starved for a few more days and then a horse was sent into the pen among them. A lion leaped on the horse and tore its side. The horse was shot right away, but its fresh blood spurting did the trick with those lions. They lashed and ripped at one another in a swirling, snarling pack fight that was photographed by hidden cameras for the most exciting animal scene in the film.

As for added scenes with the human actors, they were shot on indoor and outdoor sets. Some of them were made by superimposing studio action on footage shot in Africa. (This was before the perfection of the valuable "process screen.")

Fortunately, Van Dyke had the foresight to bring back from Africa with the troupe the giant black native he had got to play Renchero, the loyal gunbearer of Trader Horn. He had been a tribal farmer in Africa. Mutia Omooloo was his name. He proved as capable and impressive as any of the white actors in the film.

To get Mutia to leave Africa, a companion had to be brought along with him. A neighbor named Riano was chosen. He had worked as personal porter to Van Dyke. The law of the British colony required that a white Afrikander be brought along to act as guardians for the natives. He also served, when needed, as interpreter.

The foreign visitors were a source of lively interest and amusement at the studio. A small kraal was built for them on the back lot and it was there that they happily lived. Being devout Mohammedans they butchered and cooked their own meat.

After a few weeks, however, the Afrikander asked if he might speak with Van Dyke about a matter of some embarrassment but the utmost urgency.

"What is it now?" growled the harassed director.

"These natives," the Afrikander began, "well, you see, in their village back in Africa, Mutia has eight wives and Riano has six. So they have—how would you say?—the habit of women. But they have had no women since they left Africa. So, you see, they are getting very restless. Maybe soon they will get difficult, unless—"

"You don't have to draw a picture," said Van Dyke. "I get what you mean."

He mentioned the matter to Thalberg. A certain element of policy was involved. Thalberg suggested that Kid Slickem, the studio bootblack and his sometime servant, be sought for aid. Slickem was up to the assignment. He just happened to have some lady friends who were highly congenial and obliging. The gate to the back lot was left open that evening, and all was peaceful for awhile in the kraal.

However, the favors provided were but a meager and tame substitute for the kind of connubial attention that Mutia and Riano were accustomed to. As the days wore on after the picture was finished and they were being kept on for its première, they again began to get restless and felt an urge to expand. One night, with some boys from the back lot, they slipped off and went downtown to a certain Negro establishment on Central Avenue. There they were having a fine time—just like home, almost—when Mutia discovered that he was missing a wrist watch of which he was most proud. With a whoop that rattled the windows, he snatched a little whore off her feet, clasped her by the ankles and started using her on the other girls like a club. A force of brave men was quickly assembled, and Mutia was subdued and returned to the back lot.

A few days later, certain symptoms developed that caused some natural alarm. Mutia was taken to a hospital in Culver City and put to bed for observation. This disturbed him. When no one was watching, he calmly got out of bed, escaped from the room via the window and started hoofing it back to the studio. He was caught up with a few minutes later, walking solemnly down the middle of Washington Boulevard, wearing nothing but a short hospital nightgown and trailed by a rapidly increasing mob, to which he paid not the slightest attention. He was a man of great dignity.

When the gala première of *Trader Horn* was finally held at Grauman's Chinese Theatre in Hollywood, Mutia and Riano refused to be present unless they could bring their back-lot lady friends. This had not been anticipated at such a momentous affair. However, the demand was conceded. The two Africans appeared in full native dress. Their companions were in the loudest bargain-basement finery.

Poor Mutia. He was taken to New York for the grand opening of the picture there, then he and Riano were returned to Africa, per the agreement made when they were taken away. The studio lost track of him thereafter. But what tales he must have told when he got back home! He certainly had his moment of triumph in helping to advance the fortunes of Metro-Goldwyn-Mayer.

And fortune conspicuously attended the showing of *Trader Horn*. It was one of the top money-makers of 1931. It encouraged the studio to make other outdoor adventure films with sound. Even the leftover African footage was soon put to profitable use in a new series of *Tarzan* films, which Van Dyke was set to making with Johnny Weissmuller as the star.

But the personal trials and tribulations that were endured in the making of *Trader Horn* continued to afflict some of its people. Two years after the film was released, Edwina Booth filed a suit for $1,000,000 against Metro-Goldwyn-Mayer. She claimed that her health had been ruined by the hardships she was made to undergo in Africa, that her marriage had been broken by her long absence and that she had been sued for alienation of affections by Duncan Renaldo's wife.

The lawyers for the studio attempted to argue that Miss Booth had been exposed to no unusual occupational hazards, and that, even if she had, she should seek recompense for her illness through workmen's compensation in California. Her lawyer, Emil K. Ellis, countered by recalling that California law required that notices of the state's specifications be posted in prominent places where people worked and that, unfortunately, no such notices had been placed in the wilds of Africa. The studio finally settled for $37,000.

There were certain ungracious intimations that the poor woman was faking, that she was simply seeking publicity. But, three years later, she died in California of a mysterious and wasting blood disease. Her reign as the White Goddess was fleeting.

That completed the weird drama of *Trader Horn*.

CHAPTER XIX

OLD STARS AND NEW

GRETA GARBO was the last of the studio's big stars to be exposed to the challenge of sound. The reason generally given is that Thalberg and others were fearful of what she could do with her voice. She spoke in a deep, throaty fashion and with a Swedish accent that you could cut with a knife. The question was whether she would maintain her illusion of supreme femininity.

Already such fine exotic ladies as Pola Negri, Vilma Banky and Raquel Torres had demonstrated that their accents were likely to be their ruin, as had some of the home-grown favorites. As one English critic complained, "The voice of feminine Hollywood is a pentecostal calamity!" The peril of permitting Greta Garbo to destroy her popularity by speaking words was one which the studio people naturally wished to postpone.

Also a strong consideration was the fact that she was the studio's most popular star in foreign countries, especially in Europe, where silent films were still being generally shown. Thus a proof of her vocal prowess was not an immediate must. And, of course, there was still that question of the predominance of talking films in the spring of 1929, when Miss Garbo returned to Hollywood from her first trip home to Sweden and was ready to go to work.

She was put in two silent pictures, *The Single Standard* and *The Kiss*, before Thalberg and Mayer decided that the time had come when she would have to talk. Then great care was given to the selection of an appropriate vehicle for her. Eugene O'Neill's moody play, *Anna Christie*, was finally hit upon. It had to do with the somewhat sullied daughter of a Swedish sea captain—a rough and realistic young woman who naturally spoke with a strong trace of the mother tongue.

The fact that she would attempt the transition was known as they were finishing *The Kiss*, a high society drama similar to *The Trial of Mary Dugan*, in which Greta was directed by the distinguished French craftsman, Jacques Feyder. There was an air of depression on the set as they wrapped up the last scene. The usual concluding "set party" was tacitly foregone. It was known that this was more than a critical turning point for the Swedish star. It was also the last silent picture at Metro-Goldwyn-Mayer.

The time, for the record, was November, 1929.

Actually, the making of *Anna Christie* was a simple matter for the elegant star. Clarence Brown, who had brought her together with John Gilbert in *Flesh and the Devil*, directed it, and he saw to it that Miss Garbo thoroughly rehearsed all her scenes. She had memorized her lines to crisp perfection and approached the microphone with the same calm confidence and authority that she showed towards everything.

When the picture was ready for presentation, the promotion campaign was "Garbo Speaks!" as though that was one of the most momentous occurrences since the dawn of time. At least, it captured the public's fancy. Greta's opening line, as she came out of the fog and the nighttime into the back-room of a waterfront saloon, "A viskey for me, kid—an' don't be stingy," became a popular expression all over the world. The picture was entirely successful, and Garbo was happily wed to sound.

Marie Dressler

For all the excitement and importance of *Anna Christie* in Garbo's career, it was even more wonderful and propitious for the opportunity it gave another great star. This was Marie Dressler, who had the supporting role of Marthy, the bloated old boozer that was Anna's big-hearted friend. Miss Dressler's magnificent performance not only helped Garbo look great but it dramatically brought back into the limelight this aging and fading custard-pie comedy queen.

It had been a long time since Marie Dressler had made herself conspicuous on the screen in that primitive nickelodeon classic, *Tillie's Punctured Romance*. She had had her ups in vaudeville and movies. She had also had her downs. It was in one of these depressing phases that she was rescued from near-oblivion by some good friends.

One day in 1927, Frances Marion, who enjoyed (and deserved) the position (and recompenses) of a top scenarist at Metro-Goldwyn-Mayer, received a letter from Elisabeth Marbury, an important literary agent in New York, asking if there wasn't something she could do to "help Marie."

The old star had done some small-time vaudeville and a couple of one-reel comedies in France, but she was at the end of her resources, Miss Marbury's letter said. "Isn't it possible for you to write a part for her in a movie and give her a little work? . . . You know Marie; if she were starving, she wouldn't accept a cent from anyone."

Miss Marion ran through the stories that the studio had bought and came up with one called *The Callahans and the Murphys*, written by Kathleen Norris. The title at once suggested Marie Dressler and

Polly Moran, the latter a clever Irish comedienne under contract to the studio. It was a flimsy story but Miss Marion went to work on it, built it up with Miss Dressler in her mind's eye and then slipped the completed scenario on Thalberg's desk.

A few days later, he told her he had read it and liked it. "Who do you see in it?" he asked.

"Polly Moran," Miss Marion answered casually.

"Yes, she'd be good as Mrs. Murphy," Thalberg said. "But whoever plays Mrs. Callahan must be a dramatic actress as well as a comedienne."

"Do you remember Marie Dressler?"

Thalberg nodded.

"She's the only actress who could do it justice," Miss Marion said.

"But I haven't heard of her in years," answered Thalberg.

"You haven't!" Miss Marion's tone was anguished. "Why, she's one of the greatest comediennes on Broadway. That's just it. If we want to get her back in pictures, we'll have to give her a big salary—say, $2,000 a week."

Miss Marion stopped short. Thalberg's eyes were boring through her. He despised a lie.

"Irving," Miss Marion finished lamely, "Marie's a friend of mine. She needs a job."

"I thought so," he answered quietly. "I'll talk it over with L. B."

The next time Miss Marion saw Thalberg, he began to speak solemnly:

"My theory is that anybody who hits the bull's-eye—it doesn't matter in what profession—has the brains and the stamina to do it again. So I figure a woman who scored as often as Miss Dressler did should be able to repeat. She's probably been the victim of bad writing—and bad advice."

A twinkle came into his eye.

"Send for her. We'll start the picture as soon as she gets here. And her salary will be—$1,500 a week."

The Callahans and the Murphys did not hit the bull's-eye. Even though it delightfully amused the audience that saw it at the preview and Miss Dressler and Miss Moran were cheered by the crowd, it raised a storm of protest from the Irish when it was put into national release. This reaction was entirely dumbfounding to the Irishmen at the studio, especially to Eddie Mannix, who supervised it, and to its Irish-descended director, George Hill. They thought they had a picture the Irish would dote on. Instead, the Loyal Sons of This and That raised hell. Loew's received so many protests that it had to withdraw the film. It seems the Irish societies were most offended at the two old biddies, played by Miss Dressler and Miss Moran, being so indecorous as to pour needled beer down their fronts.

Despite the fiasco with this picture, Thalberg did not lose hope for Miss Dressler. He let her do another picture, *Bringing Up Father*, also with Miss Moran. This one was no world beater. They were having trouble finding further roles, when Miss Marion, who was writing the screen play for *Anna Christie*, suggested they let Miss Dressler play Marthy, the old sot. Thalberg was entirely for it. Mayer and others were opposed. But Thalberg and Miss Marion won them over. Miss Dressler was a hit in the film.

That's when the sun broke through, in the late afternoon of her career.

For it just so happened that another fading veteran of the silent screen was simultaneously being rejuvenated under somewhat similar circumstances by Metro-Goldwyn-Mayer. He was Wallace Beery, a former Keystone comedy cutup and Paramount character star, whom Thalberg and Mayer had decided to risk giving another chance in *The Big House*, a prison picture which Miss Marion also wrote. Beery's sentimental performance of a condemned convict in this film did a great deal for him with the public—and with the doubters in the company. It was thus determined to team him with Miss Dressler in a boozy comedy called *Min and Bill*.

The memory of this lusty, tearful picture about an old pot-walloper and his wife is, no doubt, green in the minds of millions who saw it back in those deep Depression days. For it was released in November, 1930, to a public that was starving to be fed with just the sort of sentimental assurance of family affection and confidence that this film contained. And it was one of the great popular pictures of 1931. For her performance in it, Miss Dressler deservedly received an Academy award, and she and Mr. Beery became as popular as any of the great glamour stars. *Min and Bill* was the sort of picture, with the sort of characters, that could only be done with the facility of articulation of personality afforded by sound.

After this, Miss Dressler and Mr. Beery were among the lions at the studio. Through the early 1930's, they were Metro-Goldwyn-Mayer's top money-making stars. Her immediately subsequent pictures were *Emma* and *Tugboat Annie*, and his were *The Secret Six*, *The Champ*, with Jackie Cooper, (for which *he* won an Academy award), and *Grand Hotel*. Their good fortunes were due in large measure to the audacity of Thalberg and Mayer.

The demand of the "talking" pictures for actors who could, first of all, talk naturally set the scouts to beating the bushes for actors who might do. Among the earliest recruited was a skinny young fellow who had been a fair success on Broadway in a play of Edgar Selwyn's called, *Possession*. This was Robert Montgomery.

While playing in *Possession* in the fall of 1928, Montgomery was asked to take a screen test for a role opposite Vilma Banky in a picture Samuel Goldwyn was about to make. The test was unsatisfactory. Goldwyn and the director agreed Montgomery looked much too young to give even the slightest illusion of being attractive to the svelte Hungarian. However, Edgar Selwyn got the screen test to show to his brother-in-law, Nicholas Schenck, and persuaded him to hire the young actor. Montgomery was thus signed up in New York—to a five-year contract, with yearly options, at $350 a week to start.

When the greenhorn arrived in Culver City, they looked him over with displeasure and dismay. He wasn't their idea of an actor—at least, not for romantic roles. However, they dumped him in a picture —an early rah-rah musical-type of thing—entitled *So This Is College*, which had the young Elliott Nugent as its star. Montgomery was supposed to play a fullback, but he was so gentle-looking and so thin that Director Sam Wood had them pad him to the point where he could barely move. Understandably, after that experience, he was loaned to United Artists for *Three Live Ghosts*.

However, he was hustled back to Culver City to appear opposite Joan Crawford in her first talking picture, *Untamed*, and then he was teamed with Norma Shearer in a plush affair called *The Divorcée*. His air of refinement in this picture convinced Thalberg that they had a young man who was right for their high-society assignments. He was cast with Garbo in *Inspiration* and was on his way.

Gable Moves In

Montgomery was rolling along nicely when there came on the lot one fine day a rangy and hungry-looking fellow whom various people at the studio had seen here and there in various items and thought likely for "heavy" roles. He had been signed to a two-year contract, with options and with hope that he might prove a fair rival for, say, Chester Morris, who was a rascal of modest renown. His hair was dark, his eyebrows heavy, his ears huge and he had a broad and villainous leer. Such was the status of Clark Gable when, in December, 1930, he joined the studio.

This boy was no stranger to Culver City. He had been there before —first as an extra in *The Merry Widow* (with Mae Murray and John Gilbert, you recall), and later to make a screen test at the urging of Lionel Barrymore.

Barrymore had got to know and like young Gable when the foot-loose kid was playing with him in a West Coast stock company production of the old stage hit, *The Copperhead*. Gable, at that time, was working in the stock company of Louis O. Macloon, and Barrymore had said he would like to help him in any way he could. Thus when Gable returned to Los Angeles in 1930, after a period of acting in New York, to play the role of Killer Mears, the condemned criminal, in the West Coast production of *The Last Mile*, Barrymore said he would introduce him, via a screen test, to the people at Metro-Goldwyn-Mayer.

The screen test was unconvincing. For some reason, Gable appeared in a South Sea island get-up with a flower behind one ear. However, an agent, Minna Wallis, had seen him and got him a job in a Pathé western, *The Painted Desert*, starring William Boyd, the actor who was to come to fame later as Hopalong Cassidy.

Gable was cast as the "heavy." He had to grow a beard and learn to ride. While they were on location in Arizona, he was a very unhappy young man. Boyd would try to encourage him. Once he took him to Flagstaff and introduced him to some girls. They said, "Is *this* the guy you were telling us about? Good gravy!" And when Boyd said, "What's the matter with him?" they said, "*Everything!*"

After that, Miss Wallis got him a bit in a Warner Brothers film, *The Night Nurse*, and was negotiating for a long-term contract at R-K-O, when Thalberg indicated that he would like to have him at Metro-Goldwyn-Mayer. Gable deliberated, then took the latter bid. He remained under continuous contract to the studio for twenty-five years.

The young man's first job at Culver City was as a milkman in *The Easiest Way*, one of those high-society dramas which had Constance Bennett and the aforementioned Mr. Montgomery in leading roles. Gable's part was incidental, but he played it so vigorously that people who saw the "rushes" were asking, "Who *is* that guy, anyway?"

He was cast next opposite Joan Crawford in *Dance, Fool, Dance*, then with Wallace Beery and Jean Harlow, a new charmer, in *The Secret Six*. And then came the picture that got him public attention and some fame. It was *The Free Soul*, in which he was permitted to slam Norma Shearer into a chair—a piece of violence that was every bit as shocking as Jimmy Cagney's contemporaneous squashing of a grapefruit in Mae Clark's face.

Clarence Brown, the director of the picture, which was a solemn tale of the rebellious daughter of a drunken criminal lawyer, had requested Gable for the role of a gangster with whom the young lady carried on a flirtatious affair. He had seen the actor around the studio and was struck by his agile, vicious grace. (Everybody now was detecting Gable's powerful suggestion of masculine sex.) Brown felt he would be a proper menace to the pathetically reckless society girl.

However, audience reaction to the film when it was released was the reverse of what was expected. Instead of disgust for the gangland brute who gave the young lady her come-uppance, sympathy went out to him. He was treating a naughty little teaser exactly as she deserved. When he was ultimately shot by the girl's fiancé (Leslie Howard), audiences were grieved. They were less interested in the rest of the story of the girl and her father (Lionel Barrymore).

Gable was the sensation of the picture. He would not continue in his next film, which was *Polly of the Circus,* with Marion Davies, without a substantial hike in his salary. He was getting wise.

The rise of Beery, Montgomery and Gable significantly paralleled the decreasing popularity of the studio's high-salaried male silent stars—William Haines, Ramon Novarro, John Gilbert and, of course, Lon Chaney, who was cut down by death. The standard explanation for their subsidence is that their voices did them in; they simply were not able to sound convincing when they talked. This was one reason for their passing—a very important one. But there were other reasons, including the mediocrity of their stories and the extravagance of their acting styles.

Haines, for instance, was ebullient in much the same fantastic way as was Harold Lloyd, the famous silent comedian whose popularity also waned with sound. The style was essentially pantomimic; it appeared a little silly with words. Although Haines made a dozen or so pictures after *Alias Jimmy Valentine,* he steadily lost ground and finally gave up in 1933. Happily, he became one of the most fashionable and successful interior decorators in Hollywood.

Novarro also continued to make talking and musical films, but his type of exotic, romantic hero was doomed by the realism of sound. He flared up briefly in *Mata Hari,* with Greta Garbo, in 1931; then terminated his long connection with the studio after doing *The Cat and the Fiddle,* with Jeanette MacDonald in 1935.

Good-by Yaquee

As for Gilbert—the incomparable Gilbert—his decline was something else again. The cruel eclipse of this flamboyant silent actor was one of the toughest real-life dramas of Hollywood.

The irony was that nobody at the studio was worried about him when sound made its fateful appearance. If any star could talk, they figured, it was Jack! Indeed, he was always talking. The difficulty was to make him stop. This born-in-a-trunk child of the theatre—could *he* handle dialogue? Ha!

Thus there was no anxiety, such as they later had for Garbo, when Gilbert began on his first talking picture in early 1929. He had just signed a new, sensational contract to make four pictures in the next two years at $250,000 a picture. "This is one of the most important moves in the history of our organization," said Nicholas Schenck. The continuation was considered most fortunate because other studios were attempting to woo the popular star.

His first picture was entitled *Redemption*. It was based on Tolstoi's *The Living Corpse*. (The ominous implication was treated as a joke.) Fred Niblo was the director, and from the start, the thing went bad. The "rushes" were bleakly disappointing and there was a high, squeakiness to Gilbert's voice. Something was wrong with the story. They worked over it for several months and finally shelved it temporarily while Gilbert was put to work on another film.

This was a Graustarkian romance entitled *His Glorious Night*. It, too, was strangely disappointing. When it was released in the fall of 1929, audiences laughed at Gilbert. They laughed at the strangeness of his voice. But they also laughed at the extravagance of his love-making with Renee Adoree. It was ludicrous when done to a flow of language. Suddenly the great silent lover was made to appear clumsy and verbose. They hadn't yet come to realize that "talking pictures" were not just silents with words.

Unfortunately, the studio powers then decided to resurrect *Redemption* and reshoot some scenes. With so much money invested in it, they couldn't afford to throw it away. The salvage job was unsuccessful. When the picture was released the following spring, shortly after Garbo's *Anna Christie*, it was a dismal, embarrassing dud. The coincidence of the great star in two fast failures virtually finished him with his fans.

Through this one year of cruel deflation, Gilbert became progressively confused and depressed by his curious inability to conquer the new medium. He had suddenly, whimsically married Ina Claire in May, 1929. She, a brilliant stage actress, had returned successfully to the screen with the coming of sound. Her success and advice were no help to him.

"The white voice! The *white* voice!" she would say. Gilbert would look at her blankly. He had no idea what she meant.

They were divorced in 1931.

The rest of the story is pathetic. Gilbert was put in further films—in *Way for a Sailor*, with Wallace Beery, in which he pitifully tried to act tough; then in *Gentleman's Fate, Phantom of Paris* and *West of*

Broadway. But the magic was gone. From a light-hearted, hail-fellow actor who drove his racy roadster onto the lot with the top down, shouting to companions, he became a morose and bitter man who drove in with the top up and sneaked quickly to his dressing room.

In 1932, he was given one more chance for glory when Greta Garbo insisted that he should be her leading man in *Queen Christina* instead of a young English actor who had been signed for the job. This was a virtually unknown fellow by the name of Laurence Olivier.

For a brief spell, Gilbert was again the old Jack, full of swagger and bounce. But the picture did nothing to help him. The old Gilbert-Garbo fire was out. And the studio now had young Clark Gable to step into the faded veteran's shoes.

Gilbert made his last appearance in *The Captain Hates the Sea,* a multi-character melodrama in which he had a minor role. For two years, he lived in grim seclusion in his home, high on Linden Drive, divorced from Ina Claire and his fourth wife, Virginia Bruce, and brooding darkly on the injustices he felt had been done him.

Drink now became his singular solace. He was nasty and brutal to old friends. Marlene Dietrich occasionally went to see him. Then even she stayed away. Finally, one morning in January, 1936, his valet found him dead. His heart, strained by alcohol and anguish, had failed. He was then thirty-eight.

His old friend, Irving Thalberg, was one of the pallbearers at his funeral.

Rest came at last for "dear Yaquee." For him, the big parade had gone on by.

CHAPTER XX

THE WHITE HEAT OF THALBERG

THOSE who worked closely with Thalberg during these wonderfully tense and exciting years of transforming the medium of the motion picture through the device of sound had nothing but awe and admiration for the vigor and range of his creative mind, for the graciousness of his way with his associates and for his amazing capacity to work.

He would arrive at the studio in the morning not later than ten o'clock, spend all day with his several supervisors, taking part in assorted conferences, selecting stories and casts, preparing scenarios and going over pictures in the works. The evenings he would spend seeing "rushes," editing pictures or attending previews of new films.

He had a remarkably bizarre but convenient theory about fatigue. It was that you only get tired when you are bored. Since he was never bored with what he was doing, he never tired. That was the only rational explanation for his seemingly inexhaustible energies.

Thalberg was a great one for previews. He believed firmly in testing finished films against the actual responses of audiences to try to discover their flaws. He had a theory about this too: "The difference between something good and something bad is great, but the difference between something good and something superior is often very small." Therefore he insisted upon laboring to find out what the good films lacked that kept them from being superior. To add that something, he had films remade which was within the realm of reason in those days of less astronomical costs. "Irving doesn't make pictures, he remakes them"—they used to say.

During the first years of sound, the place for previews was one Fox theatre in San Bernardino, where they had the only projection equipment outside the studio suitable for running the uncompleted films of Metro-Goldwyn-Mayer. (The system then practiced at the studio was to shoot the picture and the sound track separately and not put them together on the same film until the release prints were actually made.) Thus, two or three times a week, the whole contingent of people from Culver City would descend upon that single "San Berdoo" theatre and sit through a preview of a film. The regular customers became so preview-conscious they acted like guinea pigs. Often the same picture was "previewed" there two or three times!

One of Thalberg's few diversions was card playing. He was mad for bridge, and seized upon every spare moment he could possibly find to play. That inspired a happy arrangement for getting to those previews at "San Berdoo;" Thalberg, his supervisors and others would go out in a Pacific Electric interurban streetcar. The car would be brought onto a siding alongside the studio in the afternoon and would be amply stocked by Kid Slickem with an assortment of delicatessen and pop.

Then, about six o'clock, Thalberg and others would get aboard, the bell would clang and the old red car would start out on its circuitous and specially routed run to San Berdoo, while inside Thalberg and his companions were furiously playing cards, smoking cigars, eating delicatessen and having a fine old time. A remarkable camaraderie was established and maintained in that old car, full of the smell of pickles, cigar smoke and the vagrant fume of film.

On the way back, the occupation was different. No matter how good the picture was, it usually got ripped to pieces by the people going home in the car. The next morning, Thalberg would hold a conference with the picture's supervisor, director, writers and all whose work might be called into question and they'd decide what, if anything, should be done. Criticism and difference of opinion were encouraged. Thalberg did not want to be "yessed." He would make, and take responsibility for, the final decisions. But he forced an exhaustive analysis.

During a conference, he might sit there flipping a gold coin in the air or turn to some other business while his associates talked. But it was notable—and eventually legendary—that his attention never strayed. He had the phenomenal facility of being able to do two or three things at once.

His manner, however, was not Caesarian. He was not lofty, nor did he try to dictate. He treated his associates—and especially the actors—with the deference that he thought their talent was due. One time, a group of supervisors decided they'd had about enough of that nervous coin-flipping habit, so, when Thalberg took out his coin and started flipping it, they also took coins out of their pockets and started flipping them, too. Thalberg grinned and put his coin back. He seldom flipped it again.

To be sure, he was jealously guarded by his secretaries and outer-office staff. And, as time went on and the studio flourished, he was made more and more difficult to see. But this was not on his instruction. It was a part of the general spread of an aura of executive importance that emanated from Mayer.

Once, the playwright, Moss Hart, was kept waiting in Thalberg's outer office for several hours by an adamant secretary who simply would not permit him to go in. When Hart finally did burst into the office, he was sputtering with unconcealed rage. Thalberg let him sputter for a few minutes. Then he smiled and said sweetly to him, "Oh, you're not going to be temperamental, too—are you? Not *you*, Moss." Hart melted and sat down.

Thalberg's skill at cutting pictures and spotting the weaknesses in them after they were put together was one for which he was justly famed. The supervisors and other people at the studio came to depend upon him as an infallible "doctor" when their pictures were in need of care.

Introducing Helen Hayes

Instances of his diagnoses and prescriptions for treatment were innumerable. But one of the clearest examples of his capacity in this line was in the case of the difficult production of *The Sin of Madelon Claudet*. Here was a case in which a picture was not only saved from dismal ruin but the reputation of a fine actress was miraculously preserved. The actress, who was making her first appearance in the new sound films, was Helen Hayes.

Back in 1927, Miss Hayes had appeared in a play entitled *Dancing Mothers*, which Edgar Selwyn produced. It was a come-down for the talented actress, who had won fame in such plays as *What Every Woman Knows* and *Coquette*. However, Selwyn loved it. He was also very fond of Miss Hayes. He vowed he would make a movie star of her, when he later went to Hollywood.

This generous resolution was remembered by him when, in 1930, he found himself a writer-director at Culver City with an assignment to do a thing called *Lullaby*. Now, *Lullaby* was an old play which Selwyn had also produced and which had been just as bad as *Dancing Mothers*. It was about a French girl who was deceived in love, became an unmarried mother, was separated from her infant boy, turned whore and, as an old woman, avoided sailors because she knew her son was one.

This was the play which Selwyn wanted Miss Hayes to do as a film.

The actress was playing in New York in *Petticoat Fever* when the call came. Selwyn had persuaded the studio to sign her. She agreed and the deal was arranged. Miss Hayes' husband, Charles MacArthur, the distinguished playwright, had worked in Hollywood. It was much against his wishes that his wife signed to do *Lullaby*.

His apprehensions were supported when he heard the film would be supervised by Harry Rapf. He knew Rapf's reputation and his ludicrous lack of taste. The prospect of Helen Hayes entrusting her film debut to him was frightening. MacArthur shuddered when he peeked at telegrams to his wife from Culver City—telegrams saying such as, "Think we have the strongest script in years. Awaiting your arrival. Harry Rapf."

Finally, MacArthur decided to go out to Hollywood ahead of his wife and reconnoiter the situation. He called on Thalberg first. Thalberg was leaving for a European vacation and said he would not be around for *Lullaby*. MacArthur then did what he acknowledged to have been a wicked and unethical thing. He persuaded Nellie Farrell of the typing department to let him sneak a look at the script. All his fears were justified. It was a terrible piece of cheese.

The general story of the play was followed, except that, at the end, the old drab did meet her son in a North African seaport, inadvertently identified him to some thugs who were lurking to seize him. And before the eyes of the horrified mother, the lad was killed.

MacArthur returned to his friend, Thalberg. "I've violated a rule," he said. "But, my God, this thing would sink Garbo!"

"All right, I'll put you on the script," Thalberg replied. "Change it any way you wish."

Miss Hayes was due at the studio in ten days to go before the cameras. MacArthur felt this was no time for the niceties. He ripped into Selwyn's script. He had to retain the basic pattern of the mother-son relationship, but he wanted, at least, to give the woman some solid reason for becoming a whore. In this task, he knew he had to be mindful of the sensibilities of Mayer, who was deeply reverential about mothers. This compelled some considerable subterfuge. He could see that most of the people at the studio didn't give a hoot about Helen Hayes. Some of them had never heard of her. A fellow in the casting department called her "Miss Haines." And a chap from publicity asked MacArthur what was her "specialty."

The script was still being rewritten when Miss Hayes arrived and shooting began. The actors would be on the set at nine in the morning; MacArthur would arrive five minutes later with the pages they would shoot that day. He frankly borrowed a good bit from the recently successful *Madame X*. He also tried to lighten the drama with some comedy relief. His most important alteration was to change the character of the son. Instead of his being a sailor, he was a doctor, for whom the mother had secretly prostituted herself in order to earn the money to put him through medical school.

With Selwyn lovingly directing, they finally got the picture done. Judging by the "rushes," some of it was pretty good. Samuel Goldwyn came to the studio while they were shooting, took one look at Miss Hayes and forthwith signed her up for *Arrowsmith*, which he was about to produce. When Mayer saw the rough cut of the picture, he wept openly and proclaimed to all and sundry it was the greatest picture he had ever seen.

But MacArthur was dubious and nervous. He saw what he feared was a major flaw. The mood broke completely in the middle. The first half was light and bohemian; the second half was a maudlin "mammy" song. He slipped in to see Bernie Hyman, who was the closest deputy for Thalberg while the latter was away. "Mayer's on fire for this thing," he told him. "He wants to open it at the Astor. What do we do?"

Hyman tried to arrange for a preview far enough away from Hollywood so that the wise-guys and vultures wouldn't be there to gloat over its possible faults. But Mayer wouldn't hear of that. He insisted they show it right in Hollywood.

The preview was a horror. The picture laid a bomb.

Mayer's enthusiasm died quickly. "Maybe if we reshoot a third of it—" he said. MacArthur began to have nightmares. His guiltless, trusting wife was in a daze. This was to be her debut in the movies! . . .

Then Thalberg returned.

He ran the picture at his home on a Saturday evening. Surprisingly, he liked it very much. He allowed it needed some fixing, but said it could be done. Right off, he spotted the bad transition of mood in the middle of it. On Monday morning he had MacArthur, who was writing on another picture, return to *The Sin of Madeleine Claudet*.

Thalberg's key suggestion was that they have a delivery-room scene wherein the unmarried French girl, disillusioned and bitter at being with child, would refuse at first to look at the baby when it was brought to her. Then, as her eyes did turn upon it, her expression would slowly change and, out of the shadows of her torment would come the first evident rush of mother-love. This turned out to be a scene of some daring. It made the whole character of the film, and provided the delicate transition in the development of the girl.

Thalberg followed this suggestion with an order for a later scene in which the now old lady, still unknown to her successful doctor-son, would go to his office in Paris. She would look around proudly, touching things, until a nurse would rebuke her. Then the doctor would enter—her unsuspecting son! He would treat the old lady kindly, put his head softly against her breast to hear her heartbeat (having conveniently mislaid his stethoscope) and thus give the worn, adoring mother a blissful chance to feel the closeness of her boy.

Thalberg's final suggestion was that the whole thing be framed in a prologue and epilogue, by which the story of the mother would be told to the petulant and restless wife of the young doctor, causing her to realize how great a woman's sacrifice could be.

Miss Hayes, then shooting in *Arrowsmith*, went back to Culver City to do the new scenes. (The old doctor-friend who told the story was Jean Hersholt; the young doctor-son was Robert Young.) The actress tried to model her performance of the aging Madeleine Claudet after the great French physicist, Madame Curie, whom she had met one summer aboard a ship.

Neither Miss Hayes nor her husband viewed the finished film for several months. Then, one day, they saw emblazoned on the marquee of the Capitol Theatre in New York the title that *Lullaby* had been given—*The Sin of Madelon Claudet*. Impelled by a morbid curiosity, they slipped into the theatre. The house was so crowded that they had to take separate seats.

The succeeding experience was disturbing. Each of them wriggled and moaned as particular scenes, all too mindful of prior torments, came on the screen. Eventually, the person sitting next to Miss Hayes became so annoyed that he moved his seat and MacArthur, watching his wife as much as the picture, scrambled over to her side. Together, they held hands in the darkness and resigned themselves to their mutual pain.

Apparently their moans and whispers were close to disorderly, for soon a man sitting behind them leaned forward and thumped MacArthur on the arm.

"Say, mister, if you don't like this picture, we DO!" he said. "Now, either you and the lady keep your mouths shut or I'll call an usher and ask him to put you out of here."

MacArthur and Miss Hayes muttered apologies and slid down into their chairs. For the first time, they noticed that people all around them were unashamedly sniffling and mopping their eyes. The two stayed a few minutes longer. Then, as a crucial scene approached, they quietly got out of the theatre. Their departure was not noticeable.

The Sin of Madelon Claudet was very successful. It was voted one of the best films of 1931 and Miss Hayes was given an Academy award for her performance.

No mention was ever made—at least, not in public—of Thalberg's lifesaving salvage job . . .

The Lunts

The eagerness of the producer to obtain for Metro-Goldwyn-Mayer the services of the best dramatic talent in the American theatre, as soon as sound was established, led at this same time to his getting the famous team of Alfred Lunt and Lynn Fontanne to come to Culver City and do *The Guardsman*, one of their most arch and adult romps.

The deal for the play and the performers was made by Robert Rubin in New York. The Lunts first met up with Thalberg in the lobby of a Chicago hotel. They warned him they wouldn't be able to do any swimming or riding horses or falling off cliffs. Thalberg laughed and told them the movies had gone beyond those things. A few minutes later, a studio press agent entered leading a young lion on a leash.

When the celebrated couple reached Culver City, ready to begin the film, they were really quite tense and apprehensive. They had never acted together in films and had frank misgivings about how they would be. The first day they went to the studio they drove up in an old Ford car. The gateman would not admit them. Thalberg was away at the time, and they felt so hurt and unhappy, they went straight back to their hotel. Some furious and anxious telephoning brought them in the next day.

They still say around Culver City that there never has been on the lot two more "professional" people than Alfred Lunt and Lynn Fontanne. Their director was Sidney Franklin. He approached with almost paralyzing awe the job of giving directions to these famous people of the stage. He could have spared himself the worry. They were more frightened than he and depended upon him with child-like confidence to tell them what to do. Every time he was ready with a new setup, he would find them off in a corner rehearsing their lines, diligently running through their business, taking meticulous care with everything. At the end of each reading, they besought Franklin to tell them how it was. One day, an old Culver City stagehand gave Lunt reassurance. "Don't be nervous," he said. "I think you're good."

A memorable occasion on this production was when they shot a scene of Miss Fontanne in a bathtub. She came on the set wearing a bathrobe, which she took off as she stepped into the tub. The only unusual thing about this was that she revealed herself nude to the waist. There were gasps and cries of amazement. People went rushing to fetch screens. They'd never seen anything like this in latter-day Hollywood. The Lunts insisted it was all right; they liked to "feel what they were doing" when they worked.

The scene was shot with the camera trained on Miss Fontanne's handsome back, but at a point where a bell sounded off right, she swung around towards it, with startling consequence. "Cut! Cut!" yelled Franklin. Miss Fontanne couldn't understand. Since the bell came from the right, she naturally turned in that direction. Franklin had the bell sound thereafter from the back of the set. That day's "rushes" of *The Guardsman* were long cherished at the studio.

This uncommonly sophisticated picture was done in twenty-one shooting days at a cost of $374,000, including the salaries of the stars. Even so, it was not too popular. It was a little ahead of its time. And, of course, the average movie-goer was not familiar with Lunt and Fontanne. However, Thalberg would have liked to put them in other films, but they could never find precisely the right vehicle on which all could agree. Thus, *The Guardsman* was the first and last film this distinguished couple ever did.

The urge for more sophisticated pictures was upon Thalberg now. Although the range of his taste spanned many areas, he tended towards the "classier" things with sound. The casting of his wife, Norma Shearer, in such svelte and brittle films as *The Last of Mrs. Cheyney, The Divorcée* and the more complex and profound *Strange Interlude* indicated his interest and confidence in such things. His enthusiasm was stimulated by his associate and close friend, Paul Bern.

Probably his most successful and rewarding achievement in this line, in those critical years of the early 1930's, was the production of *Grand Hotel*, a cosmopolitan, multi-character picture which did wonders for the stars of Metro-Goldwyn-Mayer.

Screen rights to the story of this picture, which was originally a novel by Vicki Baum, were acquired in a most unusual fashion. They were bought for $6,000 flat, with a proviso that the company would finance a production of an adaptation of the novel on the New York stage. This was done, with Herman Shumlin producing the play for $55,000. It was a huge success. The company got back its production investment, with a profit. It thus had the screen rights of a valuable property free and clear.

Grand Hotel told the interlocking stories of several people in a Berlin hotel, and it was Thalberg's idea to make it with top performers in the studio. He used Greta Garbo, Joan Crawford, Wallace Beery, Lewis Stone, and Lionel Barrymore, and he hired Lionel's famous brother, John, to play a role that Jack Gilbert might have had, if his contract hadn't called for his being paid an exorbitant sum. Edmund Goulding directed. Aside from the phenomenal success it had, after its gala première at the Astor Theatre in New York on April 12, 1932, and the fact that it was selected by the Academy as the best film of that year, it is memorable as the picture that gave Joan Crawford a new eminence as a dramatic star and the press department's practice of publicizing Garbo by only her last name.

They were beginning to acquire the regal manner at Metro-Goldwyn-Mayer.

CHAPTER XXI

THE PRESSURE TELLS

THALBERG was driving, ever driving, through these productive years, and inevitably, without his knowing it, the pressures were beginning to tell. He and Norma had built themselves a new home—an imposing French provincial chalet—on the ocean front at Santa Monica after the birth of their first child, Irving, Jr., whom Norma carried while she was doing *The Divorcée*. (She had urged Thalberg to let her do that picture by having some elaborately sexy photographs made of herself by the studio photographer. Thus she proved to her husband that she could look a femme fatale. Towards the end of the shooting of the picture she had to make frequent use of large fans!) Irving and Norma now cut loose from his parents and moved into the new house in the summer of 1931, after a trip to Europe, which was taken largely for Thalberg's health.

But the troubles that began accumulating in 1932, mainly the insistent demands for studio economies that the national Depression brought on, taxed the strength of Thalberg, who was not physically strong, anyhow. The increasing momentum of his progress was stretching the tension on his nerves. It was under these circumstances that a sad event, which occurred late that summer, greatly shocked the producer and threw him into a strangely morbid mood.

It was Labor Day—fair and lazy. The studio was closed and Howard Strickling, head of publicity, was relaxing at his beach house when a call came from Norma Shearer. Her voice was choked with excitement.

"You'd better go right up to Paul Bern's house," she said. "Something terrible has happened. Irving just got a call."

"What's the matter?" asked Strickling.

"Paul's been found dead!"

Strickling leaped in his car and went racing through Beverly Hills to Bern's home. As he roared up winding Benedict Canyon, he met the big car of Mayer coming down. He flagged it. Mayer was inside, pale and shaking.

"Paul has killed himself," he said. "I've got the suicide note in my pocket."

Mayer had been one of the first to arrive after being summoned by

Bern's butler who had found the body lying sprawled on the living-room floor. The body was nude. A .38 caliber revolver was lying beside it and a .38 caliber bullet hole was in the head.

"We've got to get that note right back," said Strickling. "You should never have lifted it. Let's go!"

Police were swarming around the house when Mayer and Strickling got there. The note was turned over to them. (It was later grabbed by a reporter whom Strickling caught just as he was dashing off with it.) The note was to Bern's wife, Jean Harlow, the beautiful blonde actress whom he had wed just two months before, after she had made a much ballyhooed picture, *Red-Headed Woman,* for Metro-Goldwyn-Mayer.

It was a pathetic little missive. It said simply:

> Dearest dear:
>   Unfortunately this is the only way to make good the frightful wrong I have done you and to wipe out my abject humiliation. You understand that last night was only a comedy.   PAUL

The news, as it spread, was a sensation—one of those stark Hollywood violences, made to order for the lurid newspapers and the gossip-hungry fans. There was a strong breath of scandal about it. Jean Harlow was a luscious-looking twenty-one-year-old girl whose alleged romances with several actors—most notably William Powell—at the time of her surprise marriage to the forty-two-year-old Bern were common gossip in Hollywood.

There were also hints of a romance with Clark Gable just before the death of Bern. Indeed, Gable was on a fishing trip with Harlow's stepfather over that Labor Day week end. Strickling, who knew this, trembled lest the two hear of the tragedy and come charging up to the house together while all the reporters and photographers were there. Fortunately, they didn't. That tempting tip-off for the scandal-mongers was kept concealed.

More particularly—and more fascinating—the shooting posed a mystery. As pieces of information were assembled, the possibility of murder darkly loomed. What did Bern mean by that comment, ". . . last night was only a comedy"—that is, *if* he wrote it? Had Harlow been with him in their home?

She claimed she had spent the night at her mother's, elsewhere in Beverly Hills. Her story was that she and Bern were expected to have dinner at her mother's home that night and that Bern had sent their cook and butler over to prepare the meal. Harlow was there, but her husband never arrived, she said. She went to bed. The next day, the butler, returning to the house, found Bern dead.

However, neighbors reported that they had heard an automobile drive away from the Bern house sometime after midnight. It was going so fast the tires screamed as it rounded a turn. Was it Harlow—or someone else?

A few days later, there came an amazing revelation. It was acknowledged that Bern had been supporting a woman, a long-time friend, named Dorothy Millette, who sometimes called herself Mrs. Paul Bern. It was discovered that she had been staying in a San Francisco hotel, but checked out the day after Bern's death and disappeared that night from a river boat going from San Francisco to Sacramento. One week later, her body was found by two fishermen at the river's edge. It was assumed she had drowned herself.

There were lengthy and tantalizing investigations. Harlow, hysterical, could not appear. Confusing and contradictory testimony was given by several witnesses, including Mayer. A verdict of suicide was finally rendered. "The motive is undetermined," the coroner said. But this didn't satisfy the curious. To them, the case remained a mystery.

Indeed, it was reopened six months later before a grand jury and more tantalizing evidence was then brought forth. For instance, it was said that Miss Harlow and her mother had been in San Francisco two weeks before the death of Bern and that a woman closely resembling Miss Millette had been seen entering their hotel room. Also it was discovered that Miss Millette had subsequently been in Los Angeles and that a "mysterious woman in a pink dress" had been at Bern's house the day before he was found dead. Again the dark finger of suspicion moved towards Miss Harlow, who was by now one of Metro-Goldwyn-Mayer's important stars by virtue of *Red-Headed Woman* and a subsequent film with Clark Gable, *Red Dust*. But again the verdict was suicide, and this time the case was closed for good.

Despite the general suspicions, it was believed by most of Bern's close friends that he did take his life, on account of an exceedingly intimate condition that caused him deep chagrin. The fact was that he, a small man, was what the doctors call "infantile." And his notable interest in beautiful women was believed to have been a device by which he gave an appearance of being a Don Juan and compensated himself for his cruel inadequacy. His friends thought he wooed and married Harlow, a much-publicized siren, because of the opportunity it gave him to prove his charm to the world, and that he did kill himself because of some "abject humiliation" that occurred. There was a strong emphasis placed upon sexual prowess among the elite in Hollywood.

The irony was that Harlow, for all her appearance of voluptuousness, was not the hot-blooded female that she was imagined to be. She was an average, amiable woman, not stupid but not too bright, whose several romantic and matrimonial difficulties were clues to her emotional passiveness. She died five years after the death of Paul Bern, almost as shockingly as he did, of a brain swelling caused by uremic poisoning, after an illness of ten days. She was then at the height of her oddly come by fame, a sex symbol in American motion pictures and one of Hollywood's undying myths.

Whatever the ghastly circumstances of Bern's death may have been, it plunged Irving Thalberg into a sad, philosophical, resentful mood. Bern had been much more to him than a helpful associate. He had been a sort of private transmitter of the atmosphere and culture of a world of sophisticates with which Thalberg as a youth had no contact and which the maturing man was coming to enjoy. Professionally, Bern was one of his "senses," his "feeler" in the realms of literature, theatre and high-class music, about which Thalberg was avid to know. To lose him was not only distressing but it opened a dangerous cavity.

Furthermore, this morbid experience suddenly brought Thalberg up against an anxiety that was always eating on him. That was his own mortality. He was a chronic health-worrier who insisted that the rheumatic fever of his youth had left him with a heart condition that would cause his death before he was forty years old. He always carried pills in his handkerchief pocket. Norma had learned to use a hypodermic needle so she could give him injections if he were seized with a "heart attack" at home or on a trip. Bern's death inevitably caused him to reflect on his own passage in this vale of tears.

There were other disturbing factors. Schenck had been on the studio's neck all year because pictures had not been coming through with absolute regularity. A couple of the inexorably scheduled weekly releases had been missed. Schenck would call Mayer about them, more insistently each time this occurred. Mayer would take it up with his head of production, who became increasingly peeved. Also Thalberg had been forced to take a 35 per cent salary cut in July as part of the sweeping program of pay cuts and economies that was being imposed in all the studios. Thalberg was in a state of tension where something was bound to pop.

The Big Blow-Off

It did, one day in September, a few weeks after the death of Bern. Mayer signaled the situation by telephoning Schenck in New York. "You'd better come out here as soon as you can," he said.

Among the countless celebrities who flocked to the Metro-Goldwyn-Mayer lot was this bearded British playwright, outwalking his escort, Marion Davies.

About the same time came Winston Churchill, who was guest of honor at a memorable studio luncheon. Here he is flanked by his solemn hosts, William Randolph Hearst and Louis B. Mayer.

Shortly before mysterious tragedy struck, Paul Bern and his bride, Jean Harlow, at their home (1932).

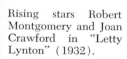
Rising stars Robert Montgomery and Joan Crawford in "Letty Lynton" (1932).

Schenck sensed that this was no nonsense, and got on the train to the Coast.

He was met by Mayer and Rubin, and they went right away to Schenck's hotel. Mayer put the situation bluntly:

"Thalberg claims he isn't well. He is asking to be relieved of his contract."

This sounded suspicious to Schenck, who remembered what followed the Fox deal. He wanted a better reason for Thalberg's beef than his health.

"I believe the boy is getting spoiled," said Mayer. "People are telling him how good he is. I believe it is turning his head a little. There are all kinds of offers." (That was the truth: Thalberg was being handsomely propositioned by several other studios.)

Later, the producer was called in. Mayer's apprehensions were correct. Thalberg was blunt about it. He wanted to break his contract right away.

Schenck said, "Irving, that is silly. You have a contract up to 1937. I have no right to release you. I don't own the company. You are a valuable man." (Two years previously the contracts of the "Mayer group" had been extended from 1932 to 1937.)

"I don't feel well," said Thalberg. "The responsibility is too great. I would like to go away and come back and then see what I want to do."

Thalberg asked for a year's leave of absence. Schenck told him it could not be arranged, that the organization continued and prospered solely on the quality of its personalities and brains.

The first meeting ended on that note. Thalberg was stubborn. Schenck was stern.

The talks continued for several days, becoming more acrimonious all the time. At one point, Schenck tried to reason with Thalberg.

"Now, Irving, after all, you are a youngster. You are not prepared to retire. You will have to work somewhere else, do something. The government will tax you, no matter what you do."

Thalberg would not be moved in his purpose.

The exchanges between the two became so violent and personally abusive that even Mayer was shaken and appalled.

"I was watching Schenck," he later reported. "His fingernails were purple as he held onto the side of his chair. Irving was riding him terribly hard and driving him. He told Schenck he didn't give a damn; that he (Schenck) was cold as ice, that he wasn't even human just as long as we made lots of money for the company. Oh, it was just fierce! And Schenck kept yelling back, 'Damn it, I've been decent and right with you! This is a corporation! I've got legal responsibilities!' Oh, it was hell! We (Mayer and Rubin) got out of the room."

Thalberg was harried and desperate. He said he had no concern about whether the company went on, that he was not getting enough out of it to warrant his working himself to death.

Schenck finally saw he wasn't bluffing.

"We'll sue you for damages," he said.

Thalberg laughed in his face. "We'll meet that later." And he walked out of the room.

Now Schenck was stuck with his problem. He went into conferences with Mayer, Rubin and Edward Loeb, the studio lawyer, and they decided among themselves that the only way to pacify Thalberg was to give him more money for what he did.

Already his partners in the "Mayer group" had been compelled twice, in the past three years, to increase his portion of the yearly "bonus" the group received out of the net profits of Loew's, Inc. In December, 1929, they raised his portion from 20 per cent to 30 per cent, with Mayer surrendering the difference from his portion and Rubin continuing to receive 27 per cent. And again, on April 7, 1932, they changed the split so that Mayer and Thalberg now received 37½ per cent each. Money was Thalberg's one avidity. "What the hell do you do with all of it?" Schenck once asked. That was an ingenuous question—coming from Schenck, especially.

Since it was obvious that an increase in salary was out of the question at that bad time, and since neither Mayer nor Rubin felt they should give up any more of their cuts, the conferees came up with what they thought a happy solution all around. It was to give options for Loew's stock to all three members of the "Mayer group." The idea was broached to Thalberg. He said he would be interested only if he were allowed to buy several hundred thousand shares, then selling around sixty, for ten dollars a share.

"That is silly," Schenck told him. "You know I cannot go back to my directors and then to the stockholders to approve such a deal."

However, Schenck returned to New York with the idea and went right away to call upon Winthrop Aldrich at the Chase National Bank. Aldrich was head of the banker group administering the Film Securities Corporation, which was then holding the William Fox block of Loew's stock.

Schenck told him the whole story and asked his professional advice.

"What about you and Bernstein?" Aldrich asked, when he got through.

"How do you know about Mr. Bernstein?" Schenck said.

"Oh, I know all about Bernstein," Aldrich said, "I've never met him but I know all about him." Then he continued, "The whole thing sounds all right to me, but I want to think about it and talk to a few people. I will talk to you in a day or two."

When Aldrich called Schenck back to his office a few days later, Sidney Kent was there. Kent was then general manager of Paramount, but he was being groomed by the bankers to take over the presidency of Fox Films.

"I feel, Mr. Schenck, that I am going to recommend this deal to the people I represent," Aldrich said. "But I also insist that you and Bernstein make a contract with this company for the same length of time and also have an option for stock."

Schenck resisted the suggestion—of a contract, anyhow. "I believe I can do better service to our company by being free," he said. The logic of that contention was a little hard to understand. Aldrich told him he thought it would be healthier for the company if he were tied up.

Thalberg and Mayer were called to New York, where the stock option deal was arranged. It was finally settled that Thalberg would be permitted to buy up to 100,000 shares of Loew's common stock, between December 1, 1934, and March 1, 1939, at thirty to forty dollars a share, no matter what the market price. The shares would be automatically issued out of the surplus authorized by the corporation's charter and the purchase price would be paid to Loew's, Inc. Mayer would be permitted to buy up to 80,000 shares on the same terms, and Rubin 50,000. The contract with the "Mayer group" was extended to December 3, 1938.

At the same time, Bernstein was put on a contract that ran to December 31, 1939 at a salary of $104,000 a year and given an option to buy 50,000 shares of Loew's common on the same terms as given the "Mayer group." He continued to receive his cut of 1½ per cent of the net profits of Loew's, Inc. Schenck was continued on an outright salary of $130,000 a year, with 2 per cent of the net profits of Loew's, Inc. He successfully resisted signing a contract at that time by foregoing a stock option deal.

The Depression may have hit the movie business, but it evidently hadn't hurt too badly the lions of Metro-Goldwyn-Mayer. . . .

Illness Strikes

Thalberg drove forward for the next two months. Then, one night in late December, on reaching home in a state of near exhaustion, he drank a bottle of ginger ale and was seized with a piercing discomfort that sent him stumbling to his bed. His constant anxiety swarmed upon him. Norma and the doctors were quickly called.

Inevitably, it was imagined that he was suffering a heart attack.

Mayer was alerted immediately. He hurried right over, bringing his own doctor with him. He was a "bug" on doctors, all the time. His doctor endorsed the heart diagnosis. Mayer immediately called Schenck.

"Irving is very ill," he told him. "We think it's a heart attack."

Schenck rushed to California. This was really dire. Mayer met him and took him to the home of Thalberg. Norma received them, graciously. She appreciated their calling but she couldn't let them see Irving. He was not to be disturbed. Schenck went back the next day—and the next. He was still not admitted to Thalberg's room. This struck him as ominous. Maybe Mayer was right about the heart. And the grim thought agonized him: If Thalberg went, who was going to keep the pictures moving at the studio?

Mayer offered a suggestion: how about his son-in-law, David Selznick; why not try to get him to Culver City to produce the big films? Selznick, who was then head of production at R-K-O, was one of the "wonder boys" of the movie business. He was twenty-nine. He had married Mayer's daughter, Irene, in 1930—much against her father's will. But now he looked very good to Mayer as a possible adjunct to the staff at the studio.

Schenck was for it. They made Selznick an offer. He and his wife thought it over carefully. Then he struck a deal to go with the company at $4,000 a week on a two-year contract, with a vice-presidency in Metro-Goldwyn-Mayer and his pick of the stories and the talent available at the studio. Quite a deal!

When Mayer went to Thalberg's home and told him about it, Thalberg, somewhat improved, was so enraged he virtually chased Mayer out of the house. Not only was he resentful that the deal was made without first consulting him, but he had his strong suspicions of what was going on. Thalberg had nothing against Selznick. They were friends, socially, and were mutually respectful as producers. But he didn't like the prospect of change.

Thalberg's confinement to bed lasted for a few weeks. Then, in mid-January his physician, Dr. Philip Newmark, issued a report: "Mr. Thalberg had a heavy attack of influenza that lasted several days," it said. "Although he was quite ill, he recovered nicely. However, he is far from being in good condition. He is all tired out and needs rest. I do not consider it necessary, at this time, to send him away, as he is quite comfortable at home."

As to the rumors that Thalberg had suffered a violent heart attack, Dr. Newmark said that his patient's heart "has not been any too strong, and that is another reason why I have insisted that he take a long rest." But a supplementary report by Dr. Robert W. Langley indicated that a "coronary thrombosis" had occurred.

The situation was critical. Thalberg was away from the studio. Whether he would return was problematic. And the wolf was at the door.

Then, in February, it was agreed that the ill producer should take a long vacation, that he should go to Europe to his favorite spa, Bad Nauheim, and rest.

Before he left, he received a long letter, a remarkable communication, from Mayer. It said:

> Dear Irving:
>
> I cannot permit you to go away to Europe without expressing to you my regret that our last conference had to end in a loss of temper, particularly on my part. . . . When I went to see you, I was wearied down with the problems I have been carrying, which problems have been multiplied because of the fact that the partner who has borne the major portion of them on his shoulders was not here. Instead of appreciating the fact that I have cheerfully taken on your work, as well as my own, and have carried on to the best of my ability, you chose to bitingly and sarcastically accuse me of many things, by innuendo, which I am supposed to have done to you and your friends. Being a man of temperament, I could not restrain myself. . . .
>
> And now, let me philosophize for a moment: Anyone who has said that I have a feeling of wrong towards you will eventually have cause to regret their treachery, because that is exactly what it would be and what it would be on my part if I had any feeling other than what I have expressed in this letter towards you. I assure you I will go on loving you to the end. . . .

Thalberg, on his part, spent several days writing and discarding drafts of a letter to Schenck, attempting to express his objections to the new arrangements at the studio and answering Schenck's evident criticism of the care and patience with which he had been making films. His tedious pains with this letter (which was simple and brief, when finally sent), indicated his deep hurt and his discomfort at having to boast of what he had achieved.

A few days later, the Thalbergs, Irving and Norma and their small son, left Los Angeles aboard the S.S. *California* for a slow trip through the Panama Canal and around to New York. They were accompanied by their now close friends, Helen Hayes and Charles MacArthur (and their small daughter, Mary). Helen had just wrapped up a second film for the studio, *White Sister*. She had worked late the night before the departure to finish it.

For the first time since he had come to California with Laemmle as a spindly boy, Thalberg was leaving the film community for an indefinite—perhaps permanent—stay. The studio and all its worries were behind him. He was shaking its dust from his feet.

The portents of calamity in his leaving were paralleled by others on all hands. While the Thalbergs were at sea, the bank closings were ordered by the new President, Franklin D. Roosevelt, and several Hollywood studios were temporarily shut down. An earthquake shook the Los Angeles region and an influenza epidemic raged on the West Coast. It was grimly suspected by some Californians that the world was coming to an end.

On his arrival in New York, Thalberg seemed cheery. He laughed at rumors that the studios might stay closed and at suggestions that the national emergency spelled the doom of the motion picture industry.

"Hollywood can never be doomed, except by producing bad pictures," he said. "These money troubles, I think, are only temporary. Art has never been fostered by finance."

Thalberg himself knew all too well how ironic were his words.

Still accompanied by the MacArthurs, the Thalbergs sailed from New York in March. Just before sailing, he told reporters, "They overdiagnosed me on the Coast. I have had myself checked by several doctors in New York and their reports were satisfactory."

The party, on arrival in Europe, went directly to Germany and Bad Nauheim. It was there that Thalberg's friend, Dr. Franz Groedel, operated his famous sanitarium and dispensed his treatment of heart ailments with the carbonated waters of the spa. Thalberg, who had been there in 1928 and 1931, had a child's faith in him.

But this was two years after his last visit—a critical time in Germany. Dr. Groedel was part-Jewish and, just before the Thalbergs arrived, some hoodlums had smeared swastikas on the windows of his health hotel. The doctor had indignantly demanded that the hoodlumism be erased, which it was, but the incident was ominous. The doctor's clientele, mainly rich American business magnates, thought it wise to go elsewhere that year. The place was practically empty and quite dismal during the gentle spring months the Thalbergs were there. The local gauleiter was in residence, and would nod to them, with a sinister air, in the dining room.

Thalberg did not realize it, but, in many ways, it was well after noon.

CHAPTER XXII

THE OLD ORDER CHANGETH

THE ILLNESS and absence of Thalberg threw the studio into a state of gloom. Supervisors who had come to depend upon him were virtually demoralized as the pictures then in production suddenly became their responsibilities, without any aid from their mentor or shouldering of blame by him. Bernie Hyman once told his associates: "So long as Irving is here, we're all great men." Now Irving was gone, perhaps forever, and they felt pretty helpless and small.

Likewise, there was a vast uncertainty right after Thalberg left as to what the exact organization of future operations would be. Would the present group of supervisors continue to function individually, with—or without—the collaboration of an overall production head. What was to be the status of David Selznick in the studio? Until Mayer came forth with an announcement of arrangements for carrying on, they weren't even sure—most of them—whether they were going to continue to have jobs.

And, to make matters worse, the conditions then prevailing in all of Hollywood were about as bad and discouraging as they could possibly be. The effects of the national Depression were weighing heavily on the industry, the closing of the banks by President Roosevelt early in March seemed the cue to calamity. Serious thought was given to suspending all activities, while the sorely hit companies readjusted to the woeful state of affairs.

To stave off disaster, an organization of all the Hollywood producers, led by Mayer, proposed that all studio workers, including producers and stars, should take a 50 per cent reduction in their salaries over the next eight weeks. This proposal was supported by the Academy of Motion Picture Arts and Sciences, which had become the virtual labor representatives of the various talent groups.

This brought a howl from the smaller people who not only opposed a salary cut but suspected that the Academy was being used as a "company union" under Mayer's and the other producers' thumbs. It was clearly remembered that the Academy was originally dreamed up by Mayer, back in 1927. He proposed it to Conrad Nagel and Fred Niblo one Sunday at his Santa Monica home, and he personally gave the big dinner party at the Ambassador Hotel at which the organization was launched. It was Mayer's idea that the film makers should have an association of their elite, which would give due recognition to achievement and represent the talented people in various ways. That it came to be the contract arbitrator between the studio heads and the talent groups was a significant and eventful development that was assisted considerably by Mayer.

However, the alignment of the Academy with the producers in March, 1933, was a bit too thick for the little people. They balked, and most of the studios were closed for a couple of days while they feverishly sought a compromise. This was got by having the burden of pay cuts fall upon the higher salaried executives and stars. They were politely invited to "cooperate" in the "national emergency." Most of them agreed. But as one wag put it, "Can you cooperate with an electric chair?"

Thereafter the functioning of the Academy as a labor representative gave way, for reasons that are obvious, to the rising screen talent guilds.

In the midst of this cheerless situation, Mayer, backed by Schenck, proclaimed that an entirely new system of production would be instituted at the Culver City studio. Instead of the Thalberg system of several supervisors working under one man, which had become more unwieldly as film making became more complex with sound, they would henceforth operate in "units." Each supervisor would have his own autonomy in the production of each picture, with Mayer in overall command but not inclined to get deeply involved in the creative process or give instructions, except in matters of policy.

Stories would be asked for by the individual supervisors, instead of being assigned, as they had been. Their choice was subject only to Mayer's approval and to the availability of the material desired. Writers, directors and actors would be drawn from the studio contract pool, or brought in from outside, when it was felt necessary, again subject only to the approval of Mayer. The actual production of the pictures would be entirely the supervisors' responsibility. Mayer wasn't likely to look at them until they were previewed in theatres.

In keeping with this new system, Mayer instituted another change, which was also in line with his concepts of managerial distinction and showmanship. Supervisors would henceforth be called "producers" and the credit line, "produced by," would be put at the beginning of all pictures, in advertising and such. Theretofore, only one supervisor, Hunt Stromberg, had obtained the formal designation of "producer" or got his name on a film. Thalberg had eschewed this ostentation. He had never advertised his name. "If I had to tell people I made a picture, putting my name on it wouldn't help me," he said.

The men who now moved into the position of "producers," in addition to Stromberg, were Harry Rapf, Bernie Hyman, Eddie Mannix, Larry Weingarten and Al Lewin, who had been upped to full supervisor following the death of Paul Bern. Mannix, a "Schenck man" from way back, was made a vice-president, too. Mayer had also brought in from the outside, as soon as Thalberg took ill, two men who had been producing elsewhere, Walter Wanger and Lucien Hubbard.

And, of course, there was David Selznick. He was the big boy of the lot.

David and the Goliath

Selznick was more than a new messiah—he was even more than Mayer's son-in-law—when he moved into Culver City. He was the bold heir of the fabulous Lewis J. Selznick, one of the lusty producing pioneers. Dave and his older brother, Myron, who was an agent in Hollywood, were almost unique in the picture business: they were second-generation peers.

This fortunate descent from a father who had studiously tutored his sons to take care of themselves in the picture business (or any other business, for that matter) by "living big" undoubtedly accounted for the vigor, self-confidence and noblesse oblige with which the youthful Dave Selznick vaulted his way to the top in Hollywood. In less than six years—beginning in 1927—he rose from seneschal to Harry Rapf in Culver City to vice-president and ace producer in that studio.

The ascent was marked with pyrotechnics. Selznick got his first job by arguing Rapf into hiring him, nominally as a reader of scripts, at $100 a week on a two-week trial.

Rapf had initially protested. "Readers don't get that kind of money," he said.

"I know they don't," replied Selznick. "But I'll do more for you than read scripts. I'll help you fix them. I'll write titles. I'll do everything that has to be done to them."

Rapf was intrigued with the prospect. "Come to work on Monday," he said.

But before Monday rolled around, Selznick received a telephone call from Rapf. "I've got bad news for you, Dave. Mr. Mayer says he won't have anybody by the name of Selznick working at this studio."

Mayer and old Lewis J. Selznick had never been what you might call close.

Then Selznick read in the papers that Nicholas Schenck was in town. He had once met the latter, with his father, under circumstances that had impressed Schenck favorably. So he went to see him at his hotel, and recalled himself to him.

"Of course, I remember you, Davie," said Schenck. "What are you doing in this town?"

Selznick explained he was making himself available for employment.

"Anything I can do for you?" asked Schenck.

"You can gamble $200 on me," Selznick answered, quick as a flash.

"What do you mean, gamble $200?" Schenck was immediately intrigued.

"Just tell them out at your studio to give me a job for two weeks," Selznick said. Then he explained the situation.

"Call me at the studio this afternoon," Schenck snapped.

Selznick called. A secretary told him that everything had been arranged. He went to work the following Monday as a sort of assistant to Rapf.

They gave him a hole in the wall and a typewriter. Before his two weeks were up, he had suggested three stories, titled two pictures and rewritten a couple of scenarios, in addition to making himself useful to Rapf in other ways. At the end of two weeks, his pay was doubled and he was given a permanent job. A few months later, he was upped to $300 and made Rapf's assistant on the production of the Tim McCoy western films.

Woody Van Dyke was the director on the McCoy films at that time, and Selznick and he got together and decided to make a reputation with them. The McCoy films were a pretty cheap product, budgeted at about $80,000 each, but they served a commercial purpose at the bottom of the schedule of the studio. Selznick and Van Dyke concocted a scheme for shooting two at once, with setups on either side of the camera, each with a separate company, and McCoy going back and forth between them. Through this saving of time, they were able to bring in two pictures for only about $10,000 more than the cost of one.

It was then that the studio bought *White Shadows in the South Seas*. Stromberg was assigned as supervisor and Van Dyke was put on it, too. One day Thalberg stopped young Selznick and said, "How would you like to supervise this film?" At least, that's what Selznick thought he said.

"There's nothing I'd like better!" the young man answered.

"Then go tell Stromberg," Thalberg said.

Selznick rushed to see the supervisor, who had worked for his father at one time. Stromberg gave him several instructions as to how the film was to be made. Selznick expressed disagreement. Stromberg then explained that he was not to be the supervisor, that he was just to serve as his assistant with the shooting unit that was to go to the South Seas.

"You mean, just the *unit manager?*" Selznick hit the roof.

In those days, the "executive dining room" was in a bungalow on the lot. Selznick had not been asked to eat there, but this day he barged in at lunch time and sat down. As the various supervisors entered, they looked at him curiously. The last man in was Thalberg. He glanced at Selznick casually. "Oh, Dave, I'm glad you're here," he said. "I want to talk about *White Shadows.*"

"And I want to talk about it, too!" Selznick said. "I think the whole thing's being done wrong! I think—"

Thalberg cut him short. He said he agreed with Stromberg's ideas, and was going on to explain, when Selznick interrupted to expound on what *he* thought should be done. In the middle of one of his sentences, Thalberg got up from his chair, flung his napkin on the table and deliberately walked from the room.

It was as though someone had spit in the potatoes. Men looked at Selznick in horror and edged away from him contemptuously. As Selznick himself got up to go, Rapf hissed at him, "I can't square this! How dare you talk to Irving that way!"

The next day, Thalberg and Selznick met in a corridor.

"I didn't like the way you talked to me, Dave," Thalberg said. "I have to ask for your apology."

Selznick was polite but stubborn. "I don't feel I have anything to apologize for," he said.

"Then I must ask for your resignation," said Thalberg.

"You have it," replied Selznick. "When do I leave?"

Selznick popped over to Paramount, went through something of the same routine of offering himself on a trial arrangement, landed a $300-a-week job and, within a couple of years, was being boosted for head of the studio. B. P. Schulberg, who held that position, early told him, "You're the most arrogant young man I've ever known."

Meanwhile, he had met, courted and married Mayer's younger daughter, Irene, who was, in the Hollywood peerage, every bit as much a personage as was he. She and her sister, Edith, had been carefully sheltered and raised, according to the dictates of their father, who had some patriarchal notions about the home. He was highly offended when young Selznick began to court his little girl. When they announced that they intended to get married, he almost had a stroke.

At the least, he would not permit it until Irene's older sister was wed. This she was, in March, 1930, to a young assistant producer, William Goetz. Irene and Selznick were married one month later, at a quiet ceremony in the home because Mayer's father, Jacob, who lived with them, had died ten days before. Mayer would not speak to the bridegroom at the wedding, and he grudgingly gave his blessing to Irene.

However, he did speak to Selznick shortly after that, when the young man walked away from his job at Paramount.

"How dare you give up that contract!" he yelled. "And you married to *my* daughter!"

"I didn't like the setup," Selznick told him. "And besides, I have other ideas. I want to produce on my own."

Mayer scoffed at the notion.

"All right, it takes courage," Selznick said. "But if I haven't got courage at twenty-eight, when will I have it?"

His father-in-law was frankly doubtful. "Let's see where you go from here," he said.

Selznick's first maneuver was to take himself and wife to New York, along with Lewis Milestone, the director, with whom he hoped to form an independent producing company. His purpose was to get financial banking and then a distributor for the films they would make. But he couldn't seem to rouse any interest. All the doors in the industry were closed.

One night, he and Irene were having dinner at the home of Nicholas Schenck. Joe Schenck was there. He suggested that Selznick might like to come to work for him at United Artists as a producer.

"Did Mayer have anything to do with this suggestion?" Selznick asked.

"What's the difference," said Joe. "How about it?"

Selznick thanked him and declined. By now, he had more than a suspicion that he was being blocked from independent production by the influence of his father-in-law.

"But I'm not going to let L. B. Mayer keep me from what I want," he told Irene. She agreed, and they set themselves to thinking who might be impervious to any possible persuasion by Mayer. They came up with David Sarnoff, president of the Radio Corporation of America, the powerful and industrially ambitious parent of R-K-O. Selznick went to see him.

Sarnoff liked the young fellow. He arranged for him to have a job. Within two years, Selznick was head of production at R-K-O. It was in this job that he established himself as a man to mark, with such films as *A Bill of Divorcement*, for which he brought Katharine Hepburn and director George Cukor to Hollywood; *The Animal Kingdom*, with Ann Harding, and, of all things, *King Kong*, produced by Merian Cooper, under Selznick's sponsorship. It was while he was pondering whether to continue with R-K-O that he got his attractive offer to go to work for Metro-Goldwyn-Mayer.

Selznick was weighing the alternatives when his father died. That was in January, 1933. At the funeral, his mother told him the last thing his father said was, "Tell Dave to stick to his own people; the only people you can depend on are your own." On his way home from the funeral, he decided to accept the offer from his father-in-law.

For all the attractiveness of it, he very soon discovered that the row he had to hoe at Culver City was going to be a long and difficult one. All of Thalberg's good friends were resentful and deeply suspicious of him. They naturally felt that he was using his relationship with Mayer to get Thalberg's job.

"The son-in-law also rises" became the cruel gag all over Hollywood.

It wasn't that the hiring of an in-law was such an odd or contemptible thing by the ethics of the motion picture business. Every company and studio had its quota of the bosses' relatives. There were more Loews and Schencks, in-laws and cousins (and in-laws of in-laws), in New York and in other branches and subsidiaries of Loew's, Inc., than you could get into a fair-sized room. When the word "nepotism" got wide usage in connection with the Selznick episode and Hollywood people rushed to their dictionaries to find its meaning, they were very much let down. They thought it meant something unusual, some sex deviation, perhaps.

Indeed, within two months after Selznick went to work for Metro-Goldwyn-Mayer, there occurred an example of favoring relatives that still holds the record in Hollywood. That was the private arrangement by which Nicholas Schenck and Mayer put up $750,000 each for Joe Schenck and William Goetz, Mayer's other son-in-law, to join with young Darryl F. Zanuck in starting the new Twentieth Century Pictures company and then arranged for them to borrow Wallace Beery to play in *The Bowery*, one of their first successful films.

No, it wasn't so much the employment of Mayer's son-in-law that the friends and associates of Thalberg resented. It was the placing of him on a par with their beloved *genius loci* and the extension of preferential treatment to him. They made no bones about their feel-

ings. Selznick was snubbed and shunned almost as bluntly as he had
been at that luncheon when Thalberg left the room. He was treated
so brutally and badly that it even got under his skin, to the point
where he would go home at the day's end, throw himself on the
bed and cry.

But his wife, Irene, comforted and cheered him. "Let them yam-
mer," she said. "You can still take the best that the studio has to work
with. Serve your term—and *make some films!*"

Selznick accepted the challenge. He started a picture called
Dinner at Eight. . . .

Meanwhile, the dismal conditions throughout the film industry
showed no immediate improvement. At last, the magnificent balloon
of physical expansion and yearly profits had been punctured after
a quarter-century of erratic rise and had plunged towards the ground
in seeming wreckage. It was wondered whether it ever again would
rise.

In January, Paramount-Publix and R-K-O went into receivership.
The Fox company was in sad disorder, and Warner Brothers was in
a bad way. Total revenues in the motion picture business had
dropped by half in two years, it was said. The disaster was felt most
keenly and most dangerously in the theatres.

Indeed, it was because of the big expansion of theatre building
and acquisition on the wave of sound that the companies which had
indulged in it were now in financial distress. With the great fall-off
in attendance that began in 1931, these companies were unable to
find the money to pay off their mortgages and bonds. Economies in
their studios wouldn't begin to take care of their debts. They were
in real trouble. Bankruptcies and reorganizations were compelled.

It was in this darksome period that the conservative policies of
Marcus Loew and Nicholas Schenck toward the acquisition of
theatres were fully and happily justified. Because they had not
plunged Loew's, Inc., into the wildly competitive race for supremacy
in theatre holdings, and because they had steadfastly held to safe and
cautious methods of financing their real estate, the company was now
in the soundest condition of any in the industry.

Of course, there had been a drop in its income. From a peak gross
of $130,000,000 declared on its annual statement in 1930, the com-
pany's total revenues declined to a low of $81,000,000 in 1933. Net
income fell off in the same period from $15,000,000 to $4,000,000.
Even so, the company continued paying dividends on its stock right
through the Depression. Loew's was the only film company that did.

One other reason for its continuing solvency was a new policy for
renting films which the company's head of distribution, Felix Feist,

put into effect in 1931. Where Loew's had previously followed the standard policy of renting its films for 30 per cent of what they grosséd in the theatres, the new Feist plan set up a sliding scale of percentage charges. The company's seven designated top films of the year would rent in a 35 per cent bracket, the next seven would rent for 30 per cent and the remaining product of the company would go for no less than 25 per cent.

This sliding-scale rental policy later became common in the industry. But at the time Loew's announced it, the reaction was as violent as had been the rebellion of the theatre operators when the exchanges broke away from the "ten cents a foot" selling practice of the old Trust. A huge rally of exhibitors, frankly labeled "The Metro National Protest Meeting," was held in New York. Some twenty-six exhibitor organizations, representing some 7,000 theatres, sent protestors. Feist ably espoused the fairness of the plan. The exhibitors let off steam—claiming, as usual, that they would be ruined. None were; not by the Feist plan anyhow.

Thalberg Returns

Four months after their departure for Europe, Thalberg and his family returned to New York. Gossip was hot in movie circles as to what he was going to do. Already the *Hollywood Reporter*, which often seemed to have a remarkable acquaintance with Mayer's thoughts, had suggested editorially:

> Those who want to guess on the Thalberg situation are of the opinion that the present conduct of MGM's production will not be touched by Thalberg. . . . The guessers figure that Thalberg has no desire to go through that drudge of single-handedly running MGM, that he has ideas that mean more to him than the power, dictatorship and personal glory that go with the handling of a big production organization.

That was, of course, the role of Mayer.

The Thalbergs, Irving and Norma, spent a week at the home of the Nicholas Schencks on Long Island. That awful, hysterical quarrel of the previous fall was forgotten. Thalberg, minus his tonsils, had put on fifteen pounds, looked fine and was in good spirits. But he was in no great hurry to reveal his plans. If and when he reached an understanding with Schenck, he would leave for Hollywood, he said.

"The important thing is that Irving is back in the best of health he has ever enjoyed," beamed Schenck.

Thereafter, the Thalbergs tarried and had a good time in New York. A month later, his arrangement with the head of the company was leaked to the press. As anticipated, he would not return as over-all head of production at Metro-Goldwyn-Mayer. He would have his own separate production unit, which would turn out six to twelve pictures a year, and he would have first call on all talent—stars, directors, writers, cameramen—at the studio. Structurally, his position was to be the same as that of Selznick and other producers on the lot, except that he was to be the most important and would probably make the most films.

What wasn't even vaguely suspected at that time, let alone leaked to the press, was that Thalberg had made a strong endeavor to persuade Schenck to free him from his contract so he could set up his own independent company. He wanted to be shed of all restraints and obligations, but to this Schenck would not agree.

It is notable that he continued to draw the same salary and get the same cut from the "bonus" of the "Mayer group" that he had previously received.

He and Norma returned to Hollywood in August. Soon he was back at the studio. His old friends flocked around him, in the vain hope that nothing really had changed. . . .

During his stay in Europe—having leisure, for the first time—Thalberg permitted himself to do some serious thinking on subjects outside the realm of films. He even committed to paper some surprisingly weighty ideas about economics and the American social system, which promptly went into his files. He was shy to reveal his scholarly interest, which actually flowed in a rather awkward, rigid vein. But he felt his mentality expanding, and he particularly enjoyed the intellectual exercise.

On one subject, however, he was an expert. That was the subject of films. And, in an article gestated during his absence, he let himself go unstintingly. It was called "Why Motion Pictures Cost so Much" and was published in the *Saturday Evening Post* of November 4, 1933. It was a sort of exegesis on all his difficulties during the previous year, when New York was clamoring for more product and demanding economies, at the same time.

Spending money on pictures, to make *good* pictures, was only wise, he said, and he cited the improvements that resulted from spending more money on *Ben Hur* and *The Sin of Madelon Claudet*. The real sins of the industry, he insisted, were the foolish attempts to maintain too many theatres and the overstaffed sales forces and distribution systems required to service them. To maintain these organizations, the producers were forced to make too many films. The consequence was too many poor pictures and a spiral of waste and public apathy.

The resentments accumulated in the years Thalberg labored to turn out schedules of between forty-four and fifty pictures a year to serve the theatre-minded men in New York burst forth in this article, which ended with these admonitory words:

> To continue the present destructive policy of rushing out pictures poorly made, of destroying stars by robbing them of their glamour and their ability to give distinguished performances, of bewildering the best creative efforts of the best writers through forcing them to work on silly material and rushing them on good material, of loading down good pictures with the production costs and selling expenses of pictures which nobody wants to see—to continue any such suicidal policy is to continue giving the one inescapable answer to the question of why pictures cost so much and to invite a condition of public apathy in which there won't be any pictures at all.

It took twenty years for the wisdom of Thalberg's reasoning to sink in.

CHAPTER XXIII

THE COMPETITIVE URGE

THE PROPHECIES of ancient Troy's Cassandra were no more insouciantly ignored than were the warnings that Irving Thalberg issued in the fall of 1933. His forecast of peril in the practice of producing so many films caused industry policy makers not the slightest concern. They went right on clamoring for pictures to be made as hurriedly and abundantly as they were before and during the height of the Depression, which, for the motion picture business, was that year.

Indeed, the demand for output was even more pressing than it had been, because of a change in exhibition that had developed during the lean and hungry years. This was the practice of showing two pictures (and sometimes three) for the price of one—a come-on for bargain hunters which was labeled the "double-feature" or "double bill." The practice was not new; Loew's had tried it in some of their theatres as early as World War I. But it became widely prevalent and popular when the public had little money and lots of time to spend, and it stuck thereafter as a fixture of the system of mass-selling films.

The spread of the double-feature brought the death of "combination vaudeville," which had already begun to wither as a popular-price theatre custom with the intrusion of sound. The endowment of films with voices and music rendered them esthetically and economically supreme over the tired and familiar "live acts" that had continued to rotate on the "combination" bills. Now the programs of "double-features" and assorted "shorts" filled up the time, and the movies finally took absolute possession of the field of "family entertainment" into which they were modestly born.

Thus, the increasing competition to get more elaborate and attractive pictures on the screens stimulated more production. And as the Depression passed, all the studios stepped up their endeavors to excel with stories and stars. The fact that the margin for improvement was vastly extended with the mastery of sound made it possible to develop new subjects of refreshing variety and literacy. The possibilities proved much more inspiring than Thalberg at that time foresaw. As a consequence, the mid-1930's were—despite everything he said— great years for American movies. They were particularly great and prosperous for Metro-Goldwyn-Mayer.

It was notable, however, that the pictures produced while Thalberg was away did not make the studio's usual showing on the lists of that year's best films—with one significant exception. That was Selznick's production of *Dinner at Eight,* a contemporary multi-character drama on the order of *Grand Hotel.* It was based on a popular stage play by

George S. Kaufman and Edna Ferber which the studio obtained for
$110,000 in highly competitive bidding (and with the friendly
assistance of Joe Schenck, who bought it from his pal, producer Sam
H. Harris, for United Artists and then resold it to Metro-Goldwyn-
Mayer). And, in his casting of it, Selznick heeded the advice of his
wife by taking fullest advantage of the studio's abundant talent pool.

He drew Marie Dressler, Wallace Beery, Jean Harlow, John and
Lionel Barrymore, Lee Tracy, Billie Burke and Jean Hersholt to play
the various dinner-party guests, and he brought to the studio George
Cukor, his new recruit from the Broadway theatre, to direct. The
script was written in four weeks by Donald Ogden Stewart and
Herman Mankiewicz, and the whole thing was before the cameras
for no more than twenty-four days! The finished film, which cost
$420,000 complete, was in the Thalberg tradition—a modern drama
with quality and "class."

All of the performances were excellent, but that which Marie
Dressler gave as a gaudy and comical dowager was a particular
triumph for the fine old star who had been spreading her talents
mostly in a run of homely comedies with Polly Moran. She also
turned up with Wallace Beery in the explosive *Tugboat Annie*,
simultaneous with *Dinner at Eight*.

From that immediately impressive—and, for Mayer, particularly
gratifying—success, Selznick raced on to the production of *Night
Flight*, a high adventure film about airmail pioneers in South America,
based on a novel of Saint-Exupery. His cast for this was Clark Gable,
Robert Montgomery, John Barrymore and the Thalbergs' friend and
companion (recently returned from Europe), Helen Hayes. Selznick
followed that with *Dancing Lady*, in which Gable again was co-
starred, this time with jazzy Joan Crawford and a new boy from
Broadway, Franchot Tone. This one—a backstage story—included
several songs. Selznick got a good young team to write one, Richard
Rodgers and Lorenz Hart, who had done one score for a picture called
Hot Heiress before signing with Metro-Goldwyn-Mayer. He also had
Robert Benchley, Ted Healy and Fred Astaire in his show-world
cast. The hit song was appropriately expressive of Selznick's pull:
Everything I Have Is Yours.

Then, before the year's end, he had started *Viva Villa!*, a rowdy tale
of the fabulous Mexican bandit, with Wallace Beery in the title role,
and *Manhattan Melodrama*, with Gable, Myrna Loy and William
Powell, the latter brought to the studio from Paramount. No one
could say the son-in-law didn't rise to the occasion that year.

Meanwhile, the bitterness and resentment of other producers
towards him had been absorbed into a thickening climate of competition among all of them at the studio. The old "team spirit"

generated by Thalberg, the all-for-one-and-one-for-all attitude, had gone with the setup of "units." Now every producer was on his own, angling and playing politics for the most promising stories, writers, directors and stars.

Thalberg himself discovered, very soon after his return, that making pictures under the new system was going to be quite different, even for him. He had already told Schenck his misgivings as to its practicality. He feared the primary aim for *quantity*-output would destroy everything he had labored to build—the value of stars, the respect for writing and the allowance of time for people to create. He foresaw deterioration in the quality of pictures and the spread of internal strife. Now he was to test by hard experience the justification for his anxieties.

He started with several promising projects. His first picture was to be a high-society drama called *Riptide*, in which Norma Shearer was to star. Norma had not appeared in a picture since her sentimental but successful *Smilin' Through* in the fall of 1932. During her husband's illness and absence, she had stayed constantly at his side. The personal risk in such devotion greatly impressed Hollywood. Now the community was curious to see how successful would be her return.

Thalberg also had a story—a novel—by Stefan Zweig, which Robert Rubin had purchased for him while he was away, on the thought that he would want it for Norma. It was *Marie Antoinette*. Nine weeks of disappointing writing had already been put on it, and it looked to be "destined for the junk pile" when Thalberg took it over and started working on it. Further, he had in mind a talking version of Michael Arlen's *The Green Hat*, which had been done as a silent picture with Greta Garbo and titled *A Woman of Affairs*. He also had an interesting novel, purchased the year before—Pearl Buck's *The Good Earth*. These, with some other tentative projects, promised to keep him busy for a while.

But he ran into trouble with *Riptide*. Charles MacArthur was expected to do the script, then balked at it, fearing the story. It was about an American girl who married an English noble and later had what appeared an affair with a dashing American playboy while on vacation in southern France. "Fists across the seas," MacArthur tagged it. Eddie Goulding finished the script and directed the film, which also had Robert Montgomery, Herbert Marshall and Mrs. Pat Campbell in the cast. But for all Miss Shearer's charm and beauty, which were carefully emphasized, to the delight of her still loyal and ardent admirers, *Riptide* was not a distinguished Thalberg film.

While in the throes of its production, he wrote a long letter to Schenck, voicing his dissatisfaction at the way things were going for him. He was not able to get the writers he wanted, and he complained that "the utmost humiliation has attended the delay in the signing of the contracts with the people that I have engaged." This caused him to lose Elissa Landi, whom he believed he could have developed into "a real star," he said. And he also complained that Mayer had refused to let him take over Franchot Tone.

"I have never found the men in this institution so completely demoralized and uninspired," he wrote. "Our standards have slipped . . . tremendously. The pictures that I see, while far from bad and some quite good, are juvenile, immature, uninspired and lacking that finish that characterized our product for so many years. If, however, they are financially successful, I presume that is definite proof that we are on the right track."

He wrote to Schenck again a few weeks later in an even more biting and cynical vein:

> I am frankly dismayed at the satisfaction that you have expressed and Louis has expressed with the pictures and the setups for the present and the future. . . . To me the enthusiasm expressed for mediocre pictures possessing a certain ingredient of obvious audience entertainment, and the wild cheers that accompany pictures possessing considerable merit are disconcerting to the painstaking effort that I, as a producer, might care to exercise.

He then went on to cite several instances in which he had been unable to get the writers and directors he wanted for his films. "I have been forced to work with the continuously available and out-of-work writers I can pick up," he said. It was clearly implied that his bitterness was directed against Mayer.

However, he persisted in his efforts. His life was in the making of films, and since he was bound to the studio by his contract, he was determined to do the best he could. Fortunately, his spirits were bolstered when he was able to begin production on a film that much intrigued him: *The Barretts of Wimpole Street.*

This romantic drama of Elizabeth Barrett and the poet, Robert Browning, had been a great and world-famous stage hit, with Katharine Cornell and Brian Aherne. It was precisely the sort of material that Thalberg sought to put on the screen. He saw it as eminently suitable for Norma Shearer, even though she did not; she was doubtful of playing an invalid poetess and having to spend half the picture on a couch.

By a grotesque coincidence, however, Marion Davies had fallen in love with the play and was eager to do it as a picture. Her wish was backed by William Randolph Hearst. They even did screen tests of Miss Davies as Elizabeth Barrett to convince Mayer that she should have the play. Miss Davies made up for it in a black wig, which hung shroudlike around her gamin face. Mayer knew she was unsuited to the dramatic role. Besides, Thalberg wanted the play for his wife.

This time, Mayer was entirely on his side. He tried to discourage Hearst. That took considerable doing. The great publisher was angry and dismayed. He always entertained the hopeless notion that Miss Davies should play serious dramatic roles. Suddenly the name of Norma Shearer no longer appeared in the Hearst press. A very delicate situation prevailed in the studio. Then Miss Shearer paid a call on Miss Davies; they had a between-us-girls talk and Miss Davies came to the conclusion that Elizabeth Barrett was really not for her.

The cloud passed, but that disappointment was not forgotten by Hearst. He was beginning to get the idea that his protégée was not appreciated at Metro-Goldwyn-Mayer.

Thalberg's production of *The Barretts of Wimpole Street*—and Miss Shearer's performance in it—were among the top achievements of their respective careers. Sidney Franklin was the director. Fredric March was got to play the Browning role and the rising British actor, Charles Laughton, who had recently been at Paramount, was recruited for Elizabeth's tyrannical father. The settings and costumes were handsome, and Franklin caught the poetry of the play. A leading reviewer put it fairly: "Hollywood could make no more fitting answer to its critics than this. . . ."

The Mercurial Selznick

The impressive momentum that Selznick accumulated for himself in his first year as a Culver City producer was maintained as he carried on. With a strong taste for literary classics, he chose to do Charles Dickens' *David Copperfield,* and he got an excellent picture out of it, with director George Cukor's splendid help. Mayer wanted them to use Jackie Cooper as the inimitable Dickens lad. Jackie was then held in great affection because of his performance as the loyal son of Wallace Beery in *The Champ.* "He's a wonderful kid," Mayer insisted, but Selznick and Cukor shuddered at the thought of the tow-headed, snub-nosed American youngster as David Copperfield.

Fortunately, on a trip to England to scout locations (which were never used) and to pick up some background footage, Cukor came upon an amazingly attractive little fellow named Freddie Bartholomew. He flashed the word to Selznick that he had found a Copperfield, and Selznick wired back to grab him. The boy was brought to this country with his aunt, which required some complicated maneuvering, for the child's parents proved difficult. However, it was well worth it. Freddie was most winning in the film and became established by it as one of the memorable child actors of all time.

Charles Laughton started as Micawber, but it was soon recognized he wasn't right for the role. So Selznick went to Paramount and made a hasty arrangement to borrow W. C. Fields. The substitution was providential. Fields' Micawber was a masterpiece.

Nick Schenck had serious misgivings about the length of the finished film. It ran for two hours and thirteen minutes, which was painful to the theatre-minded man. "How long can it be?" Schenck pleaded. "How long is it good?" Selznick replied. He won the point with that argument. Schenck agreed it was good all the way.

It is not too clearly remembered that Selznick also used Freddie Bartholomew in his production of Tolstoi's *Anna Karenina*, with Greta Garbo and Fredric March as the stars. Garbo, now in the empyrean, so far as stardom was concerned—and at a salary of $250,000 per picture—was barely averaging one picture a year. In her period of more frequent appearance, she had played the tragic Anna in the silent *Love*. Little Freddie, as the wistful son of the wayward lady, came close to stealing the show.

Despite his success in the studio setup, Selznick still had the desire to be an independent producer—to make pictures on his own, away from a factory organization and free to operate as he chose. His passion for independence was the same as that which Thalberg now had. Both men were convinced of the necessity of taking time and care in making their films, beyond that comfortably permitted by the pressures of a studio.

So, on a proper occasion in the middle of 1935, he announced that he wanted to break his contract and go on his own. He had finished *A Tale of Two Cities*, another Dickens film, and had been making tentative arrangements with outside interests to form his own company. Mayer tried to dissuade him, and even spoke of cutting him in on the bonuses of the "Mayer group." "You'll fail! You'll fail!" his father-in-law told him. But Selznick would not be discouraged. "I'm thirty-two," he answered. "I can afford to fail."

When Thalberg heard of his intentions, he congratulated him on his courage. "You are doing the right thing," he told him. "I'd like to invest in your company."

And so, a few months later, when Selznick formed Selznick International, which was subsequently to be the parent of *Gone With the Wind*, one of the great motion pictures of all time, he did so with $100,000 which Thalberg put up in the name of Norma Shearer. That was a small token of the confidence and respect that Thalberg now had for him.

CHAPTER XXIV

HAILS AND FAREWELLS

WHILE Thalberg was working on *The Barretts of Wimpole Street,* he was also engaged in producing *The Merry Widow* and thereby escorting on her way one more of the feminine luminaries that helped to give the studio its glow. She was Jeanette MacDonald, a striking redhead with a voice like a bell who became a romantic symbolization of the sturdy opulence of Metro-Goldwyn-Mayer.

Miss MacDonald was a musical comedy actress who had been grabbed up by Paramount in the first wild scramble for pretty singers after the switch to sound. She had done four good pictures for that studio—*The Love Parade, The Vagabond King, One Hour With You* and *Love Me Tonight*—before the first musical cycle ended and left her, along with other singers, temporarily at liberty. She was in France, on the Riviera, in the spring of 1933, when she got a double invitation to go to work for Metro-Goldwyn-Mayer.

By now, a second musical cycle was generating on the strength of the popularity of the Warners' recent and novel, *Forty-second Street.* Mayer, who had spotted Miss MacDonald and tried to get her when she was still at Paramount, now resumed his endeavors to coax her to his studio.

As it happened, the Thalbergs were also on the Riviera that spring, having proceeded thence from Bad Nauheim. Their path and that of Miss MacDonald crossed at Cannes, where the beautiful singer was living in elegant style. They became friends and frequent companions after Miss MacDonald generously loaned her very special chauffeur-hairdresser to Norma Shearer to do her hair. Thalberg was then in hopes of starting his own company, and he was angling to sign Miss MacDonald when she got a bid from Mayer.

The latter clinched the deal when he promised that the singer's first picture would be a very special and spicy musical comedy that had been "made to order" for her. It was called *I Married An Angel* and had to do with a heavenly creature who wed a mortal man and very quickly lost her heavenly attitudes. The script had been written by Moss Hart from a Hungarian play, and the original musical score was composed by the studio's new team of Rodgers and Hart. Miss MacDonald returned with enthusiasm on a two-picture contract to Metro-Goldwyn-Mayer.

But her inauguration was not too propitious. When she reached the studio, she was told that *I Married An Angel* simply could not be done. The industry had lately committed itself to the moral restraints of a strict Production Code, and Joseph Breen, the code's administrator, had turned thumbs down on the unangelic show. Sadly, *I Married An Angel* was consigned to the studio shelf—from which it was removed five years later and turned into a Broadway hit, thence to serve (under more relaxed conditions) for one of Miss MacDonald's last films at Metro-Goldwyn-Mayer!

With that out for the present, however, the fiery redhead was dubiously assigned to *The Cat and the Fiddle*, a recent acquisition from the musical comedy stage. Ramon Novarro was tapped to be her co-star. He was rapidly on the wane. Miss MacDonald went into the venture with displeasure and anxiety. To make it worse, Bernie Hyman, the producer, had fiddled with the Otto Harbach book. The production was commendable mainly for the Jerome Kern musical score.

When that picture was finished, Miss MacDonald was again at loose ends. Mayer had nothing to offer that she was eager to do. Then he broached *Naughty Marietta,* an old Victor Herbert show. This didn't overwhelm her, either. She had "story approval" and was hard to please. One day Mayer got her in his office—Herbert Stothart, the studio's musical director, was there—and he undertook to convince her that *Naughty Marietta* was the picture she should do. He praised her, he told her touching stories of the stars whose careers he had planned, then he offered courteous suggestions as to how she should strive for an emotional quality in her singing style. Suddenly, to her astonishment, he got down on his knees and began singing the Jewish lament, *Eli, Eli,* in a most serious and tremulous way. Miss MacDonald was genuinely affected by the uninhibited sentiment of the man. Tears came to her eyes. He got up humbly. "That's the way you should sing," he said.

The experience disarmed her completely. *Naughty Marietta* it would be. Mayer took her hands and assured her, "You trust me and you'll be a happy girl!"

Meanwhile, another pending project was running into a snarl. That was the production of *The Merry Widow*, which Thalberg was planning to do. He had got Ernst Lubitsch to direct this first sound version of the operetta of Franz Lehár, which had been a smash hit for the studio as a silent film. And he was trying to get as leading lady the talented but difficult Grace Moore.

Miss Moore had a characteristic objection. Thalberg had signed Maurice Chevalier to play the role formerly done by John Gilbert.

Chevalier's contract specified that he was to have top billing. His name was to head the cast and be uppermost in the advertisements. Miss Moore would not agree to that, and Chevalier would not surrender. The casting had reached an impasse.

Oddly enough, it was Thalberg who had put Chevalier on the road to Hollywood. He had called upon the great French music-hall singer in Paris in 1928 and had tried to interest him in a contract with Metro-Goldwyn-Mayer. Chevalier at first would not believe that the thin, boyish-looking fellow who came to see him was the famous head of that important studio. Then he agreed to do a silent screen test, which turned out very well. Too well. Before Thalberg could clear the terms of the contract with Mayer and Schenck, Jesse Lasky of Paramount, who was in Paris, saw the test and signed Chevalier for his studio. Thus the Frenchman's first Hollywood appearance was in *The Innocents in Paris*, following which he was with Jeanette MacDonald in *The Love Parade*.

Now the thought of another association of the two presented itself. If Miss Moore would not accept the top billing of a co-star, maybe Miss MacDonald would. Mayer passed the problem to Thalberg. He got the singer in his office, and again she was subjected to an earnest and eventually convincing argument. Thalberg didn't sing *Eli, Eli*, but he gave Miss MacDonald a moving talk on the higher aspects of star performing and how unimportant billing was. She again surrendered to persuasion and agreed to do the *Widow* role, with billing beneath Chevalier. No greater self-denial hath any star.

That settled, they leaped into the production, holding *Naughty Marietta* until it was done. The whole thing went off very nicely, even though Chevalier had put on some weight and fit too snugly into his uniforms. *The Merry Widow* was given a gala première in New York and was hailed as a "Lubitsch confection." As usual, Thalberg, unassuming, took no billing for himself.

The outcome of that confusion might have been arranged by a happy fate. In the first place, Grace Moore, having turned down the commitment, was at liberty to accept an offer from Columbia a short while later to do *One Night of Love*, which was, by far, her most memorable picture and one of the best of all operatic films. And, in the second place, the delay of *Naughty Marietta* compelled a hunt for a leading man for it, which ended with the "discovery" of Nelson Eddy, who had been a wash-out in pictures up till then.

Eddy had been brought to the studio a year or so before on the urging of Ida Koverman, who was now private secretary to Mayer. Miss Koverman had seen the big blond baritone do a concert in Los Angeles and had joyfully told Mayer about him. A contract was arranged and Eddy was given one song number in a vaudeville-family picture, *Broadway to Hollywood.* (Another fledgling in it was Mickey Rooney, who played the son of the vaudeville team as a child.)

So minor was Eddy's performance that he wasn't even mentioned in most of the reviews. Neither was he mentioned as a participant in *Dancing Lady,* with Joan Crawford, in which he again had one song. Indeed, he made such a weak impression that he had become discouraged and was taking lessons to improve his dramatic acting, when *Naughty Marietta* came along and Mayer persuaded Hunt Stromberg, the producer, to give him a chance in it.

Stromberg and others had misgivings. The big song that Eddy would have to sing, *Ah, Sweet Mystery of Life,* was the theme song at Forest Lawn Cemetery, they warned. But Eddy was cast with Miss MacDonald and the rest is history. *Naughty Marietta* was a winner, and Jeanette MacDonald and Nelson Eddy became a team that enjoyed phenomenal popularity and helped to establish the operetta as a particular specialty of Metro-Goldwyn-Mayer. On the huge success of *Naughty Marietta,* the two were cast in *Rose Marie.*

Good fortune was now heaping its blessings. Miss MacDonald was talking one day with a former title-writer, Robert Hopkins, who said he had a story that should be a "natural" for her and Clark Gable. It was a story of a Midwest girl who went to roaring San Francisco shortly after the century's turn and became a favorite singer in a Barbary Coast cabaret. The owner was a rakish adventurer who naturally fell in love with the girl and continued to pursue her when she went on to the local opera house and became the toast of the Nob Hill swells. The climax of the story, said Hopkins, would be the San Francisco earthquake and fire of 1906, in which the rake would prove his courage and devotion by wading through fire and ruin to find the girl. Hopkins wanted Miss MacDonald to help him push the story "upstairs."

She was delighted with it, and urged it first with Eddie Mannix and then with Mayer. It had the sound of a strong adventure drama that would also permit her to sing a variety of songs. The "upstairs" people liked it, but Gable was not then available. Miss MacDonald said she'd rather wait for him than go into a production of the operetta, *Maytime,* scheduled next for her. She was then being paid "per picture" and the delay would mean she wouldn't draw pay while waiting. But the prospect of the San Francisco yarn so pleased her that she was willing to make the sacrifice.

There was a hitch, however. Gable didn't like the idea. He wasn't interested in playing with Miss MacDonald. "She's a prima donna," he said. "I just sit there while she sings. None of that stuff for me!"

However, he was impressed when Mannix told him that the singer was willing to give up some pay in order to have him in the picture. The project was finally okayed.

Bernie Hyman and John Emerson were its producers. Anita Loos was put on the script and Woody Van Dyke was made director. They wrote into the story a rugged mission priest who was the friend of the cabaret owner. A contract player, Spencer Tracy, got the role.

Mr. Tracy

This Tracy was a bit of an enigma. He had been with the studio for something less than a year, during which time he had played in three pictures. In all of them he had tough-guy roles. In his first, *Murder Man,* he was a hard-boiled newspaper-reporter-sleuth. (Another newcomer in it was a tall, skinny lad from Princeton and theatrical stock, James Stewart. He played a droll reporter they called "Shorty." This helped to distinguish him.) Tracy's next film was *Riffraff,* with Jean Harlow. In this he was a gangster type. His third was *Whipsaw,* with Myrna Loy. Again an unsavory character.

Such was the kind of "type casting" that he had been subjected to since he had been signed up by Fox from the Broadway cast of *The Last Mile,* in which he played the original part of Killer Mears. Obviously, he was regarded as another Clark Gable type. (Gable, too, played the part of the Killer in the West Coast company of *The Last Mile,* you recall.) And, just as obviously, Tracy was not too happy in the roles. He came to be looked on as something of a "troublemaker" at Fox. When his contract was not renewed at that studio, he was taken on by Metro-Goldwyn-Mayer which had previously borrowed him for *The Show Off.* The studio was also having a little trouble with Gable about the same time. The building up of potential replacements was a way they had of disciplining the stars.

Anyhow, the casting of Tracy to play a priest in the new Gable-MacDonald film, which they had decided to call *San Francisco,* was a departure of some audacity.

They had fun making the picture. The first time Gable came on the set to play a scene with Miss MacDonald he had such a garlicky breath the actress could barely get close to him. She suspected he was letting her know his general opinion of prima donnas. A few days later, he unbended enough to ask her if she would kindly tell him why she had waited for him to be in the film. She looked him square in the eye and answered tartly, "Because you have so much sex appeal." He snorted and stalked off in high dudgeon. But they still had a lot of fun.

The "special effects" for *San Francisco*—the earthquake and the outbreak of fire—were among the most realistic ever done by a Hollywood studio. The spectacle of shivering and tumbling buildings, of great fissures opening in the earth, of bursting water mains and human panic, which continued for ten minutes in the film, was a stupendous re-enactment of an awesome debacle. It was done by putting full-sized sets on rockers and hydraulic jacks which were made to move so as to shake and then tumble the "buildings." For panoramas, they also used some "miniatures."

One "effect" was *too* clever, however. That was a shot in which Gable, shoving and clambering through crowds and wreckage, searching for the girl, was suddenly trapped and buried beneath a falling brick wall. It was a brilliant piece of illusion, terrifyingly real. So fatal appeared the calamity that when the actor came scrambling out from under tons of "bricks," which were nothing more than painted cardboard boxes, it was wholly incredible. Audiences roared at the first preview. The shot, so carefully made, had to be cut.

San Francisco was exciting and successful—a story of an extraordinary city and romantic people—and it thoroughly justified the confidence Miss MacDonald had in it. It was particularly propitious for Tracy. Out of it he emerged an actor of distinction and stature, which he has ever remained.

His playing of the priest in *San Francisco* came simultaneously with his appearance in another fine film, *Fury*, which was actually in production at the same time. Here again was one of those pictures that developed more or less fortuitously.

Largely responsible for it was a young fellow, Joseph Mankiewicz, who had been with the studio briefly as a writer and then as an assistant producer in the unit of a new man, Sam Katz. While still a writer, Mankiewicz had been invited by Norman Krasna to collaborate with him on a screenplay about an innocent man arrested as a suspected kidnaper and almost lynched by an outraged mob. The two never got to the screenplay, but when Mankiewicz later became an assistant to Katz, he began beating the drum for the Krasna story and begging permission to make it into a film.

Neither Katz nor Mayer liked the idea. They said it was too brutal and grim. But Mayer, who thought Mankiewicz had promise, told him he could go ahead. Mayer often backed the enthusiasms of young hopefuls, even in things he himself didn't like, on the theory that giving them chances to fall on their faces was the only way to have them learn. (Of course, some did fall on their faces; those were charged up to profit and loss.)

In this case, Mayer went even further. "I'll let you make it, and what's more," he said, "we'll put as much into this picture and behind it as we do for any picture this year. Otherwise, if it fails, you'll always say we didn't get behind it properly."

The story was bought from Krasna, who had almost forgotten it by now. He had to call Mankiewicz from New York and get him to refresh his memory so he could put it down on paper when the story editor, Sam Marx, offered him $25,000 for it. Mankiewicz asked for Tracy to play the leading role, and he settled to have Fritz Lang, an expatriate German, to direct. Lang had made some famous films for Ufa before being signed by Metro-Goldwyn-Mayer. Then he had languished for two years with nothing to do. His assignment to *Fury* came when he was about to give up hope. In the cast were Sylvia Sidney and Walter Brennan. The finished picture was universally hailed as one of the great sociological film dramas that surprisingly came out of Hollywood in those years. It combined with *San Francisco* to establish Tracy as a top American star.

In this period of astral propagation, another stellar personality that emerged out of the creative ferment of the studio was the astonishing Myrna Loy. Miss Loy's contact with Culver City had been established at the time they were making *Ben Hur,* when she—then an insignificant dancer—was one of many somewhat virginal-looking girls tested for the role of the Madonna, which Betty Bronson got. As an anomalous consolation, Miss Loy was given a tiny job as the mistress of one of the Roman generals who sat in a box and watched the chariot race.

After that she worked for Warner Brothers in many pictures, including *Don Juan,* the first Vitaphone sound feature, and the musical film, *The Desert Song.* In the latter, she played a harem beauty, which tagged her for Oriental roles. Her almond-shaped eyes and broad cheekbones made her the type for sin. Over a period of several years, she gravitated from boudoirs to opium dens.

Thalberg liked her in a minor Fox picture and signed her for Metro-Goldwyn-Mayer. She was in *Emma* with Marie Dressler and then was farmed out all over Hollywood. Her home studio also found her convenient for some six pictures in 1933, including the aforementioned *Manhattan Melodrama,* with Clark Gable and William Powell. Although she was again a shady lady, it was her good fortune that Woody Van Dyke, who had directed her in two previous pictures, was the director of this film, for out of it he got the notion that she should definitely have a change of atmosphere.

Indeed, he had a specific story for her and Powell that he thought would do the trick. It was a light-hearted, sophisticated mystery thriller about a private detective and his wife. The idea was that the couple should be wholesome and debonair while engaged in the perilous business of catching criminals. It was from a Dashiell Hammett novel, *The Thin Man.*

Mayer thought Van Dyke slightly daffy when he asked if he could do it with Miss Loy and Powell. Both people, he said, were "heavies." They wouldn't go in comedy. However, Van Dyke insisted that they both could be made to be droll, and that Miss Loy, if scrubbed up and dressed properly, could be a typical well-bred American wife. Furthermore, he guaranteed to make the picture at a minimum cost. That had a cheerful sound about it. Mayer convinced, said, "Go!"

With his usual expedition, Van Dyke shot it in sixteen days. Miss Loy knew something weird was happening to her when, for her opening scene, the director had her enter a room with an armful of bundles, trip and fall flat on the floor. She thought it mad, but it made a killing entrance. With that scene, a new Myrna Loy was born. She and Powell, too, were darling in *The Thin Man,* an unforgettably amusing film.

The addition of Miss Loy to the line-up of top female stars at the studio was both fortunate and timely, for in the same year that she "arrived," the pampered Marion Davies departed. And that grand old trouper, Marie Dressler, died.

Miss Dressler made just one more picture after *Dinner At Eight.* That was *Christopher Bean,* a tender story about the widow of a posthumously famous artist, based on a play by Sidney Howard. Even at the time she made it, she was suffering from cancer—a fact which was found out by Mayer after he had sent her to the country's top specialists and was told she could not be cured.

They gave her a wonderful party on her sixty-fourth birthday in November, 1933. One of the studio's huge sound stages was the appropriate setting for the affair. The food was fine. There were bright and charming speeches. Miss Dressler responded humorously and made quite a comical thing of cutting a birthday cake that was eight feet tall. Most of the 700 diners sensed this was farewell to a great and much-loved star. Some suspected that she, too, sensed it, but they couldn't tell from the way she took her bows.

She hadn't the strength for another picture. Slowly, she declined, and—brave to the end, her friends reported—she died in the summer of 1934.

The departure of Miss Davies was less poignant. She and Hearst had grown more dissatisfied with her position at Culver City after the *Barretts of Wimpole Street* episode. The actress, allegedly getting a top salary of $10,000 a week, appeared in only one picture—*Operator 13* with Gary Cooper—in 1934. That, incidentally, was the only picture Cooper ever made at Metro-Goldwyn-Mayer.

Then she and Hearst decided she must do *Marie Antoinette*.

Whether this urge was actually prompted by Hearst's weird fixation that his star should be a dramatic actress or whether it merely evolved from temperament aroused by the knowledge that it was to be a Norma Shearer vehicle was open to some disagreement. In any event, Mayer knew he was faced with another emotional crisis with the petulant Miss Davies and Hearst.

This one he handled boldly.

"Tell you what I'll do," he said to Hearst, whom he wished to maintain not only as a promotional asset but as a personal friend. "Even though it would hurt you and Marion, I'll let you have *Marie Antoinette*, if you'll pay full cost of the production. What's more, we'll distribute it free, until you've got back your money. Then you pay us *double* the usual distribution costs."

This was a put-up-shut-up challenge, for heretofore all Miss Davies' films and the other Hearst Cosmopolitan productions had been financed by Metro-Goldwyn-Mayer, with Hearst simply sharing in their profits. It was a foolproof arrangement for him.

Mayer's proposition stopped him. He declined to bet on *Marie Antoinette*, which already had accumulated a formidable pre-production cost. He took a trip to Europe, and shortly after his return, he made a quick deal with Warner Brothers to move Miss Davies and Cosmopolitan over to them. Thus the unique association that had continued since the merger of Metro-Goldwyn-Mayer was ended in a fit of vexation. Before the end of the year, Miss Davies' fabulous bungalow was dismantled and rolled off the Culver City lot.

No one, not even Mayer, was heartbroken to see it go.

CHAPTER XXV

THE *RASPUTIN* CASE

THE YEAR 1934 was witness to the conclusion of a chain of events that was an outrageous comedy of errors, as viewed from a sidelines seat, but was far from funny or rewarding to the people of Metro-Goldwyn-Mayer. This was the culmination of the famous "*Rasputin* case," which was one of the studio's prize fiascos and a precedential issue in the legal history of films.

The "comedy" actually started in the summer of 1932, when the studio—still under Thalberg—announced with justifiable pride that it was going to make a picture starring Ethel, John and Lionel Barrymore. The three had never acted together, either in films or on the stage, and the sideliners immediately began chuckling about the battles they imagined would occur when these three celebrated star performers and scene-stealers got together in the same film.

Anticipation was heightened by the word that the picture would be the story of the Russian monk, Rasputin, and his wicked influence upon the family of the Czar. Lionel would be the mad Rasputin; Ethel would be the pitiful Czarina who fell beneath the spell of the fanatic when he seemed to work a miraculous cure upon her sickly son, and John would be the Czarist prince who murdered the monstrous monk in order to end his fatal reign. The prospect of theatrical fireworks was as fine as it could possibly be.

Somewhat disappointingly, the turmoil did not develop among the stars but in the office of Bernie Hyman, the supervisor, and in the struggle to get the film made. The first draft of the screenplay was a hodgepodge of regal Russian pageantry, with orgies among the Czarist princes, naked women and Slavic sin. Charles Brabin, who had a distant Russian background, was brought in to direct. This was the same Charles Brabin who had been dropped as the director of *Ben Hur*. In order to accommodate Miss Barrymore, who had an early fall commitment on Broadway, they started the picture before the script was ready. The production was a rat race all the way.

One writer after another was set to work on the unruly script. Finally, Charles MacArthur was elected to put it into shape. He barely stayed one day ahead of the actors, so frequently were changes and rewriting required.

Rather than fight with each other, the stars fought with the director and with the script. Ethel, particularly, was outraged at the treatment of the Russian nobility. She fumed at the perversion of the Czarina, at the way she was asked to speak her lines. "You forget," she said to Brabin, "I knew Her Majesty personally!"

Another time, she reminded the assembled company that the Russian czar was a cousin of England's reigning King George V. Some of the people were suspicious. How could the Russian czar be related to the English king? The tendency was to treat the whole subject as though it were something that had happened in medieval times. Eventually, a discreet reminder from a local British officio caused them to tame the characters of the Czar and Czarina. "They became Mr. and Mrs. Hoover," MacArthur said.

However, other liberties were taken. Hyman wanted "shock progression," he averred. So he called for a scene in which the Mad Monk would violate one of the beautiful young ladies of the court. At first, she was just a lady-in-waiting. Then she was made a princess and was engaged to be married to John Barrymore's "Prince Chegodieff," as they called him, the heroic assassin of Rasputin in the film. The lovely English actress, Diana Wynyard, was the bewildered performer of this "Princess Natasha" role.

As a capstone to all these difficulties, Brabin proved unsatisfactory again. They had to find someone to replace him. In a wild search for an old Russian hand, they hit upon Richard Boleslavsky, a rather colorful émigré Pole. His recommendations were that he had been an actor with the Moscow Art Theatre and had served in World War I as an officer in a troop of Polish Lancers. His adventures had been described in a lively book, *Way of a Lancer*, published only that spring. The Barrymores had read it and thought that Boleslavsky would do, despite the fact that his previous experience as a film director was exceedingly slim.

The change did not help matters greatly. The jokers finally claimed a better title for the film would be *Disputin'* so extensive were the quarrels in getting it made. Thalberg was in on the battles, but he let Hyman have a free hand. In the end, for all the problems of production, the film came out rather handsomely. So proud, indeed, was Hyman, that he took his pen in hand and dashed off a bit of composition that was put as a preface to the film. It read:

"This concerns the destruction of an empire, brought about by the mad ambition of one man. A few of the characters are still alive. The rest met death by violence."

How the legal department ever let that preface get by is a mystery of studio operations that was never satisfactorily explained. Here, again, was the most fatal "error" that contributed to the "comedy" of this film.

Titled *Rasputin and the Empress,* the picture was presented at the Astor Theatre in New York two days before Christmas, 1932. It was greeted enthusiastically, but some of the pundits observed that, within its rather awesome melodrama, there were many historical inaccuracies. Indeed, someone made the suggestion that MacArthur should get the Academy award for the best original story of the year. One ominous note was sounded by Richard Watts of the New York *Herald Tribune.* "It achieves one feat which is not inconsiderable: it manages to libel even the despised Rasputin," he wrote.

Through the winter, spring and summer of 1933, the picture was shown to much success and admiration in this country and abroad. In Great Britain, they called it *Rasputin, the Mad Monk,* because of a national hesitation about using the terms of royalty.

Then one day, a New York woman lawyer, Fanny Holtzmann, turned up in Hollywood with the word that she represented Prince Felix and Princess Irina Yousepoff, exiled survivors of the Russian royal family. She said her clients were caused great pain and humiliation by the aspersions they felt the picture cast upon them. It seems that the prince was the man who was generally accepted as the assassin of the Mad Monk and, since he was married to the princess, it was implied that she must be the "Natasha" who was represented as having been violated by the brute. This besmirching of the princess' virtue was a libel, Miss Holtzmann said.

The people at the studio were not too troubled. Claims of libel against picture companies were becoming quite common, especially after the addition of sound to films. Only three years before, ex-Prince Danilo of Montenegro had obtained an award of $4,000 from a French court on the claim that he had been libelously portrayed as the character Prince Danilo in *The Merry Widow.* (They protected themselves by calling the character Captain Danilo when Maurice Chevalier later played the role.) The general practice was to defend libel actions, particularly when the studio felt it had an airtight case, as it did with *Rasputin and the Empress.* Miss Holtzmann was told she could sue.

Actions were filed simultaneously in New York and London. In New York, the firm of Buckley & Buckley was got by Miss Holtzmann to represent the Yousepoffs. In London, she got Sir Patrick Hastings, a famous trial lawyer, to be their advocate. Damages of $2,000,000 were claimed in each separate suit.

The acumen of filing in London became apparent when the case was first called there, and it was evident that the Yousepoffs would be favored by some strong royalist sentiment. The princess, indeed, was a cousin of King George V. It was at his personal request, Miss Holtzmann avowed privately, that she had undertaken "to do something for the poor Yousepoffs." The Russian couple were living at the time on one of the royal family's small estates near Windsor.

The trial proved a public sensation when it went on in the winter of 1934. The courtroom was daily packed with titled people and London's social elite. Sir Patrick made his case for the plaintiff by setting out to show that the characters of Prince Chegodieff and Princess Natasha in the film could have been drawn from no other models than the Yousepoffs. And, to establish the identity of Prince Felix, he called on him to tell how he slaughtered Rasputin in a St. Petersburg cellar eighteen years before. Spectators in the court were chilled with horror as the Prince calmly recounted the grisly tale, which corresponded in many details with the story as told in the film.

Sir William Jowitt, another famous lawyer, who was got as defense counsel for Metro-Goldwyn-Mayer, attempted to discredit the prince's story and to show that the characters in the film could have been based on other people. But that one line in the preface Hyman wrote—"a few of the characters are still alive"—was repeatedly cited by Sir Patrick to claim they could only mean the Yousepoffs.

In an effort to circumvent the claim of libel, Sir William asked the plaintiff's witnesses whether they thought any the less of Princess Irina because of the scene of Natasha's violation in the film. To a man, they said they did not. However, the maneuver was futile, as was Sir William's ultimate attempt to force from Prince Felix an acknowledgment that "an American lawyer, Fanny Holtzmann, has been exploiting your wife." Even though some spectators horse-laughed when the prince emphatically denied there had been any suggestion that the suit was "dishonorable," Sir William's hint was considered most impolite.

In charging the jury, Sir Horace Avory, the eighty-two-year-old judge, left no doubt that he thought the verdict should be guilty, and he quoted from Shakespeare's *Rape of Lucrece* to convey how the film's "vile libel" of the Princess' virtue had deprived her of "a thing dearer than life." He later acknowledged he had never viewed the film.

The jury, which had twice seen the picture, deliberated for two and a quarter hours, then upheld the claim of the Princess and set the extent of damages at $125,000. While the figure seemed small in comparison with the amount of damages asked, it set a precedent for other suits pending against all theatres that had shown the film in Great Britain.

Metro-Goldwyn-Mayer appealed the decision. In doing so, Sir William tried to hold that the offense was, at most, one of slander, in that the film did not maintain that the Princess voluntarily submitted to Rasputin but was unquestionably raped. (In a case of slander, it would have been necessary for the plaintiff to prove the precise extent of damages and not leave that to the jury to decide.) But the appeals court judge was as chivalrous as was old Sir Horace. "When this woman is defamed in her sexual purity," he said, "I do not think the precise manner in which she has been despoiled of her innocence and virginity is a matter which a jury can properly be asked to consider."

As might have been anticipated, the appeal was categorically denied, and J. Robert Rubin hastened to make an out-of-court settlement with Fanny Holtzmann as quickly as he could.

Already Hyman's prosy preface and the scene of Natasha's violation had been cut. Now it was a matter of bargaining to buy off the pending suits. It was agreed that the film company would apologize to the Princess and publicly proclaim that the character of Natasha in the picture was "purely fictional." This it did. It also paid to the plaintiff a sum of money, for which it was agreed that all claims would be dropped by the Princess, including the suit still pending in New York.

The exact amount of this settlement has never been publicly revealed. It is carried on the books of the company as $185,000—$125,000 to the Princess and $60,000 to Miss Holtzmann. However, it was generally reported at the time that $750,000 was paid to the Princess and the company absorbed some $380,000 in "costs." Miss Holtzmann remains cryptic on the subject.

"The settlement," she says, "was for a lot more money than they'll admit at Metro-Goldwyn-Mayer." It is quite possible that the company could have paid more than the books officially specified out of an unaudited contingency fund of around $1,000,000 that it regularly noted on its annual report.

In any event, the project of *Rasputin and the Empress* cost a lot, not only in human energy and legal expenses, but in the purchase of future protection for films. For it was after this sobering experience that all studios carefully stated in more or less these words on their every release:

"The events and characters in this film are fictional and any resemblance to characters living or dead is purely coincidental."

That is what came of Bernie Hyman taking his pen in hand.

CHAPTER XXVI

THE LAST OF THALBERG

APPROPRIATELY, Thalberg's so-called "genius" came to its fullest flower in the three years of toil and vexation that he had with his own unit at the studio. For in these years, he made the pictures that consolidated his fame as the most brilliant creative producer ever to work in Hollywood.

Following his satisfying triumph with *The Barretts of Wimpole Street*, his next fine picture was *Mutiny on the Bounty*, a film composite of the popular trilogy of *Bounty* novels, written by Charles Nordhoff and James Norman Hall.

Shortly after Thalberg's return to the studio, Frank Lloyd, a freelance director, came to him with a very attractive proposition. Lloyd had privately acquired the screen rights to *Mutiny on the Bounty*, which had been published the year before, and options on the two sequels that were to follow, *Men Against the Sea* and *Pitcairn Island*. Lloyd's offer was to sell the screen rights to Thalberg, whom he held in great esteem, with the proviso that he (Lloyd) would be signed up to direct the projected film.

Thalberg leaped at the offer. The story of the terrible mutiny on the British ship, *Bounty*, in the South Pacific in 1789 was an epic of mighty adventure, and Lloyd was a fine director. This was a conjunction of potentials that promised a splendid film.

Several months were spent preparing the screenplay. Thalberg gave the job of arranging the story-line to Carey Wilson, his old *Ben Hur* scenarist, who provided a much needed expert hand at blocking out the stories of the mutiny in the *Bounty* and the subsequent trip of Captain Bligh and his men in an open boat across 4,000 miles of sea. Then a new young playwright, Talbot Jennings, was hired to write the script, with Al Lewin, Thalberg's previous story editor, working as his production associate.

Charles Laughton, whom Thalberg had got from Paramount for *The Barretts of Wimpole Street*, was signed on early for the key role of the master of the *Bounty*, Captain Bligh, whose tyranny and sadism caused a group of his men to mutiny. Franchot Tone (failing Robert Montgomery) was cast as the loyal Midshipman Byam. For the role of Fletcher Christian, the stalwart leader of the mutineers, Thalberg insisted on Clark Gable.

But Gable didn't want the role. He felt the important character in the drama was Captain Bligh, who would be played by a polished British actor with an accent that would put his own drawl to shame.

What was more, Gable feared the knee breeches and sailor's pigtail he would have to wear, and he was superstitious about having to shave his familiar mustache, which went against British navy rules.

Eddie Mannix finally talked him into it. "You've got the personality for Fletcher Christian," he said. "And, besides, you're the only guy in the picture who has anything to do with a dame." That was true. It was Christian's consorting with native girls in Tahiti that led, in part, to the mutiny. Gable trusted Mannix. The mention of the girl did the trick. In the end, his performance of Fletcher Christian was one of the best he ever gave.

As an incidental sidelight on this casting, it is interesting to recall a contretemps that developed shortly before they started shooting the film. One day Thalberg summoned Wilson. "We've got a problem," he said. "The foreign department has turned up another *Bounty* film."

Sure enough, they had a little four-reel picture called *In the Wake of the Bounty,* which had been made very crudely and with a pick-up cast of actors by an Australian, Charles Chauvel. It had some good scenes of Pitcairn Island, and then, in flashback, it roughly told the story of the mutiny in the *Bounty* and the flight of the mutineers. It was not a very good picture, but Thalberg didn't want it to interfere with his costly production, so he bought the film rights from Chauvel.

"I've got an idea," he told Wilson. "Our audiences still don't know very much about the *Bounty*. So you take this film and cut it down to one reel. Use the Pitcairn Island footage, and tell a little of the *Bounty* history. We'll release it ahead of our picture and it will whet the appetites of audiences."

Wilson sat down with the little picture and ran it several times. The more he watched it, the more he became fascinated by a tall, handsome bucko who played Fletcher Christian. The part was all but edited out of the one-reeler, which was released as *Pitcairn Island Today,* but Wilson could not forget the actor. He was a very energetic young man.

Some months later, Wilson was invited by Marion Davies to a party to meet a team of Australian golfers. And among them, by George, was the unknown guy who had played Fletcher Christian in that picture and was about to start acting for Warner Brothers. It was Errol Flynn.

The filming of *Mutiny on the Bounty* was a herculean job, and Thalberg took great pains with it. Lloyd started shooting in Tahiti in February, 1935, to get background footage. A replica of the *Bounty* was built from an old sailing ship and this did service for all the outdoor shipboard scenes. Much of the outdoor filming was done off Catalina Island and in the Straits of Santa Barbara, where a tragic and

costly accident occurred. They had been shooting scenes of the cast-
aways in the long boat, with the cameras mounted on a barge. A storm
came up and the unit raced for shelter, but the barge was capsized
in the waves. The cameras were lost, with all that day's footage, and
an assistant cameraman was drowned.

Location accidents were not uncommon. There was the memorable
accident on *Ben Hur*. Later, while Clarence Brown was making *The
Trail of '98*, the last of the big silent epics, he lost three stunt men in
one fell swoop during the filming of a scene of gold prospectors shooting a Klondike river rapids in canoes.

After the Santa Barbara accident, Thalberg ordered the remaining
long-boat stuff shot in the studio, with the boat mounted on rockers
to give the effect of the rolling of the sea. One day, he had them rolling
it so wildly that the actors were groaning with mal de mer and the
technical advisers were forced to mention that no boat could survive
such a storm. It was with obvious disappointment that Thalberg
admitted they should tone it down.

Mutiny on the Bounty was presented in November, 1935. It cost
close to $2,000,000, but it was worth it. It could not be duplicated for
three times that cost today.

While he was working on *Mutiny*, Thalberg had gone ahead on his
third fine film of this period, which was *Romeo and Juliet*. His decision
to do the Shakespeare classic, with his wife in the role of Juliet, was
made when it was found they would have to further postpone the
oft-delayed *Marie Antoinette*.

"You're in a spot," he said to Norma, one evening while they were
dressing. "What are we going to do for you?"

Norma, looking at herself in a mirror, answered idly, "I think I'd
like to do Juliet."

Thalberg started, then broke out laughing, for Norma was conspicuously pregnant with her second child and, at that moment,
scarcely had the figure of the fourteen-year-old Veronese girl.

But the idea was not so idle. Both had had it in the backs of their
heads ever since Norma did the balcony scene with Jack Gilbert in
The Hollywood Revue. Now Thalberg, thinking upon it, agreed the
time was ripe. His decision may have been influenced slightly by the
fact that the Warners were about to do *A Midsummer Night's Dream*,
with the great German artist, Max Reinhardt, imported to direct.

Norma had her baby—a daughter, Katherine—on June 13, 1935, and
a few days later, Thalberg's intention to do *Romeo and Juliet* was
announced. Both Mayer and Mannix were dead against it. Mannix
flatly affirmed that "the masses" did not want Shakespeare. Mayer
later came to agree that a fine production of the classic might be good
for the studio's prestige. But both he and Mannix urged Thalberg

to keep the budget down. He estimated he could do it for $800,000. That didn't sound too bad.

Norma, fired with enthusiasm, prepared herself for the role by working diligently on her diction with Constance Collier and Mrs. Robinson Duff. At the suggestion of John Barrymore, who was to play Mercutio, she also worked with a Mrs. Carrington. The latter directed her to read poetry—pages and pages of it—out loud, every day. Norma wanted to catch the cadence of Shakespeare's iambic pentameter without speaking in the classic manner. She wanted to make the language vital and real—to speak like a motion picture actress so the dialogue would be comprehensible to general audiences.

The selection of a Romeo was difficult. Fredric March declined the role because he said it could not be played by any actor without strutting a little bit. Three English actors were considered—Leslie Howard, Robert Donat and Brian Aherne. Eventually, Howard was selected. George Cukor, Selznick's friend and one of the few stage directors who had managed to master the sound film medium, was named to direct.

The production was planned on a grand scale. Talbot Jennings prepared the script, with a Cornell professor, William Strunk, Jr., as technical adviser—"to represent the interests of the author," as he said. Meticulous attention was given to maintaining the dialogue and poetic content of the play, and great care went into the planning of the medieval sets and costumes. Agnes De Mille was hired by Thalberg to create the dances for the Capulet's ball (a lot of which later went into the discard because of the length of the finished film).

It is interesting and so indicative of the unpredictableness of making films that one of the best and most complex scenes in the picture, the critical "potion scene," was done with the least amount of trouble. It was shot on a Saturday morning, while Thalberg was away. He had gone to the desert for the week end with a couple of writers to work on another script, with the understanding that nothing was to be shot during his absence, other than some minor things. He always insisted upon seeing every important scene rehearsed before it was shot.

However, it was found this Saturday morning that the set scheduled for that day's shooting was not fully dressed. The only one ready was Juliet's bedroom. So Cukor said to Norma, "How would you like to try the potion scene? Let's just knock it off and see what we get."

The scene was written so that the whole thing, from the point where Juliet's mother left the room, right through Juliet's long soliloquy to her drinking the potion and falling on the bed, was to be done in one shot, without a single cut. This called for a great deal of cueing of camera movement and lights. They hadn't so much as rehearsed it, but Norma was up in her lines, so they went ahead and worked it out carefully. Then, just for luck, they made a shot. One take —that's all. "Okay, print it! We'll let Irving see it Monday," Cukor said. The stagehands seemed strangely silent.

They never made the shot again.

When they looked at it Monday morning, they agreed it could not be improved. It had an intimacy and spontaneity that no amount of rehearsing could achieve. Thalberg was a trifle peeved at them for shooting it when he wasn't there. But he had the good sense to realize that fussing wouldn't fool anyone.

The negative cost of the finished picture was $2,066,000, way above the original estimate. It brought in, during its period of amortization, just $9,000 more than that. What with the costs of advertising and distribution, it worked out to a loss of $922,000, which brought forth the "we told you so's." But the response of critics and the literate customers was excellent. Thalberg felt the effort justified.

As evidence of his old-time flexibility, it must be noted that he was engaged, during the months he was working on *Mutiny on the Bounty* and *Romeo and Juliet,* in finishing *A Night at the Opera,* with the Marx Brothers; *Riffraff* with Jean Harlow and Spencer Tracy, and in making preparations for *The Good Earth.* Not mentioned was the fact that he was also giving counsel to Bernie Hyman and other friends.

The Marx boys were among his favorite people. He personally enjoyed their madcap japes and was confident of their potential, when they were cast in a decent property. A year after they had left Paramount, where their last picture, *Duck Soup,* was a flop, he got them to Culver City and put them to work on an original farce. It was to be a spoof of the opera, and the Marx boys were nervous because they had the burnt child's anxiety about the humor of their material. So Thalberg made a suggestion: why not put together the key comedy scenes, rehearse them, call them *Scenes from A Night at the Opera* and take them out on the road—play them "live" in "presentation" houses before regular audiences?

This struck the Marx boys as brilliant, but maybe they didn't know that it fitted the theory of pretesting that Thalberg had at the beginning of sound. The experiment was gratifyingly successful. Some first-class material was proved. Thalberg himself "caught the act" when it got to San Francisco and enjoyed the sense of trouping with a show. It might be mentioned that *A Night at the Opera* did much better, financially, than *Romeo and Juliet.*

The Good Earth was a different proposition. Like *Marie Antoinette,* it had been on Thalberg's schedule since his return in 1933. The first problem was getting a "clean script" from Pearl Buck's story of a Chinese peasant and his wife who went through a poignant life cycle of toil, success, ruin and humbleness. Thalberg had people working on it for almost a year and a half—Frances Marion, Claudine West, Tess Slesinger, and Talbot Jennings, who was now his favorite fixer of scripts. Al Lewin was again his associate.

While the script was in preparation, George Hill was chosen to direct. He took a unit out to China, early in 1934, and spent several months shooting background and collecting masses of costumes and props. Among the assorted stuff he brought back were two live Chinese water buffalo, which became prominent features of the landscape of a complete Chinese village and farm that were built in a suburb of Los Angeles. Paul Muni was got to play the Chinese peasant and Luise Rainer was cast as his wife. She had just played Anna Held in *The Great Ziegfeld*, one of the studio's most lavish and successful musicals. This new role was quite a jump.

Then, one morning, just before they were ready to start shooting, Hill committed suicide. There was no indication that it was because of the film. However, this meant a delay in starting. Victor Fleming was next assigned to direct. He became ill while making final preparations, and Sidney Franklin was hastily called. It was under his able direction that the picture was made.

There were other difficulties. The Chiang Kai-Shek Nationalist government was unhappy about the making of the picture. It was fearful that it would reflect upon the conditions of the peasants in China. To allay these fears, Thalberg suggested the Chinese government assign its own observer. It sent a young Nationalist army general, Ting-Hsui Tu, who arrived with his wife and two children and rapidly became a genial and popular companion of the people working on the film. Tu was a devoted singer. He had a fine repertory of Chinese songs, from which Herbert Stothart, the musical director, selected themes for the picture's musical score.

Sometime before the picture was finished, Tu and his family suddenly disappeared. Attempts to find out what had happened, where he had gone, were to no avail. Later the Chinese consul in San Francisco showed up and announced solemnly that he had been instructed to take Tu's place. It seemed that poor Tu had committed the error of entertaining a disfavored Chinese general in Los Angeles and thus was suspected of having been corrupted into permitting a bad picture about China to be made. The company missed Tu's smiling countenance and his native songs.

To evidence the studio's responsibility, Lewin invited Lin Yutang, the Chinese writer, and the distinguished scholar, Hu-Shi, to look at the almost finished film. They were delighted with it and simply would not believe that it had not been shot in China, so authentic were the sets. Lin wrote copiously to friends in China, assuring them they need have no fears. Invented especially for the picture was a locust plague that constituted the dramatic climax. It made an awesome and convincing spectacle.

Unfinished Business

In 1935, Thalberg completed legal arrangements to have his own independent company—the I. G. Thalberg Corporation. This was something he had wanted desperately ever since his extended "vacation" in 1933. His relations with Mayer had grown more painful until the two men barely exchanged words. The deterioration of their old friendship was something that even their studio associates could not entirely understand.

It was undoubtedly the consequence of frictions between their different personalities. Within both were natural impulses of resentment and jealousy. The growth and success of the studio in the decade since they had taken command were things in which both men, in their fashion, took particular personal pride. When they disagreed on changing the system, it was inevitable that their strong egos should clash.

Mayer later explained the rupture as a purely operational result of their frequent disagreements over talent when Thalberg first returned.

"I wouldn't yield and Irving wouldn't yield," he said. "Thalberg wanted first call on all and every artist on the lot. I told him, 'I will have to throw up my hands! Irving, you ought to be fair. You are going to place me in a position that I am going to flop . . . I will give you every darned thing you want, as if you were my own son, but I've got to run that plant successfully.'"

Thalberg was bitter, Mayer acknowledged. "He didn't want to stay there at all."

The arrangement finally made was that Thalberg would have his own company after December 31, 1938. That was the date on which his contract with the "Mayer group" and with the studio would expire. The deal was that his company would be financed by Metro-Goldwyn-Mayer, with Loew's, Inc., guaranteeing the obligation, and that Thalberg's company would release its films through Loew's. The difference from his then prevailing status was that he would have complete autonomy in his choice of stories and signing of writers, directors, actors and staff.

Significantly, the arrangement provided that the contracts of all artists who were attached to the Thalberg unit between the signing of the agreement and the date the new company was to start would be assigned to the latter. Bernie Hyman was also to go with the new company. Thalberg waived a continuing bonus from the "Mayer group" in favor of the profits from his own films. He was to have a salary of $2,000 weekly, and the agreement was to extend for ten years.

But Thalberg never knew the experience of having his own company. Time was running out for the producer who had used time so prodigally. He moved from the production of *The Good Earth* to a grandly projected *Camille,* in which he would have Greta Garbo and a new young man, Robert Taylor, who was being developed as a star. He was also making ready to do *Maytime,* with Jeanette MacDonald, and another Marx Brothers film, *A Day at the Races.* And, of course, there was still pending that mammoth *Marie Antoinette.*

One Sunday morning in August of that last year, 1936, Al Lewin was sitting with him beside the swimming pool of the Santa Monica home. Norma was paddling with baby Kathy at the shallow end of the pool, and five-year-old Irving, Jr., was delightedly discovering how to dive. It was a peaceful, relaxed family picture that Lewin looked upon, and he could not resist an observation.

"You know, Irving," he said, "I'd be nervous, if I were you."

"Why?" Thalberg asked, a little baffled.

"Because you've got too much," Lewin replied. "A beautiful wife, lovely children, a gracious home, unbounded success, universal admiration and the affection of your associates. It's too much for one man, Irving. The gods are jealous of people like you."

Thalberg smiled and said nothing. One month later, he was dead.

The end came with shattering swiftness. Thalberg had gone with some friends to spend the Labor Day week end at his favored Del Monte Club in Monterey. He had exercised, got overheated and then sat down to play cards. By morning, he had developed a mean cold. He returned to Santa Monica and went to bed. Within a few days, he had pneumonia and his condition grew progressively worse.

Again the old terror seized him—the fear that his heart would go. His Bad Nauheim friend, Dr. Groedel, was immediately summoned from New York, where he had recently set up practice. He was at Thalberg's side in twenty-four hours. But there was nothing he could do for the patient, who might have been saved with sulfa drugs as an anodyne for the pneumonia. But sulfa was not quite yet in use.

There is a touching little legend that Thalberg's last words to Norma were, "Don't let the children forget me." It makes a likely sentiment, for the modest producer sometimes said this, when he was in his melancholy moods, insisting to a gently chiding Norma that he was going to die young. In the same vein, he would say to her.

"You'll marry some guy who will get all my money when I'm gone."
Then he would break out of his doldrums and warn, "Just don't marry
an actor, that's all!"

Actually, the patient was in a coma for several hours before he died,
unconscious of his final, fitful contest, inside an oxygen tent. Once,
towards the end, he asked Norma to hold his hand as he whispered
the Lord's Prayer. His communications thereafter were feverish,
feeble and to no avail.

The end came on Monday morning, September 14, 1936. Al Lewin
and Jack Conway were keeping vigil in the living room downstairs
when a nurse came and told them their friend—their thirty-seven-year-
old hero—was dead. Lewin remembers that little Kathy was crawling
about on the floor, playing and laughing in the bright sunlight—a
poignant touch that might have been in a Thalberg film. Mayer was
called and arrived a little later. His eyes were welling with tears.

The funeral of Irving Thalberg was one of those grotesque affairs,
peculiarly marked by the freakishness and mob sentimentality of
Hollywood. It was held in the Jewish temple of Rabbi Mangin, to
which admission was strictly limited to the family and a few hundred
hand-picked friends, associates and community elite. Several thousand persons—mostly sightseers—stood outside behind police lines
and gawked. As each recognizable mourner arrived and entered, the
crowds behaved as they would at a première.

The behavior inside was no less curious. A distinct murmur arose
when Myrna Loy walked down the aisle. A soft sigh of appreciation
came when Freddie Bartholomew entered, immaculate in a Fauntleroy
suit. (He had recently appeared in David Selznick's first independent
production, *Little Lord Fauntleroy*.) Nicholas Schenck and a party
of executives had flown out for the funeral from New York. They
constituted a formidable phalanx in the fore of the congregation.

The services themselves were simple. Grace Moore sang the
Twenty-third Psalm, and Rabbi Mangin, who had officiated at the
wedding of Thalberg and Norma, spoke the prayers. Sitting stoically
with Norma were Irving's father and his strong-willed mother,
Henrietta. She had lived for the power and the glory and now the
death of her golden boy.

Burial was in Forest Lawn Cemetery.

Five months later, *The Good Earth* was released, bearing this
simple foreword:

"To the memory of Irving Grant Thalberg, we dedicate this picture
—his last great achievement."

This was only the second time his name had ever appeared on a film.

CHAPTER XXVII

THE MONARCHY OF MAYER

IT WAS said by Charles MacArthur, the playwright and sardonic wit who had run up a salient service record in the 1930's at Metro-Goldwyn-Mayer, that working there after the death of Thalberg was "like going to the Automat." The excitement to mental salivation and the gusto to feast on and enjoy the business of creating movies that Thalberg inspired was gone, he said. The studio lost its savor without the presence or the aura of its famous chef. It became a mere mass-producing combine, a huge motion-picture dispensing machine.

That may have seemed a slightly biased estimation, coming from a loyal friend, or perhaps it betrayed a lack of taste buds for the particular flavor of Mayer. But it gave a fair indication of the character of the post-Thalberg regime. The sense of an inspirational influence, a *genius domus,* the studio had while he was there, even under the unit system, existed no longer when he was gone. There was little or no sense of closeness or creative participation with Mayer, who was now the supreme administrator, free of the partner towards whom he combined a cold feeling of envy with a profound professional regard. The air that emanated was one of remote authority.

The first and most poignant necessity that followed upon Thalberg's death was that of dissolving the unit which he had headed with such success. The task of editing *The Good Earth* and carrying through with *Camille* was handed to Bernie Hyman, his closest, most trusted friend. Hyman was told by Eddie Mannix that he need spare no expense to make those last films as good and reflective of Thalberg as possible. Mannix, the rough-and-ready bruiser, had his own brand of sentiment. *Maytime* was given to Hunt Stromberg and *A Day at the Races* was left in the hands of its capable and increasingly respected director, Sam Wood.

Al Lewin, who had been Thalberg's assistant, despondently quit the studio, acting on a clause in his contract which permitted him to cancel it if Thalberg was not there. Mayer took this as a personal insult and would not speak to Lewin for several years—until he wanted him for a job in 1940. Then they agreed that there had been a mistake.

More awkward and personally distressing was the ugly disagreement that arose over the contract of Norma Shearer and the settlement of the claims of the Thalberg estate. Shortly after the death of her husband, Norma herself fell ill with pneumonia. Then, grieved and exhausted, she decided she wanted to retire. Financially, she was able. In the twelve years that Thalberg had drawn a salary and bonus payments from Metro-Goldwyn-Mayer, he got more than $5,000,000. What with profitable purchases of optioned stock and the posthumous rights to a residual interest in the bonuses of the "Mayer group," he left to his wife and family an estate that was estimated to be worth between $8,000,000 and $10,000,000. Norma was calculated to be one of the richest women in Hollywood.

However, the company had invested over $400,000 in *Marie Antoinette,* which had been carefully tailored to her measure, and Schenck and Mayer did not want to let her go. But with the settlement of the estate uncertain and Norma in no mood to carry on, it was agreed that her contract would be canceled, upon her payment of $50,000.

A solution of the question of the monies that Thalberg's heirs were entitled to receive from the "Mayer group" profits was more complicated. The lawyers for the estate, for Thalberg's partners and for Loew's, Inc., found that the various percentage contracts that had been drawn and redrawn over the years were vague and ambiguous. They wrangled for six months. The Thalberg lawyers claimed his estate should continue to draw his full share of the profits; the "Mayer group" lawyers claimed it shouldn't get anything.

Finally, when Schenck got wind of rumors that the company was trying to "do Norma in," and he sensed the indignation and resentment that was felt by Thalberg's old friends, he called for a compromise settlement. It was that Thalberg's estate would receive his full share of all profits paid to the "Mayer group" up to the conclusion of its contract at the end of 1938. Thereafter it would receive 4 per cent of the net profits earned by pictures more than half completed in the period from April, 1924, through December, 1938.

This was a generous settlement, and by it the Thalberg estate has received more than $1,500,000 as its share of profits since 1936. The estate still partakes of income accruing from the rental of the studio's old films.

As a condition of this settlement, Norma Shearer agreed to return to the studio on an exclusive contract to make six pictures over a period of three years at a salary of $150,000 a picture, which was what she was getting before Thalberg died. The first of her pictures, by common understanding, would be *Marie Antoinette.*

Thus the last unpleasant squabble over the share of earnings that would go to Thalberg—or his heirs—was concluded. It is doubtful that he would have been satisfied.

An ironic sequel to this settlement was that Nick Schenck finally agreed, a few months later, to sign a contract to remain as president of Loew's, Inc., for ten years. His salary was to continue at $2,500 a week, he was also to continue to receive 2½ per cent of the net profits of the company *and* he was to be given the options on the 48,492 shares of common stock that Thalberg had not exercised. That was an exchange of perquisites at which the fates might well have smiled. . . .

For all Mayer's imperiousness and discord with Thalberg before the latter's death, it was noticeable that he seemed to endeavor, in the months that followed, to take on some of Thalberg's qualities. He was a man of violent reactions. His mind was stubborn, his patience was short, and his emotional reflexes were unpredictable to a bewildering and terrifying degree.

Once, at a Studio Club dinner dance the winter before Thalberg died (the Studio Club was an organization of Metro-Goldwyn-Mayer employees) Mayer made a shocking scene when Ted Healy put on an innocent parody of Charles Igor Gorin, the singer, hitting a high note, after which Healy launched into a current "mammy" song. Mayer, exploding with anger, shoved the comedian off the stage. "You're supposed to use your judgment," he thundered. "You're not supposed to make fun of such a great singer as Igor Gorin—or Allan Jones!" The startled guests laid the ugly outburst to the sentimentality and pugnacity of their boss.

Another time, Mayer leaped out of his desk chair and socked one of his producers in the nose because of a minor disagreement. This was typical.

But after the death of Thalberg, a brief change came over him and he evidently tried to administer the studio with solicitude for individuals and with self-restraint. This change was not unconnected with the increased requirement to maintain a flow of high-class pictures demanded by New York. He knew that the making of motion pictures was a task of extreme complexity which depended upon delicate human factors, including loyalty and pride. He tried, in his fashion, to encourage these feelings in the people at Metro-Goldwyn-Mayer.

The pressure for quality pictures was stronger than it had been because of a new selling plan developed by Al Lichtman for the distribution department. Lichtman, whose career in film business had been erratic since the days when he started the old Alco Company, out of which Metro grew, had been hired by Schenck as his executive assistant in October, 1935, following his resignation as president of United Artists because he and Sam Goldwyn couldn't jibe. The first task to which Schenck assigned him was to survey the distribution setup of Loew's and try to find a way to pull more rental for pictures than was being got with the Feist "sliding scale."

Lichtman put eight months on the study. He visited all the company's exchanges in the United States and Canada, and, sure enough, he and William Rodgers, who had succeeded Feist as sales manager, came up with a scheme whereby more money could conceivably be got. It was that Loew's would agree to deliver to its theatre customers between forty-two and fifty-two pictures a year, with the percentage terms for the rentals of the big ones to be set individually only after they demonstrated their drawing potential in thirty key theatres. Thus, the more a film grossed in its first engagements, the higher the percentage rental asked for it.

This new plan, which would probably have given Marcus Loew a heart attack in the old days, was put into operation in June, 1936, and the following year the gross returns from film rentals were up $6,000,000 over the year before. Whether this was due to the plan, entirely, or in part to the quality of that year's films, which included *Mutiny on the Bounty, San Francisco* and *The Great Ziegfeld* (for which they got the top rental of 50 per cent of the gross), could not be specifically determined. But it was proved that better films could be sold to fetch higher terms than were customary. So better films were in greater demand. Mayer went at the job of trying to provide them, with a renewed enthusiasm and energy.

The year before, Lichtman, visiting the studio and studying the organization, had found that Mayer, while brilliant, perceptive and capable of developing talent to a remarkable degree, was (in Lichtman's words) "the worst manager I ever met in all my life."

"He would waste all sorts of time talking and telling people what a great man he was," Lichtman said. His interest in politics was also consuming a great deal of his time. This made for a lack of cohesion and decisiveness in the operation of the studio. Lichtman imparted his opinion to Schenck, who asked him to talk to Mayer. He did. The consequence was an endeavor by Mayer to discipline himself, especially after Thalberg died.

It was at this time that the previous legal status of Metro-Goldwyn-Mayer as a separate corporation, wholly owned by Loew's, Inc., was abandoned and the assets of the studio were incorporated with those of the parent company. Then an effort was made to allot more clearly the responsibilities of Mayer's staff. Eddie Mannix was designated general manager and Mayer's right-hand man. Bennie Thau was titled Contact Officer to deal with the creative personnel. The post of Administrative Executive was given to a new man, Sam Katz. And Joe Cohn was promoted from studio manager to co-ordinate a somewhat fluid B-picture producer corps.

Katz was another small Napoleon in the motion picture industry.

When he was little more than a boy in Chicago, he had joined with the Balaban brothers to form the Balaban & Katz theatre circuit, out of which he emerged a wealthy man shortly before the circuit went into financial reorganization in 1932. Schenck, prone to favor men with theatre training, gave him a job in October, 1934, and sent him to Culver City to be "an added arm of management," as he said.

Mayer happened to be in Europe at the time Katz was signed, and was not pleased with the addition. He questioned the qualifications of the theatre man to enter the area of production, and wondered why he was there. But Katz was a Schenck appointee, so Mayer had to find something for him to do. He first assigned him to oversee the "B" producers, the men making the low-budget films. Later, he gave him general supervision of the production of musical films. In this position, his first adminstrative project was *Broadway Melody of 1936*, which, despite the evidence of its title, was released in 1935.

This echo of the studio's original musical had a score by Nacio Herb Brown and Arthur Freed, from which the most memorable number was *You Are My Lucky Star*. The star performer was Jack Benny, but most of the attention went to a couple of new personalities, Robert Taylor and Eleanor Powell. Taylor, fresh out of Pomona College, had the intolerable name of Spangler Arlington Brugh, until it was changed by studio fiat. He was given his first break in this film—and also, by some aberration, his first and only chance to sing. They thought he might make a musical actor, but the consensus was that his one song, *I Got a Feeling You're Foolin*, expressed the general feeling perfectly. He was spotted thereafter in straight dramas and made his first big hit in *Camille*.

Miss Powell, brought on from Broadway, turned out to be a nimble dancing star and was a familiar figure in many of the studio's subsequent musicals. She quickly replaced Joan Crawford as the perennial dancing girl, releasing that durable lady for exclusively dramatic things.

On the strength of *Broadway Melody of 1936*, Mayer decided that Katz was what they needed to organize the production of musical films. This was a kind of product that got to the heart of Mayer. (Whenever they played a score for him, they always built up the violins, confident that the G-string would soften him as quickly as anything.) So Katz was encouraged to assemble a formidable force of musical talent, with such men as Arthur Freed, Jack Cummings (who was Mayer's nephew) and John Considine Jr., working under him. In this area, he absorbed the prior functions of the waning Harry Rapf and was a logical appointee to Mayer's staff of executive producers after Thalberg's death.

The accumulation and control of all the talent that he could get to the studio was now Mayer's acknowledged obsession. He believed in what he called "strength in depth," and endeavored to make this the keystone of the continuing power of Metro-Goldwyn-Mayer. With a deep enough talent pool to draw from and with enough available stars, he saw no reason why the studio could not continue to produce the most formidable films. The obvious weakness of his theory was that it took more than sweeping commands to talent and stars to get great pictures. It took enthusiasm, work—and time.

An evidence of the application of Mayer's theory and the consequences of it was in the critical production of *Marie Antoinette*. Here was a project on which Thalberg had expended years of work to get what he felt was needed in the way of a script. He had knowingly had his writers balance the drama to converge in Norma Shearer as the French queen, and he had long beforehand selected the sensitive painstaking Sidney Franklin to direct. It is fair to assume that Thalberg wanted to make this big historical drama his chef-d'oeuvre.

There was certainly no lack of ambition when they resumed work on the film. Mayer and Stromberg instructed Cedric Gibbons, the studio's head designer, to prepare the most exquisite and impressive settings that could be conceived. Versailles itself was slightly tarnished alongside the palace Gibbons whipped up. He did some exquisite reproductions of the buildings of eighteenth century France. Ed Willis, the head of the prop department, was sent to Europe to buy furniture and rugs. He stocked his department for all time with the antiques he bought for *Marie Antoinette*. The costumes were nigh museum items. There were 152 roles to be garbed. The studio's great technical departments were triumphantly tested on this film.

And a good cast surrounded Miss Shearer. Tyrone Power was borrowed from Twentieth Century-Fox to play the dashing Count Fersen, the lover of the tragic Marie. Robert Morley was imported from England to play Louis XVI, the role which Thalberg had meant for Charles Laughton, and John Barrymore was got for Louis XV. There was no scarcity of talent to make the picture go.

Then, with all that, what did Mayer do? He decided to change directors because he feared that Franklin who abhorred a "tight schedule," would take too long to shoot the film. Instead of carrying on with the careful craftsman who had labored with Thalberg on the script, Mayer made a producer of him. Then he and Stromberg assigned Woody Van Dyke, the notorious "fast-shooter," to direct *Marie Antoinette*. Mayer asked Miss Shearer if she was willing. She was on a spot. She knew Mayer was nervous about a prolonged schedule, which would have added heavily to the cost, and she felt, under the circumstances, that this was a delicate time to object. "Put Van Dyke or anyone you want on it," she told Mayer helplessly.

That was a sad surrender which she thereafter rued. Van Dyke did the huge historical drama in a fast, modern pageant style. Miss Shearer believed that Franklin would have given it the sweep of tragedy. Despair that she had neither Thalberg nor Franklin to guide her in her most demanding role was with her throughout the picture and after it was done. *Marie Antoinette* was a big show-film of which neither Miss Shearer nor the studio could be too proud. It might well have been an example of saving money where it could do the most harm.

On the other hand, some good breaks came elsewhere. Lou Lighton, a new producer whose command was so middling that the wags referred to his as the "indirect Lighton unit," surprised everyone by piloting a good company to achieve *Captains Courageous*, a picture of Gloucester fishermen, from Rudyard Kipling's tale. Its story of a spoiled English boy who falls off an ocean liner, is picked up by a Portuguese fisherman in the Grand Banks and learns the hardships and rewards of the fishing trade, came out extremely well, with Freddie Bartholomew as the English lad and Spencer Tracy as his savior. Tracy wasn't keen for the role. He was nervous about the Portuguese accent, but he was directed well and won his first Academy award. (The following year he got his second "Oscar" for his performance of Father Flanagan in *Boys Town*.) Tracy had rapidly ascended to rank alongside Clark Gable.

Leo Goes To London

The importance of the British market, not to mention other English-speaking areas around the world, was concretely made evident by Loew's, Inc., in 1936 when a threat loomed that American motion pictures might be squeezed out of the British Isles.

The chain of Gaumont-British theatres, into which William Fox bought in 1929 and which, as a consequence, was now owned to the extent of some 47 per cent by Twentieth Century-Fox, became available for purchase. The Ostrer brothers, who held the controlling shares, were interested in selling, and the word was that a rival chain (Associated British) was angling to buy them out. This would have put the major theatres in the British Isles in the hands of one corporation, which might then have discriminated against any American company's films.

This tacit and vital information got to the ears of Arthur Loew, head of the company's foreign operations, who only the year before had been dissuaded by Nicholas Schenck from leaving the company to join a combine maneuvering to take over R-K-O. Loew had resigned as a director of Loew's, Inc., and had indicated he intended to leave, when Schenck prevailed upon him to remain, with promises of his eventually becoming president. Schenck also raised his salary to $3,500 a week and gave him 5 per cent of the profits from foreign business in excess of $3,640,000 a year. Loew, then thirty-six, was beyond question a productive and valuable executive.

On the news of the Ostrer's intention, Nick Schenck and his brother, Joe, who was then chairman of the board of Twentieth Century-Fox, began negotiations to buy a share of the Ostrers' holdings for their two companies. This was again an instance of the Schenck brothers working hand in glove to accomplish a profitable purpose, even though they were the heads of rival concerns. But the deal fell through when the Ostrers did sell to Associated British, whereupon Nick Schenck arranged to buy a half interest in the holdings of Twentieth Century-Fox. The price was $3,500,000. This gave the company a slight hold, and it also provided a legal channel for removing earnings of the company's films from Great Britain.

With the British economy in peril, heavy restrictions were being placed on the export of funds, especially for luxury items such as motion pictures, and an attempt was also being made to protect the British film industry by putting a quota on the import of pictures from abroad. Out of every five feature films distributed by a company in Britain, at least one had to be made in that country. This led the American distributors to acquire what they called "quota films"— British-made pictures of any quality that would give them license to bring in their own.

At first, Loew's, Inc., followed the policy of all the American companies, which was to finance a few British producers or purchase outright completed British films. But this soon appeared a wasteful process, in that the British-made films were generally so poor that they could not be sold in their own country, let alone in other markets of the world. Furthermore, United Artists was in a stronger position because it had Alexander Korda, one of its partners, producing for it in London. So Schenck and his associates decided to open their own studio in England and make their "quota" pictures as an extended operation of Metro-Goldwyn-Mayer.

A studio was acquired at Denham, outside London, and Michael Balcon, who had been head of production for Gaumont-British, was employed to run the place. Operations were begun in the summer of 1937 with the production of *A Yank at Oxford*, an appropriate film to symbolize the clasping of commercial hands across the sea.

Mayer was not strongly in favor of the decentralization of production that this compelled, but he had to go along with the project, so he made the best of it. He sent a good company from Culver City. Jack Conway was dispatched to direct, with a script prepared by studio writers. It had to do with a sort of Frank Merriwell American type as a Rhodes scholar at Oxford. And Robert Taylor, Lionel Barrymore, Maureen O'Sullivan, Edmund Gwenn and several others were cast to go to England and make the film, to be joined by some English performers.

The selection of Taylor for the key role represented evolution. A few years previously, Robert Montgomery would have been a natural for it. But, by now, Montgomery was maturing into more adult and sophisticated roles. Besides, he was not in best favor with Mayer and others at the studio. Two years before, on a visit to London, he had seen a play called *Night Must Fall*, about a psychopathic killer, which he was determined to do as a film. Mayer, Thalberg and Stromberg were against it; they thought it would be a damaging role for him. But Montgomery, who was always ambitious for variety, held out until they let him do the thing. He told them the roles he had been doing had got "a little difficult to tell apart."

The resistance persisted right up to the preview. A trailer was even made (but never released) which clearly implied that the choice of the role was entirely Montgomery's responsibility. When the film was received with enthusiasm, the studio people changed their tune. But Mayer now looked upon Montgomery as something of a problem boy. Also, the fact that the actor was the president of the Screen Actors Guild, which was heatedly battling with the producers for a basic contract, did not endear him to Mayer. It was evident that a place for Robert Taylor was opening in the top echelon.

Unknown to his multiplying fans, however, he came to stardom with agony and dread. The task of facing the public and reporters was terrifying for him in those first years. Being a primly handsome fellow, with a predominant widow's peak in his hair, he was naturally the butt of some sarcasm and occasional journalistic ridicule.

Shortly before he left for England, he was in Arizona, when a girl plopped herself into his lap and then reported that sitting on the lap of her boy friend was more fun. This got some minor circulation and caused Taylor great chagrin. When passing through Chicago on his way East, he was afraid to get out of the train. In New York, a reporter asked him whether he had hair on his chest. He was literally so shaken by the experience that he could hardly face the mobs of clamoring fans and, on the ship going over to England, he flatly balked at having to meet the British press.

Howard Strickling, head of studio publicity, happened to be in

Europe with Mayer, who was over to start the British production. He got a wire from his man aboard the ship asking if they might sneak Taylor into England, the actor was that terrified. Strickling wirelessed back "nothing doing," and hopped to London, where he and Jack Conway joined the press going down to Plymouth to meet the liner. He put it up to the reporters candidly. Taylor was a decent guy, he told them, but he was frightened. What would they do? They agreed to play fair with Taylor. Strickling was given a few minutes alone with him and in that time convinced the actor that this was a critical moment in his career. Then he brought Taylor forth to face the news hawks. The interview went off swimmingly. It marked a turning point in the relations of Taylor with the press.

A Yank at Oxford was a happy production. The British enjoyed watching it made and were much amused when the filming company was shooting scenes in the university town. There was one ugly clash, however. Balcon had hired an English girl at a more than moderate salary to play the second feminine lead. Mayer was outraged at this. He thought Balcon should have hired a cheaper girl, and he loudly berated him for his extravagance in front of the whole company. Balcon, a calm and courteous gentleman, took that as his cue to resign, which he did a short while later. Victor Saville was put in charge of the studio. The actress to whom Mayer objected was an oncoming star named Vivien Leigh.

Out of the British setup came the first film of a Bernard Shaw play. That was Gabriel Pascal's production of *Pygmalion*, with Leslie Howard and Wendy Hiller as the stars. Then came the excellent film version of A. J. Cronin's fine novel, *The Citadel*, which King Vidor directed and which had Robert Donat and Rosalind Russell as stars. Also in the cast of this drama of a young English doctor who was torn between a fashionable Harley Street practice and humble service in a Welsh mining town were Ralph Richardson, Cecil Parker, Emlyn Williams, Francis Sullivan and Rex Harrison. It was an outstanding example of Anglo-American cooperative work.

It was, too, the film by which Miss Russell came to the wide attention she deserved. Theretofore she had been a studio second-stringer and tacit backstop to Myrna Loy. Time and again she was cast in pictures that were intended for the rebellious Miss Loy, only to be pulled at the last minute when Miss Loy came to terms. Finally, she did get into one—*Rendezvous*—with William Powell. That was her most important picture prior to *The Citadel*. After the latter, Miss Russell was one of the studio's top stars.

That trip Mayer made to England in 1937 to launch the company's productions at Denham was productive in other ways. It resulted in his signing two ladies of some later consequence. They were Greer Garson and Hedy Lamarr.

Mayer was in his London hotel room one evening with Howard Strickling and Ben Goetz of the London office. Suddenly he flung down the paper he was reading and let out an anguished cry. "What's the matter with you fellows?" he hollered. "Why don't you tell me what's going on?" Strickling and Goetz were bewildered. This could be anything. "Here's a show at the St. James called *Old Music*, and you didn't tell me it's in town!"

There was no use trying to stop him. To Mayer, *Old Music* could mean only one thing. He had been buying old music all over Europe that trip. So now he insisted, without question, that they go to the St. James that night. When they got to their seats, they discovered *Old Music* wasn't a musical show at all and, to Mayer's further annoyance, they discovered it wasn't very good. But along in the first act, a beautiful redheaded actress came out on the stage and Mayer jumped as though someone had hit him. A fast reference to the program showed the name of the actress was Greer Garson. Mayer insisted he must meet her right away.

Goetz set up an appointment for supper at the Savoy after the play, and Miss Garson showed up, a radiant figure in a strikingly becoming gown. She had hastened home from the theatre and put on the best thing she had. Mayer was overwhelmed and arranged a screen test within the next few days. He ordered a special gown and saw that the test was made with the greatest care. A contract was signed and Miss Garson was instructed to come to Culver City as soon as her play closed.

During this same stay in London, Mayer met another handsome girl—a dark-haired actress named Hedy Keisler, who had been in a Czecho-Slovakian film, *Ecstasy*. An agent brought her to see him, and Mayer was favorably impressed, but he hadn't made up his mind to sign her when he was ready to leave London for home. He had boarded the *Normandie* at Southampton and was standing at the rail looking down at other passengers, coming aboard from the tender, when, lo, he beheld Hedy Keisler moving demurely in the crowd! She was playing the part of a sort of guardian to a fourteen-year-old violin prodigy, Grisha Goluboff, returning to America from engagements in Europe. Mayer had put them both under contract by the time they reached New York. He had also changed the name of Hedy from Keisler to Lamarr.

Unfortunately, on their arrival, certain of the ship news reporters recalled that Hedy had made something of a sensation by appearing in *Ecstasy* in the nude. It caused her extreme humiliation when they mentioned this delicate fact to her. The next day, the story was in the papers and Miss Lamarr was in tears. Howard Dietz, head of Loew's publicity, was called to her hotel by Mayer to straighten out this terrible situation.

"Did you appear in the nude?" Dietz asked.

"Yes," Miss Lamarr answered shyly.

"Did you look good?"

"Of course!" she snapped.

"Then it's all right," Dietz assured her. "No damage has been done."

Miss Lamarr very soon became familiar with the peculiarities of American publicity.

It so happened that neither Miss Garson nor Miss Lamarr was put to work right away. The studio was then so full of glamorous ladies that there weren't enough stories to go around. Miss Lamarr was finally started on a picture called *I Take This Woman* which was stopped and started so often that the wags said a better tag would be *I Re-Take This Woman*. Finally, she was loaned to Walter Wanger to score her first American hit in *Algiers*.

As for Miss Garson, she just sat at the studio with nothing to do, occasionally being screen-tested and drawing her salary of $500 a week. She was about to return to England, when Sam Wood saw a test of her and decided he could use her in a small part in a new picture that he was going to direct in the British studio. The role was the bride of a young school teacher, who appeared in only a few scenes and then died. But she meant a great deal to the story. The picture was *Good-by, Mr. Chips*.

Again a stellar female performer emerged from one of the many fine films made in the British studio. *Good-by, Mr. Chips* was superb, with Robert Donat giving a historic performance in the title role. And because of her lovely, fragile playing of the young, brief and poignant Mrs. Chips, Greer Garson was brought back to Culver City with a virtual halo around her lustrous head. . . .

After he returned from Europe in the fall of 1937, Mayer indicated that he was restless—that he had to work too hard, that he wasn't getting support from the producers, that he wanted to quit the studio. Schenck, accustomed to such complaining as preliminary to a maneuver for a raise, tried to calm him with assurance that he would die in six months if he didn't have work to do.

"You have this wonderful position and you have this wonderful power," Schenck said. "You love that kind of thing. That is what you need and what your nature demands."

They argued the matter for some time. Schenck met Mayer at Palm Springs and had the suspicion he thought some of the other men would join him if he bolted from the studio. The possibility of a disruption of production terrified Schenck, who knew what would happen to the company if the flow of pictures was checked. Finally, he came to terms with Mayer. The latter agreed to stay, if his own contract were extended with improvement, and if some of his men in the studio were given percentage deals.

Mayer's contract was drawn to run from January 1, 1939, for five years, with him to receive a salary of $3,000 a week, plus 6.77 per cent of the net profits of Loew's, Inc., computed after payment of a $2.00 annual dividend on the common stock. The other men who received salary increases and percentage deals ranging from .35 per cent to 1.4 per cent were Sam Katz, Al Lichtman, Eddie Mannix, Hunt Stromberg, Bernie Hyman, Bennie Thau, Harry Rapf, Larry Weingarten and Robert Rubin and Dave Bernstein in New York. A couple of months later, a very profitable secret deal was made with Mervyn LeRoy, who had been wooed by Mayer from Warner Brothers to strengthen his producer corps. LeRoy got a deal that guaranteed him $300,000 a year. At this same time, Mayer endeavored to get Dave Selznick back to the studio, but Selznick was busy and happy with his own production of a film called *Gone With the Wind*.

Thus was affirmed with profit sharings in the prosperity of the company the managerial philosophy that the producers were the key men in the studio. The monarchy of Mayer was strengthened with the establishment of a corps of titled dukes. Or, to use another simile, a lot of cats were being allowed to lick at the cream.

Dark Clouds

But three dark clouds rolled across the landscape in 1938. One was the first big rebellion of stockholders in Loew's, Inc. A minority stockholders' suit was inaugurated and tried in New York Supreme Court that year, charging mismanagement of the company, as evidenced primarily by the high salaries and percentage bonuses paid executives. This brought on a broad and detailed airing of the company's affairs. The whole complex business of the movies was startlingly and bewilderingly exposed.

Although the management was ruled innocent of the major fraud that counsel for the stockholders charged, it was not found free of certain errors in the computation of profits for the determining of percentages and such. The tremendous richness of the company made it possible for it to extend such generous inducements to its executives who had the approval of Schenck. And Schenck, himself, had the thorough endorsement of the company's rather bland directorate.

The only concern of the major stockholders was that the prosperity would prevail.

The second disturbance that cast its shadows was the accumulation of labor troubles in Hollywood—a continuing push by studio workers to get union recognition, contracts and terms. The history of this tormented struggle that extended over several years and included all groups of employees, from the actors and writers to the stagehands and hairdressers, is long and too complicated for this volume. But it deeply involved Metro-Goldwyn-Mayer. And, in one of its more sordid developments, it came right to the door of Nicholas Schenck.

In 1941, it was revealed that Schenck and his brother, Joe, acting for their respective companies, Loew's, Inc., and Twentieth Century-Fox, had paid bribes to William Bioff and George Browne, racketeer rulers of the stagehands union. The bribes had amounted to $50,000 a year from each of these two companies. Nick Schenck admitted he got the money from his company by having his New York executives make large and misleading levies on their expense accounts. When asked in court why he submitted to the demands of the labor racketeers, Schenck said, "I was afraid of what they would do." He meant he was afraid they would close his theatres by calling strikes of the projection-machine operators, who were also controlled by Bioff and Browne. And, of course, the closing of theatres was the one thing Schenck dreaded more than a stop in the flow of pictures.

Actually, Joe Schenck went to jail as a consequence of this dark affair. He was convicted first of income-tax evasion because of false statements as to the transaction with Bioff and Browne. But because of his aid to the government in prosecuting those criminals, he was allowed to plead guilty to a charge of perjury. He served four months of a one-year sentence and was paroled. Later he was pardoned by President Truman and his citizenship was restored.

The third cloud that swept across the landscape in 1938 was the launching by the Justice Department of a long-threatened anti-trust suit to compel the major motion picture companies to separate their joint holdings of studios and theatres. This large and ominous maneuver, which was formally leveled against Paramount, the target of previous government investigations, was also a vital threat to Loew's, for its success against one would rip all vertically constructed companies. Although the suit did not develop into a complete action until after World War II, it was a premonitory warning. The government was rolling up its guns. And the basic structure of the American film industry was soon to be fired upon.

CHAPTER XXVIII

MICKEY AND JUDY

THE PROPAGATION of talent at Metro-Goldwyn-Mayer was one of its peoples' proudest and most justifiable boasts. The patient development of star performers was a specialty of the studio. No other place of picture making brought forth quite the number and array of so-called performing artists as the Culver City operation spawned. And two of its most phenomenal in the great years before World War II were significantly teen-agers. They were Mickey Rooney and Judy Garland, who in their youth, were particularly reflective of the taste and sentiment of Mayer.

By chance, and then design, the path of Mickey often and fortunately crossed that of Spencer Tracy, when they were both new at Metro-Goldwyn-Mayer. As the son of Tracy's Portuguese fisherman in *Captains Courageous*, Mickey made a large contribution to that picture and a complement to the older star. Later, as the toughest of the youngsters that Tracy's Father Flanagan trained in *Boys Town*, the lad was most notably and affectionately established as the adumbration of the older star. It was appropriate that Mickey should have been the *Young Tom Edison* that preceded Tracy's *Edison the Man*.

But Mickey was not a performer who had to ride on the shoulders of anyone. He was rather a personality who had his own individual glow. His pint-sized form and youthful effervescence gave off a dynamism of their own. There was no holding Mickey Rooney at Metro-Goldwyn-Mayer.

He first went to work at Culver City in 1933, when he was already a veteran performer, nearly thirteen-years-old. A son of burlesque and vaudeville parents, Nell Carter and Joe Yule, he had been in theatrical business almost from the moment he started to breathe. At six, he was a vaudeville trouper in Will Morrissey's Revue. Then he played Fontaine Fox's cartoon character, Mickey McGuire, in a series of short films produced by Larry Darmour. So he could get the job in the first place, his mother dyed his blond hair black. And to give him professional identity, they called him Mickey McGuire. Later, when he was dumped from the series, Darmour forced him to abandon the familiar name. His mother suggested he call himself Mickey Looney. Wisely, they modified the gag.

Mickey was "between engagements" when David Selznick happened to spot him one night putting on quite a cute performance in a pingpong tourney at the Ambassador Hotel. He invited the kid to Culver City. Mickey was out the next day and was hired on a week-to-week basis. Selznick wanted him to play Clark Gable as a boy in *Manhattan Melodrama*, but Mickey was first put to work, appropriately, as the son of the vaudeville couple (Frank Morgan and Alice Brady) in *Broadway to Hollywood*. Then Selznick used him in *Manhattan Melodrama*, and after that he was steadily employed. He was well-known when he was loaned to Warner Brothers to play Puck in *A Midsummer Night's Dream*.

Mickey eclipsed Jackie Cooper as the studio's leading boy star when he was cast as the younger brother in *Ah, Wilderness!* Then there developed competition in Freddie Bartholomew. The studio played this duo wisely. First it cast the two in *The Devil Is A Sissy*, with Mickey as a tough New York street kid and Freddie as a visiting boy, under the direction of W. S. VanDyke. Then it teamed them in *Captains Courageous*, again contrasting the personalities of the lads.

Mickey was all over the place by this time, tripling in brass and bassoon. But little did he—or anyone—reckon what was in store for all of them when he was cast in a low-budget picture called *A Family Affair*.

This was a little story of an average American family, based upon a modest play, *Skidding*, by Aurania Rouverol. The father was a small-town judge who got in trouble with his family and friends when he rightly refused to give permission for a chiseling contractor to build a local water line. Political enemies, resenting his action, threatened to besmirch his older daughter's name, and his younger daughter was angry and resentful because her sweetheart had expected to get a job. That's about all there was to it, except that there was a young son who stoutly upheld his father. Andy was his name. The name of the family was Hardy. That was *A Family Affair*.

In addition to Mickey Rooney, who was Andy, a minor role, Lionel Barrymore was cast as Judge Hardy, Spring Byington was his wife, Cecilia Parker was the younger daughter, Julie Haydon was the married one and Sara Haden was Aunt Millie, a limpid but forthright old maid. George B. Seitz was the director. It came out a pleasant little film in April, 1937, and it cheerfully went down the line. No one at the studio gave it another thought.

Mickey went on to other pictures. One of these, *Thoroughbreds Don't Cry*, was a story of a hard-boiled jockey who lived in a boarding house where also lived a young girl with a considerable singing voice. In this role they cast Judy Garland, a promising youngster on the lot.

Judy had come to the studio in 1935, when she was a fat little girl of eleven by the name of Frances Gumm. Mayer had auditioned the youngster when she was playing vaudeville with her mother and two older sisters—the Gumm Sisters, they were billed, The mother played the piano, the daughters sang. Little Frances struck Mayer as a child with talent, and he put her under short-term contract to the studio, where, as a preliminary to all else, they gave her a more euphonious name. Mainly for the purpose of testing her, she was teamed with another pretty child, then under similar contract, to do a musical short. The short was called *Every Sunday* and Deanna Durbin was the other girl.

Mayer was in Europe when it was ready. He saw it on his return and gave orders that the two children should be put in a picture as a team. Then, to everyone's horror, it was discovered that Deanna's contract had been allowed to lapse and that she had been grabbed by Universal. Mayer nigh took the place apart.

The loss was unfortunate for Judy. Her contract was renewed, but for months she was allowed to go idle. Then they loaned her to Twentieth Century-Fox for a bit in a college musical, *Pigskin Parade*. More months passed, then one day at a studio party, Judy got up and sang some lyrics that Roger Edens, a promising lad in the music department, had written to the tune of *You Made Me Love You*. They were called *Dear Mister Gable* and offered as a paean to Clark.

Everybody thought it darling, so they hastily cast Judy to sing the number in *Broadway Melody of 1938* (released in the summer of 1937), after which they gave Judy a chance with Mickey in *Thoroughbreds Don't Cry*. Both did very well in it and ably demonstrated their style.

Meanwhile, the Lucien Hubbard unit that had produced *A Family Affair* was reorganized, with Joe Cohn as head man. He had a bunch of young Turks under him, including Carey Wilson, Sam Marx and Sam Zimbalist. They howled and hooted at one another and turned out a lot of little films. Several months later, William Rodgers, the company's sales manager was on the Coast and, in moving around the studio, dropped by to talk with them. He told them that, of all the unit's pictures, some of the best responses were got from that little film with Lionel Barrymore and Mickey Rooney, *A Family Affair*. Why not make a couple more pictures about that family, Rodgers proposed. Cohn, always open to suggestions, agreed it was a good idea.

He talked it over with Carey Wilson. They decided the best laughs had come from the few little scenes in which Judge Hardy had conversations with his son—such as that when the Judge frankly stated his moral philosophy and Andy, a pragmatic character, thought he was being scolded for not washing behind his ears. The stories would be constructed with emphasis on the father and the son.

A *Family Affair* had ended with Andy getting interested in a girl. Cohn and Wilson decided they would make Andy's interest in girls the minor theme.

Aurania Rouverol wasn't able to write the sequels, but she sold the rights to her characters, so they got Kay Van Riper, who had done the script for A *Family Affair*, to write the screenplays, with the members of the unit blocking out the stories and Wilson polishing Andy's dialogue. The second show, *You're Only Young Once*, had the family going to Catalina Island for a holiday. There Andy discovered the excitement to be got from kissing girls. The complication of the older daughter was discreetly dropped and nothing more was said about the peril of the Judge losing his job.

There were three major changes in casting. Lionel Barrymore was in England working on A *Yank at Oxford* when they were ready to start shooting, so they got Lewis Stone for the judge. Stone was a veteran contract player of even longer lineage at the studio than Barrymore. Then Fay Holden was cast as the mother instead of Spring Byington and Ann Rutherford was brought in as Polly Benedict, Andy's steady girl. George Seitz continued as the director.

The only thing notable about the second film was that Stone and Mickey seemed to give the father-son relation a new warmth and sincerity. This was further developed in the third film, *Judge Hardy's Children*, which came along four months after the second. In this one, Andy asked his father if it was normal that he should want to kiss every pretty girl he saw. By now, Andy's adolescence was becoming the major theme.

For the fourth in the series, they got an out-of-work lawyer, William Ludwig, to write the script. He added a complication in the form of a little girl visiting next door. She was a neighborhood nuisance, until it was discovered that she could sing. Indeed, she was the daughter of a musical comedy actress. Judy Garland was cast in that role. *Love Finds Andy Hardy* was the title of this fourth film.

Suddenly, when it was previewed, all the executives were there, from Mayer on down, and all were singing the praises of the Hardy films. The word had got out that they were grossing three or four times their cost. And well they might, for they were genuinely charming, warm and likeable little films. Mickey Rooney was the new sensation and Andy Hardy was the all-American boy.

The happy flush of triumph: Judy Garland and Mickey Rooney at a party in their honor following the preview of "Love Finds Andy Hardy" (1938).

Paul Muni and Luise Rainer in Thalberg's last film, "The Good Earth" (1936).

Patriarchal Louis B. Mayer poses amid the visiting Edsel Ford family and a group of his own studio "children": front row, l. to r., Mickey Rooney, Cora Sue Collins (center), Freddie Bartholomew and Jackie Cooper (1935).

A key scene in the incomparable "Gone With the Wind," showing Scarlett O'Hara (Vivien Leigh), Rhett Butler (Clark Gable) and Melanie (Olivia De Havilland) (1939).

Carey Wilson gave a party for the company on the night that fourth film was previewed, and Mickey and Judy, as guests of honor, were showered with admiration and applause. Still very much kids, the happy youngsters accepted their plaudits graciously. This may have been the most wonderful evening in both their famous careers.

After *Love Finds Andy Hardy*, Mayer got devoutly interested. He gave emphatic instructions that the Hardy series should not be "improved."

"Please don't try to make them any better," he said. "Just keep them the way they are. The only thing you've got to worry about is not insulting the friends you have made."

This became a Mayer fixation. Here was the sort of thing about which he felt himself most knowing—the Average American Family. In one picture, they had a cute sequence in which Andy, forlorn and distressed because his football team had lost that afternoon and Polly Benedict was having a date with a handsome naval lieutenant, sat at the dinner table without eating anything. His mother asked what was the matter and he answered, "I'm not feeling so good." "I think it must be his liver," Mrs. Hardy said anxiously to the Judge, who replied, "If what's ailing Andrew is his liver, a lot of boys are suffering liver trouble."

When they came to that sequence at the preview, Mayer yanked Wilson's arm violently. Wilson knew by this that he was furious. Later, going home in the car, Mayer blasted the producer's ears off. "I thought you told me you were brought up in your mother's kitchen! You lied to me!" he screamed. "So you've insulted the American home and mother!" Wilson was confused. "Anybody who has been brought up in the kitchen knows that the average American boy at sixteen is hungry *all* the time!" Mayer said.

He insisted they make a retake in which Andy thanked his mother for her concern and assured her that her cooking was excellent, but— et cetera, et cetera.

Another time, Mrs. Hardy was ill and they feared she would die. Wilson, flowing with tenderness, had written a long prayer for Andy to say. But, having learned his lesson, the writer showed it to Mayer before they shot the scene. "Who the hell wrote this prayer?" Mayer bellowed. Wilson confessed he did.

"You see, you're a Hollywood character. You don't remember how a boy would pray. All right, shoot it," Mayer said. "We'll go to the preview and see if it makes people cry. If it does, you can keep it in the picture. But if it doesn't, you will shoot this prayer—!" He fell upon his knees, lifted his eyes to heaven, clasped his hands and murmured with choking sobs, "Dear God, please don't let my Mom die, because she's the best Mom in the world. Thank you, God."

Wilson, being a smart man, abandoned his prayer forthwith and shot Mayer s.

They had early discovered that the Judge was as critical as Andy in the films, and that most of the laughs on Andy's lines were developed by showing the Judge's wise reactions to them. The man-to-man talks between the father and the son were the heart of the films.

Mayer kept saying, "Don't go crazy because you have an oil-well in this boy. Be careful. If you let Andy's relationships with the girls predominate, you'll lose your audience."

In *Love Finds Andy Hardy*, they had Andy needing eighty dollars to complete payments on a jalopy to take a girl to the dance. Mayer said to keep that in mind: the big thing with Andy was having the jalopy, not the girl. He warned against too much kissing. "You know girls," he said. "Don't let them get in situations where they kiss automatically." And he insisted that Andy's respect for his father should be frequently indicated with plenty of "sirs." Mayer took great pride in the Hardy series. He considered it his own masterpiece.

The rest of the "Hardy" story is woven closely into the fabric of Metro-Goldwyn-Mayer. As a consequence of the early success of this series—and also as a consequence of Mayer's compulsion to keep costs within reasonable bounds—the Cohn unit was importuned to come up with another good series idea. It did. One day Carey Wilson read a magazine story called *Whiskey Sour* by Max Brand. It was set in a general hospital and had to do with an old, experienced doctor and a young, enthusiastic interne. Right away, Wilson saw the similarity to the basic character relationships in the Hardy films.

Wilson went to Cohn with the idea. He didn't have to talk very hard. "Joe, what are the vital things in life? They settle around birth and death. And who is usually present in these crises. The doctor, of course. Whenever you are in trouble the doctor comes into the house a small god." Cohn liked the idea. They got hold of Max Brand.

He turned out to be an extraordinary fellow by the real name of Henrik Faust. He was full of endless stories of old Doctor Gillespie and young Doctor Kildare, as he called his two key characters. So they went to work on the new series, calculating in advance that the stories would be constructed so each would lead on to the next. For old Doctor Gillespie, they decided to use, again, Lionel Barrymore, who was now back from his stint in London. For Doctor Kildare, they got Lew Ayres, an earnest, intense young actor whose own philosophies were not unlike those of the character he was to play. Harry Ruskin and Willis Goldbeck wrote the scripts from stories supplied by Brand. Harold S. Bucquet was the director. Some time after the medical series was underway, they discovered to their astonishment that Bucquet was a devout Christian Scientist.

Just before they were ready to start shooting the first of the series, *Young Doctor Kildare*, they learned the sad news that Lionel Barrymore had become so crippled with arthritis that he could not walk or stand. He would be confined to a wheel chair, perhaps for the rest of his life. This seemed, of course, to put an end to his acting career. But Wilson, Ruskin and Goldbeck came up with a happy thought; why not let Doctor Gillespie be a wheel-chair-ridden man? This was gratefully accepted. They set things up so as to get quite a shock with the first entrance of the old doctor in his wheel chair, and then they hastily wrote a new scene in which Dr. Kildare discovered that Doctor Gillespie was suffering from cancer. This gave added courage and noble character to the philosophical old healer of others.

Thus the famous *Doctor Kildare* series was started because of the success of the Hardy films. Later the studio started the *Maisie* series to give itself three low-budget series going at the same time.

The Hardy films were immensely valuable for another strictly intramural reason. They were an excellent showcase and testing area for young talent that came to the studio, especially the promising young actresses who were paraded before Andy's cavalier eye. If they stood up in his estimation, they were likely to be okay. The first notable graduate of this screening was Judy Garland, as we have seen. After her performance in *Love Finds Andy Hardy* she was cast in *The Wizard of Oz*, and thus came to the fulfillment of one of the classics of the musical screen.

The horrible thought is that Judy Garland would not have been in this film if Mervyn LeRoy, the producer, had been able to get his way. LeRoy wanted Shirley Temple to play Dorothy, the Kansas farm girl who was carried by a tornado to the magical Land of Oz, there to meet the Tin Woodman, the Scarecrow and the Cowardly Lion. He held out hopefully for Shirley, but she was tied up by Twentieth Century-Fox. So he settled for Judy, who was touted by Mayer and Arthur Freed. The latter erstwhile song writer had been promoted to associate producer of this film.

The musical score by Harold Arlen and E. Y. Harburg was strong. And the cast, which included Jack Haley as the Tin Woodman, Bert Lahr as the Cowardly Lion, Ray Bolger as the Scarecrow and Frank Morgan as the Wizard of Oz, gave plenty of promise. But the rushes of the first few weeks of shooting under director Richard Thorpe were strangely lacking in fantasy and charm. LeRoy soon stopped the shooting, scrapped most of the footage and began all over again with Victor Fleming as director. Fleming did a sensitive job. The "rough cut" was much too long, however, and at one point they pulled a couple of songs and considered dropping them to shorten the picture. *Over the Rainbow* was one.

There are many nice and sentimental reasons for remembering *The Wizard of Oz*—not the least of which is the elevation it gave Judy Garland as a star. But one of the nicest is the thought of the pleasure it gave the British in the autumn of 1939 when they were waiting in anxious trepidation for the Nazis to strike. A year later, Australian soldiers borrowed one of its liveliest tunes, *We're Off to See the Wizard*, as their favorite marching song when they were fighting Rommel in the Libyian desert. And "wizard" became a word of highest praise.

CHAPTER XXIX

THE MIGHTY *WIND* ARISES

OF ALL the motion pictures produced since the screen began, the one that has reached the most people and may fairly be judged most popular is the epic production of Margaret Mitchell's famous novel, *Gone With the Wind*.

This fabulous motion picture, which was given its world première in Miss Mitchell's home city of Atlanta on December 14, 1939, could itself be the subject of a novel, or a full-length historical review, so fantastic and significant is the saga of the trials and tribulations of getting it made. It was more than three years in preparation, it ran to exceptional cost and length, and it worked up more public excitement before its release than any film had ever stirred. The response when it opened was phenomenal. It has earned three times as much as any other film (with the possible exception of *The Birth of a Nation*). And it still does great business whenever it is shown.

That Loew's should have been the main participant in the profits of this vast film, which was actually produced by David Selznick through his Selznick-International company, was a stroke of good luck as fortuitous as its inheritance of *Ben Hur* or its even more fortunate acquisition of Rex Ingram's *The Four Horsemen of the Apocalypse*. As in those two prior instances, the privilege was virtually dumped in its lap. The break came mainly because Clark Gable was under contract to Metro-Goldwyn-Mayer.

This is the story of how it happened that David Selznick made *Gone With the Wind*, Loew's, Inc., made a lot of money and the picture itself made history.

When Selznick left Culver City in 1935 to form his own independent company and produce films the way he wanted to, he got most of his financial backing from a rather surprising source. That was the prominent Whitney family of Long Island and New York, headed by the dapper Whitney cousins, Cornelius V. and John Hay. These two gentlemen, along with their sisters, Mrs. Joan Payson, Mrs. Flora Miller and Mrs. Barbara Henry, advanced some $2,400,000 to launch Selznick-International. This represented three-quarters of the money put up. The rest of the financing came from Myron Selznick, David's brother, ($400,000); Robert and Arthur Lehman, New York bankers, and John Hertz ($300,000); and Norma Shearer and Irving Thalberg ($100,000). Selznick himself did not invest any money—only his skill and his time—but he owned a little more than half of the company.

With a three-year contract to release through United Artists,

Selznick's first film was *Little Lord Fauntleroy,* with Freddie Bartholomew, his own original discovery, whom he now borrowed from Metro-Goldwyn-Mayer. His next was *The Garden of Allah,* with Marlene Dietrich. He was busy with this in the early summer of 1936, when a wire reached him from Kay Brown, his New York story editor, urging him to buy film rights to a new Civil War novel entitled *Gone With the Wind.* Margaret Mitchell, the author of the novel, was unknown in the literary world.

The circumstances of the publication were intriguing. The novel had been picked up by a representative of the publisher, Macmillan, while scouting through the South. It was first intended for spring publication, but then a late acceptance of it by the Book-of-the-Month Club as its July selection set back the date until late June. Thus Miss Mitchell's literary agent, Annie Laurie Williams, was able to send advance copies of the novel (not galley proofs, as has often been recalled) to all the story editors of the film companies simultaneously.

Although two or three of the editors got excited, including Selznick's Miss Brown, there was a surprising lack of interest in the novel among the major studios. The general feeling was that Civil War stories had been played out with *The Birth of a Nation.* Paramount had lately come a cropper with a big one, *So Red the Rose,* starring Margaret Sullavan. Also, the heroine was a "bitch." And besides, Miss Williams' asking price for the screen rights—$100,000—was considered exorbitant. The only bid of any consequence from a major quarter came from Darryl Zanuck of Twentieth Century-Fox. He offered $35,000, which Miss Williams promptly declined. The author, who had come to New York from Atlanta for the book's publication, was shocked. She thought that a princely sum.

Meanwhile, Selznick, on receiving Miss Brown's enthusiastic wire, which was followed by a long synopsis from her, was considerably interested, but he had strong misgivings about the problems of producing a novel of such length. However, John Hay Whitney had taken a look at the book and told Selznick that he himself would buy it and let Selznick take his time making up his mind. That was enough for Selznick. He told Miss Brown to buy. She found she could now get it for $50,000. They closed for that figure in July.

Of course, as we look back upon it, that price was an absolute steal for a story property that later came to be one of the greatest "best sellers" of record. But, under the circumstances, it was considered pretty good. This was just after publication, before the novel had begun to sweep the land—and before its heroine, Scarlett O'Hara, had become the most-talked-about woman of the year. It was only then the film community realized Selznick had a tremendous property on his hands.

No one realized it better than he did. As winter came and the sales of the novel soared, the reading public began some positive thinking as to who would play the leading roles—especially the roles of Scarlett and Rhett Butler, the bold adventurer who married her. Selznick, knowing full well the advantage of such anticipatory talk, fed it by dropping frequent rumors on his plans for casting the film.

There was early talk of Tallulah Bankhead. She was a Southerner and had the theatrical personality of the scheming, bashless Scarlett. There was also talk of Norma Shearer, who was then in retirement from the screen. In March, a "source close to Selznick" said that Miriam Hopkins and Clark Gable would have the two leading roles, with Leslie Howard to play Ashley Wilkes and Janet Gaynor to play Scarlett's sister, Melanie.

On the casting of Rhett, there was no question. Although there was some mention of Gary Cooper, the overwhelming sentiment was that Gable *must* play the role. It was made-to-order for Gable. Indeed, the enthusiasm was so strong that Selznick soon perceived he would have to try to get the popular actor, who was, of course, under contract to Metro-Goldwyn-Mayer.

His tentative feelers discovered that the studio would loan him the star only on condition that Loew's, Inc., be permitted to release the film. But Selznick was committed to United Artists to release through them until 1939. If he wanted Gable, he would have to hold back the production of *Gone With the Wind* for a couple of years.

This was a difficult dilemma. Selznick was anxious to start the film and he felt that the public's eagerness for it was building up to a peak. He had already got the eminent playwright, Sidney Howard, to work on the script, and he had announced George Cukor as director. He had put his production staff, headed by William Cameron Menzies, to the arduous task of designing the whole thing. But he still hadn't settled on his actors, especially those for Scarlett and Rhett.

In his reconnoitering for Gable, negotiations were conducted through Al Lichtman. Mayer did not want to be in the position of talking such an important deal with a relative. And Lichtman was a tough trader. He set these terms; Metro-Goldwyn-Mayer would loan Gable and put up half the production costs, then estimated at $2,500,000, on condition that it would release the film and share equally with Selznick's company in the profits, after paying off production costs and taking out 15 per cent of the gross receipts for distributing it.

Selznick had a better bid from Warner Brothers. They offered to finance production in full and let him have Bette Davis to play Scarlett, Errol Flynn for Rhett and Olivia de Havilland for Melanie, while they asked only 25 per cent of the profits. This was a very tempting offer. Selznick also received a couple of juicy bids for the screen rights. But he was determined to do the film himself.

His own general manager, Henry Guinsburg, tried to discourage him. This was really too much of an undertaking for an independent producer, he said. But Selznick stubbornly insisted that it was exactly the sort of thing that an independent could do most effectively, with creative devotion and care. It was, in its way, the sort of challenge that Thalberg would have wanted to face.

Selznick heard criticism from other sources. After a year or so had passed from the time he bought the screen rights, Joe Schenck told him he was foolish not to have got the picture done. "I would have had it finished and made a million dollars profit by now," Schenck said. Selznick replied he was hopeful they might make more than that.

Throughout the period of indecision as to Gable and the releasing deal, Selznick was continuing to produce pictures for United Artists—*A Star Is Born, The Prisoner of Zenda, Nothing Sacred* (in which Carole Lombard was starred), *The Adventures of Tom Sawyer* and *The Young in Heart.* And he was ardently conducting the screen's most celebrated "talent hunt" for the proper actress to play the Scarlett role.

There was nothing calculated about this. He truly could not decide on the suitable actress. Tallulah Bankhead had been pretty well scratched. So had Miriam Hopkins. Katharine Hepburn wanted the role. She begged Selznick for it. Cukor was all for her. But Selznick couldn't see her in it. He allowed he was looking for an "unknown."

He and his staff interviewed a hundred hopefuls and screen-tested a score or more. Among the latter were several young ladies who were then comparatively unknown: Susan Hayward, a New York model; Paulette Goddard, Evelyn Keyes, Joan Fontaine (whom he used in his later film, *Rebecca*) and a Texas girl named Margaret Tallichet. The same agent who brought him the latter also brought him a saucy little blonde by the name of Judy Turner. They screen tested her in a bathing suit, for some peculiar reason. She wouldn't quite do for Scarlett. But Mervyn LeRoy later saw the screen test and decided to use the girl in *They Won't Forget,* a stinging drama he was making at Warner Brothers. She had a small but sensational role in the film, for which she changed her first name to Lana. That started her on the road to fame.

The Selznick scouts also spotted another prospect. When they asked her if she would like to test for Scarlett, she cracked, "Are you kidding?" She was then the very minor Lucille Ball.

The quest for a Scarlett was so famous that many freakish and pathetic things occurred. One Sunday morning, a huge box was delivered at Selznick's home. It was wrapped in fancy ribbons and had a sign on it, "Open at Once." When Selznick yanked the top off, out stepped a young girl in a green dress who said, with a pitiful simper, "My name is Scarlett O'Hara, and I am here to play the role." This rather made Selznick wonder whether things hadn't gone a bit too far.

The decision to close the deal for Gable was reached in early 1938, a short while after Selznick had turned down a strong bid to return as a producer to Metro-Goldwyn-Mayer. But the announcement and the signing of contracts was withheld until August 24, because of the deal with United Artists. Selznick couldn't proceed too rapidly because of that.

At the same time, it was reported that Norma Shearer would get the role of Scarlett, and the long "talent hunt" appeared ended. But actually Norma never was signed, and a month later, there came an official announcement that she had "withdrawn" from the role. What happened was that Selznick offered it to her and she accepted it tentatively, pending the reaction of her public. But she said she got so many letters from her fans, urging her not to play the "bad woman" that she decided to pass it up. She was also strongly advised against it by the newspaper columnist, Ed Sullivan. Later, Miss Shearer acknowledged it was one of the bad decisions of her career. "Anyhow," she said, "Scarlett is going to be a difficult and thankless role. The one I'd like to play is Rhett."

So strong was public interest, fed by the popularity of the book and the publicity, that the New York *Times* regretted, editorially, when Miss Shearer declined Scarlett. A few months later, Mrs. Ogden Reid, vice-president of the New York *Herald Tribune,* told a gathering of 3,000 clubwomen that Katharine Hepburn was her choice and she understood Miss Hepburn was the choice of Margaret Mitchell, too. Miss Mitchell replied that she was neutral. "I don't know anyone in the movies who looks like Scarlett," she said.

As winter came on, it was acknowledged by Selznick that he was going to start production on the film in January, even though he didn't have a Scarlett. "I still hope to give the American people a new girl," he said. As late as December 18, it was rumored that, unless someone was found, the picture would be started with Gable and Carole Lombard in the leading roles. In that event, the director would be Gable's good friend, Victor Fleming, not Cukor, it was said. Gable and Miss Lombard were then beginning a much-publicized romance.

But that eventuality was forfended, because Scarlett had already been found, even though the public announcement did not come until January 13, 1939.

It happened in a quite dramatic fashion. Selznick's studio was the old Pathé lot in Culver City, and it was there that *Gone With the Wind* was to be made. In order to clear the back lot for the building of Tara, the O'Hara plantation home, and the outdoor sets of Atlanta, a jungle of old standing sets had to be removed. Among them were sets used in C. B. DeMille's great Biblical drama, *King of Kings*.

William Cameron Menzies had an idea. Rather than tear down these old sets, why not burn them in a mammoth conflagration and use the fire to represent the burning of Atlanta, which was to be one of the great dramatic highlights of the film? Then the lot would be clear for the new buildings and they would have one of their most important scenes completed.

Selznick jumped for the idea, and arrangements for the burning were made. The old sets were "doctored" with false fronts and the cooperation of the Culver City fire department was obtained. Since a part of the action in this sequence was the frantic flight of Scarlett and Rhett from the burning city in an old wagon which Rhett commandeered, they wanted some long shots of the couple in the wagon against the roaring fire. Two stunt men were got to play the couple. The burning was scheduled for the night of December 10.

The occasion was reminiscent of the shooting of the chariot race in *Ben Hur*. Many of Hollywood's famous people were invited by Selznick to watch. Among them was his brother, Myron, whose talent agency was one of the best.

As the moment approached for starting the conflagration, Myron had not arrived. Selznick, himself burning furiously, waited a few minutes, then told them to touch off the fire. The flames were just rising into the night sky, dozens of cameras were beginning to turn, and Selznick was in a lather, when he felt a tug at his sleeve. He looked around and there was brother Myron, accompanied by a beautiful girl.

"I want you to meet Scarlett O'Hara," said Myron, dramatically.

Selznick shot a quick glance at the young lady. And, sure enough, in the wild and fiery glow of the simulated burning of Atlanta, he saw the girl who was to play the famous role. She was a hazel-eyed, brown-haired beauty with a face that was impudent and alive beneath a large hat such as might have been worn by Scarlett. She was the English actress, Vivien Leigh.

It may have been the drama of that moment—the start of the picture, the reality of the fire, the awesome sense that the Yankees were approaching and old Atlanta was going up in flames—that prepared Selznick for a revelation, but he suddenly felt this was *the* girl.

Within a matter of six minutes, the old sets burned and collapsed. The last of DeMille's Biblical spectacle went up in the smoke of the Civil War. In that time, they got two "takes" of the wagon with Scarlett and Rhett passing across the fiery scene. Then Selznick took Miss Leigh to his office and asked her if she would test for the role.

She didn't need urging. Later, it was realized by her friends that she had been secretly hoping and angling to cop the job for more than a year. In at least two previous pictures—*A Yank at Oxford* and *St. Martin's Lane* she had played naughty, flirtatious women. And her trip to America to see her good friend, Laurence Olivier, who was busy in Samuel Goldwyn's *Wuthering Heights,* was suspiciously timed. It turned out that Myron had already made arrangements for her to be tested, through Selznick's right-hand man, Danny O'Shea.

Only four actresses were put through full color tests for the role. They were Joan Bennett, Jean Arthur, Paulette Goddard and finally Miss Leigh. Cukor directed all of them and had them do three scenes from the script: Scarlett getting into her corset, with the help of Mammy; talking with Ashley in the paddock, and drunkenly proposing to Rhett. Cukor had them play the latter with a trace of comedy. Later, when the selection of Miss Leigh was announced, one of the disappointed actresses asked if she could run her screen test at her home. Selznick's office sent it around and she burned it. But Selznick still has the negatives.

The picture went before the camera on January 26, 1938, with a scene on the steps of Tara, which had now been built on the back lot. In addition to Miss Leigh and Gable, the cast included Olivia de Havilland as Melanie, Leslie Howard as Ashley, Thomas Mitchell as Scarlett's father, Gerald, Hattie McDaniel as Mammy and Ona Munson as Belle Watling. A Gallup poll found that the American public was 35 per cent in favor of Miss Leigh.

Three weeks after shooting started, Selznick found himself dissatisfied with the tempo and style of Cukor's direction. He thought the pace too slow and the emphasis too much on the feminine characters. Gable, too, was dissatisfied. From the start, he had wanted another director. So a change was arranged. Cukor was taken off the picture and Victor Fleming, the old trouble shooter, was pulled off *The Wizard of Oz* and assigned to *Gone With the Wind*. Actually, the switch was propitious. Cukor was immediately assigned to *The Women,* while Ernst Lubitsch, who had been booked for that, was switched over to direct Greta Garbo in *Ninotchka*. They were both skillful films.

As for Fleming, he was not too happy. Both Miss Leigh and Miss de Havilland resented him. Miss Leigh kept looking at her screen tests and stuck as closely as she could to the Cukor style. When Selznick asked Fleming if he would take a share of the picture in lieu of a salary, Fleming replied, "What do you think I am, a chump?" Late in April, after ten weeks of shooting, he collapsed, and Sam Wood was called in to finish the film. Even so, Fleming got one of the ten "Oscars" that were later given for *Gone With the Wind*.

Throughout this period of shooting, Selznick was going at killing pace, feeding himself benzedrine and thyroid extract and staying up late playing poker and roulette to relax. Sidney Howard and others were still doing rewrite on the script. Selznick himself did a lot of the writing. He was constantly on the sets.

When they were something more than half finished, Selznick called Lichtman one day and told him he would like to show him some of the picture. Lichtman was eager for the chance. They had a screening that evening—a matter of some five reels. Only Selznick, Lichtman, a cutter and a secretary were in the room. When it was ended, Lichtman jumped up excitedly. "Dave, we're home!" he cried. "This picture will gross $19,000,000!"

"I'm glad you think so," Selznick said, "because I'm here to get more money from you. I haven't enough to finish it."

"How much do you need?" Lichtman queried.

"Another million," Selznick replied.

Lichtman called Schenck about it, but Schenck said he would not ask his board of directors to approve more of an investment than the original contract with Selznick specified. Lichtman then called Joe Rosenberg in charge of motion picture loans at the Bank of America in Los Angeles and told him, "Joe, I've just seen one of the greatest pictures ever made. You're a banker and a conservative man, so I hesitate to tell you entirely what I think. But I'll be conservative and promise you this picture will do a $10,000,000 gross. Will you give Selznick a loan on it?"

"Tell Selznick's man to come down and get the money," Rosenberg said. A straight bank loan of $1,000,000 was thus acquired to finish the film.

After twenty-two weeks of shooting, the final scene—an interior of Melanie's parlor in Atlanta—was done on July 1. That was the end, except for one retake and a montage, done on November 11. The picture ran four hours and twenty-five minutes at its first preview. Schenck saw it and thought it wonderful. He told Selznick not to touch it. But Selznick began trimming scenes and removed some forty-three minutes, so that it ran three hours and forty-two minutes in its final cut.

During this period of the previews, there was much discussion as to whether there should be an intermission during the showing of the picture. Selznick thought there should be. Howard Dietz, who was heading the record promotion campaign, thought there should not. Selznick's point was that human bladders could not hold out for the length of the film. He carried his point by making a check on the number of people who went to the conveniences during an experimental intermission at a preview.

For the world première in Atlanta, a tremendous celebration was arranged. The front of the Grand Theatre was decorated to resemble the portico of Twelve Oaks, one of the Georgia mansions in the novel. Selznick and most of the company were on hand, including Gable and his new wife, Carole Lombard, and the now celebrated Miss Leigh. When they got off the airplane in Atlanta, she clutched Selznick's arm. "Listen," she said, "they're playing the music from the picture." He laughed, "That's *Dixie,* dear."

There were two days of festivals and galas, during which the glories of the old South were recalled, capped by the première showing. Emotions ran rampant. At the end, Margaret Mitchell, almost weeping, told the audience, "It is a great thing for Georgia and the South to see the Confederates come back.' There was little thought in Atlanta that evening of the German cruiser, *Graf Spee,* in the Platte River or of another war that was already begun.

The New York première, two nights later—December 16—was another plush affair, held in two theatres, the Astor and the Capitol. In the lobby of the Capitol, recording the arrival of guests and stars, was a novel and amusing instrument—a television camera.

The success of *Gone With the Wind* thereafter exceeded the expectations of anyone. In the first four months of its showing, it grossed over $4,000,000 at the theatres. A unique plan for selling it had been set up by the people of Loew's. They took 70 per cent of the gross of the theatres, but they guaranteed at least 10 per cent profit to every house. In its first year, the picture took in $13,500,000 in distributor's gross. On its second release, a year later, it took in another $5,000,000. To the end of 1955, it had brought in close to $50,000,000. Since 1944, it has been owned entirely by Loew's.

Selznick sold his interest in this picture to John Hay Whitney in 1942, and Whitney, in an involved financial transaction, sold to Loew's two years later. Even though Metro-Goldwyn-Mayer did not produce it, the company has got the lion's share of the profits from *Gone With the Wind.* This was the ironic conclusion of the independent producer having free rein.

CHAPTER XXX

THE GRAVY TRAIN

THE TREMENDOUS success and profits that were reaped from *Gone With the Wind* were but the beginning of a harvest to be gathered by Metro-Goldwyn-Mayer-Loew's, and, indeed, by the whole motion picture industry, during the years that lay immediately ahead. Following a slump in net income from 1937 through 1940, a boom of unprecedented prosperity occurred through World War II and, despite many adverse circumstances, the movie business never had it so good.

The situation was eccentric. When the war in Europe began, the prospect of perilous depression for the American film companies loomed. Total restriction on the export of currency from the warring nations put such a dent in the revenues from foreign distribution that it appeared to amount to a crippling wound. Then, in 1940, when the deadly fighting commenced and the Continent became forbidden territory, the amputation was complete.

Loew's own theatres in Austria, Belgium and France were lost. In August of 1940, it was ousted from Germany, where it had attempted to maintain distribution, in spite of discouraging Nazi rules. The end came when the studio produced *The Mortal Storm,* a fearlessly anti-Nazi drama, and Herr Goebbels, hearing of it, said "Go!" That summer, a few days after the fall of Dunkerque, the company announced the closing of its British studio. The rumble of Winston Churchill's defiance sounded like a rear-guard resistance to England's doom.

But, for all the grave fears of 1940, the American film companies were cheered by a sweeping upturn in domestic business in 1941. The rise in employment and income that came as American industry went into heavy war production gave lots of people money to spend, and the movies were one of the few diversions on which it could now be spent. The spiral continued upwards as this country went into the war. The next four years were a virtual millennium for the marketing of films.

Indeed, they were so propitious and the pickings were so easy and lush that the Hollywood motion-picture makers lost contact with normality. Practically any sort of product could be unloaded profitably on a public that was virtually a captive audience for the unchallenged entertainment of films. Even with many leading actors in military service, the screen was more popular and more looked-to for the blessing of "escape" than it had ever been. Under these circumstances, the film makers became careless and fat. The unhealthiness of this obesity was to take effect after the war.

Of all the studios that prospered and grew corpulent and lax, none got more rich or more flabby than Metro-Goldwyn-Mayer.

The process of change in organization and rotation of talent that was in a state of acceleration after Mayer took full command had brought some conspicuous climaxes, even before 1941. The old stars were swinging towards the horizon and new ones were coming on. This inevitable evolution was most apparent among the actresses.

Norma Shearer, Joan Crawford, Greta Carbo and Jeanette Mac-Donald were the ladies whose days in the studio where they had had their glory were fast coming to a close. Oddly enough, Luise Rainer, a sort of comet, had already gone. After her triumphs in *The Great Ziegfield* and *The Good Earth,* she was rather sadly used in *The Toy Wife* and *The Great Waltz,* which was one of the vain enthusiasms of Mayer. Then she was caught in a picture, produced by Mervyn LeRoy, called *Dramatic School,* which made a dismal mockery of its title, and that was the fade-out for her.

Miss Shearer's poignant departure was more wistful and prolonged. After the dubious indulgence of *Marie Antoinette,* she was cast to play with Clark Gable in the film of Robert E. Sherwood's *Idiot's Delight.* Again she was disappointed in the choice of director, Clarence Brown. She would have preferred George Cukor, who was waiting for *Gone With the Wind.* Under the auspices of Thalberg, the arrangement might have been made, but Mayer and Hunt Stromberg, the producer, were unable to gratify her wish. The film was a far cry from the tragi-comedy performed on the stage by the Lunts.

Next she was cast in *The Women,* to be made from the then Clare Boothe's stinging play about the tribal behavior of wives and mistresses of the rich. It was an all-female comedy-drama, appropriate to the facilities of Metro-Goldwyn-Mayer, and, in addition to Miss Shearer, the cast included Joan Crawford, Rosalind Russell, Paulette Goddard, Hedda Hopper and Joan Fontaine. Cukor, just off the Selznick picture, was relied upon to handle the girls.

He did so with extraordinary finesse—considering that Miss Shearer was now in the somewhat vulnerable position of having no particular favor at court. Although she tried to take her status with good humor, there were times when it was a little hard to submit.

Some of the ribbing was genial. At a party, during the course of shooting, one night, Cukor was dancing with Rosalind Russell. Ernst

Lubitsch danced by and cast a knowing wink at her. "Trying to get a close-up in the picture, I see!" he purred. Miss Russell smiled and nodded. Once around the room and Lubitsch was back. "But if you want to *stay* in the picture, you'd better dance with Miss Shearer," he cracked. Miss Russell and Cukor giggled. A few minutes later, all the guests were amazed to see Miss Russell and Miss Shearer dancing together, with the latter smiling graciously. Someone had told her of Lubitsch's wisecrack, so she grabbed Miss Russell and danced away with her.

But the one really rough experience that occurred in the shooting of the film came when Miss Crawford and Miss Shearer were preparing for the only scene they had together in the whole thing. That was the scene in which Miss Shearer, playing a wife, confronted her husband's mistress, the role Miss Crawford played.

During rehearsals of a scene that is played by two people, it is courteous for each to "feed" the other lines when the director is having them practice for the shots that will be made individually. They were running through Miss Shearer's "singles," with Miss Crawford sitting in a chair to one side, "feeding" her lines—but also devoting her attention to knitting furiously with large needles that clicked. Miss Shearer took it for a few run-throughs. Then she asked Miss Crawford to stop. The latter paid no attention. She continued to knit and click. It was a highly suspicious show of rudeness. This was the first time the two actresses, who had been stars in the same studio for a decade, had been together in a scene.

Miss Shearer finally turned to the director. "Mr. Cukor," she said, "I think Miss Crawford can go home now and you can give me her lines."

Cukor was as outraged as Miss Shearer. He asked Miss Crawford to leave the set. Later, he handed her a lecture the likes of which she had probably never heard. Several stagehands congratulated Miss Shearer. But that night she received a telegram from Miss Crawford that made her hair curl. The two actresses never spoke to each other again—except, of course, to finish that particularly venomous scene.

The Women might be regarded as the last real display of the two stars in their appropriate setting at Metro-Goldwyn-Mayer. Miss Crawford did five more pictures before she left the studio in 1942, but each represented a step-down from the level on which she had been. When she pulled out and went to Warner Brothers, it was a grimly conclusive episode.

As for Miss Shearer, she still owed the studio three films. Her next was *Escape,* an anti-Nazi melodrama that closely followed *The Mortal Storm.* Then Mayer made a valiant endeavor to persuade her to take the title role in a purposeful picture the studio was planning, called *Mrs. Miniver.* It was a story of a brave English woman in the first year of the war. Mayer told her the more dramatic parts of it, but she wasn't interested. She wanted to do light, frothy comedies. This sounded too heavy to her. Beside, it was tacitly noted that Mrs. Miniver was the mother of a grown son.

Without anyone's encouragement, Miss Shearer elected to do, in quick succession, a trifle called *We Were Dancing* and then *Her Cardboard Lover,* a thin, synthetic thing. "On these last two," she later acknowledged, "nobody but myself was trying to do me in." She considered the refusal of *Mrs. Miniver* the second big mistake of her career. The first was, of course, her refusal of the lead in *Gone With the Wind.*

That finished her contract for six pictures, and she decided she was through. She had fallen in love with a handsome ski instructor, Martin Arrougé, whom she met in Sun Valley when he was teaching her and her children to ski. They were married shortly after her retirement in the summer of 1942. The wedding ring that Thalberg had given her was placed on her finger by Arrougé. . . .

Already Greta Garbo had completed her last film—a wretched comedy, *Two-Faced Woman,* in which the distinguished actress played identical twins. This was a dismal experience after the glittering success she had with her first comedy role in *Ninotchka,* under the direction of Ernst Lubitsch, in 1939. Following that memorable satire, Eddie Mannix agreed with her to start her in a new picture on September 1 of that year.

Then the war broke out and the closing of the European market, where she was always most popular, made another picture with her risky, especially at her high salary. Bennie Thau was delegated to ask her if she would do two pictures for the price of one. Garbo thought it over (it took her some time), then replied that she wouldn't make that concession but she would do one picture for $150,000. Thau asked if she would do two for $300,000. She said no, just the one. That was *Two-Faced Woman,* when they got around to it. The title did not do justice to the unaccustomed generosity of the star, who had previously been most stubborn and uncompromising where money was concerned.

There have been endless theories about Garbo—why she remained aloof, why she was never married, why she quit the screen. The mysteries will outlive interest in them, but her retirement may be explained by the simple colloquial phrase, "She'd had it." The medium had got too baffling for her.

Jeanette MacDonald was the fourth of the great ladies who

departed in 1942. She checked out with a picture called *Cairo,* which was a miserable rodomontadê. After her performance in *The Firefly,* which followed *Maytime,* she had been, by her own calculation, in the not too good graces of Mayer. He had objected to her dubbing her own voice in the foreign-language versions of the film. She went to New York and got Schenck's approval. That didn't sit well with Mayer. Nor would she later "go in and make peace with Papa," as Ida Koverman urged her to do.

"He wasn't fighting my battles after that," the singer found.

Although she did several subsequent musicals—*Sweethearts* (which was the first all-color film produced at Culver City), *New Moon, Bittersweet* and *Smilin' Through*—she had the uncomfortable feeling that she was losing ground. Nelson Eddy was being teamed with her in some films and put in others by himself. (One of his separate films, *Rosalie,* was written to fit around a song Mayer asked Cole Porter to write as close as possible to *Rose Marie.*) Then the two were teamed in *I Married An Angel,* after that musical, originally written for Miss MacDonald, had been done on Broadway, and that was the end of their famous tie-up. *Cairo* followed. Then Miss Mac-Donald left. She returned to Culver City for two pictures in 1947-48, but her popularity was spent.

Again the spots of the old stars were being crowded by the new— by the actresses who were moving forward with the inexorable pressure of change. Time and the younger generations had as much to do with pushing them on as the dissatisfactions of the older actresses had to do with their making room.

Foremost among the newcomers was Greer Garson, who had been returned to Culver City with revitalized interest after *Good-by, Mr. Chips.* Her first assignment was to play Elizabeth Bennett in a delightful dramatization of Jane Austen's *Pride and Prejudice.* Miss Garson did the young English lady so delightfully that she added vastly to her circle of friends. She next did a sentimental foray as the founder of an orphanage in *Blossoms in the Dust,* then ran rings around Joan Crawford in a comedy, *When Ladies Meet.*

Mrs. Miniver

It was shortly after she had finished this picture that Mayer called her to his office and said he had a superb assignment for her. It was *Mrs. Miniver.* He did not tell her that Norma Shearer had flatly turned it down, but even that knowledge could not have made her any more resistant to the role than she was. She knew the very popular group of pieces by Jan Struther, on which the intended film was based, and while she greatly admired them for their sense of English valor during the first dark year of the war, she could not be moved. Jan Struther's Mrs. Miniver was a settled lady. And, besides, she did have that grown son! Mayer kept after Miss Garson, but she begged him not to force her to play the role.

Poor Mrs. Miniver had had a slow time getting even this far. The essays, when they were first published in an English newspaper, were turned down by Kenneth MacKenna, story editor for Metro-Goldwyn-Mayer. Later, when they were published in book form and became very popular in the United States, MacKenna took the book home one week end to try to find out what made it tick. He realized, upon rereading it, that it conveyed something that Americans very much wanted to know—what the British were having to go through, so close to the war and the Blitz. He took the book to Sidney Franklin, who had been made a producer in 1938, and roused his interest in it. Franklin took it to Mannix, who authorized its purchase for $30,000.

Franklin was now enthusiastic. He had been looking for something that would be a tribute to the English people and the way they stood up under Dunkerque and the Battle of Britain. Although the Struthers pieces had no dramatic plot, Franklin got James Hilton and Arthur Wimperis to prepare a script. His own favorite writer who had worked with him for eighteen years, Claudine West, also had a hand in it, and later he got George Froeschel, an Austrian refugee, who had come to the studio to write *The Mortal Storm*, to help. Finally, R. C. Sherriff, the British playwright, was rung in to write the memorable scene of Mr. and Mrs. Miniver with their children in the bomb-shelter, reading *Alice in Wonderland*, while the air raid was going on. Sherriff who had done a similar scene in his classic play, *Journey's End*, was on it only a few weeks and did not get credit as one of the writers of the script.

Franklin explained to Mannix, who was sitting in for Mayer at this point, that it would be just a little story of how this one English family stood up. It might lose $100,000, he said, but he thought it should be done. Mannix agreed with him entirely and said to go ahead. So Franklin got William Wyler, who had just done *Wuthering Heights* for Samuel Goldwyn, to come on as director. Wyler was eager from the start, from the moment Franklin read the script to him instead of letting him read it himself. He thought there should be a picture that would make the onrush of the Nazis plain to the American public and that might help get us into the war. (He was later told to go easy on this point. Mayer did not want a war-mongering film. But, of course, by the time the picture was released in the summer of 1942, we were already in.)

Now Mayer was working on Greer Garson to persuade her to play the film. "I *hate* Mrs. Miniver!" she finally told him, "but if you insist, I'll do the thing!" Walter Pidgeon, who had been with Miss Garson in *Blossoms in the Dust,* was considered a fair bet to play Mrs. Miniver's husband, Clem. Richard Nye, whom Miss Garson later married, was called in to play her son.

There was some talk, at this point, of arranging it so the lad would be the son of Clem Miniver by a former marriage, but Jan Struther heard of this and protested so fiercely it was abandoned. Clem Miniver would never have been remarried if he had lost a wife, she said!

During the shooting of the picture, they had some trouble over the scene in which Mrs. Miniver encountered the wounded German pilot in her garden and later found him to be a poor, frightened boy. Wyler wanted to make him tough and vicious. "If I have a lot of Germans, I can show one nice one," he said. "But if I have only one German, and one of Herman Goering's Luftwaffe monsters, at that, I've got to make him typical." Wyler was almost pulled off the picture because of the arguments. The point was finally compromised.

Miss Garson was intent upon a good job, once she had committed herself. She asked Wyler whether he wanted her to make herself look older for the role. "Should I have the make-up department put little lines in my face and gray my hair?" she asked. "Oh, no," Wyler assured her. "You look just right as you are." When he saw this was not exactly what Miss Garson wanted to hear, he added quickly, "I mean, I *want* you to look young and vital, a youthful woman. The audience will make allowances, you may be sure."

The only complete incongruity from which Miss Garson could not be budged was that of playing a bedroom scene in a glamorous nightgown that might have been elaborate for a honeymoon. It was thoroughly impractical for sleeping, but she insisted on it. So, rather than force the issue, Wyler let her wear the nightgown of her choice.

When *Mrs. Miniver* was completed, the people at the studio knew they had a powerful picture, and they hoped to build up to its release with a big publicity campaign. But President Roosevelt saw an advance print at the White House and felt so strongly it would help American women grasp the impact of the war on their British counterparts that he requested Loew's to release it right away. This was done, and the picture immediately became one of the great inspirational dramas of World War II.

Along with its other triumphs, it took most of the Academy awards in 1942—best picture, best screenplay, best direction, best performance by an actress, best performance by a supporting actress (Teresa

Wright, who played the sweetheart of the Miniver son) and best black-and-white cinematography.

As a consequence of this picture, Miss Garson immediately became the top dramatic actress at Metro-Goldwyn-Mayer and, indeed, the most highly regarded leading lady in Hollywood. Her next appearance in *Random Harvest*, with Ronald Colman, made that sentimental film a hit of extraordinary dimensions. And when she and Mr. Pidgeon were teamed again as a husband and wife in *Mme. Curie*, a romantic biography of the discoverers of radium, the warmth of the popular reception had a glow to compare with that of the element released.

In her next film, *Valley of Decision*, Miss Garson was cast as a matriarch. This was a role to which her strong maternal channeling was inevitably leading her. Mayer, being a zealot for mothers, was enthusiastic about the trend. Miss Garson was privately unhappy. "Metro's Glorified Mama," she called herself.

This was the foundation laid down by *Mrs. Miniver*, a film that had found lodging in the hearts of people in many parts of the world and even in Britain, where it was jumped on by the critics as a glamorization of the English home. But that was the secret of the success of American movies: People liked to see themselves glamorized.

Eight years later, a postwar sequel to *Mrs. Miniver* was made by the studio. It was called *The Miniver Story* and Miss Garson and Mr. Pidgeon were again starred. It had to do with the tough domestic problems of the middle-aged couple in their country after the war. Sidney Franklin was again the producer and he wanted Wyler to direct. The latter was impressed with the story and thought it could be as good as the first, provided it was played lightly by the principals against a background of imminent tragedy. But the studio wouldn't hire Wyler. The film was a drab, inept affair. In the end, Mrs. Miniver died of cancer. It was a wretched conclusion for her.

At about the same time Miss Garson was emerging as a star, Katharine Hepburn was got to Culver City to do a film of her popular play, *The Philadelphia Story*, and then to team up with Spencer Tracy in the comedy, *Woman of the Year*. Miss Hepburn had been publicly called "boxoffice poison" by a prominent New York exhibitor, but Mayer had the courage to sign her in the face of this idiotic blast. Under George Cukor's nimble direction, she came out a mature and stylish star. She was one of the few top-flight actresses who could get along swimmingly with Mayer. Her hard Yankee mind understood him, and he shrewdly respected her. She talked like a businessman to him. He couldn't fool her with his emotional acts. The further pictures she made during the war years—*Keeper of the Flame, Dragon*

Seed and *Without Love*—were done by her with the efficiency and expedition of a full professional.

It is reflective of the studio's operation that most of the young actresses who came along in these years of largely feminine pre-eminence were alumnae of the Andy Hardy films. Judy Garland sprang from *Love Finds Andy Hardy*. In that same picture, playing a small role as a vampish young thing in a tight sweater, was Lana Turner, whom Mervyn LeRoy had brought with him to the studio. She had been standing around doing nothing, except attending the studio children's school, when she was dropped into the Hardy picture. She went up the ladder from there.

Other girls who came out of the Hardy pictures were Ruth Hussey, Virginia Weidler, Marsha Hunt, Kathryn Grayson, Donna Reed and Esther Williams, who became the studio's first sub-aqueous star.

They had a hard time hooking Miss Williams, who would rather have been a fish—or perhaps an assistant buyer at Magnin's store in Los Angeles. She was in an aquacade in San Francisco, when a studio scout first spotted her and offered to give her a contract. She said she was disinterested. Later, when she was modeling at Magnin's and hoping to work herself up to assistant buyer, an agent, Johnny Hyde, maneuvered her into an interview with Mayer. He conspired to get her out to the studio on the pretext that she was going to model a gown, and led her into Mayer's office. Mayer's first words were, "She's awfully tall." "Exactly what I say," piped Miss Williams and started for the door, but Mayer grabbed her and stood his five feet five beside her. "Have a hard time finding leading men," he said. However, attractive terms were offered, so Miss Williams agreed to have a go at films.

It happened they were already having trouble with Lana Turner. She had been teamed with Clark Gable in *Honky Tonk* and was scheduled to do another with him, when she dashed off to New York after Artie Shaw. The studio meant to teach her a lesson. They put Miss Williams in a beautiful dress, did a test and showed it to Gable. He was much impressed with the girl and said he would do a test with her. When he came on, he didn't know his lines, so he faked it by mostly hugging and kissing Miss Williams, which was unsettling for an inexperienced girl. Miss Turner returned, however, so the beautiful model (who was so tall they would have trouble finding leading men for her) was put in *Andy Hardy's Double Life* with the redoubtable Mickey Rooney, who was all of five feet one. The script had her meet Andy Hardy underwater in a swimming pool and give him a kiss. That was the beginning of Miss Williams' career as a submarine. She went from that to *Bathing Beauty*, via *A Guy Named*

Joe, and thereafter was a stellar adornment of water pictures and sequined bathing suits. Miss Williams' luscious color spectacles have been big hits all over the world.

The discovery of this superb attraction, who was, in a subtle sense, a modern, civilized, feminine version of the studio's old wood nymph, Tarzan, precisely coincided with the discovery of another great star— or, we should say two, in the same picture. The first was Lassie the collie dog.

Harry Rapf's low-budget unit had a novel, *Lassie Come Home,* by Eric Knight, about an old Scot and his sheep dog, which Rapf had decided they should do. Sam Marx was assigned as producer and Fred Wilcox was chosen to direct. Wilcox was a former test director. He was also a brother-in-law of Nick Schenck.

As a first step towards finding a collie to play the principal role, Marx advertised for dog-owners to bring their animals to Gilmore Stadium in Los Angeles for a "mass interview." (This was reminiscent of the maneuver by which Woody Van Dyke found Edwina Booth for *Trader Horn.*) No animal of suitable "personality" was spotted at that canine canvassing, so Wilcox got a professional dog trainer, Rudd Weatherwax, to scout the countryside and bring in as many collies as he might fancy as likely for a test.

Weatherwax showed up in a few days with a station wagon full of dogs and paraded them one at a time in front of Wilcox's camera. None looked exceptional. Then Wilcox noted there was still an animal in the station wagon that hadn't been brought out. It seemed that this collie, a year-old male that Weatherwax called Pal, was a cull which the trainer had recently accepted from a breeder in lieu of a ten dollar debt. He didn't even think the dog worth testing. He had just brought it along for company.

Wilcox liked the looks of Pal better than any of the other dogs. He put him before the camera and found he tested best. So Pal was the dog they selected to play Lassie in the film.

The first footage was shot by a unit on location in the state of Washington and also along the beaches outside Monterey, to simulate the landscape of northern Scotland for Lassie's climactic trek back to her home. While these scenes were shooting, Weatherwax was training Pal to "act" with people in the studio. By the time they returned to Culver City, the dog was perfectly prepared.

A Dog and a Child

It was while they were shooting in the studio that they realized the little girl they had to play a wee Scot was unable to continue because her eyes were too weak to stand the brightness of the lights.

A replacement was required. Edgar Selwyn overheard Marx and Wilcox discussing this, and said he believed he could find them a girl. Selwyn had a friend named Sara Taylor, an English actress, who had come from London to escape the Blitz. She had a pretty daughter. Maybe she would do. Marx suggested that Mrs. Taylor bring her daughter around. She did, and the pretty daughter turned out to be a darling ten-year-old, with huge, lustrous eyes, raven black hair and an exquisitely molded little face. Her name was Elizabeth and they discovered she had been trained as a small child to dance. Indeed, she had appeared in a London recital before the little English princesses, Elizabeth and Margaret Rose. Wilcox saw immediately, without a test, that this was his girl. He started rehearsing her right away. Thus Lassie and Elizabeth Taylor were fledged, shall we say, in the same film.

Lassie—or Pal—was a remarkable animal, very smart and affectionate, too. He was used in all the future Lassie pictures that the studio inevitably made. It was true they had a few dogs that looked like him to serve as stand-ins and for occasional long "stunt" shots, but reports that they had several animals to play the role were false.

Pal is still alive when this is written, but he is old and stiff in the joints. His son, Laddie, who looked much like him, took over the role for the Lassie television shows.

As for little Miss Taylor, she was next cast to play in a film about steeplechase riding in England. *National Velvet* was its name, and the ubiquitous Mickey Rooney was co-star. Thereafter she did a succession of increasingly older teen-age girls, until she came to young ladyhood completely in the delightful postwar *Father of the Bride*. She achieved her maturity as an actress on loan-out for *A Place in the Sun*.

If there appeared to be an excess of youthful talent at the studio in these years, it could be accounted for, in part, by the circumstances that so many of the male stars were going off to war. Right after *Love Finds Andy Hardy* and the casting of Judy Garland in *The Wizard of Oz*, Arthur Freed was told by Mayer to find a story for himself to produce. He knew he could not get a "big" show or be given a top musical star, so he decided to try teaming Judy Garland and Mickey Rooney, who had been so good together in the Hardy film. He got hold of a fair Broadway musical, *Babes in Arms*, and was permitted to cast the youngsters in it. The experiment was successful. Freed quickly repeated in *Strike Up the Band*.

Mickey was a wheel horse in the studio, after this country got into the war and such stars as Robert Montgomery, Clark Gable, Robert Taylor and Lew Ayres went into the services. He played everything from Hardy pictures and *Young Tom Edison* to the musicals with Judy and *National Velvet*. He was even a hoofer in the all-star *Ziegfeld Girl*. But perhaps his most bizarre experience was in *The Human Comedy*.

The story for this fantastic picture was bought from William Saroyan by Mayer, who took an extraordinary fancy to the ebullient Armenian. Arthur Freed brought the writer to the studio and introduced him to Mayer. Mayer bought the story for $60,000 and told Saroyan he would make "another Thalberg" of him. He told him he would make him a producer and also let him direct.

Things didn't work out in that order. *The Human Comedy*, which had been written by Saroyan in three weeks on the suggestion of a friend that he do a story about his youthful experiences as a messenger boy, appeared rather difficult on close inspection. It was turned over to Clarence Brown to direct, and Saroyan was given his opportunity to be a Thalberg by producing and directing a short. He did so with considerable flamboyance and a great deal of noise-making around the place. He insisted on having a grand piano in his office and spending much time in the projection room. It was later discovered that he was viewing all the old pictures he had missed over the years.

However, *The Human Comedy*, when completed was a fanciful sentimental film about a messenger boy and his whimsical kid brother, with Rooney in the former role and a youngster called "Butch" Jenkins as the kid brother. It was variously viewed as either poetry or guff. Saroyan didn't last long at the studio. When he departed he took some verbal shots at Mayer. For all that, *The Human Comedy* remained one of Mayer's all-time favorite films.

The increasing trend towards musical comedies which went on through the war came to a happy climax in 1945 with the achievement of *Meet Me in St. Louis* and the joyous *Anchors Aweigh*. The former was directed by Vincente Minnelli, who was brought to the studio by Arthur Freed, producer of the picture. They were the only ones who had confidence in it at the start. Freed had to fight to get the story, had to plead with Judy Garland to play the role and had to get down on his knees and beg Mannix to let him spend $100,000 to have a set built to be a reproduction of a St. Louis street at the beginning of the century. (That standing set, solidly constructed, has since been frequently used and rented to other companies, so that it has paid for itself many times.) During the shooting, Judy didn't get along with Minnelli—at first. (They were later married and divorced.) But *Meet Me in St. Louis* was finally a most happy film.

So was *Anchors Aweigh*. It presented the new Gene Kelly and Frank Sinatra as stars, and was produced by Joe Pasternak, who had been got to the studio by Sam Katz in 1942. Kelly had been brought from Broadway by Arthur Freed, who had seen him in *Pal Joey* and had persuaded the studio to buy his contract from David Selznick for $80,000. He had first been put with Judy Garland in *For Me and My Gal*, against the advice of several bigwigs. When the picture was a success, it was all right.

The illusion of a smoothly functioning studio that the prosperity of the war years gave was belied by internal frictions and confusions of a disconcerting sort. Mayer still didn't have his top-level operations organized efficiently, and the presence of Katz and Lichtman did not lead him to feel more secure. In the hopes of achieving some stability in studio policy, Mayer set up what he called an executive committee in 1943. It was composed of himself, Katz, Lichtman, Mannix, Thau, Weingarten and a new man in the executive ranks, James Kevin McGuinness, a former writer who had lately ingratiated himself with Mayer. It was supposed to be the function of this committee to analyze and pass upon all questions of major importance concerning production, but it was just a quaint device through which to pass the buck.

Not helping matters any was the fact that Mayer had become an ardent devotee of horse racing and was now operating his own breeding farm. He found the sport fascinating when he took to going to the track with a few friends and beheld the attention the owner of a winning horse got. The urge to join this "sport of kings" seized him, and he started accumulating race horses in 1938. He said that he intended to build his stable as he did "his" studio on "personalities." The misfortune was that this new interest drew him more and more away from his work, and the studio operation fell largely upon the executive committee, powered mainly by Mannix, Lichtman and Katz.

There had been, too, some major changes in the producer ranks. Hunt Stromberg, one of the mighties, resigned late in 1941. An illness, which left him physically shaken, caused dissatisfactions that prompted him to leave. And Bernie Hyman, the Mercutio to Thalberg, died in September, 1942. He suffered a heart attack in Harry Rapf's office, and died a few days later. He was forty-five. Mayer had already got Pandro Berman, former head of production at R-K-O, to come in as one of his reliables. And Joe Pasternak, a musical expert at Universal, was recruited by Katz.

When the time drew nigh for a renewal of Mayer's contract in 1943, he went through the usual period of bickering and bargaining with Schenck. Now there were new considerations. The increased wartime income tax took a big bite out of his annual compensations, which, for several years, had been of such swollen amounts as to make him the highest salaried man in the United States. While this may have gratified his ego, it became embarrassing to the company. And, every year, income taxes were eating more deeply into his "take home" pay.

Schenck and Mayer battled with the problem. Finally, it was agreed that Mayer would sign a contract that would tie in with a new company pension plan. The plan was worked out so that Loew's, Inc., would contribute the entire amount to cover retirement benefits for all employees of the company. Retirement pay at age sixty-five would amount to approximately one-quarter of the employee's average annual wage.

Since this would have led to such munificent retirement benefits for Mayer and other executives that the government would certainly have hollered, it was settled that Mayer would take a $2,500 a week salary and allow that his total compensations, salary and bonuses, would not exceed $300,000 a year. The pension plan also specified that the retirement benefit of any employee should not exceed $49,500 a year. Mayer's new contract thus represented a limitation and gave the appearance of sacrifice by him.

Unquestionably, he was happy to see a generous retirement plan inaugurated by the company and was willing to endure some self-denial for it. But, in order to have it work, other studio executives accepted a limitation of $200,000. More compensation than that was academic, anyhow.

As for the company's contribution, the government was paying about 85 per cent of it, since the whole thing was coming out of earnings that would otherwise have been highly taxable. The plan went into effect on March 1, 1944. The Internal Revenue Department studied it very closely, but couldn't find a weakness by which to knock it out.

By this interesting arrangement, Mayer continued with the company.

CHAPTER XXXI

NEW SON IN THE SKY

THE SENSE of relief and thanksgiving that the nation felt with the end of World War II was shared in unqualified measure by the people of the film industry. They glowed with a sense of fulfilling the service of keeping the nation entertained, and they dwelt in the comfortable security that easy prosperity brought. But they were due for a violent deflation within the next decade. The fat accumulated in the war years was to be quickly and cruelly sweated off.

The picture of a bully snatching candy from a youngster best conveys a notion of the shock that sudden changes in the postwar period caused the film industry. The emergence of television as a device for entertainment in the home presented the menace of a monster within a couple of years. This thing that the motion picture people had looked upon with amusement and scorn in its prewar experimental stages now loomed as an ominous enemy. It was to steal the movies' patrons more surely and shamelessly than ever the nickelodeons stole customers from the costlier vaudeville shows.

But even before television began to freeze the public in their homes, there were other postwar changes that snatched the patrons from the movie theatres. There was the drain upon family resources that the purchase of new automobiles, washing machines, refrigerators, houses, baby layettes and all such items as were now liberated inevitably caused. There was the pull of other forms of entertainment that could again be reached easily. And there was the fact that routine motion pictures themselves had begun to pall.

A decline in the quality of movies during the war years, when talent was tight and the demands of the customers were casual, was unavoidable. But the studios were slow and gravely sluggish in getting back into prewar form. They generally persisted in the usual attitude of sublime complacency until the horses were stolen and the wolves were prowling outside the stable doors. For the reasons of executive confusion and inefficiency that we have seen, inability to readjust to the new conditions was downright chronic at Metro-Goldwyn-Mayer.

While other studios were making, at least, such pictures as *The Best Years of Our Lives, The Jolson Story, Gentleman's Agreement,*

The Lost Weekend, Treasure of Sierra Madre, Notorious and *Spell-bound,* the output at Culver City was topped by *The Green Years, The Harvey Girls, The Yearling, The Postman Always Rings Twice, State of the Union* and *Easter Parade.* Clark Gable, returning from service, was woefully wasted in *Adventure.* Even the Hardy series, after one attempt to get it back into operation, was dropped.

Significant was the fact that the product of the studio, which usually scored all through the 1930's with several pictures every year in *Film Daily's* annual "ten best" polls, had a total of only three mentions in 1946, 1947 and 1948 and it did not win a single major Academy award in those three years! The public might well have wondered what had happened to Metro-Goldwyn-Mayer.

More oppressive than the quality of the pictures was the financial situation of Loew's, Inc. After showing a record net income of $18,000,000 on its annual statement in September, 1946, its profits took a nose dive. Two years later, in September 1948, it showed a net of $4,212,000 which was the lowest reached by the company since the dark year of 1933.

This alarming decline coincided with the commitment of the company to bond issues totaling $55,000,000 in 1945 and 1947. These sinking fund debentures were arranged by Dave Bernstein and then Charles Moskowitz through the First National Bank of Boston and a group of insurance companies and represented the largest financing of a motion picture company ever arranged. The monies were used for clearing off old bond commitments that had been made at higher interest rates, and for further investment in new pictures. The sudden slump in profits thus came at a time when it was most embarrassing. Schenck and the board of directors were quickly crying for something to be done.

In the offing, too, there was looming a grim and imponderable peril—the consequence of a court order handed down on the last day of 1946. The Department of Justice had finally, after more than twenty years, got the courts to find that the "vertical" structure of motion picture companies as producing-distributing-exhibiting combines put them in the category of monopolies in restraint of trade. A federal court ordered that the operations of production and exhibition would have to be "divorced." Thus the great and characteristic amalgamations engineered by Adolph Zukor, Marcus Loew and their lesser contemporaries and successors were to be undone.

The court made a reasonable concession of several years in which "divorcement" was to be carried out, but the eventual effect upon the companies, and upon the industry as a whole, could not be told. Loew's, Inc., had never indicated how much of its income came from the rental of films and how much from exhibition. This was a secret that only a few men in the company knew. What would happen when the operations were divided was a dark uncertainty.

Toward the end of the war, Mayer warned his people that the easy pickings would not last, that the time would come when retrenchment would be compelled in the studio. But he warned without taking forcible action and when the time for economies came, he was unprepared and unable to enforce economies and effect productive change. His disposition to prodigality had finally caught up with him.

One thing, however, was obvious. Mayer's absorption in race horses must be dropped, if he was to be a forceful factor in the running of the studio. His absences to spend time at the race tracks had become a rueful joke. If someone asked where Mr. Mayer was and got a reply, "He's on Lot 14" or "He's on Lot 15" that was a way of informing that he was at Santa Anita or Hollywood Park. Schenck finally told him bluntly that he couldn't run a studio from a race-track box.

With sadness but a clear realization that it was something he had to do, Mayer ordered the sale of his horses. They were put on the auction block early in 1947. The cup was particularly bitter for Mayer, because most of the horses were bought by Harry Warner, who was one of his liveliest enemies. The feeling stemmed from a time when Warner berated Mayer publicly for not contributing as much to Jewish charities as Warner thought he should.

Shortly after the sale of his racing stable, Mayer was divorced by his wife. Their marriage of forty years was ended under circumstances that shocked his friends. It was testified in court that, three years earlier, Mayer had come home one day, flatly announced, "Well, I'm leaving," and cleared out of his house. Whatever his private motives, the rupture seemed unbecoming to those who knew Mayer's familiar fetish for mothers and the sanctity of the home. Nineteen months after the divorce was final, he was married again to Lorena Danker, a widow and former dancer, who was some thirty years younger than he.

While the sale of his racing stable gave Mayer more time for his job, there was no perceptible improvement in the output of the studio. The films continued to show a sameness of conventionalities, performed with characteristic slickness by the Metro-Goldwyn-Mayer stars. An unresolved disagreement between Schenck and Mayer—or between New York and Culver City—as to whether the studio should concentrate on a greater number of cheaper pictures or a lesser number of more expensive ones was reflected in the quantity of output. In 1945, the studio made thirty-one pictures; in 1946 it made twenty-four; in 1947 it was up again to twenty-nine, and in 1948 it was down to twenty-three. Regardless, the cost of production was rising every year. It rose from $56,563,000 in 1945 to $73,313,000 in 1948. In the latter year, the studio operated $6,500,000 "in the red."

A crying need for someone to do the critical job of putting new life into production, developing fresh ideas, cutting out the dead wood, was now all too clearly seen. What was wanted was someone like Thalberg in the old days. It was evident that Mayer was not the answer. A new man had to be found, an adminstrator more creative and energetic than anyone in the studio.

Mayer again went to David Selznick and besought him to return. He told him he could write his own ticket. But Selznick was not so inclined. He had just given up his own Vanguard company, which he formed after *Gone With the Wind*. He was being divorced by Irene Mayer Selznick and was paying court to Jennifer Jones. Mayer spoke to several other people. Then his eye lighted upon Hollywood's latest "boy wonder." He was Dore Schary, who at forty-three, was now considered "young."

Schary, a tall, bespectacled fellow with a calm, somewhat professorial air, was a former writer (and later producer) whose background was fairly typical of the younger crop of creative and productive personnel in Hollywood. He was entirely a creature of the post-sound era, ingrained with a fundamental feeling for cinematic communication with words. Like most of the younger people, he was rigorously intellectual and a veteran of the organizational battles of the Screen Writers Guild. His one deviation from the new type, his one affinity with the old pre-sound guard, was the fact that he had never been to college. He stopped his formal education in high school.

Schary grew up in Newark, New Jersey, where his family were caterers. His mother was a strong and forceful influence, as were the mothers of Thalberg and Mayer. His high school summers were spent as a paid hand in Catskill Mountain resorts, where he waited on table and doubled as an entertainer in customary "borscht circuit" style. Among his early associates in that area were Moss Hart and Danny Kaye.

He was attracted to the theatre and had a walk-on acting role in the Broadway production of *The Last Mile*, in which Spencer Tracy starred. Schary was one of two reporters who "interviewed" the Killer in the death-house, but he had nothing to say. Years later, he recalled himself to Tracy. "Of course, I remember you well," Tracy said. "I would look out at you every night from behind those bars and say to myself, 'Some day that young man is going to be vice-president in charge of production at Metro-Goldwyn-Mayer.'"

As part of his theatrical apprenticeship, Schary started writing plays. One which had often been optioned to Broadway managers but never produced was submitted to Columbia Pictures with an application for a junior-writer job. Walter Wanger, then a vice-president at Columbia, happened to read it. He thought it had power. He was under the impression a woman had written it, because it said "By Dora Schary" on his script. The studio hired the young writer at $100 a week.

Schary and his new wife, Miriam, took off a few months later for Hollywood, where he worked on a script at Columbia. One night at a party he met Herman Mankiewicz, who became interested in him because of his skill at a parlor word game. Mankiewicz, then a top writer, told Schary if he ever needed a job, to give him a call. Schary, grateful for the offer, did so very soon. Columbia would not raise his salary when his junior contract was up—this was in 1933, the bad year—so he casually chucked the job. Mankiewicz was true to his promise. He got his friend Sam Marx, who was then story editor at Culver City, to wangle Schary a job at $200 a week. That was the young man's introduction to Metro-Goldwyn-Mayer.

He and another tyro writer, Vance Randolph, from Arkansas, were put to work in Harry Rapf's unit. They were assigned to develop a script for Marie Dressler and Wallace Beery with an Ozark Mountain locale. The Ozarks were Randolph's special area. He and Schary wrote a comedy scene in which the speech of a couple of Ozark characters had to be translated into English by an interpreter. It was a very amusing situation, pungent and appreciative of the Ozark speech.

When the script was finished, Rapf read it. He called the writers into his office one day and, after making some harsh remarks about the story, said the dialogue lacked authenticity. Randolph, who was a colorful individual, a charming rustic in Hollywood, stood for a moment, speechless, a cud of tobacco hanging slack in his cheek. Schary was equally baffled. Then Randolph amiably drawled, "Well, Mr. Rapf, as to the story, I wouldn't be able to say. But they tell me I know more about the Ozarks than any man alive—and I reckon I do. So when you tell me this writin' ain't authentic, all I can say to you is, 'Mr. Rapf, you can take it and shove it!'" And with that he spat a nice big splash of tobacco juice on the pretty green carpet, turned and walked out the door. Schary spluttered some apologies and hastily chased after him. By the time he reached their office, Randolph had cleaned out his desk and gone. He was already headed for the Ozarks. Schary's contract was not renewed. He drew his last pay check and departed the studio on December 24, 1933.

For some little while thereafter, he and his wife had a rough time. Then Mankiewicz put him in touch with an agent who started getting

Walter Pidgeon and Greer Garson in the
bomb-shelter scene (anonymously written
by R. C. Sherriff) in "Mrs. Miniver"
(1942).

The collie dog, Lassie, and a little English war
refugee, Elizabeth Taylor, make their professional debuts in "Lassie Come Home" (1943).

Head-keepers of the Lion: Nicholas Schenck, Louis B. Mayer and Arthur M. Loew in 1950, a year before Mayer's exit from the company.

Mayer's successor, Dore Schary, and Mrs. Eleanor Roosevelt at a Jackson Day dinner in Los Angeles.

him jobs. He went from one studio to another—from Universal to Warner to Fox, then back to Universal and on to Paramount and Columbia—until 1936, when Norman Krasna got him a job writing *The Big City,* a film for Spencer Tracy, at Metro-Goldwyn-Mayer. This was a large break for him. He was on a week-to-week free-lance basis at $750 a week, and he worked on several other pictures, when John Considine called him to read the material for *Boys Town.*

The picture was planned for Tracy, Mickey Rooney and Freddie Bartholomew, but Schary spotted a weakness in having Bartholomew in such a tale. Considine agreed with him and gave him the job of writing the original story for it. Schary was sent to Boys Town to see Father Flanagan, then wrote a good solid yarn. Considine was much pleased with it. However, Tracy besought the studio not to have him do another priest so soon after his work in *San Francisco,* so *Boys Town* was shelved for a while and Schary was hopelessly shunted to his old nemesis, Harry Rapf. This was inevitably disastrous. Rapf soon gave him the air.

Once more Schary was in trouble. He had just bought himself a home and furniture (on installments), he and his wife had a second child on the way, and he had got his salary up to a figure that he had to insist upon or lose professional caste. He was out of work for almost three months. Then Leo McCarey gave him a job writing *Love Affair* with him. But a screen credit didn't go with it, so Schary was still in a hole.

Meanwhile, *Boys Town* had been made and Considine invited Schary to the opening. Eddie Mannix was there and asked him what he had been doing. Schary mentioned his tiff with Rapf. Mannix was nice about it and got him back to the studio. Then his original story for *Boys Town* won an "Oscar" and he was pretty well set. He worked on several stories in the next two years, including that for *Young Tom Edison.*

Now Schary had read a story by Paul Gallico called *Joe Smith, American.* It was a story of a war industry worker who was put through an ordeal by Nazi spies. Schary got an idea how to do it simply, so he asked Considine to let him try his hand directing it. Considine put it up to Mayer, relaying Schary's argument that, even though it was a "small" picture, it could, and should, be done intelligently. Schary didn't know it, but a policy decision had just been made to do more low-budget pictures of about the sort that he had in mind. Mayer called him to his office the next day.

"I hear you want to direct this little picture," he said. "Well, we want to make more like it. How would you like to head up a unit for making them?"

This was a bolt from the blue for Schary. He had no particular yen to produce. Furthermore, he was not encouraged by Mayer's assurance that the executive manager of his unit would be Harry Rapf. With deep appreciation of the offer, he still felt he'd rather direct.

"Why direct?" Mayer asked him. "Anybody can direct. I've watched you, my boy. I've heard you talk. You can do this job."

Schary said he was nervous about bossing other people and sometimes having to give them the sack. Mayer belittled that apprehension and urged him to take the job. Considine also encouraged him. So Schary went for it. His salary was raised to $1,100 a week, and the Rapf-Schary unit was formed. In a matter of eighteen months, beginning in 1941, it turned out *Joe Smith, American; Journey for Margaret,* a very moving little film about an English war orphan, which introduced Margaret O'Brien; *Lassie Come Home, Nazi Agent, The War Against Mrs. Hadley, Pilot Number Five* and *Lost Angel*—a remarkable assortment of interesting low-budget films.

But arguments developed. On a later picture called *Bataan,* Schary wanted to have several Negroes as prominent characters among a group of "death march" troops. Rapf opposed this notion and the executive committee supported him. They settled by letting Schary have one Negro in the film.

Then Schary wanted to make a bolder picture in which the story of the Nazi and Fascist regimes would be told allegorically in terms of an American western. The executive committee passed the idea and gave Schary permission to get Sinclair Lewis to write the script. This was somewhat surprising, since only a few years before the studio had caused a furor by starting and then stopping abruptly a plan to produce Lewis' controversial novel, *It Can't Happen Here.* It was surprising that the studio would hire him and that he would take the job.

He now put together with Schary what the latter considered an excellent script. It was called *Storm in the West* and it ended with an amazing pair of prophecies. Hyatt (Hitler) one of the villains, was cornered in a burning building and died in the flames, while Mollison (Mussolini) was shot in the back by his own men as he was trying to escape on horseback from them. His body, with a foot caught in a stirrup, was dragged head down in the mud. (Remember, this script was written in 1943.)

However, the executive committee didn't like it and ordered it shelved. Schary told them quite frankly that he would never come up with a script that he would want to do more than this. It was, he said, a crucial issue. His absolute convictions were involved. Mayer told him he would have to yield to the decision of the executive com-

mittee. So he chucked his job. His contract was still good for three years and he was earning $2,000 a week. But he told Mayer he couldn't work under such restriction. Mayer tried to urge him not to leave.

"I'm talking to you like a son," he told him. "You'll never amount to anything if you leave this studio."

But Schary was adamant, so Mayer released him. That was in October, 1943.

Even before the formal announcement of his departure, Schary was getting offers from other studios. Then one came from David Selznick, who now had his new Vanguard company, which was making pictures for release by R-K-O.

"I hear you are out of Metro because you're a difficult fellow to get along with," Selznick said. "Well, I like difficult fellows." He offered Schary $2,500 a week to come with him as a producer, plus a percentage of the profits of the pictures he made. Schary accepted the offer and was very soon on his way. He produced *I'll Be Seeing You, The Farmer's Daughter, The Spiral Staircase, The Bachelor and the Bobbysoxer* and *Till the End of Time.* Then Selznick, suspending his Vanguard company, farmed Schary out as a producer to R-K-O.

He had been working thus but a few months, when he was asked to head that studio. Selznick first opposed this, but later released Schary from his contract to take the job. He assumed his new position on January 1, 1947. He was building up a program of pictures when the studio was sold to Howard Hughes, the financier and airplane manufacturer. Schary had his misgivings about Hughes. He told him quite frankly he didn't intend to be his "echo." "If you just want somebody to take orders, you can get him for less money than you're paying me," he said.

Hughes assured Schary he wouldn't boss him, and the latter agreed to remain.

However, trouble soon started over a project aptly titled *Battleground,* a story of World War II, which Schary was very eager to do. Hughes phoned him at home one night while he was running some "dailies" in his library projection room and started to give him an argument. Schary said what he had predicted was happening and there was no point in going on. He said he wanted out and would be willing to buy the rights to *Battleground.* Hughes suggested a meeting the next day. When Schary came in, Hughes said, "I don't understand you. You're going to have to have bosses, aren't you?"

Schary answered, "Sure, but it all depends on the areas the bosses want to invade."

Hughes snapped his jaw. "You want to quit? Okay. See Rathvon!" And he turned away. Rathvon was the general manager. Schary saw him and got his release. And again he walked out of a contract, one that was getting him $4,000 a week.

As soon as the story broke on Schary's resignation, he was deluged with offers from all sides. United Artists, Paramount, Columbia, Republic wanted him. Then Mayer called and asked to see him. Schary went around and found his ex-boss most cordial and encouraging. He wanted Schary to return to Metro-Goldwyn-Mayer not as a unit producer, not as a member of the executive board, but as vice-president in charge of production! It was substantially the job that Thalberg used to have.

This sounded great to Schary, who by now had lost his fears of handling an administrative position and telling other people what to do. But he told Mayer he didn't want it unless it was understood that his right to make decisions would be respected by Mayer. The battle on *Storm in the West* still rankled. Schary didn't want to be in such a spot again.

It was on that understanding that Mayer informed Schenck he had found the man they needed. Schenck flew out secretly from New York. The secrecy was caused by Schenck wishing to avoid getting mixed up in the disquieting investigations of Communism then going on in Hollywood.

Carefully guarded meetings of Schenck, Mayer, Rubin, Charles Moskowitz, Schary, his agent and his lawyer were held in the home of Joe Schenck. A contract was drawn that clearly stated Schary would be "in charge of production" at the studio. He insisted upon the "identification" because he had often heard that Thalberg's later fights and headaches were due to the vagueness of his relationship to Mayer. Both men had started at the studio on a basis that was never legally defined. However, Schary's contract also specified that his only superiors would be Schenck and Mayer, which still left Mayer the head of the studio.

The contract was drawn for seven years and Schary's salary was set at $6,000 a week—$4,000 payable weekly and $2,000 deferred. He was to begin his new job on July 1, 1948.

Everybody was happy. Schenck felt they had a good young man who might develop into a new Thalberg. Mayer felt he had a "son" on whom he could place the heavy burdens of handling the productions of the studio. (In his enthusiasm, he told Schary he would help "make him rich," and privately loaned him $10,000 to buy some oil stocks that he himself was in.) As for Schary, he felt that he would now be free to make the sort of forthright, forceful films that he had been doing on a small scale with his B-unit during the war.

In preparation for his new functions, which would inevitably include a more or less stringent reappraisal of the pending projects of the studio, Schary hopped down to Palm Springs for a few days with a batch of scripts that were waiting final approval. Among them was one to which Mayer asked that he give immediate attention. It was a dramatization of William Faulkner's *Intruder in the Dust,* a story of a near-lynching of a Negro in a Mississippi town. Clarence Brown was eager to do it, and he wanted to use Claude Jarman, a Southern boy he had previously discovered for *The Yearling,* to play the lad whose valor saved the Negro's life.

Schary whole-heartedly approved it. This was the sort of thing that he regarded as fresh and important. Mayer was far from sure. He was always apprehensive of stories that revealed embarrassing conflicts in American life. However, he didn't make an issue. Brown was authorized to go ahead, and he later came out with one of the finest of the studio's postwar films. He shot most of it on location in Mississippi, in a stark, realistic style. Mayer was displeased with the role of the Negro, whom Juano Hernandez played in a manner to show pride and defiance. Mayer thought he should be an Uncle Tom. But Schary liked the picture immensely. The only trouble was that it came at the end of a run of pictures about Negroes from other studios. It was badly sold and poorly patronized by the public. Mayer could (but didn't) say, "I told you so."

Schary's first bold determination was to get hold of *Battleground,* which Howard Hughes had prevented him doing, and make it the way he wanted to. He put it up to the executive committee, which under him was to be rearranged into a sort of studio cabinet and editorial advisory board. The committee didn't raise any question about the purchase of the property from R-K-O. It was got for $110,000. But there was again some misgiving on the part of Mayer. He thought the time bad for a war picture; he didn't like the title, *Battleground.* Some of the executives privately whispered that Schary was making a big mistake in going against the disposition of Mayer. But the latter was philosophical about it. "Go ahead, make it, my boy," he said. "It will teach you a lesson." Schary went ahead.

He knew he was sticking his neck out. So he put all he had into the film. The studio spent lots of money on it. Van Johnson, a rising star, had the principal role. Everybody in the studio realized that Schary's prestige was riding on *Battleground.*

While it was in production, Schary was going through a time of desperate tension. There were those in the executive-producer group who looked upon him with dark suspicions. Within two months of Schary's arrival, first Katz and then Lichtman resigned. The former saw the portals of the doghouse had opened for him; the latter, who had suffered two heart seizures, decided it wasn't worth while to go on.

There were other and more ominous rumblings. Schary had a reputation as one of the more liberal thinkers in the Hollywood community. Even as far back as his hassles with Mayer over *Storm in the West,* there had been disagreeable rumors that he was a "pink" or possibly a "Red." Mayer mentioned these rumors to him when they were arguing over the film. Schary snapped back by remarking there were also rumors that Mayer was a fascist. There the point was allowed to rest.

Also, when Schary was head of production at R-K-O, he was caught in the delicate situation of having to state what he would do about continuing to employ two men who had refused to answer questions of the House Un-American Activities Committee. The men were writer Adrian Scott and director Edward Dmytryk, who had worked with Schary on the production of *Crossfire,* a celebrated film on anti-Semitism, of which he was justifiably proud. He said there was nothing to cause him to suspect that the men were Communists and that the laws of California would not permit him to fire them, anyhow. This caused some papers to carry stories to the effect that "RKO head says he will hire Reds."

Subsequently the men were discharged by action of the R-K-O board, and Schary, after weighing his position, decided to go along with that. But he continued the butt of suspicion and rumor among the arch conservatives in Hollywood.

Thus his return to Culver City was the signal for those elements in the studio to sharpen their political axes. There was particularly a group that centered around James K. McGuinness which was militantly against Schary. It was the latter's suspicion that members of this group did a lot to talk down the stories and the scripts that he approved. The situation was eminently unhealthy, and it did not noticeably improve after a settlement was made for McGuinness to leave the studio some eight months after Schary arrived. McGuinness died in 1950. His coterie then faded away.

Battleground was still in production, amid these various studio tensions, when another and more ominous disagreement between Schary and Mayer occurred. This was over the preparation of a script for *Quo Vadis,* which had been one of the studio's pending projects for a matter of several years. Indeed, it had been considered by Thalberg before he died, and several attempts had been made to get it started by various people since then. Shortly after Schary returned, it was resurrected and put in the hands of Arthur Hornblow Jr., a producer at the studio for six years.

During the fall and winter, Hornblow and a couple of writers worked on it. His idea was to make it with a strong, modern point of view, not in the old DeMille tradition of the Biblical spectacle. He brought in young John Huston, a latter-day King Vidor, to direct. Schary discussed their project with them and approved their general ideas.

Shortly after this, Hornblow came forward with ninety pages of script which he showed to Schary and to Eddie Mannix, with a frank admission that he wasn't too pleased with it. Mannix apparently passed the word to Mayer, for the latter called Schary the next day and asked him what he thought of the script. Schary said he thought it excellent. Mayer said he thought it terrible. Schary stood by his opinion and suggested they put it up to Schenck.

This was a new development. An appeal over Mayer's head was a form of procedure that even Thalberg had delicately eschewed. Schenck came back with a reminder to Mayer that they hadn't been able to get a satisfactory script on *Quo Vadis* under his aegis, so now he felt they should let Schary have his way. The realization struck bluntly: Schenck had sided *against* Mayer.

The rest of the story of the production of *Quo Vadis* is long and involved, almost as long as the story of its epic predecessor, *Ben Hur*. As in the case of the latter, the producer and the director were changed and the picture emerged quite different from what it was intended by Hornblow and Huston to be. In the end, it was a huge commercial victory for the traditional spectacle concept supported by Mayer, but Schary won the first round in the tussle that was inexorably building to a knockout affair.

Then *Battleground* was finished. From its first preview, the evidence was clear that it was a rousing war picture, destined for popularity. The sales department got behind it and a thumping big première was given it in New York in the summer of 1949. Sure enough, the public went for it. The money began to roll in, and Schary's first individual project was handsomely vindicated. Schenck, recollecting the circumstances of the production of *The Big Parade*, saw a striking parallel in this experience. Perhaps the studio did have its new Thalberg.

The triumph of *Battleground* lifted Schary's prestige immeasurably. He assumed a considerably larger stature around the studio. The fulfillment of his convictions also helped his self-esteem. He was able to continue "in charge of production" with a great deal more confidence.

In the next year or so, a spate of pictures that had quality and appeal were laid down. There was *Father of the Bride,* a top-drawer comedy with Spencer Tracy and Elizabeth Taylor in the title roles; *The Asphalt Jungle,* a carbolic crime film which Hornblow and Huston did while waiting to get started on *Quo Vadis* (before they were removed); *King Solomon's Mines,* a tremendous African adventure film which somewhat duplicated the experience of making *Trader Horn;* and *An American in Paris,* a handsome and spinning musical comedy, with Gene Kelly starred. These were the top in a flow of product that was noticeably improved.

Battleground

But the relations between Mayer and Schary were not keeping comparable pace. Their clashes on stories and issues were becoming more frequent and sharp. Two crises arose simultaneously over things Schary wanted to do. One was a script by Ben Hecht called *Europa and the Bull.* The other was *The Red Badge of Courage,* the classic Civil War story of Stephen Crane.

Schary had already made arrangements for John Huston to direct the latter film and Gottfried Reinhardt to produce it. Then he was laid up with an aggravating back that he had injured shortly after he arrived in Hollywood and that was now giving him a lot of pain. While he was out, Mayer got Huston into his office one day and, in a half hour of strong persuasion, argued him out of wanting to go ahead with *The Red Badge.*

"What have you got here?" Mayer asked him. "In thirty-five years we've had two wars—two terrible wars, with millions slaughtered and whole cities destroyed. And you're going to make a picture about boys in funny caps, shooting pop-guns, and try to make people think this is terrible. Dave Selznick was too smart to try that. He wouldn't show you the Civil War battles in *Gone With the Wind.*"

Huston and Reinhardt capitulated. They asked Mayer to pick them another script. "If I do, it'll be roast beef and potatoes," he told them. However, to play it fairly, he now sent the script of *The Red Badge of Courage* to Schenck and asked him to give an immediate answer on what he thought of doing it. (It was, indeed, a rare thing for Mayer to send a script to Schenck; the fact that he did indicated he was rattled, was losing his confidence.) In a few days, Schenck telephoned him. "The boys here think you may be right," he said. "But, at the same time, you may be wrong. You admit it. Why not let Schary have his way."

Then Mayer got a letter from Schary—a "beautiful letter"—in which the latter said he would go along with Mayer on *Europa,* it could well be "too satirical," but he could not abandon *The Red Badge of Courage,* which he understood Mayer had persuaded Huston and

Reinhardt not to do. Mayer was so moved by the letter he immediately summoned the two men and said, "As a personal favor to me, won't you take this thing and make it. I may be wrong." Thus, amid much emotion, *The Red Badge of Courage* was resumed.

The later story of the making of this drama has been told in anatomical detail by Lillian Ross in a book called *Picture*. It is a witheringly close-to account of the problems and the personal eccentricities of a group of people making a film. It also gives an isolated picture of the tension between Schary and Mayer. They continued to have their disagreements about the project right up to the time it was released. The film was a "box-office failure," but it was a succès d'estime.

This time, on the basis of dollars, the decision went to Mayer.

There were further disagreements, which was natural and healthy, indeed, in a field of operations as uncertain as the making of films. Schary wanted to make a couple of pictures starring Larry Parks and Edward G. Robinson. Both men were in the bad graces of the House Un-American Activities Committee at the time. Mayer opposed the projects. Schenck first upheld Schary on Parks, and Mayer accepted the decision. But when he heard that Schenck had okayed Robinson, he called and asked if he was not to be supported.

"What do you mean?" Schenck said.

"Maybe it would pay to call the head of the studio!" replied Mayer.

Here was the rub of the tension. Mayer felt that he was the man to make the final decisions, and that Schary shouldn't be going over his head to Schenck.

Only a short while before this—in February, 1949—the studio threw the famous celebration of its twenty-fifth anniversary, with a tremendous luncheon on a sound stage. It was a show to put in the shade that hopeful little gala that Mayer assembled on the studio lawn away back in 1924. He himself was at the center of the galaxy of studio stars. This was the sort of attention that Mayer expected and considered his due. Shortly after, his contract was extended for another five years.

Thus it was galling to him as one after another issue on which he locked with his own chosen "head of production" was referred past him to Schenck, and, in virtually every instance, Schary was upheld.

On the other hand, Schary's feeling was that Mayer was opposing him on matters which were vital to his effective functioning as production chief. As soon as the trouble between them started, he paid back the money Mayer loaned him to buy oil stock.

This sort of thing continued until early in 1951, when renewals on several executive contracts were due. Mayer had recommended that stock options be bestowed, but had heard nothing more about it. Then suddenly Schenck informed a group of six executives, of which Schary was one, that they were receiving options. Mayer heard it later and was enraged, not because the options were given (he had recommended this) but because Schenck had bestowed them without even letting him know in advance. (It was later explained that Schenck had tried to reach Mayer by telephone before spreading the happy word.)

The options were given for the purchase of Loew's stock at $16.44 a share. Schary received options on 100,000, Arthur Loew received options on 40,000, and options on 25,000 each were given to Bennie Thau, L. K. Sidney, and Charles Moskowitz and Joe Vogel in New York. It was startling to many that Eddie Mannix, who was an old and devoted friend of Schenck, did not receive a similar bonus. He was considered to be in line. But Schenck said that Mannix was a "sick man" and that he therefore could not recommend to the directors that they recompense him. The reasoning was hard to understand—especially by Mannix, who had long been one of the studio's sturdiest hands.

It was later calculated by persons close to the situation in the studio that the conflict was clarified at that point: it was between Mayer and Schenck and was thereafter irreconcilable. Many tactful and desperate efforts were made by some who saw what was coming to head it off. Schary was urged by studio veterans to make a show of acquiescence towards Mayer, to flatter and cajole him. In that way, he could get what he wanted, they said. But Schary was not inclined to play the toady. And, besides, the old fat was in the fire.

Once Schenck got Mayer on the telephone and said, "Louie, what's wrong? Why can't we get together? Let's meet someplace and talk this out."

But Mayer replied, "No, I've got a temper. If I hit you, I'll kill you, Nick. I'm just waking up and I don't like it!"

He felt he was being deliberately pushed aside.

Then a story appeared in the papers one day saying that Mayer intended to resign. Schary read it and went directly to him and asked if it was so. Mayer said it was. Schary asked him if they couldn't reconcile their quarrels.

"What do you mean?" Mayer answered. "Are you going to save my job for me?"

While they were talking a phone call came through to Mayer from Robert Rubin in New York. Rubin had also seen the stories (or heard about them) and was alarmed. He asked Mayer if they couldn't do something to make him change his mind. Mayer answered, "Nick and Dore want the studio. Well, they can have it and choke on it!"

Rubin, distressed to distraction, cried out, "It's all because of *Battleground!*"

Schary, sitting there and hearing the conversation, asked Mayer just what did he mean. Mayer replied by accusing Schary of simply wanting to make speeches and win plaques. He charged him with being a publicity seeker, because Schary frequently appeared before religious and educational gatherings. This was his interest, comparable to Mayer's in politics.

Mayer couldn't understand why Schary was having trouble with his back. "You get on a train and go someplace to make a speech, then you come back tired!" he said. The personal abuse was violent.

Finally Schary said he wasn't going to sit there and take it.

"I'll talk about my work," he said. "I'll talk about that as long as you like. But I'm not going to talk about my personal activities."

"You're doing a lousy job!" Mayer said.

With that Schary got up and left.

Word of the clash spread quickly. Mayer let it be known around that he had told Schary off with good measure and that he did not intend to resign. Schary was angry and baffled. He felt like quitting himself, but he was advised he would thus be creating a situation where Schenck would have to choose between him and Mayer.

With the studio buzzing and jittering, Schary went to Palm Springs. Schenck called him there and said he had got a full report of the clash from Mayer. He asked Schary not to make an issue of the unfortunate affair and to make another endeavor to reconcile with Mayer on his return.

Schary did. But again Mayer attacked him as a seeker of publicity. Schary again said he wouldn't listen.

"You'll listen!" Mayer roared at him.

"That you can't make me do!" Schary answered. And again he took a walk.

This time Mayer called Schenck and said, "It's either me or Schary. Which?"

Schenck said he would answer him by letter.

Previous to this, Schenck had had L. K. Sidney bring the records of the studio to New York and had made a careful analysis of the achievements of all the producers, before and after Schary came. Now he wrote to Mayer and informed him the analysis clearly showed that there had been an appreciable improvement in the product since Schary was there. As a consequence, Schenck advised him that he was going along with Schary.

The implication was obvious. Mayer would have to resign.

He called his old guard into his office and showed the letter to them.

Bennie Thau cried. L. K. Sidney almost fainted. Mannix threw the letter down with a howling curse and fled the room.

This was the end of the ball game. There was nothing else to be done.

Mayer announced his resignation on June 22, 1951, the same to be effective on August 31. But he left the studio before that, without saying any formal good-byes or making a handsome gesture of farewell to his old associates that many expected of him.

There were rumors that he intended to take some of the top stars with him and also some top producers. It was inconceivable that "the king" could possibly go into exile in the Hollywood community.

But no one left the studio to join him, and the likelihood that he would return to production at the head of another studio or in an independent organization faded fast. His only formal association with motion pictures since he left Metro-Goldwyn-Mayer has been as an investor and officer in the Cinerama enterprise.

A couple of weeks after the announcement of Mayer's resignation, Schary and a group from the studio met in Chicago with Schenck and others from New York. There it was decided that Schary would have full command of all studio operations, with a three-man executive board composed of Mannix, Thau and Sidney to function directly under him. The old guard did not rebel or surrender. It discreetly closed ranks to carry on.

In November, after some negotiations, it was agreed that Loew's, Inc., would pay Mayer $2,750,000 for his residual rights in all the films that were made in the studio under his tenure. A special clause was even put in the federal tax law, after some discriminate lobbying by the tax lawyer for the studio, which made it possible for Mayer to pay the minimum 25 per cent tax on his money as a capital gain.

No one could say that this old warden of the lion did not get his share.

CHAPTER XXXII

OLD LION, NEW JUNGLE

THE QUIP was made that Dore Schary, in ascending to full command of the studio, "became mayor of Rome while it was burning," and the joke was peculiarly apt. Conditions both within and without the company were such that, no matter how able he was, the chances of re-establishing the old magnificence of Metro-Goldwyn-Mayer were quite remote.

In the first place, the studio was burdened with a tremendous financial overhead and an inordinate roster of contract players for the limited number of films being made. The insistence of Mayer upon maintaining a large staff of producers and stars on long-term contracts to provide the advantage of what was boastfully termed "strength in depth" had resulted in an overload of high-priced and not always too active personnel. The studio had some 4,000 employees to make an average of twenty-nine pictures a year.

This burden, bequeathed to Schary, could be lessened in one of two ways: by rigid economies and reductions or by a step-up in the manufacture of films.

The first of these possibilities would obviously place in jeopardy the essential maintenance by Schary of the cooperation of the creative personnel. Already considerable resentment was felt against him personally. Just as the old friends of Thalberg had grumbled when Selznick came in, now the old Mayer associates suspected and secretly belittled the new man. They found a new gag that kidded his enthusiasm for "idea" films. The studio, generally known for "escapist" pictures, had "sold its soul for a pot of message," they said. If Schary was to have the confidence and support of the critical personnel, he would have to be shrewd and diplomatic about how he imposed economies.

On the other hand, the question of increasing the studio's output of films called for basic policy decisions that were largely over his head. They involved the amount of money that the company wished to invest and the size of the inventory that Loew's, Inc., could hope to sell. These decisions, and, indeed, the decisions on all the films that Schary wanted to make, were resolved in the last analysis by the head of the company, Nick Schenck.

While Schenck was initially generous in his disposition to let Schary have his way in choosing particular pictures, he represented a formidable check upon the judgment and creative freedom of the head of the studio. Schenck was notably cautious and conventional in his calculations of what films should contain. His concepts of screen entertainment were laid down in the prosperous years of romance and glamour in motion pictures, when Leo the Lion was in his prime. He tended to be agreeable to Schary's ideas, but the latter realized that he could not safely ask for approval of anything that departed too far from the norm. This absolute dependence of Schary and his three-man executive board—Mannix, Thau and Sidney—upon the final okay of Schenck bound him pretty thoroughly to the traditionalism of New York.

And, of course, the state of the film business, when Schary took command in 1951 and thereafter, was not conducive to a return to the extravagance and multiplicity of production that had previously characterized the Lion's share. The expansion of television was now extending free entertainment into the homes of millions and millions of people who had been habitual customers of films. The inevitable loss of these customers, first for virtually all films, as people acquired their television sets, and then for the routine entertainments that they could see on their video screens, rapidly changed the size and nature of the potential motion picture audience. The market for the so-called "program picture" was radically reduced. The only hope of obtaining large attendance and profit was in exceptional films. And, for these, the response of the public was erratic and unpredictable. The area in which the Lion had formerly prospered had undergone incalculable change.

There was nothing wrong with the top pictures that came out of Metro-Goldwyn-Mayer in the period immediately succeeding Schary's establishment as head of the studio. *Ivanhoe,* which he had first intended to make when he was head of R-K-O, was a rousing costume adventure picture. *Singing in the Rain,* produced by Arthur Freed, was a superior musical comedy which amiably satirized the confusions and artistic pretensions of the early days of sound. *Pat and Mike,* with Spencer Tracy and Katharine Hepburn; *The Prisoner of Zenda, Scaramouche* and *Million Dollar Mermaid* (with Esther Williams) had the usual class and casts of the studio.

Likewise, the charming picture, *Lili,* produced by Edwin Knopf, came in the new regime of Schary. It emerged from a gentle fantasy which was not looked upon too kindly when it was proposed to Schenck. But they badly needed a story for Leslie Caron, the little French dancer who had been launched with Gene Kelly in *An Ameri-*

can in Paris, so the picture got the go-ahead. Schary also pushed *Julius Caesar,* which Joseph L. Mankiewicz directed and produced; *Mogambo,* which took Clark Gable and Ava Gardner into the wilds of Africa, and *The Band Wagon,* as nifty a musical as ever came out of Metro-Goldwyn-Mayer.

There was nothing wrong with the top pictures. There were just not enough of them. But that was now a common cry of anguish in all the Hollywood studios.

A year after Schary's promotion, the problem of the huge overhead was tackled in a fashion reminiscent of the Draconian measures taken to meet the crisis in 1933. To the studio's 4,000 employees, including producers and stars, assembled outside the largest sound stage one morning in July, 1952, Schenck, who had come out from New York to convey personally the bad news, announced that executives earning more than $1,000 a week would have to take pay cuts of from 25 per cent to 50 per cent for one year. This applied to executives of the studio and also executives of Loew's Inc. Schenck himself was submitting to the full reduction. He thus served notice that an economy drive was on.

Included would be a reduction in the number of long-term contract employees, not only stars and players, but producers, directors and writers, too. And Schenck added significantly that the budgets of films would be watched to eliminate factors of "waste that have resulted from lush operations during lush years."

Thus the passing of the era of munificence was acknowledged at Metro-Goldwyn-Mayer.

The Erosion of the Stars

Already the list of star performers was being eroded by circumstances and by death. Mickey Rooney and Judy Garland had departed. Wallace Beery had died. Mickey had not been congenial after his return from World War II, which he entered as a private in the Army early in 1944—even though a new seven-year contract had been drawn for him while he was away which assured him $200,000 a year. His first picture, *Love Laughs at Andy Hardy,* was a vain attempt to warm up the old stew, and he proved a disappointment in *Words and Music,* in which he played the song writer, Larry Hart. Mickey then took to complaining about his billing, about his roles. He was angry and particularly caustic because he had not been cast in *Battleground.* Finally, the studio settled his contract, and Mickey bid the old home lot adieu.

Judy's departure was splattered with unpleasantness and distress when she, too, was released, in 1950, and allowed to go her way. For several years before that, she had been more or less emotionally disturbed and had clashed with Mayer and others on the choice and production of her films. Judy got along poorly with her mother, who had driven and pushed her since she was a child. This antagonism toward her parent was something that Mayer could not understand or abide, and he persistently sided with the mother in trying to compel or discipline the girl.

Judy suffered a serious nervous breakdown in May, 1949, when she was far into the production of *Annie Get Your Gun*. She was finally put on suspension and sent to a sanitarium in Boston at the studio's expense. Betty Hutton was got to replace her in the picture and the footage containing Judy was scrapped.

Upon her return some months later, she was assigned to do *Summer Stock*. Again they began having trouble after the picture was well along. This time a psychiatrist who had treated her in Boston was brought to Los Angeles, and with him and other doctors to attend her, Judy was able to finish the film.

At this point, the story of what happened is open to dispute. The studio claimed that it put her on vacation status for two months, after which she reported that she was rested and able to go to work. She claimed that she had been promised a year's vacation after *Summer Stock*, but was recalled to replace June Allyson in *Royal Wedding* when it was learned that Miss Allyson was going to have a baby. The studio said that Judy was anxious to take the role.

In any event, trouble started again within a few days. Judy, unhappy and uncertain, caused innumerable delays. One morning, in her bathroom, she nicked her neck with a piece of broken glass. The cut was superficial, but it showed the state she was in. Finally, after more interruptions, it was mutually agreed that her contract should be dropped. "It was felt that every opportunity should be given to Judy for her complete happiness," Mayer said.

Jane Powell replaced her in *Royal Wedding* and Ava Gardner was assigned to the role in the pending production of *Showboat* that was hopefully but vainly held for her.

Judy later explained her behavior by saying, "I was a very tired girl."

A somewhat similar difficulty, three years later, further deprived the studio of another star performer, Mario Lanza, who had been catapulted to fame in the title role of *The Great Caruso*. Mr. Lanza had a very impressive voice, but he was a temperamental fellow and inclined to extreme corpulence. With great difficulty, the studio got him to get his weight down to 200 pounds for his next picture after

The Great Caruso. It was called *Because You're Mine*. But thereafter he became a problem with which the studio was unable to cope. He recorded a musical sound-track for *The Student Prince*, but was so obese that they did not dare put him in the picture. Edmund Purdum was assigned to play the role, with Mr. Lanza's voice delivering the musical numbers. The popular singer had to be let go.

As regrettable as was the necessity to abandon these youthful and still potent stars, the studio was in the position of having to look out for itself. It could not maintain high-salaried people who did not work steadily or who did not produce an appreciable return of revenue.

The ultimate exercise of realism along these lines came in March, 1954, when both, Greer Garson and Clark Gable were allowed to cast off from the studio. Miss Garson's impact in pictures had been on a slow decline ever since *The Valley of Decision*. She had played a succession of roles that had been increasingly embarrassing and discouraging to her following. One of the cruelest was in *Adventure*, in which she was haplessly teamed with Gable. It was his first picture upon his return from war. The slogan used to promote it was one of the corniest ever coined: "Gable's Back and Garson's Got Him." Critics said they both got what they deserved.

Significantly, Miss Garson was a strong admirer of Mayer. After he went, she felt her prospects for the kind of stardom she had known were dim. "We are not making the big romantic type of picture that is my forte," she said. Several promising roles tagged for her went aglimmering. One was in a project that Schary got Carl Sandburg to write, an epic story of the growth of America, called *Remembrance Rock*. It was never made as a picture. (Sandburg later put his material into a novel.) Another was in a biography of the opera singer, Marjorie Lawrence. Eleanor Parker got that one when the picture was done as *Interruped Melody*.

Miss Garson's last work at Culver City was in a soggy little film called *Her Twelve Men*, which she did after playing a small role in *Julius Caesar* as Caesar's wife. With a few months still to go on her contract, she asked for and got her release. She received a sizable pension, having been with the studio for fifteen years.

Three days after Miss Garson's severance, Gable's contract expired and was not renewed. For all his continuing popularity, he was too expensive at $300,000 a year. His last film but one, *Mogambo*, was ironically a temperate remake of *Red Dust*, the hot adventure picture he did with Jean Harlow in 1932. After twenty-two years, the old favorite was a little battered but still able to convey a strong charge of masculine magnetism toward Ava Gardner and Grace Kelly, a striking new arrival. Gable took his departure without fuss or sentiment. He had made some fifty-four pictures in his record career of twenty-three years with Metro-Goldwyn-Mayer.

And the following year, Spencer Tracy closed out with the studio. He was acting in *Tribute to a Bad Man,* when he complained he couldn't go on. He said the distress caused him by working on location in high altitudes was too much. The studio took him off the picture and got James Cagney to do the role. Then, by "mutual agreement," Tracy's contract was dissolved. His length of time with the studio had been twenty-one years.

As the old "planets" departed, the group of younger stars was also diminished. Van Johnson, Esther Williams and Jane Powell went. Lana Turner and Gene Kelly were put on contracts that called for their services in only one picture a year. This became a standard arrangement that allowed the studio to have an option on the performers but relieved it of the expense of maintaining them. The old boast of "more stars than there are in the heavens" had to be allowed to lapse.

Remaining, however, were Robert Taylor, Ava Gardner, Elizabeth Taylor, Cyd Charisse (a talented dancer who had been brought along in musicals with Fred Astaire), little Leslie Caron, Debbie Reynolds and Grace Kelly (until she married a prince).

Miss Kelly was one of those phenomena such as occurred at Culver City in the golden days during the few years that she was ascending. She had been signed to a contract by the studio when director John Ford asked to have her as the second female lead in *Mogambo.* He had admired the cool, obscure young actress in a small role in the independent film, *High Noon,* which was her first break in motion pictures after having been tested by several studios. Automatically, Metro-Goldwyn-Mayer put her under contract, She scored a hit in *Mogambo* and was launched. Thereafter she was loaned out abundantly until brought back to Culver City to do *Green Fire.* She was then the rage of film fandom and one of the happiest assets of the studio, when she met and married the Prince of Monaco and discontinued her film career to reign serene as the Princess of Monaco. Her contract still had four years to go.

The Moving Finger Writes

In these years of vastly changing conditions in the motion picture industry, Metro-Goldwyn-Mayer and Loew's Inc., were not alone in their difficulties. All of the Hollywood studios and the established motion picture companies were compelled to make drastic retrenchments and adjustments to save their corporate lives. If there was a noticeable difference in the methods and procedures of Loew's, Inc., it was in the slowness of its changes, reflecting the caution of Schenck.

While the other major companies, beginning with R-K-O and continuing with Paramount, Warner Brothers and Twentieth Century-Fox, submitted reluctantly but inevitably to the demands of the "consent decree" and divorced their producing and distributing functions from their operations of theatres, Loew's, Inc., succeeded in finding reasons for delay and obtained periodic postponements from the remarkably patient courts. Although it set up Loew's Theatres, Inc., as a subsidiary in 1954 to carry on the operation of its 105 theaters, it still had not effected its "divorcement" ten years after the "consent decree."

There may have been hope that a remission might have finally been got through this delay. There was also the problem of dividing the liabilities of the company. Loew's, Inc., was exceptionally saddled with sinking fund debentures of more than $30,000,000. It had to find a formula for dividing this burden between the producing-distributing corporation and the theatre company. Schenck went at it slowly, loathe to finalize the split. But so long as "divorcement" was postponed, so long was the company delayed in getting itself adjusted to the new order in the industry.

Schenck also counseled caution toward the rush to larger screens which moved the industry following the independent inauguration of Cinerama in 1952. He had looked at this new giant screen process when it was still in its demonstration stage and had considered it impractical for general use. He remembered that his and other companies had tried to raise interest in a new giant screen back in 1930. King Vidor had shot *Billy the Kid* in a wide-film process that had permitted it to be exhibited on an enlarged screen in several specially equipped theatres, but the public had not been overly excited. Schenck was skeptical toward the new thing.

He continued to maintain caution after Cinerama was released and Twentieth Century-Fox, shrewdly sensing a chance to ride with this popular novelty, came forward with a more practical wide-screen process, known as CinemaScope. On the strength of extraordinary promotion and the eagerness of theatre men for a "shot in the arm," CinemaScope was established. Then Schenck accepted it. Installations were made in Loew theatres and CinemaScope pictures were filmed at Metro-Goldwyn-Mayer. The pattern of watchful waiting was almost identical to that followed with the development of sound.

Likewise, the acknowledgment by Loew's, Inc., of the challenge of television was slow. In common with others in the industry, it acted as though the new thing was a nuisance that would pass. Even as it became obvious that television was closely akin to the nature and means of motion pictures, Schenck and his associates continued to keep Loew's, Inc., out of it. In this way, they felt they weren't abetting their upstart competitors.

The attitude indicated a failure to appreciate the change that was happening to habits of the American people and, as a consequence, to the commerce of films. The salient fact was that television had become a fixture in the average home, as much a convenience of modern living as the automobile or telephone. The wisdom for motion picture merchants was to offer theatrical product of exceptional appeal, while possibly servicing video on a lower level and using the medium to ballyhoo films.

Eventually, Loew's, Inc., decided in 1955 to develop a bi-weekly video program, called *The M-G-M Parade*—half-hour shows of short subjects and clips from old Metro-Goldwyn-Mayer films. The shows were so poorly assembled they did no justice to the studio's prestige. The program was continued for eight months and then went off the air.

But Schenck's most questionable caution was in keeping the company away from the trend to independent production units that was sweeping the industry. With the break-up of the vertical structures of the large companies and the reduction of pressure for product on the "divorced" studios, most of them found it economical and stimulating to arrange for some, if not all, their product from independent producers, rather than having their films made entirely by studio personnel. This was a throw-back to the early arrangements of the old Metro and First National groups.

However, Loew's, Inc., was tardy in permitting movement in this direction for Metro-Goldwyn-Mayer. The delay proved costly. Some of the better independents were snapped up by other studios.

In these circumstances, with the entertainment world in a state of flux and with the financial statements of Loew's, Inc., showing a fall in profits from year to year, it was inevitable that the company's stockholders, especially those who held large blocks, and the holders of its debentures should have grown anxious and even alarmed. The charge that the company had become sluggish, that it was not acting positively, that it was like an old lion defying stalkers was spoken openly. The question of Schenck's continuation as president and chief architect of policy was raised. It was noted, not without clear implications, that he was past seventy.

For three or four years, the necessity of a successor to him was discussed within the circle of the board of directors. The most generally approved candidate was Arthur Loew, son of the founder. He had been eminently successful in building up the foreign operations of the company over three decades.

Loew was a cool, quiet individual, a man of inherent modesty and good taste. He had a lot of the shrewdness of his father and a thorough knowledge of the business of films. Further, and most impressive, Loew's International, under him, was now delivering about half the total income of the company.

But Loew was not eager to have the burden of the presidency. He liked his job and knew too well the problems accumulated in recent years. Also, he was in his mid-fifties, close to the age at which his father had died. He consistently declined importunities that he become the head of Loew's, Inc.

Now was exposed a weakness that had been foreboded for several years. That was the curious absence of a predetermined replacement for Schenck. Through all the time of his preeminence as the main spring—"the General," as they called him—of Loew's Inc., he had strangely neglected to designate and develop a likely young man to take over from him.

Schenck's closest and most trusted associate was Charles Moskowitz, former head of theatre operations and successor to Dave Bernstein as treasurer. But Moskowitz was in his sixties and was popular almost exclusively with Schenck. The latter's endeavors to promote him were strongly opposed internally.

Another possible successor was Joseph R. Vogel, a diligent man who had been head of theatre operations since 1945. Vogel had worked for the company, in the theatre branch, since he was a lad. He was now pushing sixty. He was logical, but he lacked the endorsement of Schenck. Leopold Friedman was out of the running, being close to seventy. J. Robert Rubin, who might have been considered, had retired for reasons of health. (Like his partner, Mayer, he departed, in 1954, with a handsome settlement of $1,200,000 for his residual interest in the company's post-1924 films.)

Finally, the pressure of the directors to find a successor to Schenck grew so acute that Loew, sensing a crisis, agreed to take the job. He made it clear in private parleys, however, that his tenure would be tentative, that someone would have to be found to replace *him*, if the going got too rough.

His election as president of Loew's, Inc., was announced on Dec. 14, 1955. It was the first time an heir of a major pioneer in the American film industry had actually reached the top position his father had held.

Schenck, as befitted a president emeritus, was moved into the newly created position of Chairman of the Board.

Within a few months of his promotion, Loew let it be known that the producing-distributing arm of the company would enter the television field. It wisely arranged to lease its old pictures for showing on television, instead of selling its backlog outright, as other companies were doing with theirs. In this way, it kept control of its old pictures, while standing to earn several million dollars a year profit from them.

The company also began to ally itself with television stations in various localities, and it announced that it would eventually go into the production of entertainment for video. Thus a bridge with the television industry was constructively designed.

Loew took positive steps in other quarters. At the annual stockholders meeting, which he "chaired" (by even showing up he performed a formality that Schenck had oddly avoided over the years), he announced the entire elimination of all executive profit-sharing plans and a reduction in the amount the company was paying into the pension fund. He compelled certain studio economies. He made several independent production deals. He battled to straighten out the tangle of the funded debt that was delaying "divorcement." Loew tried.

However, stockholder criticism and pressure continued stubbornly. Progress towards a pruning of "dead wood" was felt to be too slow. And the strong investment banking interests that were now asserting themselves obstinately through representatives on the board of directors were displeased with the operation of the studio. They were shocked to hear that a deficit of $3,000,000 might be shown in studio operation in the year 1955-56. This would be the heaviest operating loss since the critical $6,500,000 deficit in 1947-48.

Inevitably, blame and resentment were heaped upon Dore Schary. He was the traditional scapegoat, as head of the studio. His long-standing "old guard" enemies, both within and without the company, renewed the whisper campaign against him. He was even criticized for his active participation in Democratic Party politics. Arthur Loew was strong for him, but other powerful elements on the board of directors were against. Among them now was Schary's old sponsor, Schenck.

Apres Moi?

Such was the state of agitation when, on Oct. 3, 1956, the trade paper *Variety* flashed the information that Loew had resigned as president. The news was flabbergasting to the film industry. It was incredible that Loew, so generally respected, should give up the job within a year. Even those who knew of his reluctance were amazed that he should resign and that the fact should be "leaked" to a trade paper before a successor was named.

Loew frankly admitted the pressures and problems were too much for him. His health was beginning to suffer. That's why he chucked the job, he said. He had indicated to the directors that he intended to do so, several times, but no move was made to replace him. So he laid his resignation on the line. It was to be effective by the end of the year.

Now Schenck came back into the picture. As chairman of the board, he was head of the committee to find a new president. The tough and tenacious "General," who had been restless with little to do, made a surprising endeavor to get Sol Siegel into the job. Siegel was an independent producer who had made one successful film, *High Society,* for Metro-Goldwyn-Mayer. It was difficult to understand his nomination until it was realized that he was being touted to act as president from offices on the West Coast. In such an arrangement, the New York office would probably be headed by Charles Moskowitz. And behind Moskowitz would be "the General."

That negotiation fell through.

For two weeks, uncertainty existed. Rumors flew thick and fast of various people, some outside the company, who would get the job. The disquieting thing was that Loew's Inc., regarded for so many years as the Rock of Gibraltar of the film industry, should appear so unsettled "upstairs."

Word got around that the directors—especially two or three who were not employees of the company—were determined to have no more of Schenck. There was now criticism not only of his continued influence on policy but of the presence of nepotism that he had tolerated in the company for many years. It was known he had relatives scattered throughout the home office, the studio and the various subsidiaries and theatre concessionaires.

The crux of this executive crisis was the powerful shadow of Schenck.

Then, on Oct. 18, it was announced that Joe Vogel had been picked to ascend from the head of Loew's Theatres to the presidency of Loew's, Inc. Arthur Loew would return to his old job as head of Loew's International and would also assume the position of Chairman of the Board. Schenck would give up that position to become Honorary Chairman of the Board, a purely nominal title.

This was plainly his exit from Loew's, Inc.

The fact was acknowledged a month later when Howard Dietz informed the press that Schenck would retire completely at the end of the year.

Thus the sturdy veteran who had weathered so many storms and had reached the peak of his authority in the showdown with Louie Mayer took his departure from the company he had served for fifty years, unwept by the very "stockholders" he had said so often he strove to "protect."

His was not the only departure. Within a month of assuming the presidency, Vogel called Dore Schary to New York and threw him to the wolves. Schary submitted his resignation as head of the studio, effective at the year's end, even though his contract had thirteen months to go. He took $100,000 in settlement. This, with the $900,000 in deferred salary he had coming, to be paid at the rate of $100,000 a year, gave him some balm for his injured pride.

Bennie Thau, a veteran in Culver City, was assigned to administer the operation of the studio.

With this dramatic upheaval, we may logically bring to a close this story of an entertainment empire and the people involved in it. The character of it, if not the empire, was dissolved with the passing of Schenck. An inevitable alteration was due in the years ahead.

What this would be, under pressures of continuing industry change and the vigilance of powerful stockholders, was no more sure than what lay ahead for the mutable nexus of the industry itself. Stockholder ire was still vengeful at the end of 1956, but stockholders have always been tractable when dividends roll in. The possibility of improving profits was the indomitable hope on which the new wardens of the Lion looked for sustenance.

And as a wistful observer cast back on the years—back to the days of the nickelodeons, the growth of the theatre chains, the great mergers of studios and theatres, the bewildering arrival of sound, the picture triumphs of the Nineteen Thirties, the vast prosperity during World War II—it was hard to imagine that there could ever be an end for Loew's, Inc., and the Lion. At least, it was hard to imagine a world of motion pictures without them.

INDEX